Medieval and Post-Medieval Occupation and Industry in the Redcliffe Suburb of Bristol

Excavations at 1–2 and 3 Redcliff Street, 2003–2010

Edited by Mary Alexander

Medieval and Post-Medieval Occupation and Industry in the Redcliffe Suburb of Bristol

Excavations at 1–2 and 3 Redcliff Street, 2003–2010

Edited by

Mary Alexander

Excavations and Observations of Medieval and Post-Medieval Tenement Blocks at 1–2 Redcliff Street, 2007–2010

by Jonathan Hart and Mary Alexander

with contributions from P.L. Armitage, A.J. Arnold, E. Besly, S. Cobain, A. Crawford, P. Davenport, D. Dungworth, D.M. Goodburn, R.E. Howard, R. Jackson, R. Leech, Q. Mould, D. Smith, C. Philpotts, E.R. McSloy, V. Taylor, S. Warman and K. Wilkinson

Excavations at 3 Redcliff Street, 2003

by Peter Davenport, Simon Cox and Richard Young

with contributions from J. Athersuch, N.P. Branch, R. Gale, C.P. Green, L. Higbee, R. Leech, E.R. McSloy, G.E. Swindle, S. Warman, A. Vaughan-Williams and A. Vince

Cotswold Archaeology Monograph No. 8

Cotswold Archaeology Monograph No. 8

Published by Cotswold Archaeology
Building 11, Kemble Enterprise Park, Cirencester, Gloucestershire GL7 6BQ

Copyright © Authors and Cotswold Archaeology 2015

All rights reserved. No part of this publication may be reproduced, stored in a retrieval system, or transmitted in any form or by any means, electronic, photocopying, recording or otherwise, without the prior permission of the copyright owner.

ISBN 978-0-9934545-1-6

British Library Cataloguing in Publication Data
A catalogue record of this book is available from the British Library

Mapping in 1–2 Redcliff Street figures 1.1, 3.1, 3.7, 3.12, 3.15, 3.17, 3.19, 3.20, 5.3 and 3 Redcliff Street figure 1.1 is reproduced from the Ordnance Survey on behalf of the controller of Her Majesty's Stationery Office, © Crown Copyright Cotswold Archaeology Ltd 100002109.

Front cover: Medieval Ham Green B jug, early 13th century
Back cover: Back cover: 14th century tenement buildings; Detail of Ashmead's map 1855; Glazed condiment dish in the form of a boat

Cover design by Lucy Martin, Cotswold Archaeology
Produced by Past Historic, Kings Stanley, Gloucestershire
Printed by Henry Ling, Dorchester

CONTENTS

List of Figures   vii
List of Tables   ix
Summary   xi
Acknowledgements   xiii
Preface   xv

Excavations and Observations of Medieval and Post-Medieval Tenement Blocks at 1–2 Redcliff Street, 2007–2010

Chapter 1: Introduction
1.1 Topography and Geology   1
1.2 The Historical Background for Bristol by Roger Leech and Chris Philpotts   3
1.3 Project Aims and Objectives   3
1.4 Excavation and Post-Excavation Methodology   4

Chapter 2: Historical and Archaeological Background
2.1 Documentary Evidence by Roger Leech   6
2.2 Archaeological Background   12

Chapter 3: Fieldwork Results
3.1 Introduction   14
3.2 Geoarchaeological Deposits   14
3.3 Period 1: early 12th to mid 13th centuries   14
3.4 Period 2a: late 13th to mid 14th centuries   20
3.5 Period 2b: mid 14th century   24
3.6 Period 2c: mid 14th to early 15th centuries   26
3.7 Period 3: early 15th to late 17th centuries   29
3.8 Period 4: late 17th to late 19th centuries   32
3.9 Period 5: late 19th to late 20th centuries   34

Chapter 4: Finds
4.1 Pottery by E.R. McSloy   37
4.2 Medieval Ceramic Roof Tile by Angus Crawford   53
4.3 Coins and Tokens by Edward Besly   54
4.4 Objects of Metal and Worked Bone by E.R. McSloy   54
4.5 Clay Mould Debris by E.R. McSloy   60
4.6 Copper-Alloy Working Debris by David Dungworth   65
4.7 Objects of Worked Stone by E.R. McSloy and Victoria Taylor   73
4.8 Clay Tobacco Pipes and Pipe Kiln Assemblage by Reg Jackson   73
4.9 Glass and Glass Waste by E.R. McSloy   76
4.10 Architectural Stone Fragments by Peter Davenport   76
4.11 Leather by Quita Mould   78
4.12 Worked Wood by D.M. Goodburn   84
4.13 Tree-Ring Analysis of Timbers by A.J. Arnold and R.E. Howard   92

Chapter 5: Biological Evidence
5.1 Animal Bone by Sylvia Warman   96
5.2 Fish Bones by Philip L. Armitage   101
5.3 Plant Macrofossil and Charcoal Remains by Sarah Cobain   104
5.4 Insect Remains by David Smith   121
5.5 Geoarchaeology by Keith Wilkinson   132

Chapter 6: Thematic Discussion
6.1 Early Development of the Redcliffe Suburb   137
6.2 Development of the Plots   138
6.3 The Medieval Buildings   140
6.4 Industry, Economy and Trade   141

Excavations at 3 Redcliff Street, 2003

Chapter 1: Introduction
1.1 Previous Work   147
1.2 Excavation and Post-Excavation Methodology   147

Chapter 2: Documentary Evidence by Roger Leech
2.1 The Redcliff Street Area   149
2.2 Documentary Evidence for the Site   149
2.3 Conclusions   150

Chapter 3: Fieldwork Results
3.1 Introduction   151

3.2 Period 1: Geological Strata 151
3.3 Period 2: Early Reclamation and Settlement Activity (later 12th to mid 13th centuries) 151
3.4 Period 3: Medieval Expansion and Industrial Activity (mid/late 13th to 15th centuries) 155
3.5 Period 4: Early Post-Medieval Industrial Activity (15th to 18th centuries) 160
3.6 Period 5: Later Post-Medieval Activity (late 18th to 19th centuries) 165
3.7 Period 6: Modern Development (19th to 21st centuries) 165

Chapter 4 Finds
4.1 Medieval and Later Pottery by Alan Vince 169
4.2 Ceramic Building Material by Alan Vince 173
4.3 Metalwork by E.R. McSloy 174
4.4 Crucibles and Copper-Alloy Casting Waste by E.R. McSloy 175
4.5 Clay Tobacco Pipes by E.R. McSloy 175
4.6 Stone Roof Tile by E.R. McSloy 175
4.7 Glass by E.R. McSloy 175
4.8 Perforated Fired-Clay Fragment by E.R. McSloy 176
4.9 Wooden Artefact by E.R. McSloy 177

Chapter 5 Environmental Evidence
5.1 Overview by Sylvia Warman 177
5.2 Animal Bone by Lorrain Higbee 177
5.3 Mollusca by N.P. Branch, C.P. Green, G.E. Swindle, A. Vaughan-Williams and J. Athersuch 178
5.4 Archaeobotanical Remains by N.P. Branch, C.P. Green, G.E. Swindle, A. Vaughan-Williams and J. Athersuch 179
5.5 Lithostratigraphy by N.P. Branch, C.P. Green, G.E. Swindle, A. Vaughan-Williams and J. Athersuch 179

Chapter 6 Discussion
6.1 Early Landscape Reclamation and Settlement 181
6.2 Expansion of the Medieval City and the Early Industrialisation of the Redcliffe Suburb 181
6.3 Industrial Activity in the Post-Medieval Period 182
6.4 Late Post-Medieval and Modern Redevelopment 183

References 185

Index 197

List of Figures

Nos 1–2 Redcliff Street

1.1	Site location of 1–2 Redcliff Street and 3 Redcliff Street (scale 1:2000)	2	
1.2	The site under excavation, looking south-west	4	
2.1	Historic features and archaeological excavations in the Redcliffe suburb. Scale 1:4000	7	
2.2	Hoefnagle's map of Bristol of 1581 (detail), showing site location	8	
2.3	Ashmead's map of 1828 (detail), showing site location and street numbering used between 1775 and the 1880s	9	
2.4	Goad's Insurance Map 12 of 1887 (detail), showing site location	11	
2.5	Deed plan of the mid 19th century for Nos 18–20 Redcliff Street (also shows No. 17) (BRO 36722, Box 4)	12	
3.1	Plan of Period 1: early 12th to mid 13th centuries. Scale 1:250	15	
3.2	Period 1 pit 3177 at Nos 16/17 Redcliff Street. Scales 1m and 0.3m	16	
3.3	Wattle hurdle in Period 1 pit 3066 at Nos 16/17 Redcliff Street. Scales 1m	16	
3.4	Period 1 drain 1773 and surface 2009 at Nos 16/17 Redcliff Street, looking north-east. Scales 2m	17	
3.5	Wattlework drain 1773 at Nos 16/17 Redcliff Street under excavation, looking west	18	
3.6	Wattlework in pit 3173 at Nos 16/17 Redcliff Street. Scale 1m	18	
3.7	Plan of Period 2a: late 13th to mid 14th centuries. Scale 1:250	21	
3.8	Little Thomas Lane in Period 2a	22	
3.9	Buildings 2A and 2B of Period 2a with Period 1 pits also visible, looking south-west. Scales 2m	23	
3.10	Period 1 pit 3151 and Period 2a Building 2A wall, looking south-east. Scales 1m	23	
3.11	Building 2C of Period 2a, looking south-west	23	
3.12	Plan of Period 2b: mid 14th century. Scale 1:250	25	
3.13	Period 2b cistern 1604. Scales 1m	26	
3.14	Period 2b circular stone-built hearth 1417/1419 looking north-east, with Period 2c water butt 1352 to the right of the 1m scale	26	
3.15	Plan of Period 2c: mid 14th to early 15th centuries. Scale 1:250	27	
3.16	Period 2c furnace 1845. Scale 1:400 approx.	28	
3.17	Plan of Period 3: early 15th to late 17th centuries. Scale 1:250	30	
3.18	Period 3 furnace 1426	31	
3.19	Plan of Period 4: late 17th to late 19th centuries. Scale 1:250	33	
3.20	Plan of Period 5: late 19th to late 20th centuries. Scale 1:250	35	
4.1	Pottery vessels nos 1–17 from Period 1. Scale 1:4	47	
4.2	Pottery vessels nos 18–27 from Periods 1 and 2a. Scale 1:4	49	
4.3	Pottery vessels nos 28–38 from Periods 2a, 2c and 3. Scale 1:4	51	
4.4	Illustrated objects of metal nos 1–5. Scale 1:1	56	
4.5	Illustrated objects of metal and worked bone nos 6–11. Scale 1:1	57	
4.6	Illustrated objects of worked bone nos 12–13. Scale 1:1	58	
4.7	Illustrated object of worked bone no. 14. Scale 1:1	59	
4.8	Photographs of clay mould fragments. Scale 1:2	63	
4.9	Drawn fragments of clay mould. Scale 1:2	64	
4.10	Photographs of crucible fragments (nos 1–2) and clay mould fragments (nos 3–5) subjected to metallurgical analysis. Scales 1:2 for nos 1–2 and 1:3 for nos 3–5	66	
4.11	Photographs of copper-working debris nos 6–7. Scale 1:2	67	

4.12　A *(left)*: Scanning Electron Microscope (SEM) image (back-scattered electron detector) of crucible from context 1463 (fabric 1, sample 4). An example of the carbon-rich temper is indicated with a white arrow. B *(right)*: SEM image (back-scattered electron detector) of crucible from context 1392 (fabric 2b, sample 8)　68
4.13　Stone spindlewhorl cat. no. 4. Scale 1:1　73
4.14　Stone jetton mould. Scale 1:1　73
4.15　Clay pipes nos 1–5. Scale 1:1　75
4.16　Objects of leather nos 1–4. Scale 1:3　81
4.17　Objects of leather nos 5–8. Scale 1:3　82
4.18　Object of leather no. 9. Scale 1:3　83
4.19　Interpretation of a 12th-century style stave wall construction based on interrupted sill beams (end wall). Scale 1:50　85
4.20　Period 1 post base 2072 (left) and 3055 (right). Scale 0.3m　87
4.21　Period 1 grooved oak building timber 1876 with felling date of 1176–1201. Scale 1:5　88
4.22　Period 1 oak post base 2104 with axe-cut end and hauling hole. Felled 1150–60. Scale 1:5　88
4.23　Interpretation of hauling timbers using oxen　89
4.24　Beechwood lidded container from Period 1 pit 1932. Scale 1:2　90
4.25　Timber 2113, felled 1229–54, from Period 2a well 1822. Scale 1:10　90
4.26　Woodscape of parent trees for 11th to 13th-century timbers and roundwood　92
5.1　The proportions of the ecological groupings of Coleoptera　128
5.2　The proportions of the synanthropic groupings of Coleoptera　129
5.3　Location of the geoarchaeological boreholes. Scale 1:1250　133
5.4　Cross section through the deposits revealed in the geoarchaeological boreholes　134

No. 3 Redcliff Street

1.1　Excavation Areas 1 and 2 showing monolith and borehole (BH) locations. Scale 1:500　148
3.1　Area 1, Period 2a: later 12th to mid 13th centuries. Scale 1:100　152
3.2　Area 1, Sections AA and BB. Scale 1:50　153
3.3　a: Board 1048 and associated pit 1049. b: Board 1048 after lifting. Scales 1m　153
3.4　Area 2, Period 2b: later 12th to mid 13th centuries. Scale 1:100　154
3.5　Area 2, Sections CC and DD. Scales 1:100 and 1:50　155
3.6　Area 1, Period 3b: mid/late 13th to 15th centuries. Scale 1:100　156
3.7　Area 1, Wall D viewed from the south. Scale 1m　157
3.8　Area 1, Section EE. Scale 1:50　157
3.9　Area 2, Period 3b: mid/late 13th to 15th centuries. Scale 1:100　158
3.10　Area 2, Wall E/F viewed from the west. Scale 1m　159
3.11　Cistern A viewed from the north with incoming drain visible top right. Scale 1m　160
3.12　Area 1, Periods 4a and 4b: 15th to 18th centuries. Scale 1:100　161
3.13　Area 2, Periods 4a and 4b1: 15th to 18th centuries. Scale 1:100　162
3.14　Area 2 cellars, general view from the east　163
3.15　Area 2, Period 4b2: 15th to 18th centuries. Scale 1:100　164
3.16　Area 2, west end of Cellar 1. Period 4b2 alterations (in brick) to stonework of Period 4b1　165
3.17　Area 2, Period 5 modification of Period 4 cellars: 15th to 18th centuries. Scale 1:100　166
3.18　Areas 1 and 2, Period 5: late 18th to 19th centuries, plotted against early 19th-century ground plans (based on BRO P/StT/Ch/3/31, fol. 20). Scale 1:250　167
3.19　Ashmead's map of 1855　168
3.20　Areas 1 and 2, Period 6: 19th to 21st centuries, plotted against the 1884 Ordnance Survey boundaries. Scale 1:400　168
4.1　Medieval pottery. Scale 1:4　174

List of Tables

Nos 1–2 Redcliff Street

4.1	Quantities (sherd count/weight in grams and rim EVEs) by deposit type and period	38
4.2	Composition of the pottery assemblages from Periods 1–3 by fabric type	39
4.3	Composition by fabric type of the larger pottery groups associated with the occupation of Period 1	41
4.4	Medieval ceramic tile fabrics (Bristol Roof Tile Fabrics; BRF) by period	54
4.5	Clay mould fragments by period, context and object 'class'	61
4.6	Cauldron/posnet rim diameters derived from cope and core rim mould fragments	62
4.7	Weights of different metallurgical materials examined by period (kg)	65
4.8	Crucible fragments	65
4.9	Samples selected for scientific examination	67
4.10	Chemical composition of the crucibles, mould and slag	69
4.11	Composition of copper alloy (including droplets within crucibles)	70
4.12	Leather from a Period 1 floor and associated drain, and Period 2a occupation layer, at No. 17 Redcliff Street	79
4.13	Waste leather by count and dry weight	80
4.14	Dated tree-ring samples listed in potential felling date order	94
4.15	Results of the cross-matching of site sequence BRCASQ01 when first ring date is 1057 and last ring date is 1163	94
4.16	Results of the cross-matching of site sequence BRCASQ02 when first ring date is 1066 and last ring date is 1161	94
4.17	Results of the cross-matching of sample BRCA2113 when first ring date is 1129 and last ring date is 1214	95
4.18	Results of the cross-matching of sample BRCA1537 when first ring date is 1168 and last ring date is 1253	95
4.19	Results of the cross-matching of sample BRCA3187 when first ring date is 1169 and last ring date is 1273	95
4.20	Results of the cross-matching of sample BRCA2101 when first ring date is 1424 and last ring date is 1498	95
4.21	Results of the cross-matching of sample BRCA2010 when first ring date is 1479 and last ring date is 1551	95
5.1	Animal bone from Period 1 deposits by species	97
5.2	Animal bone from Period 2 deposits by species	99
5.3	Summary counts (NISP) of the identified fish bones by period and taxa	102
5.4	Frequency of conger eel bones from Periods 1–2c in comparison with other medieval sites in Bristol	104
5.5	Plant macrofossils from Period 1 deposits at Nos 12, 13–15 and 17 Redcliff Street	106
5.6	Plant macrofossils from Periods 1, 2 and 3 deposits at Nos 17, 18 and 19 Redcliff Street	111
5.7	Charcoal species	116
5.8	The insect remains	122
5.9	The proportions of the ecological groupings of Coleoptera	128
5.10	The proportions of the synanthropic groupings of Coleoptera	129
5.11	AMS radiocarbon dating results. The radiocarbon date was calibrated using the IntCal04 curve (Reimer *et al.* 2004) and OxCal 4 software (Bronk Ramsey 2008)	132

No. 3 Redcliff Street

4.1	Basic pottery quantification with concordance with Bristol Pottery Type series (BPT)	170
4.2	Pottery quantification by period	172

Summary

This volume is concerned with excavations at two adjacent sites in the Redcliffe suburb of Bristol. Excavation at Nos 1–2 Redcliff Street took place across ten historic properties fronting onto the street. The evidence included well-preserved structural and industrial remains dating from the colonisation of the Redcliffe suburb in the 12th century through to the later post-medieval period. In the early 12th to 13th centuries the buildings were of timber construction and activity in the backyards was dominated by the cloth-dyeing industry. Waterlogged conditions preserved structural timbers, pit linings and abundant environmental remains including evidence for vegetable dyes and insect remains. Leather shoes and off-cuts typical of a cobbler's workshop were also well preserved. The pottery from this period was the largest assemblage of its kind from the city to date, and the dating of the site sequence was augmented by dendrochronology of structural timbers. In the late 13th century construction in stone of boundary walls and house footings replaced earlier building plans and solidified the tenement layout until the 19th century. A pair of well-built town houses in adjoining tenements suggest a joint venture in the early 14th century. The dye-pits of the earlier period were replaced by stone-built, circular hearths. The mid/late 14th or early 15th-century casting of lead-bronze cauldrons or posnets was evident from mould and crucible fragments, and the presence of a furnace. The industry was developed in several plots and additional furnaces were constructed. Structural features of the later furnaces suggest these were some of the earliest examples of reverberatory furnaces, which represent a technological advance on earlier types of furnaces. Extensive rebuilding in the 17th century included the amalgamation of two properties and the establishment of a sugar refinery.

The discussion and interpretation of the site evidence has been augmented by documentary and historical research and is examined within the context of previous excavations and investigations within the Redcliffe suburb, and in particular the evidence for the development of the wharves at Redcliffe to which the activity at 1–2 Redcliff is intimately linked. In the wider sphere the economic fortunes of the site and the growth and decline of the various trades and industries represented in the evidence can be seen to reflect some aspects of the economic history of the port of Bristol as well as casting light on new technological advances. Other significant aspects of the site evidence include architectural fragments of 14th to early 16th-century date that may relate to the medieval church of St Thomas's and a large assemblage of clay pipes and kiln material which can be dated with some precision to the period 1651 to 1654.

The second excavation occurred at No. 3 Redcliff Street on the opposite side of Thomas Lane from the first site. Investigation occurred in two areas, both at some distance from the original street frontage as a result of road widening in the 19th century. The earliest evidence had been severely reduced by the deep foundations of later cellars, but included foundations for stone walls dating to the late 12th to early 13th centuries, representing property divisions that survived into the 19th century. The excavations included parts of three tenements numbered 21–23 in the 18th and 19th centuries. Hearth bases, stone surfaces and cisterns dating to the mid 13th to 15th centuries may be linked to the cloth-dyeing industry; a prominent occupation in the Redcliffe suburb in this period. The evidence included the bases of two circular dye-vat hearths of typical 14th-century design. Crucible fragments linked to copper-alloy working were found in 13th to 15th-century contexts. Fired-clay mould fragments and a large quantity of scrap and misshapen lumps, probably representing spills or other waste from copper-alloy casting, were identified in both 19th-century and unstratified contexts. A source for this waste material may have been the copper-alloy casting furnaces dating from the late 14th to the late 17th centuries excavated at Nos 1–2 Redcliff Street. The evidence for cloth dyeing was replaced in the 15th century with structures relating to unidentifiable industrial activities. This included substantial resurfacing in Area 1 and a stone-lined square pit in Area 2. Building activity of this period also included two substantial cellars towards the rear of the tenement at No. 22. The 17th-century documentary sources link the property owners and occupiers to various trades of which cloth-working predominated, whilst distilling features amongst the occupations documented in the 18th century.

The discussion and interpretation of the excavated remains from both sites has been augmented by documentary and historical research which, combined with evidence from other excavations in Redcliffe, further enriches the story of the urban development and economic history of this important suburb of Bristol.

Acknowledgements

The work at 1–2 Redcliff Street was made possible by the financial support of Hanover Cube LLP who developed the site on behalf of Scottish Widows for Her Majesty's Court Service. Particular thanks go to Chris Richards of Hanover Cube for his close involvement in the project and his support throughout. In their role as enabling works contractor, Sanctus Consulting were instrumental in ensuring that the fieldwork proceeded smoothly and safely, and for this our thanks go to Peter Cooke, Managing Director, and Site Manager David Budden. We are also grateful to Bob Jones, City Archaeologist for Bristol City Council, for monitoring and advice during fieldwork, and for comments on an earlier draft of this report.

The fieldwork was managed for Cotswold Archaeology by Mark Collard, Simon Cox and Richard Young. The excavation was directed by Chris Pickard, and thanks are owed to all the excavation team who worked with him and on the later watching brief. Sylvia Warman provided on-site sampling advice. Mat Jane, Claire Lorrain and Phil Marter of ARCA drilled the geoarchaeological boreholes and Keith and Myra Wilkinson undertook laboratory examination of the cores. The post-excavation programme was managed by Mary Alexander, and Jon Hart and Chris Pickard undertook the site analysis, which was carried through into the publication stage by Jon Hart. X-rays and metalwork cleaning were undertaken by Karen Barker Antiquities Conservation Service. The leather was conserved by Cardiff University, Commercial Division and the waterlogged wood by Wiltshire Council Conservation Unit. The assessment of the plant macrofossils was carried out by Julie Jones. The illustrations were produced by Angela Aggujaro, Jon Bennett, Damian Goodburn, Lorna Gray, Peter Moore and Aleksandra Osinska. A draft text was edited for publication by Neil Holbrook.

Philip L. Armitage would like to thank Dr Alison Locker for allowing access to her unpublished report on the fish bone assemblages from Victoria Street, Bristol, and for providing a copy of the published report on the fish remains from St Thomas Street and Redcliff Street. Roger Leech thanks the staff of the Bristol Record Office for assistance in locating documents, most especially Alison Brown for her help in checking details of palaeography, and also Pamela Leech for all her help and support.

Westmark Developments Ltd provided the funding for the work at 3 Redcliff Street. Particular thanks go to Tony McGorrigan, Project Director for Westmark, and Elfyn Haycock of King Sturge, acting on behalf of Westmark as Project Manager. We are grateful to Bob Jones, City Archaeologist for Bristol City Council, for monitoring and advice during fieldwork, and for comments on an earlier draft of this report. The fieldwork was managed for Cotswold Archaeology by Simon Cox. The excavation was directed by Kevin Colls and Richard Young and thanks are owed to all the excavation team who worked on the excavation and on the later watching brief. Peter Davenport took the site analysis through to the publication stage, aided by Peter Rowsome. The post-excavation programme was managed by Martin Watts and latterly Mary Alexander. X-rays and metalwork cleaning were undertaken by Esther Cameron. The illustrations were produced by Jon Bennett, Lorna Gray, and Peter Moore. The text was copy-edited by Dr. Rachel Tyson. Martin Watts commented on an earlier draft of this report.

Preface

This volume is concerned with two excavations bordering Redcliff Street, one of the principal streets of a suburb on the opposite bank of the Avon from the late Saxon *burh* and subsequent Norman castle of Bristol. The two sites lie on the eastern side of Redcliff Street, separated by Thomas Lane. Development of the Redcliff and Temple Fees in the 12th century on the alluvium of the Avon floodplain resulted in the formation of an urban suburb that grew to rival in size the built-up area of Bristol itself. The potential of the archaeology in Redcliffe is well recognised, with a number of excavations on the western side of Redcliff Street in the 1980s revealing spectacular preservation of medieval waterfront structures (Jones 1991 provides a summary of this evidence). By the turn of the 21st century redevelopment of former industrial premises in Redcliffe for offices and residential accommodation was in full swing, and the integration of archaeology within the planning process led to opportunities for excavation and analysis. The financial crisis of 2007–8 caused a temporary hiatus in the pace of redevelopment but at the time of writing a number of schemes have been dusted off and are being actively promoted, so doubtless opportunities for further investigation will occur before too long. Like many historic towns and cities in Britain the pace of excavation has not been matched by a commensurate level of analysis and publication. A number of important excavations, both pre and post the formalisation of archaeology within the planning process in 1990, remain unpublished. Cotswold Archaeology, however, is proud of its record of publication in Bristol and this volume builds on work at two other sites in Redcliffe (55–60 St Thomas and 26–28 St Thomas Street) published in 2011 (Watts 2011b) and our extensive excavations in partnership with Pre-Construct Archaeology in advance of the Cabot Circus shopping centre in the Broadmead suburb (Ridgeway and Watts 2013). A published baseline of analysis is therefore emerging, not only of the stratigraphic sequences but also of the crucial finds and environmental data. These corpora will be crucial in informing future decisions on how to manage the impact of future development on the historic environment of Bristol and facilitate the effective deployment of resources devoted to future investigations. The need for synthesis of archaeological work in Bristol remains pressing, and the City Archaeologist Bob Jones is to be congratulated on his continuing devotion to press forward with the publication of the long-awaited Bristol Urban Archaeological Assessment.

The economic fortunes of Redcliffe fluctuated over time, just like any urban centre, but the continued use of the area for industrial and craft activities into the post-medieval and modern eras has often had the effect of truncating or puncturing earlier archaeological deposits. At the main site reported in this volume, 1–2 Redcliff Street, the levels of preservation of 12th to 14th-century deposits and structures were much better than might have been expected given the results on adjacent sites. No preliminary evaluation of 1–2 Redcliff Street was possible due its use as a car park, and this is a salutary lesson on the dangers of inferring (or assuming) too much from work at other sites. Waterlogging of the lower levels of the excavation also resulted in the recovery of high quality finds and biological data sets. These are some of the best fully analysed and published assemblages from medieval Bristol, and serve to demonstrate once again the just how good the quality of the archaeology found in the City and its suburbs can be. Interpretation of the archaeology of both sites reported in this volume has been greatly aided by the detailed documentary research undertaken by Dr Roger Leech, although as is now commonly recognised, each type of evidence needs to be evaluated in its own right, and attempts to shoehorn one source into a framework provided by the other can be a futile and misleading exercise.

We hope that this volume will make a contribution towards furthering appreciation of the archaeology of Bristol and demonstrate what commercial archaeology can achieve in urban environments. Cotswold Archaeology recently celebrated the 25th anniversary of its formation. During that quarter century work in Bristol has figured strongly in our portfolio of projects, and the skill required to excavate and analyse deeply stratified complex urban archaeology continues to challenge our field and post-excavation teams. But it is a test we readily accept as it is a privilege to be afforded an opportunity to investigate the history of one of the great historic cities of Europe and the regional capital of the South West of England.

Neil Holbrook
Chief Executive, Cotswold Archaeology
August 2015

Excavations and Observations of Medieval and Post-Medieval Tenement Blocks at 1–2 Redcliff Street 2007–2010

by Jonathan Hart and Mary Alexander

with contributions from P.L. Armitage, A.J. Arnold, E. Besly, S. Cobain, A. Crawford, P. Davenport, D. Dungworth, D.M. Goodburn, R.E. Howard, R. Jackson, R. Leech, Q. Mould, D. Smith, C. Philpotts, E.R. McSloy, V. Taylor, S. Warman and K. Wilkinson

Chapter 1
Introduction

Between May 2007 and May 2008 Cotswold Archaeology (CA) carried out an archaeological excavation at 1–2 Redcliff Street, Bristol (centred on NGR: ST 5907 7276; Fig. 1.1). The project was undertaken at the request of Hanover Cube LLP, on behalf of Scottish Widows Fund and Life Assurance Society, and was designed to mitigate the impact of the construction of new offices and a basement car park. The work included a watching brief, undertaken during initial construction groundworks between December 2009 and January 2010. Prior to the excavation, the site was a car park.

The site fronts the eastern side of the northern end of Redcliff Street. The Church of St Thomas the Martyr, a medieval foundation largely rebuilt in the post-medieval period, is located immediately to the rear of the site and the River Avon lies to the west, behind properties fronting the other side of Redcliff Street.

1.1 Topography and Geology

The modern ground surface is at approximately 8.5m AOD and the underlying geology is Mercia Mudstone (informally known as Redcliffe Sandstone) overlain by fluvial gravels of the Avon Formation with silts, clays and sands of the Wentlooge formation lying above (Chapter 5.5). Alluvial clay was exposed as the earliest deposit during the excavation although the underlying Triassic deposits were exposed within several boreholes.

The Holocene stratigraphy of central Bristol is broadly understood as a result of many geoarchaeological borehole investigations since the late 1990s. Fluvial gravels of the Pleistocene Avon Formation (Campbell *et al.* 1999) are overlain by alluvial deposits of the informally defined Wentlooge formation (Allen and Rae 1987), with both units topped by 'made ground' (including archaeological deposits) of medieval and later date. The thickness of the Wentlooge formation and made-ground deposits depends on topographic location, but the broad trend is for sites in the centre of the valley and in westerly locations to have thicker Holocene stratigraphies than those on the valley sides and in easterly positions.

The term 'alluvium' in this context is a catch-all title used to describe the (geologically) recent fine-grained deposits of the Holocene (*c.* 11,500 years ago to the present), including archaeologically important organic muds and peat, that formed in riverine and intertidal environments. Fluvial gravels of Late Pleistocene date (*c.* 128,000 to 11,500 years ago) provide the

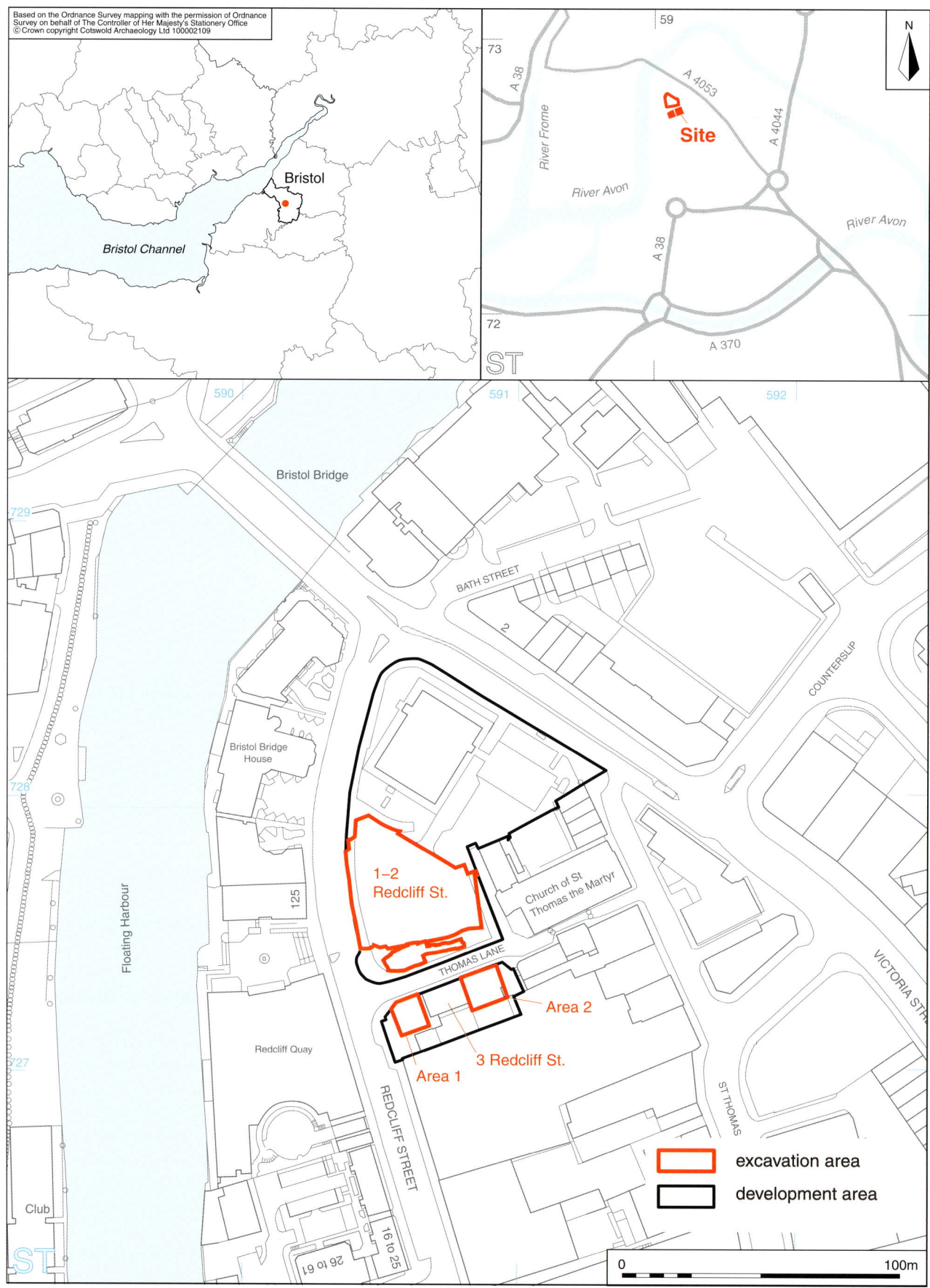

Fig. 1.1 Site location of 1–2 Redcliff Street and 3 Redcliff Street (scale 1:2000)

earliest Quaternary infill (Bates 2003). Deposits of the youngest Pleistocene gravel terrace have been identified on previous investigations in the Avon valley in central Bristol, including the Harbourside Development, Canon's Marsh (Wilkinson 2011a), and in the Redcliffe suburb at Redcliff Backs (Wilkinson 2004), 55–61 Victoria Street (Wilkinson 2007a), 32–36 Victoria Street (Wilkinson 2008a) and 55–60 St Thomas Street (Wilkinson 2011b). Investigations at Cabot Circus (Wilkinson 2013) demonstrated a similar sequence in the Frome valley to that seen previously in the Avon valley. Evidence from Harbourside indicates that, during the initial stages of the Holocene, marsh accretion kept pace with relative sea-level rise, resulting in the formation of the peats and organic muds, but after *c.* 3500 cal BC these organic deposits disappeared as the area became an intertidal zone, the bulk of the later deposits being mineral silts and clays. In the Redcliffe suburb radiocarbon dating at 32–36 Victoria Street (Wilkinson 2008a) demonstrated that the lower contact with the Avon Formation dates to between 5320–5070 cal BC (6280±40 BP, Beta-245646).

1.2 The Historical Background for Bristol
Roger Leech and Chris Philpotts

The origins of Bristol are obscure but it appears to have been founded in the late Anglo-Saxon period on the promontory between the rivers Frome and Avon, which was also the lowest bridging point of the Avon. It is from this bridge that the settlement took its name 'bricgstow', meaning 'the place of the bridge'. The earliest definitive evidence for Bristol comes from coins of Cnut's reign, bearing the mint mark 'bricgstow', believed to date between 1017 and 1023 (Grinsell 1986, 4; Hinton 1984, 151). The minting of coins implies that by this time Bristol must have been a *burh*, and would have possessed defences, as well as a market and some degree of trade. The latter appears to be confirmed by the first documentary mention of the town, as a port used by sea-going ships travelling to and from Ireland, in the Anglo-Saxon Chronicle of 1051 (Lobel and Carus-Wilson 1975, 3). The strength of the defences is later attested in 1067, when raiders from Ireland led by the sons of Harold Godwinson failed to take them. Settlement was centred on the crossroads of Corn Street, Broad Street, High Street and Wine Street, and was later enclosed by a stone defensive circuit (built in the early 12th century) which may have been established on the line of earlier earthen bank and ditch defences of the *burh*. Archaeological evidence for the *burh* defences is very limited, with a possible ditch discovered on the line of Dolphin Street (Watts and Rahtz 1985) and an earth bank located to the rear of Leonard Lane (Williams 1992, 54).

Bristol Castle was established in around 1080 to the east of the town. It may have started out as a ringwork, later reinforced with a large motte and ditch, and was one of the finest in Norman Britain, owing its grandeur to an extensive programme of building work initiated in the late 11th/early 12th century by Robert FitzHamon (Jackson 2006b, 5). The castle ditch was flooded with water drawn from the Frome via a leat that connected with the river some distance to the east. By 1147 the castle motte had been largely replaced with a substantial keep built of Caen stone by Robert Earl of Gloucester, the bastard son of Henry I (Lobel and Carus-Wilson 1975, 4).

Broadly contemporary with the encircling of the town with walls in the early 12th century, a number of extra-mural suburbs began to develop on formerly marginal marshland, including Broadmead, Redcliffe, Temple and the area of St Stephen's Marsh to the south of the town. However, it took a number of major civil engineering projects over a century later to provide the economic impetus for the town's rise in prosperity, not least of which was the digging of a new channel for the Frome in the 1240s to provide new deep harbourage for seafaring ships at St Augustine's Reach. Prior to this, the Frome seems to have turned eastwards further north, to join the Avon further upstream. Around the same time a replacement bridge was built across the Avon in stone, grants of murage were made for new circuits of town wall to be built around Redcliffe and Temple (the Portwall) and St Stephen's Marsh (the Marsh Wall), and Bristol began to prosper from the flourishing textile industry and the vibrant trade passing through the port (Lobel and Carus-Wilson 1975, 6–10). The walled area of the town was also extended northwards as far as the southern bank of the Frome (Jones 2006, 195).

The site lies within the suburb of Redcliffe, close to Bristol Bridge, the only dry crossing of the River Avon at Bristol in the medieval period. Development of the Redcliff and Temple Fees in the 12th century is the earliest known use of this part of the Avon floodplain, and resulted in the formation of an urban suburb that was to rival in size the built-up area of the town.

Over five or more centuries the north end of Redcliff Street was a mix of dwellings and industry. In the later medieval period industry was centred around the production and particularly the finishing of cloth. From the 16th and 17th centuries industrial processes linked to the Atlantic trades predominated, first of soap and then of sugar and its by-products. A significant part of the excavated site formed the sugar house founded by Robert Newport in 1695. Other trades included metalworking, possibly within the excavated areas.

1.3 Project Aims and Objectives

Prior to the commencement of fieldwork the principal project aims were broadly to elucidate the nature and functions of the buildings and associated structures and gardens from the earliest period of settlement in

Redcliffe. Following the completion of the fieldwork an assessment of the findings was made and the following more specific objectives were defined to guide the post-excavation process (CA 2010):

1. To elucidate the early colonisation of Redcliffe in the 12th to 13th centuries.

2. To study changes in the settlement and economic development that occurred between the 12th and 14th centuries and throughout the remainder of the medieval period.

3. To examine the development of the site between the later medieval and the earlier post-medieval periods (16th to 18th centuries).

4. To examine the remains dating to the later post-medieval through to the modern periods and establish how closely these correlate to the cartographic record of the site.

1.4 Excavation and Post-Excavation Methodology

The project comprised an excavation, two borehole surveys (Chapter 5.5) and a subsequent watching brief. During the excavation, modern dumped layers and surfaces were removed by a mechanical excavator under archaeological supervision. The archaeological features thus exposed were hand-excavated to the bottom of the archaeological stratigraphy, although some bulk archaeological layers were removed mechanically after sampling and assessment (Fig. 1.2).

During the watching brief, machine excavations were monitored until the highest significant archaeological horizon was encountered, with excavation continuing by hand thereafter. The watching brief areas comprised narrow service trenches which restricted the potential for features thus exposed to be directly correlated with the stratigraphy recorded during the preceding excavation, although in the event, the majority of the deposits identified during the watching brief proved to be make-up layers.

The borehole investigations comprised three 9–10m deep boreholes excavated by ARCA and two further boreholes excavated for geotechnical investigation by C.J. Associates and examined by ARCA (ARCA 2007).

The preservation of deposits within the site was very good, with various classes of organic materials being

Fig. 1.2 The site under excavation, looking south-west

recovered from medieval layers, including from those dating to the initial colonisation of Redcliffe. Within the southern two thirds of the site, a good stratigraphic sequence was recovered from the medieval to the modern periods with only limited truncation. In contrast, most of the northern part of the site had been occupied by modern oil stores and few remains survived. The site did not extend for the full width of the medieval and later properties, and so the Redcliff Street frontages and the rear parts of the plots were not examined. In addition to this, the two southernmost properties were only very partially investigated within an area excavated for an attenuation tank and this restricted the potential for interpreting the features exposed.

Features were phased into archaeological periods based on the stratigraphic sequence established through single context excavation. These periods were then dated, largely based on the artefactual record, but also on the morphology of certain late medieval and early post-medieval industrial features.

Following the completion of fieldwork a Post-Excavation Assessment and Updated Project Design (CA 2010) was produced which summarised the potential of the archaeological data, established updated aims and objectives for the project, and determined the content of this final report. We have adopted a traditional approach to reporting with separate sections for the Historical and Archaeological Background (Chapter 2), the Fieldwork Results (Chapter 3) and the Finds and Biological Evidence (Chapters 4 and 5). The results are summarised and their significance considered within a series of Thematic Discussions (Chapter 6).

The archive and artefacts from the excavation have been deposited with Bristol City Museum and Art Gallery under accession number BRSMG 2007/48.

Chapter 2
Historical and Archaeological Background

2.1 The Documentary Evidence
Roger Leech

The author was commissioned to research the available documentary evidence pertaining to the tenement blocks partially revealed in the excavation. A discussion of the manuscript and cartographic sources consulted can be found in the References.

The setting

Though now referred to as Nos 1–2 Redcliff Street, the area within which the excavations were situated was from 1775 to the 1880s numbered as Nos 11–20 Redcliff Street. Nos 16 and 17 were separated by Little Thomas Lane. To the north of this lane there was a series of separate tenements, for which no street numbers are available for the period before the 1880s.

Historically the site was situated entirely within the parish of St Thomas. This locality was first developed as part of the town of Bristol in the 12th century with the establishment of the fees of Temple and Redcliff. The site lay within the Redcliff Fee. A fee was an area of lordship; through rents, urban fees could yield considerable profits for their lords. The Temple Fee was granted by Robert Earl of Gloucester to the Knights Templar between 1128 and 1148 (Taylor 1875, 275–8; Patterson 1973, 173). The building of Temple Church and a preceptory followed, together with the setting out of Temple Street and the subdivision of the land either side into burgage plots. The Redcliff Fee was developed by Robert Fitzharding, being part of his manor of Bedminster (Cronne 1946, 32–3). Two main streets were laid out, Redcliff Street and St Thomas Street, each with tenement plots extending back on either side, those on the west of Redcliff Street stretching to the Avon (Fig. 2.1). Redcliff Street was the principal route to the south, towards the Earl of Berkeley's manor of Bedminster. Dendrochronological dating of structural timbers from the excavations at Dundas Wharf (Fig. 2.1, no. 3) has shown that the west side of Redcliff Street was being developed from *c.* 1123–33 and that quays were being built by 1147–8 (Nicholson and Hillam 1987, 141). The two developments of the Temple and Redcliff Fees were probably undertaken at the same time. The boundary between the two developments was the Law Ditch; this served as a drain and open sewer for the tenements on both sides, in both fees. In medieval Bristol, the term 'Law Ditch' was generally applied to the ditch which demarcated a boundary between two fees, and which often preserved its significance as a parish boundary. The tenement plots within which the site was located extended from Redcliff Street on the west to a 'Law Ditch' on the east, and it would seem that in this context the term has been applied to a ditch that played a role in defining the limit of property ownership. Further instances of this use of the term 'Law Ditch' in property deeds can be found elsewhere (cf. Leech 2004, also shown on Ashmead's map of 1828). These ditches may have held a greater significance in the early development of the suburb (see Chapter 6, below). The Law Ditch between Nos 12 and 13 Tucker Street is thought to define the eastern limit of Arthur's Fee, a fee that encompassed land surrounding Bristol Bridge, but which was later subsumed into the larger area covered by the parish of St Thomas.

Title deeds, leases and other documents provide a general picture of this part of Redcliff Street by the 15th and 16th centuries. The part of Redcliff Street closer to Bristol Bridge was a prime location for inns, providing accommodation for visitors to the town (Leech 2006, 92–3). On the east side were the Queen's Head Inn and its yard at No. 26, the Red Lion Inn and its yard at No. 7, and the Berewykesyn or Bear Inn and its yard at No. 2 (using the late 18th to early 19th-century numbering scheme). Almost opposite the Red Lion Inn was the White Horse at Nos 143–144.

In this period many other properties at this end of the street were connected with the cloth trade, which dominated life in the town south of the River Avon. In 1473 No. 3, immediately south of the Bear Inn, was

Historical and Archaeological background 7

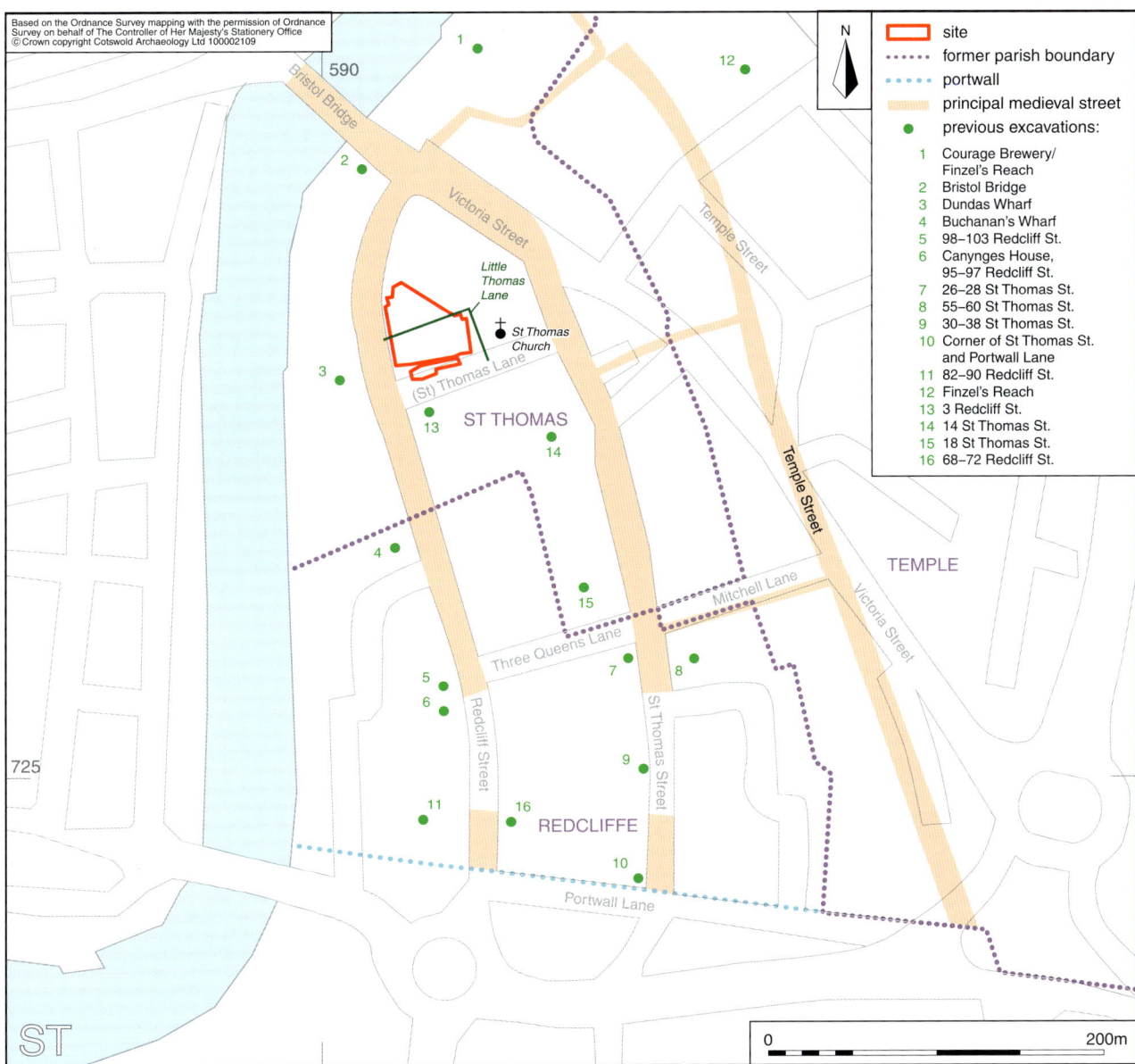

Fig. 2.1 Historic features and archaeological excavations in the Redcliffe suburb. Scale 1:4000

the hallhouse of Canynges' chantry in the church of St Mary Redcliffe and the home of William Guylham, a sheerman (Williams 1950, 227). The sheermen were probably concentrated in this part of the street, for No. 21 Redcliff Street extended back to a tenement on the south side of Thomas Lane that by 1684 was formerly known as 'the Sheermans' Hall' (BRO 05836). On the opposite side of the street No. 127 was by 1522 the home of another sheerman, Humphrey Jones. In the second half of the 15th century No. 127 had been successively the home of Alexander Newe, Edmund Newe and Richard Newe, three generations of dyers and their families (BRO P/StJ/B/D/113 and 117).

Other trades included metalworking. Thomas Elyot and William Tanner were both brasiers living in a row of properties belonging to Burton's chantry, somewhere within Nos 1–32 Redcliff Street. In 1521 Nicholas Elyott, son of Thomas Elyott late of Bristol brasier, assigned the lease of a house that his father had built on the west side of the street in or after 1463 to Thomas Olyver, a baker (Veale 1953, 1). Thomas Elyot may also have been involved in other industrial processes. In his will of 1505 he left to his son Nicholas also the '"ffate ffurneys cestren" etc' (Wadley 1886, 174); fat, furnaces and cisterns may have had more connection with soapmaking than brazing. William Tanner, another brasier two doors away from Thomas Elyot in 1454, was described as a crocker or potter in 1456 (BRO P/StMR/5163/249; Veale 1950, 58).

From at least the 15th until at least the mid 17th

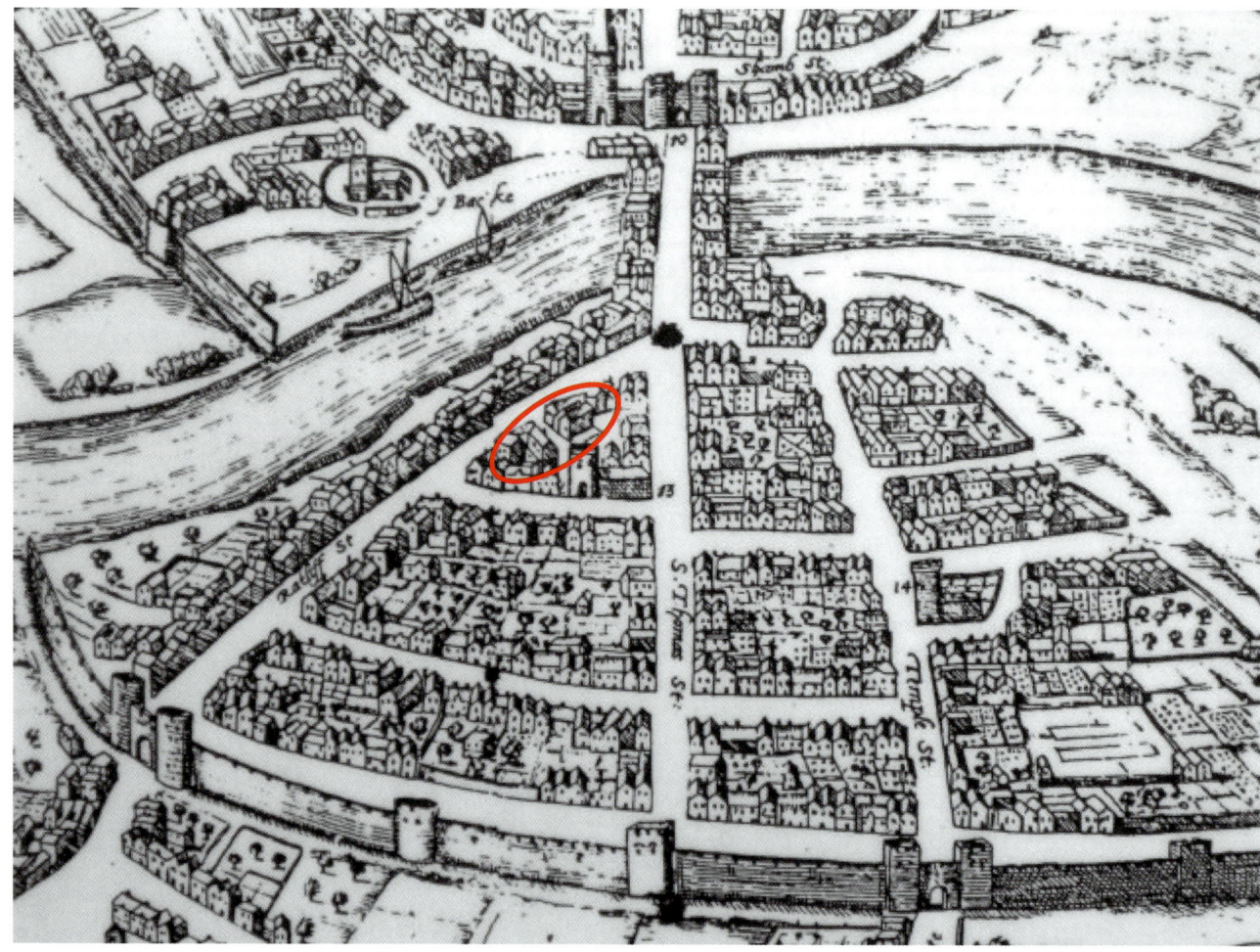

Fig. 2.2   Hoefnagle's map of Bristol of 1581 (detail), showing site location

century Redcliff Street was the home of some of Bristol's wealthiest citizens, some of whom lived at the north end of the street close to the bridge. At the end of Bristol Bridge was the Great House on Redcliff Back, illustrated by Millerd in 1673. At No. 5 an unidentified owner or occupier installed in 1637 a chimneypiece depicting St George slaying the dragon, a piece now reinstalled in a grand house in Wiltshire (BRSMG M2043; NMR Red Box for Lake House, Wilford, Wiltshire). No. 28 was in the 1670s the home of Alderman John Willoughby, prominent in the Atlantic trade; another monumental chimneypiece stood in his house (BRSMG M2098, Braikenridge Notebook E85; illustrated in Stoddard 2001, 89).

In the 17th century the north end of Redcliff Street increasingly became the location for industrial processes and trades connected with Atlantic commerce. On the west side of the street against the River Avon were the premises of soapmakers: Joseph Lewis at No. 129 in 1700; Henry Rich at No. 130 before 1668; Charles Jones the elder there after 1668, and Richard Benson at No. 138 in 1687 (BRO 28048/D13; P/StS/D/Box 6).

The soap trade relied on the importation of whale fat, in this period principally from the North Atlantic and the coast of North America.

A second industry established at the north end of Redcliff Street in this same period was the production of refined sugar and its by-products. A sugar house was established at No. 18 Redcliff Street by 1695 and continued there in operation until 1816. It is clear from the title deeds and plans that No. 18 Redcliff Street consisted of three separate tenements, thrown together to form the sugar house. Behind the sugar house and fronting St Thomas Lane and the church of St Thomas was a warehouse, still in use as a sugar warehouse in 1887 (BRO 36722, Boxes 1, 2, 4 and 7; Goad Insurance Map 12, January 1887; Fig. 2.4).

On the opposite side of the street the Bristol Distilling Company was established at Dundas Wharf, Nos 127–134, by the 1790s, possibly developing out of the business of Fear and Burgum, distillers and vinegarmakers, at No. 136 in 1775. The sugar house and distillery were certainly linked. The properties purchased for the sugar house included the Three Boars' (or Bears') Heads at No. 134 in 1775. The premises of the Bristol Distilling Company were largely destroyed by fire in September 1909 (BRO 05830 and 25641/10 and 12).

In the 19th century the landscape of Redcliff Street was much changed by widening the east side of the street. North of Little Thomas Lane, the east side of Redcliff Street was widened *c.* 1872 as part of the scheme to create Victoria Street. Nos 12–15 were purchased for street widening in 1869 (BRO 05613). No. 16 was purchased in 1872 (BRO 05615).

Between Little Thomas Lane and (St) Thomas Lane, the east side of Redcliff Street was widened *c.* 1878. The purchases of properties Nos 17–20 to be demolished in advance of widening were made in 1878 (Nos 48, 49 and 50 on the plan (BRO 06494(2) fol. 38; deeds are BRO 05830). No. 20 Redcliff Street already belonged to the City. The south side of Thomas Lane was widened *c.* 1880. The purchases of properties to be demolished in advance of widening were made in 1879 (BRO 06494(2) fol. 38). South of Thomas Lane the east side of Redcliff Street was widened *c.* 1880. Most of the purchases of properties to be demolished in advance of widening were made between 1876 and 1879 (BRO 06494(2) fol. 38). No overall plan of this scheme to the south of Little Thomas Lane (BRO Undertaking No. XII in the Provisional Orders) has been traced.

Tenements within the excavated area

The excavations were situated within the plots numbered from 1775 to the 1880s as Nos 11–20 Redcliff Street (Fig. 2.3). For few of these properties has it been possible to extend the histories of the tenements back beyond the 18th century:

The properties of Burton's chantry in the church of St Thomas the Martyr (possibly within the excavated area)

In 1454 Thomas Burton devised to the trustees of his chantry two adjacent tenements and one nearby fronting Redcliff Street, and also two tenements in St Thomas Lane opposite the south door of the church (Veale 1950, 58). In 1548 these same tenements were said to be in the parish of St Thomas (TNA E318/33/1845). Since no mention is made of their extending back to the Avon it can be concluded that they lay on the east side of Redcliff Street, within Nos 1–32, the part situated in the parish of St Thomas. These tenements, and those adjacent, can be described from north to south as follows:

A: A tenement of Thomas Parkhous, occupied in 1454 by Thomas Tadleton, latimer (an interpreter), the part extending behind Nos 2–6 occupied by Nicholas Hyle.
B: A tenement occupied by John Elyot, brasier, late belonging to Thomas Fysshe.
C: A tenement occupied by John Elyot, brasier.

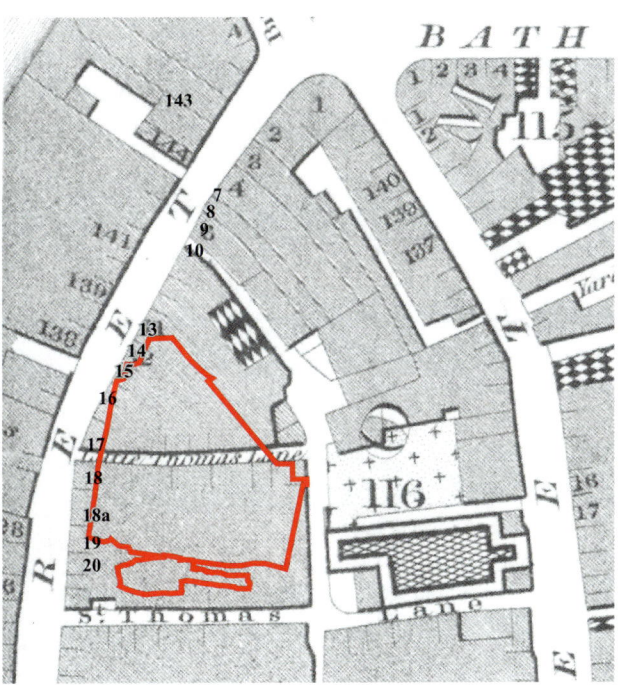

Fig. 2.3 Ashmead's map of 1828 (detail), showing site location and street numbering used between 1775 and the 1880s

D: A tenement of John Hampton of Bath, occupied by William Hone, weaver, conveyed to John Bushe of Wellow, Somerset in 1456 (Bickley 1899, 87–8).
E: A tenement occupied by William Tanner, potter, but described as a brasier in 1454 (ibid.).
F: A tenement occupied by Thomas Vyell, gent., occupied by Thomas Taillour.

Owing to the presence of brasiers (evidence for metalworking) it would be tempting to correlate these tenements with those excavated at the modern Nos 1–2 Redcliff Street. However there is no mention in the abuttals of Little St Thomas Lane or St Thomas Lane, which would have placed them firmly in this location.

Nos 11 and 12

In 1780 this was the property leased by John Croft esq. and George Watson the younger, merchant, to Thomas Cave, wine merchant, late of William Ludlow the younger, grocer [at No. 12 in James Sketchley's street directory of 1775], and now of William Mills, baker, as tenant, consisting of a tenement some years since new erected, where George Bridges the elder, distiller, lived. And the little tenement adjoining formerly of William Naish, cooper, in the parish of St Thomas, between a tenement formerly of Capel Haubury and now a warehouse late of John Crofts and George Watson and partners, and now of John Croft, Joseph Glover and James Whitchurch on the south [the property below, identified here as No. 13], and a tenement formerly of Edward Millard sergemaker [No. 10 in 1775; Sketchley] and in the tenure of Bridget Elsworthy, now of ---, on the north, extending back to the Red Lyon Inn, and part of the tenement of Capel Haubury (BRO 05613, conveyance of 1780, paraphrased; the identification of the location of this and adjacent tenements is based on the correlation of the plan for the street improvements of 1868 (BRO 07711(14b)) with the deeds of the compulsorily purchased properties, listed in the accompanying schedule of 'provisional orders' (BRO 06495(1) fols 72–4).

No. 13

In 1780 this was the property sold by John Crofts esq. and George Watson the younger merchant to Thomas Cave wine merchant, the late tenement formerly two tenements heretofore of Thomas Puxton, after of Thomas Puxton his son, after of John Page surgeon, the greater part late in the occupation of Crofts and Watson, and now of Crofts, Joseph Glover and James Whitchurch, and by them used as warehouse [No. 13 in 1775; Sketchley], bounded on the south by a tenement heretofore of Thomas Willis victualler, late of John Crofts, Joseph Glover and James Whitchurch, and on the north the tenement heretofore of George Bridges the elder [the above property, identified here as Nos 11–12], extending from Redcliff Street back to the 'Red Lyon Inn' (BRO 06495(1) fol. 72, (BRO 05613, conveyance of 1780, paraphrased)). The tenement plot is shown as No. 12 on Ashmead's map of 1828 (Fig. 2.3).

Nos 14 and 15

The deeds for the two properties commence in 1868 (BRO 05614, deeds for property Nos 7, 8 and 9 on the plan for improvements to Redcliff Street in 1868). The most likely explanation for the absence of earlier deeds is that they could not then be found.

No. 16 (immediately north of Little Thomas Lane)

In 1700 this was the tenement late inhabited by Richard Thomas victualler, and now of Daniel Jones the younger [between Little Church Lane and a tenement formerly in the possession of Simms shoemaker] extending back to a tenement lately built and held by Daniel Jones the elder (BRO 05615). In 1737 it was late of Temperance Cook and now leased to James Rigbye gent., by c. 1740 in the possession of Richard Godwin cordwainer (BRO 04043(4) fol. 36, annotated as 'NR823', here paraphrased). The tenement plot is shown as No. 16 on the Goad Insurance Map 12, of 1887 (Fig. 2.4).

Little Thomas Lane lies between Nos 16 and 17.

Nos 17–20

Nos 17–20 were purchased for street widening in 1878, Nos 48, 49 and 50 on the plan of properties to be compulsorily purchased (plan is BRO 06494(2) fol. 38; deeds are BRO 05830). By 1931 Nos 17 and 20 were in separate ownership to No. 18 (BRO 18399(3)a).

Nos 18–20

In 1409 this (or part) was probably the tenement in Redcliff Street belonging to John Droys, between a tenement also of Droys and one belonging to William Warminstre, extending from the street back to the lane opposite the porch of the church of St Thomas behind, conveyed by John Uphyll, son and heir of Simon Uphyll, to William Tamworthe clerk (BRO P/StT/D/39).

From 1695 these were the premises of John Newport, sugar baker, and then from 1696 to 1709 of he and his partner George Tyte, grocer; from 1709 to 1728 of just Tyte. From 1729 these were the premises of the Rigges and from 1795 to 1808 of Henry Bright. A deed plan of the mid 19th century shows the premises and layout of the five tenement plots within Nos 17–20 in detail (BRO 36722, Boxes 1, 2, 4 and 7) (Fig. 2.5).

In 1775 Nos 18 and 20 were the premises of Keene, Allis and Thomas, sugar-refiners (Sketchley 1775). In 1823 this was the late sugar house and all other structures formerly of Thomas Keene sugar baker, also the tenement and warehouse formerly of Keene, erected and built by Joseph Rigge on ground where a tenement called the Gun formerly stood, and where Henry Bright decd. subsequently built a coach house, stable and other offices. Also part of the property was a tenement adjoining, with two pavements and one garden, formerly of Thomas Brook haberdasher and after of Robert Rogers soapmaker, in St Thomas Lane, between Redcliff Street on the west and St Thomas Lane on the east, the tenement formerly of Richard Woodson on the south and the tenement formerly of Thomas Holbyn baker on the north. Also part of the property were two other tenements, next to and opening into Redcliff Street, formerly of Bridget Need widow and Michael Warton shop keeper, which were some time since thrown together and used as one, known as the Three Bears' Heads and then late of Edward Carter as tenant.

All these premises were greatly altered by Henry Bright between 1795 and 1808 to form a sugar house, dwelling house, two warehouses, four lofts and hauling ways, stable, coach house, three counting houses, and other buildings, for the sugar refining undertaken by Bright and Messrs Tipton, Cole and Feddens. Later the sugar house was converted into a warehouse and used as such by J. and G. Thomas (BRO 05830, abstract of title of 1870, here paraphrased; see also the deed plan of the mid 19th century (Fig. 2.5). By 1887 No. 18 comprised three formerly separate tenement plots, all now of John Thomas and Sons Ltd (Goad Insurance Map 12; Fig. 2.4).

No. 20 (part of the lands of Lord Lisle)

In 1735 this was leased to Daniel Millard, house carpenter; by c. 1740 the tenement and garden was now in the possession of John Copnor baker, from 1743 leased to Hannah Catcott (BRO 04043(4) fol. 37). By 1791 it was leased to Nicholas Poole, the precise location and component parts of his tenement

Historical and Archaeological background 11

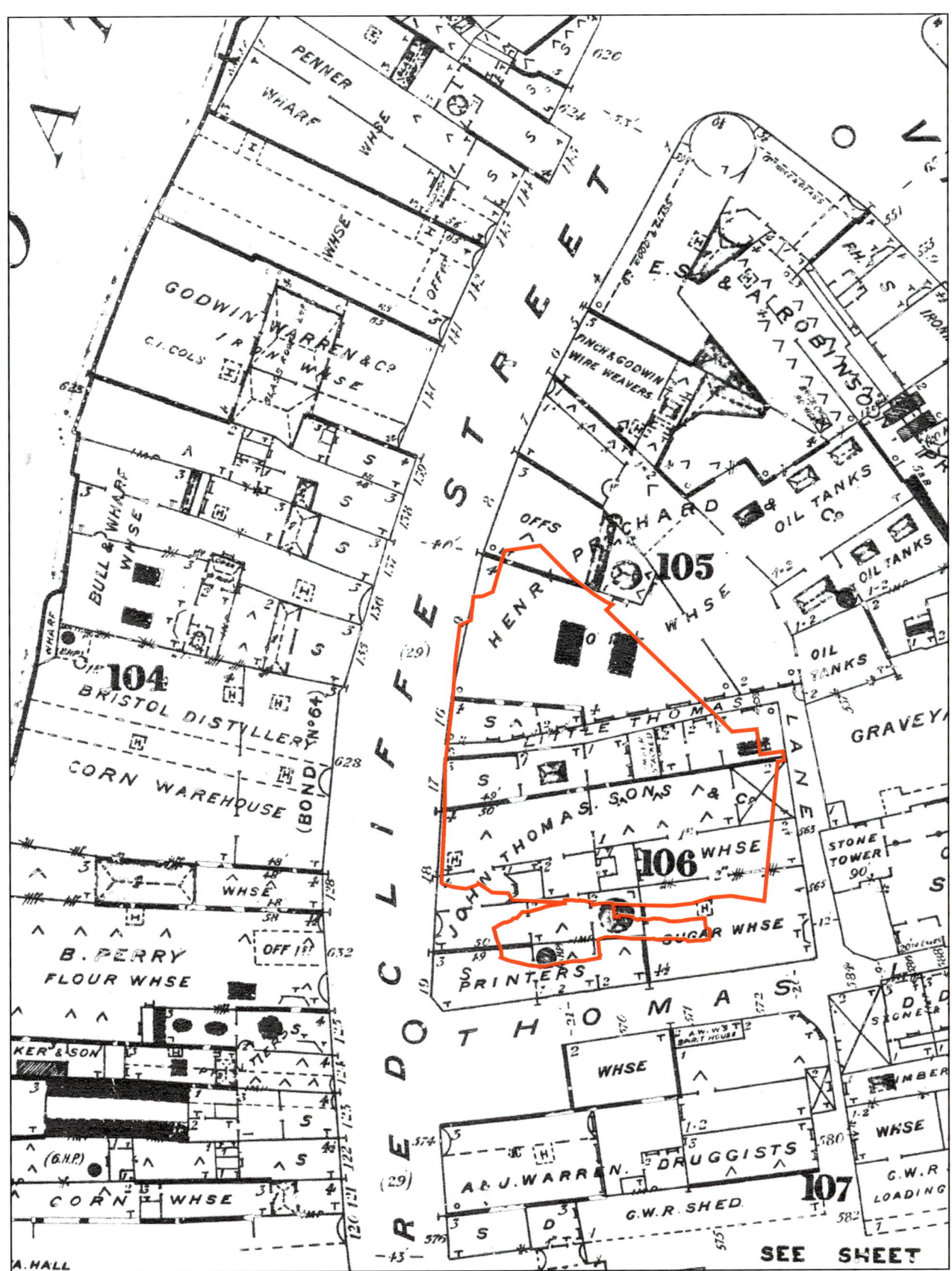

Fig. 2.4   Goad's Insurance Map 12 of 1887 (detail), showing site location

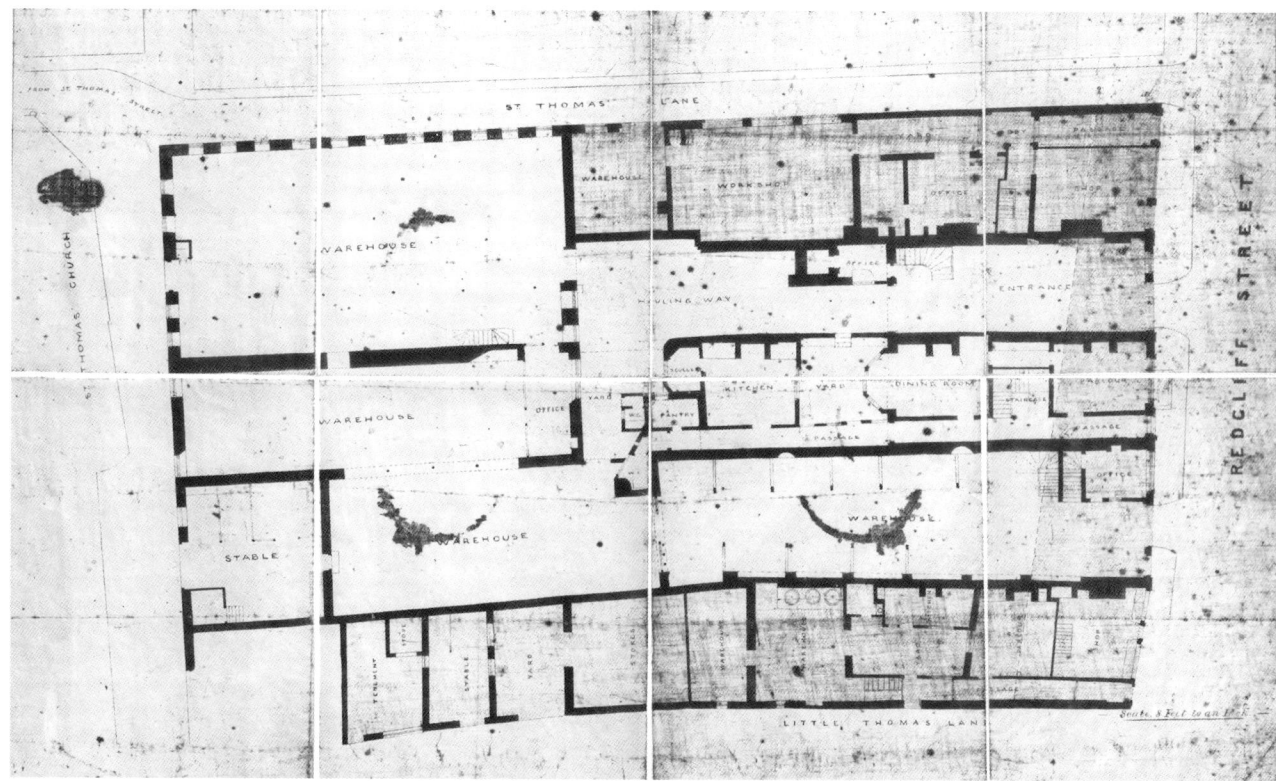

Fig. 2.5 Deed plan of the mid 19th century for Nos 18–20 Redcliff Street (also shows No. 17) (BRO 36722, Box 4)

shown on a plan ((BRO 09082(2) fol. 824; 00568(8) g, annotated 'CB 824'; 1640/37)). The tenement plot is shown incorrectly as No. 19 on the Goad Insurance Map 12, of 1887 (Fig. 2.4). Confusion had possibly arisen as a result of properties being demolished for the widening of Redcliff Street. To the south, No. 21 was designated for compulsory purchase in 1877, was absent from Kelly's Directory of 1883, and shown as an empty plot on the Goad Insurance Map 12 of 1887.

Conclusions

As will be seen, the above data can be correlated with difficulty with that from the archaeological excavations. The two substantial stone houses with garderobes of Period 2a were possibly those of John Droys in 1409. Droys was a member of the urban elite, three times mayor, in 1406–7, 1409–10 and 1414–5 (Latimer 1903, 130). The deed plan of the mid 19th century for Nos 17–20 (Fig. 2.5) shows very much the complementary nature of archaeological and historical evidence in an urban setting. The deed plan shows features not revealed by excavation and *vice versa*.

Over five or more centuries the north end of Redcliff Street was a mix of dwellings and industry. In the later medieval period industry was centred around the production and particularly the finishing of cloth. From the 16th and 17th centuries industrial processes linked to the Atlantic trades predominated, first of soap and then of sugar and its by-products. A significant part of the excavated site formed the sugar house founded by Robert Newport in 1695. Other trades included metalworking, possibly within the excavated sites.

2.2 Archaeological Background

Most of the previous archaeological recording along Redcliff Street has been undertaken adjacent to the waterfront and has demonstrated that the western side of Redcliffe was reclaimed from marsh by dumping considerable quantities of domestic and industrial debris, as well as through silt accumulation. Dendrochronological dating of structural timbers from the excavations at Dundas Wharf (Fig. 2.1, no. 3) has shown that the west side of Redcliff Street was being developed from c. 1123–33 and that quays were being built by 1147–8 (Nicholson and Hillam 1987, 141). At Bristol Bridge (Fig. 2.1, no. 2) the earliest excavated evidence for waterfront development dated to the 12th century and comprised a stone quay wall and a plank and stave revetment (Williams 1982). A wicker revetment of 12th-century date was found at 95–97 Redcliff Street (Fig. 2.1, no. 6) (Jones 1986), and structural evidence of this date was also found at Buchanan's Wharf (Fig. 2.1, no. 4) (Burchill *et al.* 1987). The earliest wharfside development at the former Courage Brewery (Fig. 2.1, no. 1) dates to the 13th century, although the 12th-century stone buildings behind the wharf show that the area was developed earlier (Jackson 2006b) and recent excavations at Finzel's Reach (Fig. 2.1, no. 12) suggest the earliest property boundaries may date to the late 11th or early 12th centuries (Kate Brady, pers. comm.). Where evidence survives it is apparent that the riverside wharves were largely infilled and replaced in the 13th century with stone structures that advanced the river frontage westwards. At Bristol Bridge the plank and stave revetment was reused as the back of a later 13th-century dock, and the possible line of the 13th-century bridge approach was also identified as a row of substantial timber piles (Williams 1981).

A large number of excavations and investigations on the west side of Redcliff Street suggest that by the 13th century the area between the street frontage and the wharves was fully developed, with evidence for substantial stone structures, for instance at Canynges House and Dundas Wharf, and for burgeoning industrial activity centred on dyeing and tanning (Williams 1981; Good 1991; Jones 1986), also found to the north of the bridgehead at the former Courage Brewery, and at Finzel's Reach, where evidence for hornering has also been suggested (Kate Brady, pers. comm.). Less archaeological investigation has taken place to date on the east side of Redcliff Street. Excavation at No. 3 Redcliff Street on the south side of St Thomas Street undertaken in 2003 was the most extensive of these investigations and is the subject of the accompanying report. Here, the earliest evidence for the development of tenement plots included the construction of stone-built walls, and was associated with pottery with a later 12th to mid 13th-century date range. A period of ground consolidation of the 13th to 14th century was followed by the construction of stone buildings fronting on to Redcliff Street and St Thomas Lane, and solidly-constructed dye vats to the rear where other evidence of occupation was also recorded. Away from the river frontage, and towards the southern end of Redcliff Street, suburban development was slightly later. Towards the north end of St Thomas Street at No. 14 an evaluation in 2002 revealed 1.4m of *in situ* medieval stratigraphy (BaRAS 2002a, 6–7; Fig. 2.1, no. 14). At 55–60 St Thomas Street (Fig. 2.1, no. 8) the burgage plots were laid out in the mid 13th century and the first substantive occupation dated to the late 13th to 14th century (Davenport *et al.* 2011). This compares with the earliest occupation at 26–28 St Thomas Street (Fig. 2.1, no. 7; Watts 2011a), and a little earlier than the 14th-century pits at Portwall Lane (Fig. 2.1, no. 10; Good 1989, 22) and at 30–38 St Thomas Street (Fig. 2.1, no. 9; Jackson 2004).

Evidence from the later medieval and post-medieval period excavations on the west side of Redcliff Street suggest mixed use of the tenement plots for warehouses, domestic dwellings and industry along with continuing development of the quays. The dyeing industry was supplemented by other industrial ventures linked to easy access to the raw materials shipped along the river, which included lime production, metalworking and tobacco. The excavated sequence at No. 3 Redcliff Street (detailed in the accompanying report) suggests a period of stasis centered on the 15th century was followed by further construction in stone including large cellars and other features probably associated with distilling.

At the south end of Redcliff Street and within the Redcliffe suburb activity was less intense with some evidence for a reversion to open ground used for cultivation and drying cloth. Early ironworking was replaced by copper-alloy casting at 68–72 Redcliff Street (Jones 1983) and there are indications that this industry took place elsewhere with clay mould fragments for casting found at 55–60 St Thomas Street in 15th to 17th-century deposits (Davenport *et al.* 2011) and in late 14th to early 15th-century deposits at the corner of St Thomas Street and Portwall Lane, the latter possibly from a bell foundry (Good 1989, 26).

Other findings in the near vicinity of the site at 1–2 Redcliff Street include the discovery of floor tiles in St Thomas Lane, probably deriving from the church of St Thomas (Bristol Urban Archaeological Database (BHER) event 48), and burials of unknown date during the excavation of evaluation trenches in the area of St Thomas's graveyard in 1994 (BRSMG 108). A paper given to the Bristol and Gloucestershire Archaeological Society in 1924 by H.C.M. Hurst refers to a conduit in the vicinity of St Thomas's Church, which was probably the culverted drainage ditch running behind the former tenement plots at Nos 1–2 Redcliff Street (BHER event 223). The post-medieval culvert roof was also identified in an evaluation at No. 14 St Thomas Street (BaRAS 2002a; Fig. 2.1, no. 14), and again at No. 18 St Thomas Street (BaRAS 2002b, 5; Fig. 2.1, no. 15).

No archaeological investigation had taken place in the development area at 1–2 Redcliff Street before the excavations which form the subject of this report. The most recent buildings on the site were offices erected in 1961. The office block occupied No. 1 Redcliff Street, with underground and overground car parking extended into No. 2 Redcliff Street. A desk-based assessment (MoLAS 1999a–c) concluded that the 20th-century building would have caused some areas of considerable truncation to earlier deposits, but enough was known about the character of the area to suggest that where deposits survived there would be a considerable depth of medieval and post-medieval remains of equal significance to those excavated on the west side of the street.

Chapter 3
Fieldwork Results

3.1 Introduction

The excavation included parts of several historic properties fronting Redcliff Street. The medieval and later street frontage lay beyond the western edge of excavation and therefore no property frontages were exposed (Redcliff Street was widened on its eastern side *c.* 1872–8). The site has been sub-divided into 10 tenement plots, given property numbers 11–20 Redcliff Street based on maps published by Ashmead in 1828 and Goad in 1887 (Figs 2.3 and 2.4). As has been detailed in Chapter 2.1 these numbers were only used between 1775 and the 1880s. The 1828 and 1887 maps show three of the properties amalgamated as No. 18. However, these properties were probably originally separate and are referred to in this report as Nos 18, 18a and 19, although the letter suffix for 18a does not have any historical derivation.

Modern cellars had extensively truncated deposits within Nos 11–15 and no archaeological remains were recorded from No. 11. Elsewhere truncation was more limited, and remains dating from the early 12th century through to the industrialisation of the area in the later post-medieval period were recorded. Aside from the issues of truncation, the quality of archaeological deposits was very good, and organic remains within medieval features were often well preserved and included timbers, wattling, leather, animal bone, horncores and other palaeoenvironmental material.

The archaeological sequence was divided into five periods based on the stratigraphic sequence, to which date ranges were derived from the artefact assemblages, supplemented for Periods 4 and 5 by the documentary evidence:

Period 1: early 12th to mid 13th centuries
Period 2a: late 13th to mid 14th centuries
Period 2b: mid 14th century
Period 2c: mid 14th to early 15th centuries
Period 3: early 15th to late 17th centuries
Period 4: late 17th to late 19th centuries
Period 5: late 19th to late 20th centuries

3.2 Geoarchaeological Deposits

The geoarchaeology encountered on the site is discussed in Chapter 5.5. Across the site, at the base of the archaeological excavations, the natural substrate recorded at between 6.6m and 6.9m AOD, comprised part of the Wentlooge formation, and consisted of bluish grey to light brown silty clay alluvium.

3.3 Period 1: early 12th to mid 13th centuries (Fig. 3.1)

This period dates to the development of the medieval fee of Redcliffe which excavations elsewhere along Redcliff Street have indicated was under way by *c.* 1123–1133 (Nicholson and Hillam 1987, 141). On the current site, this early colonisation comprised the construction of timber buildings with yards to their rears containing pits, surfaces and drains. The building evidence comprised postholes (some with timbers), beam slots and small patches of stone surfacing, which together represent the rear parts of buildings fronting the street. There was also evidence that at least some of the tenement boundaries established at this time were maintained throughout the medieval period and beyond. No dumped deposits suggestive of land reclamation were found and the features had been cut into the alluvium. In places, the alluvium was overlain by a mixed alluvium containing charcoal flecks and pottery. Period 1 spanned around 100 to 120 years, and this is reflected in evidence for repair and modification of the buildings.

Pits

Dense concentrations of pits were found to the rear of the buildings. The pits could be broadly sub-divided into two types, with the commonest comprising deep, sub-rectangular cuts with vertical sides and flat bases (Fig. 3.2), a number of which included the remains of plank and wattle linings or other internal wood or wattle structures (Fig. 3.3). These pits varied in size between pit

Fieldwork Results 15

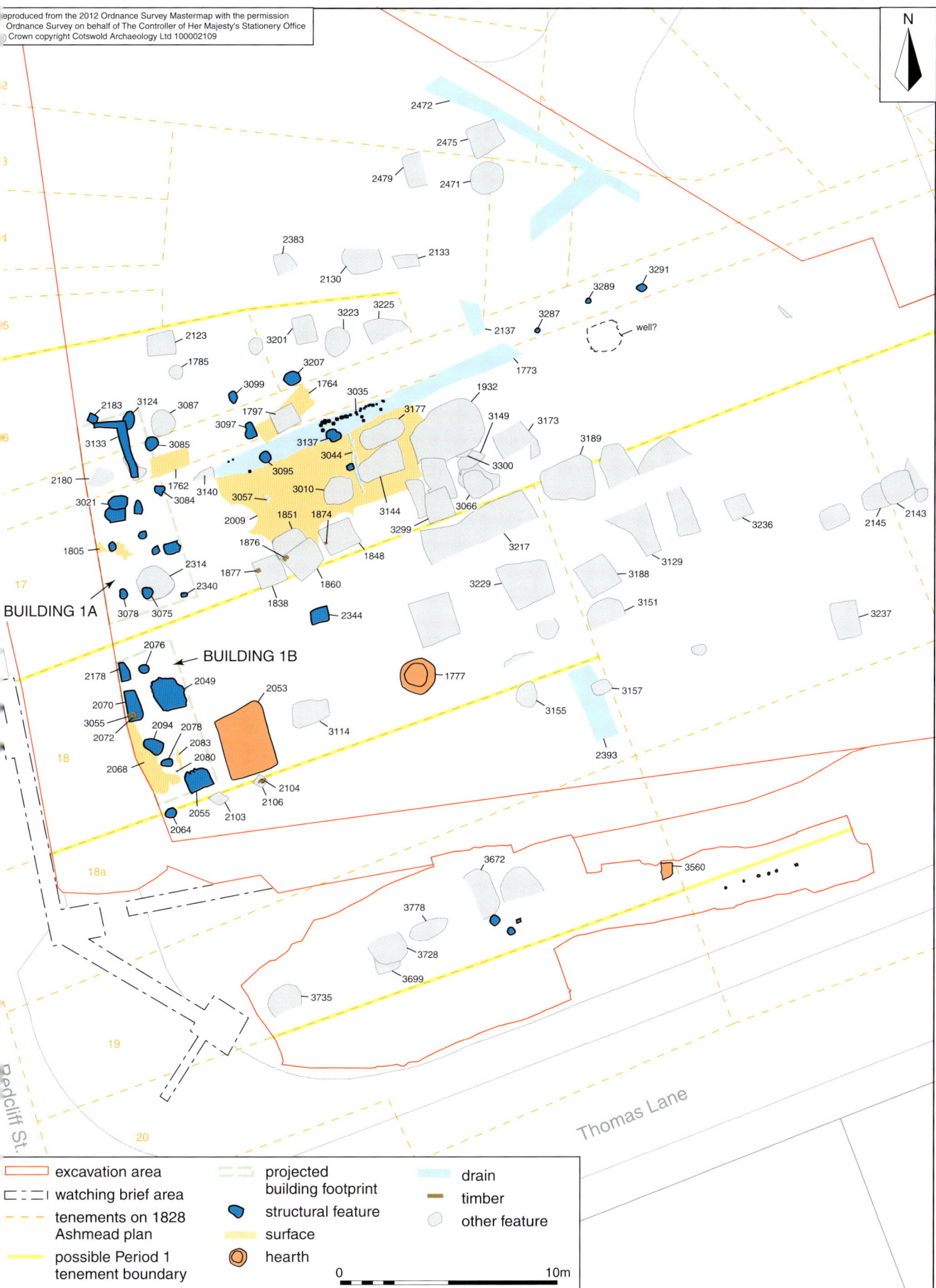

Fig. 3.1 Plan of Period 1: early 12th to mid 13th centuries. Scale 1:250

Fig. 3.2 Period 1 pit 3177 at Nos 16/17 Redcliff Street. Scales 1m and 0.3m

1848 which was 1.65m long, 1.4m wide and 1.5m deep and pit 3217 which was 5.4m long, 1.55m wide and 0.9m deep, with most examples being similar in size to the former. The second pit type occurred less frequently and comprised shallow oval/circular cuts with rounded profiles. These varied in size between pit 1785, which was 0.8m in diameter and 0.15m deep and pit 3087 which was 1.3m in diameter and 0.3 m deep.

Fig. 3.3 Wattle hurdle in Period 1 pit 3066 at Nos 16/17 Redcliff Street. Scales 1m

There was no evidence of primary silt deposits or stored material within the pits. Samples from the pit fills contained food waste and cess-related insect remains, along with animal bones that appeared to have been deposited soon after use, suggesting that the pit fills derived from the disposal of waste. Since it is unlikely that waste disposal was the primary use of the pits, given that many seem to have been carefully constructed, and occasionally lined, it would seem probable that this waste disposal is an opportunistic reuse of decommissioned features.

Along with food waste and cess, the pit fills frequently contained a high proportion of plant species associated with dyeing (weld, dyer's greenweed, madder and woad; Chapter 5.3). Some mineralised plant remains and concretions were suggestive of urine, which might reflect the presence of cess or the use of urine in dyeing. Further evidence for industrial activity contained within the pit fills was a bias in the animal bone assemblage towards skull and sawn horncore fragments, indicating that cattle, sheep/goats and pigs were being processed for hornering, although in general, butchery seems to have occurred only at domestic levels (Chapter 5.1). Many leather items, mostly worn footwear and leather scraps, were recovered from pit fills across the site and this material is suggestive of cobbling, the practice of buying old shoes for refurbishment and resale (Chapter 4.11).

It is considered that the primary function of most or all of the carefully-constructed pits probably related to an industrial process, perhaps dyeing, given the large amount of waste material from this activity, although the authors are aware that this is one of a number of possible interpretations of the pits' original purpose. An industrial use would explain the absence of any primary fills, as these features would presumably have been regularly scoured out during use.

Nos 12–15 Redcliff Street

Several pits were located to the rear of Nos 12–15. Pits 2383, 2130 and 2133 were laid out in a row, perhaps alongside a boundary between Nos 14 and 15, for which no other evidence survived. A similar row comprising pits 2123, 3201, 3223 and 3225 lay within No. 16, although whether this reflects the existence of a property boundary between Nos 15 and 16 at this date is unclear. The pits included sub-rectangular, vertical-sided, flat-based cuts, such as pit 2123, which was 1.3m long, 1.1m wide and 0.75m deep, and examples with rounded profiles, such as pit 3087 which was 1.3m in diameter and 0.2m deep. One of the sub-rectangular pits, pit 2130, contained an *in situ* oak board (2125), probably a reused building weather board (Chapter 4.12), held on its side by stakes to bisect the pit base. In addition to the finds and palaeoenvironmental remains common to most of the Period 1 pits across the site, pits 2475 and 2479 contained leather scraps likely to have been cobbling waste.

Nos 16/17 Redcliff Street

Building 1A

A series of postholes and beamslots was found towards the west side of Nos 16 and 17 which probably formed the rear of a building (Building 1A) fronting Redcliff Street. Beamslot 3133 extended across what later became Little Thomas Lane, demonstrating that this was not yet in existence, and it is likely that Nos 16 and 17 was a single tenement containing a building with a width of *c.* 8.5m between beamslot 3133/posthole 3124 and postholes 2340/3075/3078. Posthole 3084 contained a stone and plank postpad whilst posthole 3124 contained two wooden stakes. All these features were cut into the alluvium and most contained single clayey fills deposited when the posts were removed.

Postholes 2183 (post 2182), 3085 and 3021 were cut through the mixed alluvium and possibly represent repairs or remodelling of the building. Posthole 3021 contained two cleft oak boards that may have formed a postpad. Within the building, part of a Pennant sandstone flag surface (1805) survived, but too little of the building was exposed to reconstruct any floor plan. The pottery assemblage from the postholes was small, but comparable to that recovered from the mixed alluvium, and dateable to the first half of the 12th century.

Features to the rear of Building 1A

The rear part of the tenement was presumably a yard behind Building 1A and within this stone surface 2009 was laid. This surface comprised roughly-laid stones and slabs abutting the south side of wood-lined drain 1773 (Fig. 3.4). Similar surface fragments (1762 and 1764) survived to the north of the drain. The drain itself was 0.85m wide, 0.3m deep and lined with wattling held in place by a series of hazel, holly and fruitwood stakes (Fig. 3.5). The drain ran eastwards from the building for 15m, with further stake-holes (3287, 3289 and 3291) indicating that it probably emptied into the 'Law Ditch' which ran to the rear of the properties and which probably served as a drain and open sewer for adjoining tenements on both sides (Chapter 2.1). Two smaller and fragmented wattle and board-lined drains, 3057 and 3044, within surface 2009 probably fed run off from the surface into drain 1773. A post from drain 1773 (post 3035) had been felled after 1175 (Chapter 4.13), but may be part of a later building, or relate to a relining of the drain, an earlier phase of which is suggested by the presence of board fragments behind the wattling. All of the drains incorporated reused wood fragments, including two boards and a post from timber buildings, another board which might have been a former door ledge or window shutter, and a board probably originally from a clinker-built boat (Chapter 4.12). Conjoining finds from drain 1773 and surface 2009 reveal that these were open at the same time and since the surface abutted a number of pits, it was probably a work surface for activities associated with the pits, with the drains removing waste.

The pits included examples of the sub-rectangular, vertical-sided, flat-based type (between 1.5–2m long, 0.9–1.3m wide and 0.5–0.7m deep) and pits 3010 and 2314 which had rounded profiles and were 1.6–1.8m wide and 0.3m deep. Several of the sub-rectangular pits contained wooden structures, the best preserved of which was within pit 3300, a sub-rectangular cut 2m long, 1.8m wide and 0.6m deep containing two lines of hurdles set at right angles around a timber post. One hurdle ran along the pit's eastern edge, whilst the other bisected the pit just off-centre. Sub-rectangular pits

Fig. 3.4   Period 1 drain 1773 and surface 2009 at Nos 16/17 Redcliff Street, looking north-east. Scales 2m

Fig. 3.5 Wattlework drain 1773 at Nos 16/17 Redcliff Street under excavation, looking west

3066, 3173, (Figs 3.3 and 3.6), 3149 and 3299 were also wattle-lined whilst sub-rectangular pits 1860, 1848 and possibly 3299 had board linings held by stakes. At least one of the boards in pit 1860 was probably a reused roof shingle (Chapter 4.12). At least 13 examples of the sub-rectangular pits were present within this property, but many were intercutting and it is likely that only a small number were in use at any one time.

The line of the later tenement boundary between Nos 17 and 18 depicted on the 19th-century mapping of the area was respected by the buildings and pits, suggesting that it was established in the early stages of Period 1. Posts 1874, 1876 and 1877 lay to the north of the boundary between Nos 17 and 18. The posts were typical of earth-fast building posts of the Saxo-Norman period (Chapter 4.12) and were dated by dendrochronology to a felling date of 1174–1199 (post 1874) and 1176–1201 (post 1876). Since the posts were cut through several backfilled pits and were sealed by Period 2a deposits, they would seem to be a later addition. Unless these posts represent a shift in the boundary line to the north, it is probable that they supported part of an outbuilding. If this was the case, then the more substantial postholes cutting the backfill of drain 1773 (postholes 3095 and 3137), and postholes 3097, 3099 and 3207 might also have been part of this outbuilding or an adjoining structure.

Fig. 3.6 Wattlework in pit 3173 at Nos 16/17 Redcliff Street. Scale 1m

In addition to the artefactual and palaeoenvironmental remains common across the site, deposits within No. 17 contained other evidence for industrial or craft activities. This included fragments of ceramic inturned dishes from the fills of drain 1773 and pits 2314, 1838 and 1848 and from surface 2009. It has been speculated that such dishes found on other sites were for cheese making or formed the base of wattle bee hives, although other interpretations are possible (Chapter 4.1). The pit and drain fills and surface 2009 also included much of the leather cobbling waste retrieved from the excavation, and the discarded shoes amongst this material date stylistically to the mid 12th to mid 13th centuries (Chapter 4.11). Other notable finds included shears from posthole 3021 (Chapter 4.4, cat. no. 8; Fig. 4.4, no. 1); the base (and possible lid) of a wooden container from pit 1932 (Chapter 4.12; Fig. 4.24) and part of a stone mould for casting jettons from pit 3201 (Chapter 4.7; Fig. 4.14).

No. 18 Redcliff Street

Building 1B

Postholes 2076 and 2078 and stakehole 2080 probably defined the rear of a building within this tenement (Building 1B). No posts survived, but the relatively small size of the posts implied by the posthole dimensions (up to 0.45m in diameter and 0.3m deep) suggest that these supported wattle and daub walls (Chapter 4.12). Vertical-sided, flat-based pits/postholes 2094 and 2178 might also have been part of this building.

Mixed alluvium, similar to that seen at Nos 16/17, sealed postholes 2076 and 2078 and was cut by structural features likely to represent modification to Building 1B. These included postholes 2070, 2064, 2103 and 2106 as well as stone postpads 2049 and 2055, the latter features perhaps representing a change in building technique. Posthole 2070 contained wooden posts 2072 and 3055, both worked in characteristic 12th-century style (Chapter 4.12), and posthole 2106 contained an earth-fast rectangular post (2104) which tree-ring dating shows to have been felled in 1150–1160 (Chapter 4.13; a post felled 1510–1535 found within posthole 2103 alongside an undated post is assumed to be an intrusive pile associated with the construction of Period 3 Building 3A). Any doors to the rear of the property may have been in the side wall rather than the end, and it is possible that post 2072 within posthole 2070 was part of a door jamb, giving access to the rear of the building, with timber 3055 being part of a repair or packing. A patch of stone surfacing 2068 lay within the footprint of this rebuild, along with a small patch of mortar 2083, possibly the remnant of another surface or surface bedding layer. Occupation layer 2081 overlaid the stone surface and included a thin scatter of oyster shells.

Features to the rear of Building 1B

Directly to the rear of Building 1B, was a large rectangular stone hearth (2053). This comprised a rectangular base 3.25m long and 2.3m wide, built from Pennant flagstones. The stones had been scorched and were overlain by ashy layer 2052. Hearth 1777 was present 6m to the east and consisted of a circular Pennant stone base 1.6m in diameter overlain by scorched pink clay and charcoal lenses.

Sixteen sub-rectangular, vertical-sided, flat-based pits were revealed within the backland of the tenement, all of which were comparable in their morphology and fills to those found to the rear of Building 1A. For example, pit 3188 was sub-rectangular with steep/vertical sides and a flat base and was 1.85m long, 1.6m wide and 0.7m deep. Pit 3217 was unusually long at 5.4m but was otherwise comparable to other examples. Three pits with round profiles (pits 2149, 2145 and 3158) were also present and were also comparable to those found to the rear of Building 1A, being 0.75–1m in diameter and 0.1–0.2m deep. Although no surfacing was present, the pits had been laid out in rows extending at right angles to the property frontage (an impression slightly exaggerated by subsequent truncation) and it is possible that walkways existed between these.

The fills of both types of pits were similar to those at No. 17, being apparently derived from domestic waste, cess and industrial/craft residues. Samples from pit 3229 (fills 3199 and 3200) contained plant remains associated with dyeing, including abundant madder plant remains. Also present were abundant flax seeds, not found elsewhere on the site. Some of these seeds were crushed, which can be indicative of linseed oil production, which was also used in the dyeing process (Chapter 5.3). Pit 3217 contained a wood fragment, possibly part of a coopered vessel (fill 3219) from a tree felled 1152–77. The lower fill of pit 3188 included plank fragments, one of which came from a tree felled 1288–1313 (Chapter 4.13). Unless the wood was intrusive, this late date suggests this pit may have been infilled immediately before the later, Period 2 building was constructed.

The correlation of the southern extent of Building 1B and the pits with the later tenement boundary between Nos 18 and 18a shown on 19th-century mapping is striking and suggests this tenement plot was established from an early stage, although no physical remains of a boundary were present in this period.

No. 18a Redcliff Street

Few features were present within No. 18a, although the absence of structural remains comparable to those of Buildings 1A and 1B may reflect the limit of excavation, which excluded more of the area nearest the street frontage. Within the rear part of the plot, a possible drain 2393 ran across the width of the tenement. It was 1.15m wide and 0.15m deep and silted up during this period. It was cut by oval pit 3157 which was 0.9m long, 0.7m wide and 0.35m deep with steep sides and an undulating base. Two stakes in the pit base may have been the remains of a wattle lining. Two other pits dated to this period: pit 3237 was comparable to the sub-rectangular, steep-sided, flat-based pits found elsewhere whilst pit 3155 was of the rounded type. There was no evidence of a tenement boundary between Nos 18a and 19, although this might reflect the limited number of features present.

No. 19 Redcliff Street

Slightly more evidence was recorded within No. 19, comprising pits, a hearth and postholes. Again, the absence of building remains towards the plot frontage probably reflects the limited extent of excavation. Within the rear of the plot, three pits were found in a linear arrangement; although all three were truncated, it was apparent that pit 3735 was originally rounded and pits 3699 and 3672 were sub-rectangular, steep-sided, and flat-based. Pit 3672 included a wood lining and was located adjacent to three postholes which possibly supported an associated structure. Part of a hearth, 3560, survived to the rear of the pits, and comprised scorched red clay with burnt stones overlain by charcoal. To the rear of this, a line of six post/stake holes may have been the remains of a tenement boundary between Nos 19 and 20.

Dating evidence for Period 1

Saxo-Norman pottery was present in small quantities within the mixed alluvium, and the postholes were consistent in producing this early pottery, albeit in small quantities. These wares included 'motte ditch' type (BPT 6) and Bristol C wares with a late 11th to early 12th-century date range, and the handle of a Ham Green A jug dateable to *c*. 1120–*c*. 1150/60 (Chapter 4.1). Further dating for the construction of Period 1 features was provided through dendrochronological dates from structural features 2106 (felling date 1150–1160) and 1773 (felling date of after 1175) and for the plank linings of pits 1860 (felling date 1176–1201) and 1848 (felling date 1174–1199) (Chapter 4.13). Together, the Saxo-Norman pottery and slightly later dendrochronological dates suggest an ongoing phase of construction during the 12th century.

The majority of the Period 1 pottery assemblage was recovered from pit fills and dates their infilling to the mid 12th to mid 13th centuries. Typically for this period, unglazed cooking wares such as Ham Green redware (BPT 32), 'Bath A' type ware (BPT 46) and Pill/'Proto-Ham Green' coarseware (BPT 114) predominate and a date range for the assemblage of *c*. 1160/75 to 1250 is suggested by the relatively high quantities of Ham Green B compared to Ham Green A wares. Later Ham Green products which continue in use until *c*. 1275 were absent. Overall, the evidence of building repairs and of intercutting pits suggests that Period 1 extended over a long period, dated by the pottery assemblage to *c*. 1120–1250. A few late 13th-century finds were found within Period 1 features but are probably best regarded as relating to infilling prior to rebuilding in Period 2a.

3.4 Period 2a: late 13th to mid 14th centuries (Fig. 3.7)

Period 2 represents a clear break from the earlier activities. Based on the ceramic evidence, and on a *terminus post quem* provided by a dendrochronological date, there appears to be a gap of several decades (between *c*. 1250 and *c*. 1288–1313) between the end of Period 1 and the beginning of construction works in Period 2a. However, it is not clear whether this represents a true hiatus across the site or simply reflects changing depositional practices, with a decline in the number of pits towards the end of Period 1 meaning that later wares were less likely to be deposited. In any case, any suggestion of hiatus across the site most likely masks a more complex history of redevelopment within each plot. No remains were found within Nos 11–14 Redcliff Street, probably due to modern truncation, some pits and surfaces were found at No. 15, and at No. 16 hearths and two wells, with associated surfaces. Within Nos 17–20 the Period 1 pits and associated features were backfilled, some with stone rubble and clay capping deposits, and stone-founded buildings constructed above. The buildings within Nos 18 and 18a appear to have been built in a single phase and remained in use until the 18th century. Little Thomas Lane was laid out in this period and a small number of circular stone-built hearths were constructed, several of which were rebuilt throughout much of Period 2. Plant remains associated with cloth dyeing found in the backfills of pits suggest these hearths were associated with the dyeing industry. Evidence from the animal bone assemblage suggests that hornering continued on site, and a goose sternum may have been processed to create decorative inlays (Chapter 5.1). Further evidence of craft activity is provided by a spindlewhorl recovered from make-up layer 2043 (Chapter 4.7; cat. no. 1).

No. 16 Redcliff Street

Limited remains were found within No. 16. These included a highly truncated, 0.5m-wide Pennant stone wall (2013) bonded with pink sandy lime mortar which was abutted by a mortar bedding layer overlain by a patch of Pennant stone surfacing (2014). The surface had been cut by postholes 2020 and 2460, but whether these features collectively represent the remains of a building or a yard is unclear. To the south, a further posthole (2023) was present and behind these features was a small patch of make-up overlain by a skim of burnt stones, 1665, which might have been the base of a hearth, possibly comparable to the circular stone-built hearths found in plots to the south.

Fig. 3.7 Plan of Period 2a: late 13th to mid 14th centuries. Scale 1:250

Little Thomas Lane

Little Thomas Lane (named as such on Ashmead's 1828 plan; Fig. 2.3) was laid out between Nos 16 and 17 and consisted of a shallow construction cut into which a series of make-up layers and a cobbled Pennant stone surface had been laid. The surface was flanked by 0.6m-wide walls, built from randomly coursed Pennant stones bonded with reddish mortar (Fig. 3.8). The southernmost wall was interrupted by step 1455 which led from No. 17, suggesting that the walls survived above foundation level.

Fig. 3.8 Little Thomas Lane in Period 2a

No. 17 Redcliff Street

Remains within No. 17 included a few short lengths of walling, patches of Pennant stone surfacing, a drain, two wells and several hearths. Much of the surfacing abutted Little Thomas Lane, and incorporated a short length of drain 1911.

Towards the tenement frontage a patch of surfacing was associated with several circular stone-built hearths which showed evidence of rebuilding or replacement. Hearth 1724 survived only partially as a construction cut containing a pitched Pennant stone base bonded with pale grey sandy mortar. The stone base had been scorched, and the hearth was rebuilt as hearth 1637, which survived as a single course of a circular stone wall. Just to the north of this, hearth 1717 comprised a construction cut that was truncated along its western side, but which was probably originally circular and *c.* 2m in diameter. This contained a bedding layer of pinkish sandy mortar over which the partial remains of a Pennant stone base survived. It had been replaced by hearth 1712 which survived as a fragment of a stone base. To the north of this was a later hearth, 1685, which was one of the best-preserved examples on site. This survived as a circular construction cut into which a pitched Pennant sandstone base had been laid, surrounded by a Pennant stone wall which survived to a maximum of two courses. In common with the other hearth floors, that of hearth 1685 had evidence of scorching on the stones. Hearth 1685 was itself replaced by hearth 1683, which survived as a mortar bedding layer and an overlying pitched stone base. Both of these hearths appear to have been built up to, or even into, the southern wall of Little Thomas Lane, which survived only partially at this point.

A dark, organic-looking occupation layer 1812 butted the wall of Little Thomas Lane. It directly overlaid Period 1 surface 2009 and it is possible that the surface remained at least partially in use into this period. The occupation layer itself contained late 12th-century pottery and 13th-century shoes and a sample from it produced abundant madder fragments. The former presence of other surfaces within the tenement is suggested by a number of horizontal layers and by several patches of remnant stone surfacing. Built into one of these surfaces was drain 1911.

A large hearth 1776 was built partially into party wall 1794 with No. 18. It survived only partially as a clay bedding layer overlain by a charcoal spread 3.6m by 2m in extent and a squared slab. To the rear of the hearths was well 1822. This was a vertical-sided cut 2m in diameter and 2.9m deep. It was excavated to its base and one of its lower fills, 1821, included a wooden plank that may have been from a lining or superstructure and which came from a tree felled 1229–1254 (Chapter 4.13). There was a second well 1914 further to the rear of the tenement which consisted of a vertical-sided cut 1.6m in diameter which was stone-lined and partially built into the southern wall of Little Thomas Lane.

No. 18 Redcliff Street

A series of make-up layers laid down throughout the tenement raised the ground level in preparation for the construction of a rectangular stone-founded building, Building 2A, that was in excess of 15.4m long and 4.5m wide internally (Fig. 3.9). The surviving walls were constructed of a foundation of two courses of pitched limestones overlain by horizontally coursed, roughly-squared and faced limestones with a rubble core, bonded with reddish sandy mortar (Fig. 3.10). The walls forming the sides of the building were 1m wide, but to the rear they were 1.6m wide. The southern wall included sockets for three posts (3108, 3110 and 3111) suggesting that this was a dwarf wall supporting a wooden superstructure. A small stone cell (wall 3106) abutting the rear of the building may have been a garderobe, or stairwell, although no deposits relating to its use survived.

A short length of wall (1794) was present along the tenement boundary between Nos 17 and 18 and may have been the party wall between these properties. The gap between this wall and the walls of Building 2A may have been occupied by a passageway in which two small patches of a mortar surface survived.

Fig. 3.9 Buildings 2A and 2B of Period 2a with Period 1 pits also visible, looking south-west. Scales 2m

Fig. 3.10 Period 1 pit 3151 and Period 2a Building 2A wall, looking south-east. Scales 1m

Towards the western end of the building, a narrower, 0.5m-wide length of wall 3053 survived. The relatively narrow width of this wall might suggest that it was an internal partition, indicating that the original building extended further towards the plot frontage to include wall 1200. Alternatively, walls 3053 and 1200 might have defined part of a yard or outbuilding. In either case, a relatively complete circular stone-built hearth (1201) had been built into the angle of these walls. This hearth included a mortar bedding layer overlain by the surviving quadrant of a presumably formerly circular pitched Pennant stone surface with an outer wall.

Well 1445 behind Building 2A was 1.4m wide internally and lined with Pennant stone and clay. Its fill included clay mould fragments comparable to examples recovered from Period 3 deposits, suggesting that the well remained open into the early post-medieval period.

No. 18a Redcliff Street

A second stone-founded building (Building 2B) was present at No. 18a (Fig. 3.9). This survived less extensively than that at No. 18, but its construction and surviving plan were so similar as to suggest that these were built in one phase of construction, potentially by the same owner. A garderobe at the rear of this building survived, defined by walls 3107 and 3109. Wall 3109 sprang directly off the southern wall of Building 2A, which served as a party wall. However the location of wall 3112, suggests that a double wall between the properties existed further west. No further traces of Building 2B survived nearer to the street frontage.

No. 19 Redcliff Street

Relatively extensive remains were found at No. 19 and included a series of make-up layers laid down in advance of construction, along with stone foundations and walls, surfaces, hearths and a well. The walls that survived along the boundary between Nos 19 and 20 were substantial (0.9m to 1.6m wide), suggesting a building (Building 2C), that extended back almost as far as Buildings 2A and 2B (Fig. 3.11). The walls were constructed from Pennant stones with occasional limestones bonded by pinkish and yellow clay.

Fig. 3.11 Building 2C of Period 2a, looking south-west

Too little of the building survived to make an accurate assessment of its ground plan, but it included at least two to three rooms, sub-divided by wall 3561, and possibly by wall 3500, which survived just as a stub. The westernmost of these rooms contained hearth 3651 which comprised a construction cut into which a rectangular pitched Pennant stone base measuring 1.4m by 1.25m had been built. The hearth probably originally backed onto the south wall of the room against chimney stack 3540, although this relationship was lost to truncation. A blackish sandy layer 3590 found close to the hearth probably represents raked-out material and included a 13th to 15th-century copper-alloy buckle. Within the same room and to the west of the hearth there was a second circular stone-built hearth 3597. This comprised a construction cut containing a circular pitched Pennant stone surface 2m in diameter, which extended eastwards as a flue. A ring of whitish mortar surrounding the surface may have been the base of surrounding hearth wall. The hearth had been replaced by hearth 3534, which was of similar construction. Elsewhere, the room contained patches of Pennant flag surfacing along with stone drain 3649.

No features were found in the possible central room, a space approximately 2.5m wide defined by walls 3561 and 3500, which may have served as a passageway. Much of the rearmost room lay beyond the limit of excavation but a stone-lined well, 3550, had been built into the walls between Nos 19 and 20 and was probably shared between these properties.

No. 20 Redcliff Street

Very limited excavation was undertaken within No. 20. As at No. 19, the construction phase of Period 2a began with a series of red-brown clay make-up layers and three small pits containing mortar fills (3592, 3614 and 3625). Pottery from pit 3614 (fill 3615) and from make-up 3546 and 3601 indicates that construction began after the early 14th-century. Make-up layer 3675 included a silver Short Cross penny, probably dating to *c.* 1205–1217/18 (Chapter 4.3), but this was worn and may have been in circulation for a long time before deposition.

A series of fragmentary walls survived along the tenement boundary between Nos 19 and 20, adjacent to the foundations within No. 19. These included arched stonework 3800 of a type seen elsewhere in Bristol and interpreted as foundations designed for load bearing on a clay sub-base (Good 1991, 36, figs 9–10). Further evidence of efforts to improve building strength was provided by walls 3681 and 3678 which may have been buttresses. Some masonry survived above foundation level, including the base of a chimney stack 3323. Although too little of the building survived to reconstruct its groundplan, wall 3621 was 0.4m thick and may have been an internal wall. To its east, patches of stone surfacing survived, along with stone-lined drain 3641. A second drain, 3532, was present towards the rear of the tenement.

Dating evidence for Period 2a

A few of the later fills within Period 1 features contained finds post-dating *c.* 1250 and these probably relate to groundworks undertaken within the site prior to rebuilding during Period 2a. Several of the remnant hollows left by the Period 1 pits were backfilled and capped with clay and stone. Amongst these construction deposits was a small quantity of 'high medieval' pottery, most notably from pit 3066 (fill 3015) which included three Bristol and non-local jug type vessels dateable to after *c.* 1230/50, a bone knife handle, probably dating to the 14th century or later and a worn coin of 1205–1217/18, found within make-up layer 3675 at No. 20. A plank found within the backfill of Period 1 pit 3188 was probably dumped when this pit was levelled during the Period 2a construction works and provides a dendrochronological *terminus post quem* of 1288–1313 (Chapter 4.13) for this period, at least at No. 18.

Ceramically, Period 2a shows a change from Period 1 with the earlier unglazed cooking wares declining in frequency in favour of glazed Ham Green types dateable up to the mid 13th century. The absence of 'late medieval' wares from Period 2a suggests that this activity pre-dates *c.* 1350 and so Period 2a represents a relatively short time span compared to Period 1.

3.5 Period 2b: mid 14th century (Fig. 3.12)

Across much of the site, the Period 2a buildings and associated features were retained and activity within Period 2b was restricted to modifications at No 17. These included the insertion of new walls and hearths as well as a continuation of the rebuilding of the circular stone-built hearths and the creation of a large cistern.

No. 17 Redcliff Street

Well 1822 was backfilled with rubbly fill 1820 and capped with red-brown clay 1819, and a series of red-brown clay make-up layers were then laid down. Following this a 0.3m-wide wall 1654 was built over the backfilled well, and probably formed a room or yard (Building 2D) along with wall 1541 and the retained earlier walls. Patches of Pennant stone surfacing and mortar bedding survived within the room, as well as possible postpad 1650. An occupation layer (1577; not illustrated) within this area included half of all the fish bones recovered from this period (Chapter 5.2).

Within, or to the rear of, this room or yard stone cistern 1604 was constructed (Fig. 3.13). This consisted of a square construction cut with vertical edges lined to a width of 0.3m to 0.4m with roughly-squared Pennant stones bonded with grey clay, creating a shaft that was 2.2m deep and 2m by 2m internally. The walls incorporated a reused post (1741) which had a dendrochronological felling date of 1178–1203 (Chapter 4.13) and thus derived from a much earlier building.

Fieldwork Results 25

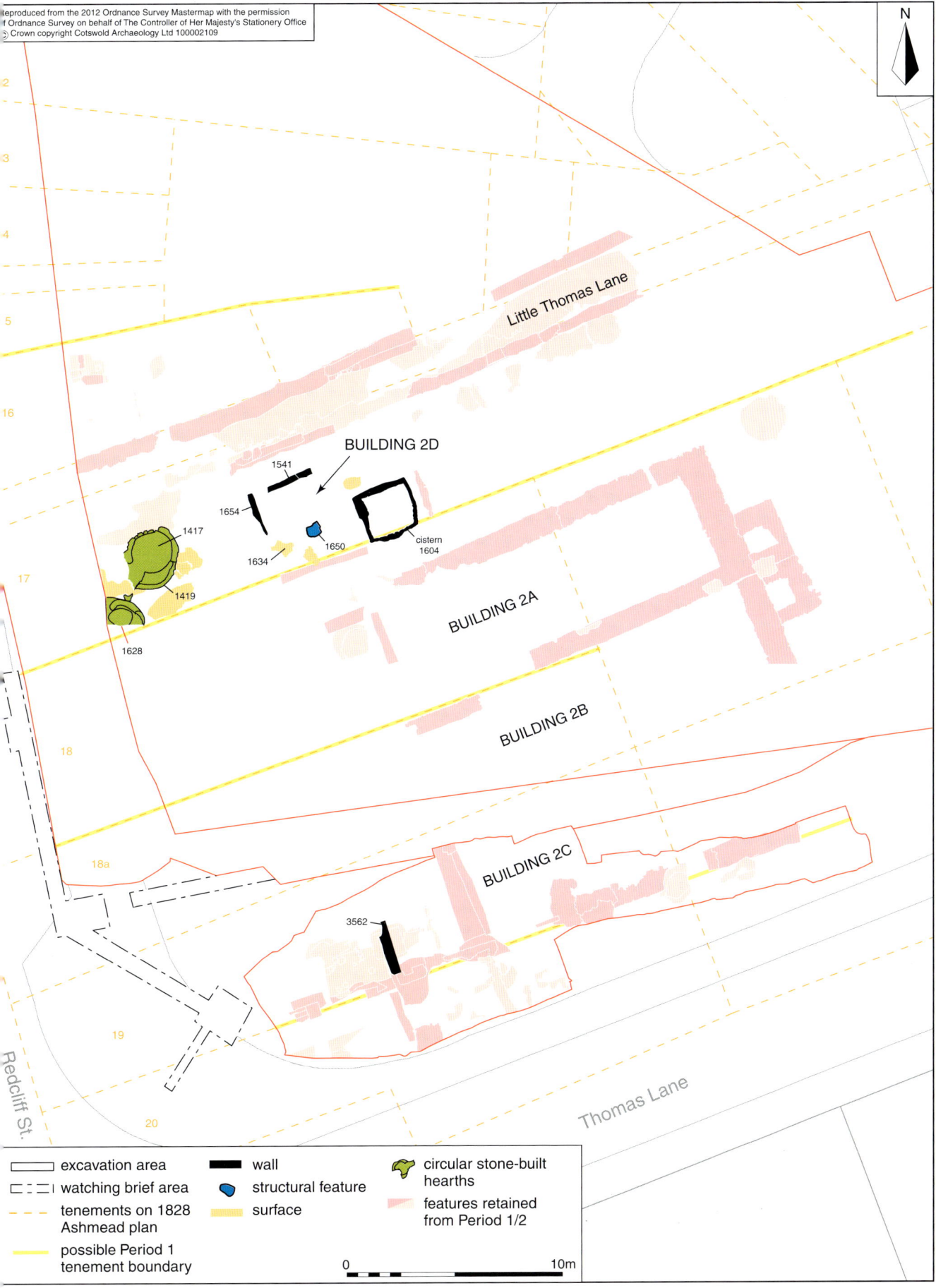

Fig. 3.12 Plan of Period 2b: mid 14th century. Scale 1:250

Fig. 3.13 Period 2b cistern 1604. Scales 1m

Towards the tenement frontage, the industry represented by the stone hearths in Period 2a continued with further hearths constructed and subsequently replaced. To the west of the new room/yard, a red clay make-up 1603 was cut by the construction cut for circular stone-built hearth 1538 (not illustrated), which survived as a sandy bedding layer overlain by a circular base of pitched Pennant stones 2.37m in diameter. Patched repairs to the base were evident and it was surrounded by a Pennant stone wall. It was replaced by circular stone-built hearth 1419 which survived only partially but was of similar construction. This had been partially demolished and the resulting material used as make-up for the construction of another circular stone-built hearth 1417 (Fig. 3.14). This was similar to the earlier structures and included a 0.5m-wide Pennant stone flue extending from the stone base through a gap in the outer wall. A further circular stone-built hearth, 1628, was built to the south, but this survived only partially. Patches of pitched and slab Pennant stone surfacing survived around these hearths, overlain in part by an organic occupation layer 1381, that contained frequent charcoal inclusions.

The cistern was filled by a series of organic deposits interleaved with thin silt layers, suggesting that this infilling occurred over a protracted period with occasional dumping into a disused feature interspersed with periods of natural infilling. These deposits were sealed by a series of organic fills of which 1723 comprised fragmented wood and fibrous red/purple organic material, and 1643 comprised abundant madder. A discarded timber (1726) within fill 1711 included a tenon typical of late 12th/early 13th-century carpentry techniques (Chapter 4.12).

Dating evidence for Period 2b

The limited extent of Period 2b features is reflected in the small size of the pottery assemblage associated with the period. The assemblage differs from that of Period 2a in that over half of the wares are 'high medieval' types. Amongst these, the plainer types of jugs in Bristol glazed ware (BPT 118L) indicate dating after *c.* 1300/25, whilst the presence of some partially glazed jugs and bottles, including from construction make-up 1603, indicate a mid 14th-century date. One tree-ring determination, suggesting a felling date 1178–1203, was obtained from stone tank/cistern 1604 and is significantly earlier than the dating suggested by the pottery. This feature produced 37 sherds from seven fills. The dating is consistent across the different fills and includes 16 sherds of types BPT 118, BPT 134 and BPT 84 suggestive of dating after *c.* 1250.

3.6 Period 2c: mid 14th to early 15th centuries (Fig. 3.15)

Period 2c comprised rebuilding at Nos 16, 17 and 20. Within the remainder of the site, the earlier Period 2 buildings were retained, and there was evidence at No. 16 that some of the earlier activities continued into this period with the construction of further circular stone-built hearths. At No. 17 a new activity was represented by the construction of a large furnace associated with the working of copper alloy.

No. 16 Redcliff Street

At No. 16 ashy make-up layer 1697, probably industrial waste, was dumped, followed by the construction of walls 1479 and 2002. Wall 1479 was 0.55m wide and constructed from Pennant stones, roughly faced on either side with a rubble core and bonded with pinkish lime mortar. Wall 2002 was of similar size and build, and included a patch of render on its northern face suggesting that these walls enclosed a room (Building 2E). Pennant flagstone surface 2022 was laid within

Fig. 3.14 Period 2b circular stone-built hearth 1417/1419 looking north-east, with Period 2c water butt 1352 to the right of the 1m scale

Fieldwork Results 27

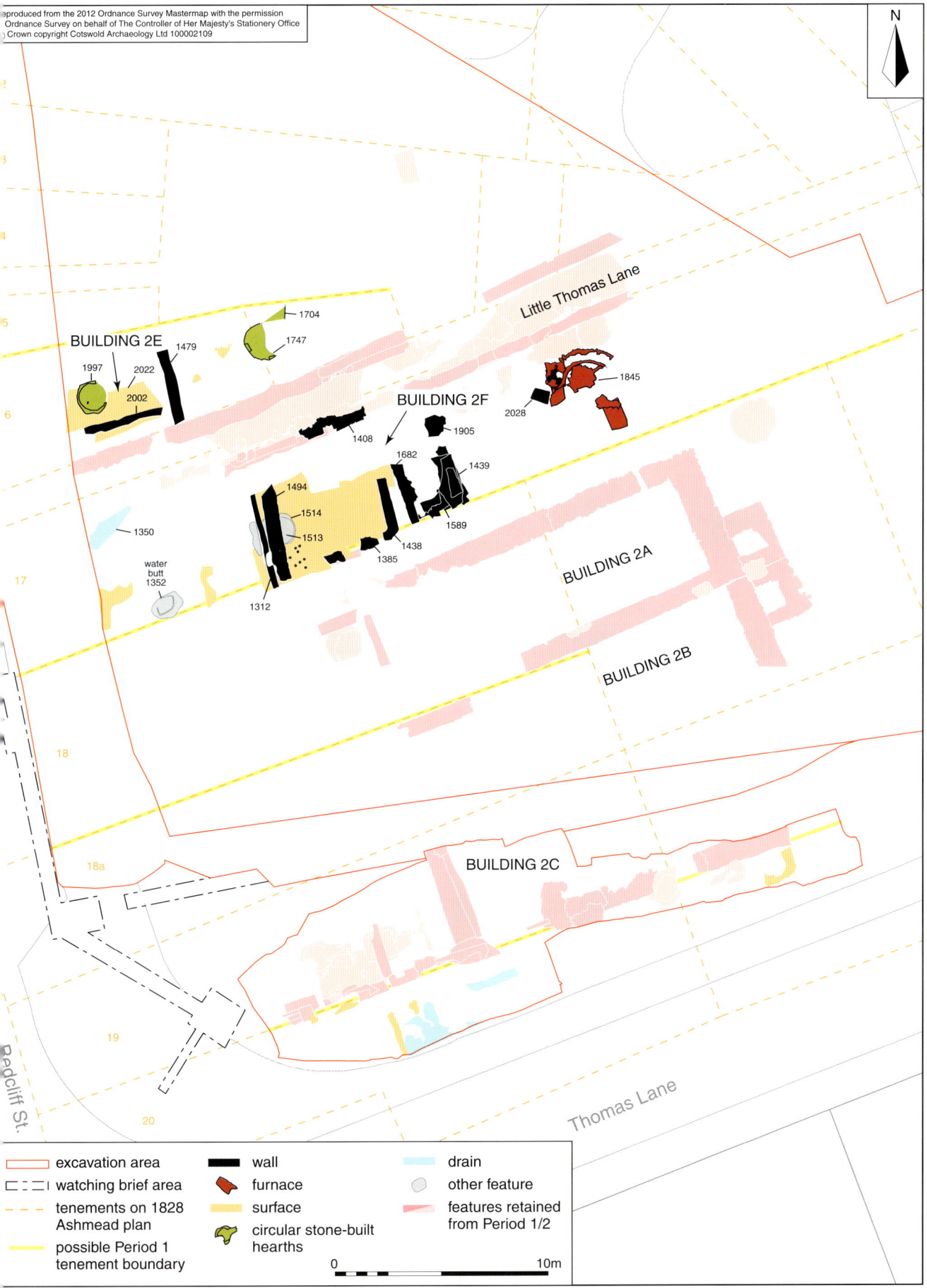

Fig. 3.15 *Plan of Period 2c: mid 14th to early 15th centuries. Scale 1:250*

Building 2E, along with circular stone-built hearth 1997 which consisted of a circular pitched Pennant stone floor, 1.5m in diameter, surrounded by a circular hearth wall. Surface 2022 was overlain by blackish occupation layer 2005 which contained a bone stylus/parchment pricker dateable to before the 15th century (Chapter 4.4).

A narrow gap between this room and Little Thomas Lane, whose walls were retained into this period, may have been a narrow passageway or storage area within which a strip of Pennant flagstone surface survived. A second circular stone-built hearth was built to the rear of the new room. The original build survived only as wall fragment 1704 although the rebuild, 1747, survived more fully as part of a circular pitched Pennant stone floor surrounded by a circular stone wall.

No. 17 Redcliff Street

The Period 2b cistern was fully backfilled with a series of cess, ash and mortar dumps and capped with clay. Above this, walls and surfaces were constructed defining a passageway between two rooms (Building 2F). The passageway was flanked by walls 1438 and 1682 and was adjoined to the rear by a small room, defined by stone walls 1905 and 1439/1589 which survived mostly at foundation level. No surfaces survived within this room.

The westernmost room was defined by walls 1494/1312, 1438 and 1408 built up against the existing tenement boundaries. An early 15th-century French jetton (Chapter 4.3) was found within wall 1494. Intercutting pits found beneath the walls may have been associated with the construction of this building and included pit 1513 which was clay lined and contained lenses of mortar. The room had been surfaced with stone, with evidence of patches of repair and contained a series of stakeholes which may have supported a structure, although no definitive plan of this was apparent. The surface was overlain by blackish occupation layers, of which layer 1341 contained a medieval lead measuring weight (Chapter 4.4, object no. 11). Occupation layer 1345 comprised reddish clay and blackish sandy silt which included clay mould fragments and two copper-alloy pins.

To the front of Building 2F the earlier Period 2 circular stone-built hearths were sealed by make-up deposits for new stone surfaces which survived as patches, along with the remains of stone drain 1350 which might have originally fed into Little Thomas Lane. One of these surface patches abutted oval pit 1352, which was 1.1m long, 0.8m wide and 0.35m deep with vertical sides and a flat base. It had been lined with clay which preserved indentations that were possibly from the metal bands of a barrel, although no further remains of this were found, and the pit possibly served as a water butt (Fig. 3.14).

To the rear of Building 2F furnace 1845 was constructed (Fig. 3.16). This comprised a construction cut onto which a bedding layer and pitched stone base were laid. The base was probably originally circular and *c.* 1.85m in diameter

Fig. 3.16 Period 2c furnace 1845. Scale 1:400 approx.

and was surrounded by a circular Pennant stone wall 1844 which survived up to ten courses high. This wall was itself surrounded by structure 1939/1940 which was the remains of a clay-domed superstructure. The stone base extended southwards for 0.65m from the furnace, presumably as a flue, and the furnace interior had been scorched. Several deposits within the furnace appear to have been associated with its use. These included grey silt and charcoal layer 1842, which overlaid the furnace floor and contained clay mould fragments for the manufacture of metal cauldrons/posnets. The casting technology for these vessels was current in England from the late 12th century until *c.* 1690/1700, but the mould shapes allow for closer dating within the late medieval to early post-medieval periods (Chapter 4.5). Two spreads of black ash found outside the furnace were probably raked-out during its use and a small pit filled with mortar to its immediate west (pit 2028) was perhaps associated with its construction.

No. 20 Redcliff Street

The limited parts of No. 20 that were exposed also showed evidence for redevelopment in this period. Make-up layers were dumped throughout the tenement and towards the frontage, a series of stone drains and surfaces were present, all of which survived only as fragments. Towards the rear of the tenement further stone surfacing was laid.

Dating evidence for Period 2c

The majority of the ceramic assemblage from Period 2c derived from make-up layers and most comprised later Bristol glazed wares, regional glazed wares and south-west French types; the greater frequency of glazed wares provided a clear distinction from earlier periods. Specifically the presence of Malvern Chase redware (BPT 197) and 'Tudor Green' ware (BPT 182) within make-up layers 1155 and 1291 for water butt 1352; drain 1350; occupation layer 1346 and dumped layer 1814, all at No. 17, indicate a date after *c.* 1400/1420, and an early 15th-century jetton was recovered from the same plot.

3.7 Period 3: early 15th to late 17th centuries (Fig. 3.17)

Period 3 relates to a period of redevelopment across much of the site. The last of the Period 2 circular stone-built hearths was levelled and infilled and industrial redevelopment relating to metalworking was undertaken at Nos 16 and 17, along with rebuilding at Nos 18a and 19. At No. 18 stone-founded Period 2 Building 2A was retained and this also seems to have been the case at No. 18a (Building 2B), although here, a new building was added towards the street frontage. Little Thomas Lane remained open, with minor modifications, although encroached upon by a furnace at No. 17.

No. 16 Redcliff Street

At No. 16 the Period 2c structures were levelled to near foundation level and sealed by make-up deposits. A stone-lined drain, 2007, towards the frontage probably fed into a former drain along Little Thomas Lane.

The major surviving development was the construction of furnace 1426 (Fig. 3.18). This was a sub-rectangular stone-built structure 2m long and 1m wide, which consisted of a floor and walls, an internal partition wall and a chimney. The presence of a chimney and partition wall suggest that this was a reverberatory furnace, a technology developed in the later medieval period for melting copper alloy for large items such as cauldrons (Chapter 4.6). Burnt deposits, some containing copper slag pieces, were found within the furnace, of which ashy layers 1405/1407 included an unfinished copper-alloy candlestick dateable to between *c.* 1400 and the late 16th century (Chapter 4.4, cat. no. 2; Fig. 4.4; no. 5) as well as clay mould fragments for similar candlesticks and for cauldrons/posnets, all of which date stylistically to the late medieval to early post-medieval periods. A further ashy layer 1429 within the furnace contained charcoal from oak, a wood suitable for maintaining the high even temperature required for copper casting (Chapter 5.3). The remains of kindling were also present, along with a small oak timber (1406) with traces of red pigment which may have been a piece of furniture or machinery (Chapter 4.12) intended for reuse as fuel. A small patch of stone surfacing adjoining the furnace was overlain by scorched clay which was probably raked-out from the furnace.

Vertical-sided, flat-based pit 1436 lay to the immediate west of the furnace. It was 1.3m in diameter and 0.3m deep and appears to have been kept clean until it was deliberately backfilled, which possibly indicates that it was a casting pit or held water for cooling. The backfill, 1392, was an ashy deposit presumably derived from the furnace, and included further crucible fragments and a 13th to 14th-century copper-alloy buckle (Chapter 4.4, cat. no. 3; Fig. 4.4; no. 6) which might have been either an accidental loss of an heirloom item, or an old item kept for remelting.

No. 17 Redcliff Street

Extensive rebuilding occurred at No. 17. Period 2 well 1914 was backfilled with deposits containing 15th to 16th-century pottery, furnace 1845 was levelled, and pit 1513 in Building 2F was backfilled with silty clay mixed with mortar lenses (the mortar possibly being construction or demolition debris). The southern wall of Little Thomas Lane was retained. The rear room of Building 2F was demolished, although the front room may have remained in use.

To the front of Building 2F stone-lined drain 1283 was built and probably fed into Little Thomas Lane. Pit 1340 comprised a rectangular cut 2.8m long, 0.95m wide and 0.45m deep with vertical sides and a flat base. It appears to have been kept clean until backfilling and may have been an industrial feature, such as a casting pit or water store.

To the rear of Building 2F there was a large number of pits and two hearths, along with associated stone surfacing. There was no indication that these features were within a former building, and they may have been in a yard, although the possibility that a former stone or timber building was present but fully removed by truncation cannot be discounted. The hearths were built up against the boundary with No. 18. Hearth 1767 was square in plan, surviving to its full width of 1.85m but was truncated along its front edge. It consisted of a Pennant slab stone base with rear and side walls. Hearth 1611 appeared to have been of similar form but survived only partially. The pits were oval to rectangular with steep to vertical sides and flat bases and were typically 1.6m long, 1.2m wide, and 0.25–0.6m deep. Pit 1815 included clay lining and it is possible that they were all associated with water storage. A number of the pits were intercutting and those that were disused contained dark ashy fills, some of which included material from metal casting. For example fill 1701 of pit 1721 contained copper slag; fill 1367 of pit 1371 contained clay mould fragments and part of a copper-alloy vessel and fill 1471 of pit 1472 contained further clay mould fragments. The clay mould fragments from these pit fills were for a range of items including cauldrons/posnets, candlesticks and chafing dishes. The cauldron/posnet and candlestick moulds are dateable to the late medieval to early post-medieval periods whilst those for the chafing dishes date to the 15th or 16th centuries (Chapter 4.5). Further dark ashy deposits covered the surfaces.

Two furnaces were constructed to the rear of the hearths and pits. Furnace 1530 projected into Little Thomas Lane. It was truncated but comprised a Pennant stone base 3m long flanked by Pennant stone walls which survived to a height of 0.8m and with an internal width of 0.8–1m. The base incorporated an oak plank from a tree felled 1268–1293 (Chapter 4.13).

Fig. 3.17 Plan of Period 3: early 15th to late 17th centuries. Scale 1:250

Period 3 furnace 1426

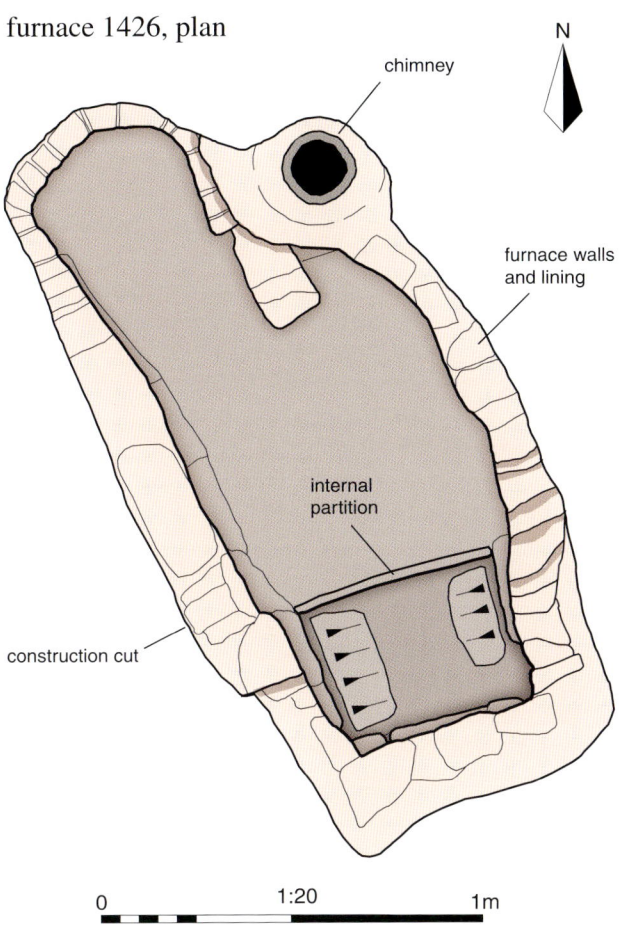

Fig. 3.18 Period 3 furnace 1426

This plank had probably been reused several times and may have originated as a weather board from a medieval building (Chapter 4.12). Although no partition wall or chimney were present, this may be due to truncation, and it is possible that this was another reverberatory furnace, particularly since it contained deposits with copper-alloy slag inclusions comparable to those within the reverberatory furnace at No. 16.

Furnace 1535 was also truncated and survived only as a construction cut containing mortar floor make-up, comparable in dimensions to the stone floor of furnace 1530, and Pennant stone walls. Surface fragments around this were overlain by occupation layer 1349 which included a handle for a cast copper-alloy chafing dish dateable to the late 15th to early 16th centuries. In this instance, the casting was flawed and the item was probably retained for recasting (Chapter 4.4, cat. no. 4; Fig. 4.4; no. 4).

The two furnaces appear too close together to have been operating simultaneously and since the backfills of furnace 1530 contained pottery pre-dating 1530 whilst those of furnace 1535 comprised a dump of 17th-century clay tobacco pipe kiln waste, it seems likely that furnace 1535 was a replacement of furnace 1530.

No. 18a Redcliff Street

At No. 18a reddish sandy clay make-up layers were deposited towards the tenement frontage in advance of the construction of new party walls with No. 18 and a new building (Building 3A). This building work would have required the demolition of the front end of stone-founded Building 2B, although it is possible that the rear parts of this were retained.

The new party walls 1526 and 1517 between Nos 18 and 18a were 0.35m wide and built from Pennant stone. Wall 1517 was built as a double wall with wall 1317 at No. 18. Wall 1517 rested on wooden piles, one of which was from a tree felled 1510–1535 (Chapter 4.13) which provides a plausible *terminus post quem* for the rebuilding within this tenement. Little remained of the structure of Building 3A, other than the 1.3m-wide arched Pennant and limestone foundations (2088) for 1m-wide sandstone wall 1182. The thickness of this wall, and the provision of arched foundations, suggests that it was load bearing and part of a building, with a room towards the frontage and a second room or corridor to its rear, defined by wall 1180. Stone surfacing survived within the building and that within the frontmost room comprised a 0.85m-wide strip of Pennant cobbles and slabs flanked by two raised stone kerbs. Within the corner of the room a Pennant stone hearth 1373 had been built onto this surface and floored with scorched clay.

No. 19 Redcliff Street

The Period 2 walls appear to have been retained in the rear part of No. 19, but towards the frontage new walls, surfaces and hearths replaced the Period 2 features. Period 2a hearth 3651 was capped with sand, circular stone-built hearth 3534 was backfilled and capped with mortar, and well 3550 was backfilled.

A new Pennant and limestone party wall 3341 was built between Nos 19 and 20. This wall was 0.5m wide, but its rear part was 0.7m wide and potentially formed part of a building. Its northern face had a lime render. Patches of Pennant cobble and mortar surfacing/make-up survived to the north of the wall and one of these surface patches abutted feature 3585. This was a circular structure 1.8m in diameter with Pennant stone walls and base, the build of which included 16th to 17th-century pottery. White lime was found on the inner surfaces of the stonework and it is possible that the feature had a function associated with lime, such as for mixing mortar. Stone-lined well 3596 was adjacent to (but presumably not contemporary with) the possible mortar mixer. This well survived only partially but had an internal diameter of $c.$ 0.5m and was excavated to a depth of 0.75m without the base being encountered.

The remains of a stone hearth, 3480, were found towards the front of the tenement. This comprised a construction cut with make-up layers over which a circular Pennant flagstone base, 1.4m in diameter, had been laid. Areas of scorching and charcoal survived on the hearth base and a ridge of lime mortar around its edges suggests that the base was originally surrounded by a stone wall. A series of postholes (3472, 3502, 3493, 3499, 3491, 3512, 3505 and 3497; not illustrated) to the rear of this hearth may have been part of a wooden structure although no obvious plan of this was apparent.

No. 20 Redcliff Street

Limited remains were exposed at No. 20. The Period 2c drainage features towards the tenement frontage may have been retained, although this is not certain. Towards the rear, a hearth and several adjacent pits were added. Hearth 3503 overlaid make-up deposits and comprised a Pennant flagstone base 1m long and 0.55m wide covered by a dark charcoal-rich layer, 3489. Three small rectangular pits (3421, 3455 and 3469) lay to the south of the hearth. These comprised vertical-sided, flat-based cuts, typically 0.8m long, 0.5m wide and 0.15m deep. They contained single charcoal-rich fills and may have been directly associated with the hearth.

Dating evidence for Period 3

Period 3 represents a clear stratigraphic break from the earlier periods, one that is also marked by the introduction of new technologies. Although the pottery assemblage from this period is large, it is only broadly dateable. The dating of the stratigraphic sequence has therefore been more reliant on other material types, particularly clay tobacco pipes, which made their first appearance on site in this period, and the copper-alloy products of several furnaces, along with their associated moulds.

Some deposits probably pre-date $c.$ 1530, based on the presence of certain ceramics (BPT 197, BPT 182, BPT 266 and BPT 287) and the absence of clay tobacco pipes and pottery types common only after $c.$ 1550, primarily the glazed Somerset and west country earthenwares. These deposits include those associated with construction in this period, such as make-up layers for hearth 3503 at No. 20 and slab surface 1487 at No. 17. Similar dating for the construction of a party wall at No. 18a was provided by a felling date of 1510–1535 obtained from a timber pile (Chapter 4.13).

Pottery types common only after $c.$ 1550 and in use until the mid 18th century were present in some deposits, along with well-dated groups of clay tobacco pipe. These deposits included the backfills of furnace 1426 at No. 16 and of pit 1340 at No. 17. The backfill of pit 1340 also contained a James I farthing dating to 1623–4 and 17th-century glass. Clay tobacco pipe fragments dating to $c.$ 1660–80 were recovered from fill 1248 of pit 1251 at No. 17. All of these deposits relate to the disuse of Period 3 features, suggesting that most or all had been decommissioned by the late 17th century.

3.8 Period 4: late 17th to late 19th centuries (Fig. 3.19)

The Period 4 features largely relate to a sugar house established by 1695 at Nos 18–19 and operating until 1816 (Chapter 2.1). The creation of this sugar house required extensive rebuilding and Period 4 therefore represents a significant change from the earlier periods. Title deeds suggest that Nos 18–19 were amalgamated into a single property within which the earlier buildings were demolished and the sugar house constructed. This survived largely at cellar and foundation level, along with drains, soakaways and several wells, reflecting the importance of water in sugar production. Extensive rebuilding was also undertaken at Nos 17 and 20. Little Thomas Lane remained open, with parts of its walls being repaired and new drainage added, and some rebuilding was evident at No. 16.

No. 16 Redcliff Street

The Period 3 features were partially demolished or infilled with deposits dating up to the 19th century. A stone party wall was built along the boundary with No. 15, with soakaway 1664 on its southern edge. This feature was sub-rectangular, vertical-sided and lined with Pennant stones bonded with greyish white lime mortar.

No. 17 Redcliff Street

The Period 3 features were levelled and backfilled with industrial and demolition debris. Furnace 1535 was backfilled with three deposits (1533, 1532 and 1470), all being debris from a clay tobacco pipe factory, including kiln fragments and waste pipes (Chapter

Fig. 3.19 Plan of Period 4: late 17th to late 19th centuries. Scale 1:250

4.8). Following the infilling of the Period 3 pits a series of cellars was added within the front parts of the tenement. The western part of the building was defined by 0.9m-thick structural walls 1145 and 1488 (the latter also formed the southern wall of Little Thomas Lane), with a number of 0.3m-wide walls between these defining a corridor leading to several cellars. All of the walls were built using Pennant stones and limestone and some had traces of lime rendering. The south-westernmost of the cellars was 5m long and rectangular and included a mortar floor/sub-floor which abutted brick hearth 1151. Alongside the hearth, a small pit had been excavated to hold metal pot 1150, which may have been placed as a sump or container. On the opposite side of the corridor, a small, square-planned cellar measuring 1.8m by 1.8m was defined by wall 1111 and adjoining to the west was a 2m-wide rectangular cellar. To the rear of these, a larger square cellar was defined by walls 1145 and 1189 and within this a series of make-up layers was laid of which layer 1236 contained late 17th to 18th-century pottery, along with clay tobacco pipe fragments dating to *c.* 1660–80. The make-up layers were overlaid by a stone surface which abutted two red brick hearth bases, 1195 and 1197, built against the southern edge of the cellar. Three small pits, 1216, 1219 and 1221 lay adjacent to these hearths. All of these pits were circular in plan with rounded profiles and were typically 0.6m in diameter and 0.3m deep.

To the rear of No. 17, oval pit 1461 was found. This had vertical sides and was 1.4m long and 2.3m wide and was at least 0.5m deep (the bottom was not reached in the excavation). It contained a single lime fill and was probably a mortar-mixing pit associated with the construction works. The pit was sealed by a rebuild (1254) of the party wall between Nos 17 and 18 which included fragments of reused church masonry, probably recovered from the demolition of St Thomas's Church in the 1790s (Chapter 4.10). Given the likely date of the reuse of this masonry, this party wall would seem to have been a later addition during Period 4, rather than part of the initial construction. A short length of wall (1448) to the immediate north of the new party wall may have defined a passageway.

Within the rear part of the plot, clay-lined soakaway 1544 was found, along with well 1489. The well was lined with Pennant stone and clay, with an internal shaft diameter of 0.85m. It was unclear whether these features were built at ground level, or within cellars.

Nos 18–19 Redcliff Street

The documentary evidence shows that by 1695 Nos 18–19 were amalgamated to create a new sugar house. This was reflected in the archaeological record by remains likely to be the sugar house which date from the late 17th century. As at No. 17, most of the surviving structures were at cellar level and cannot be related to the surviving plans of the property, which are of the ground floor level, and date to the 19th century (Chapter 2.1; Figs 2.4 and 2.5). Sugar refining requires abundant use of water and this is reflected in the provision of soakaways and drains within the sugar house and by the construction of well 1046, built within a large cellar towards the property frontage. Other features within the cellars included a brick hearth base (1101) within a cellar defined by rendered Pennant stone walls 1267, 1171 and 2067 and a small number of pits cut into the floors of several other cellars.

Within the rear of the plot, stone walls 1254, 2067 and 1233 were probably the foundations of a large room, labelled on 19th-century mapping as a warehouse. This mapping also shows that, by the 19th century at least, the rear part of Nos 19 and 20 were also occupied by a warehouse belonging to the sugar house.

No. 20 Redcliff Street

A single small vertical-sided pit, 3366, was present. It contained a single rubbly backfill, 3365 from which late 17th to 18th-century pottery was recovered and may relate to construction works in Period 4.

Dating evidence for Period 4

With the exception of No. 16, the Period 3 features all seem to have been decommissioned before the last quarter of the 17th century, which accords with the date of 1695 by which time the sugar house had been established. The sugar house operated until 1816 although a warehouse to its rear was still in use as a sugar warehouse in 1887. The east side of Redcliff Street was widened *c.* 1872–8, which involved the demolition of existing properties fronting the street, although buildings within the rear plots evidently survived and are depicted on Ordnance Survey maps of 1884. Finds recovered from the backfills of the latest Period 3 features, levelled during the Period 4 construction phase, and from Period 4 construction deposits accord with a late 17th-century date for the construction work at Nos 17 and 18–19. At No. 17 furnace 1535 was backfilled with debris from a clay pipe kiln which dates to the period 1651–54 (Chapter 4.8) although as it was imported into the site the actual date of deposition might have been later than this date range suggests. The latest fills from the Period 3 pits at No. 17 included late 17th to 18th-century pottery and clay tobacco pipe fragments dating to *c.* 1660–80 from pit 1251; 17th to 18th-century pottery from pit 1472 and a coin of 1623–4, early to mid 17th-century pottery, part of an early 17th-century pharmaceutical phial and fragments of 16th/17th-century window glass from pit 1340. At No. 16 the rebuilding appears not to have occurred until the 19th century.

3.9 Period 5: late 19th to late 20th centuries (Fig. 3.20)

Period 5 dates from the 1870s, when the east side of the

Fig. 3.20 Plan of Period 5: late 19th to late 20th centuries. Scale 1:250

northern end of Redcliff Street was widened, a process that included the demolition of properties within the site. These demolition works were undertaken to the north of Little Thomas Lane from 1872 and to its south from *c.* 1878 (Chapter 2.1). The Period 5 remains were found within the front parts of the plots, and some of the buildings within the rear parts were retained, including the two warehouses to the rear of Nos 18–20 which were still depicted on the 1887 Goad map (Fig. 2.4). Within the northern part of the site, Nos 11–15 had become part of a large oil store by 1885, and this building was still depicted, albeit unlabelled as to function, on Ordnance Survey mapping of the 1920s.

Nos 11–15 Redcliff Street

A series of cellars was built within these tenements as a single build, indicating they had amalgamated into a single property, probably the Oil Store depicted on the 1885 Ordnance Survey Map.

No. 16 Redcliff Street

The remains of two small buildings depicted on the 1884 Ordnance Survey map survived at No. 16 as cellars with extensive drains.

Little Thomas Lane

Little Thomas Lane continued to be depicted on historic mapping into the first half of the 20th century. It is last depicted clearly on an Ordnance Survey map of 1938, although maps of the 1950s and 60s show what might be the remains of the lane, with open areas to the south and several small buildings fronting Thomas Lane, one of which is labelled as a 'Ruin'. During Period 5, evidence for maintenance of Little Thomas Lane included a phase of rebuilding of the northern wall in Pennant stone and the addition of stone-capped, brick-lined drains, one of which (1239) clearly received run-off from drains at No. 17. Mid to late 19th-century pottery and a Victorian coin were recovered from fill 1238 of this drain.

No. 17 Redcliff Street

At No. 17 Period 4 well 1489 was backfilled and a series of stone-lined drains added which truncated the Period 4 walls and surfaces.

No. 18 Redcliff Street

The cellars at No. 18 were demolished and backfilled and replaced by adjoining cellars with Pennant stone and brick walls and flagstone surfaces.

No. 20 Redcliff Street

Cellars were added at No. 20, built from Pennant stone with occasional bricks and limestones.

Chapter 4
Finds

4.1 Pottery
E.R. McSloy

Pottery amounting to a total of 5,120 sherds, weighing 116.191kg (70.95 estimated rim equivalents) was hand recovered from 350 separate deposits. A further quantity amounting to 105 sherds (496g) was recovered from the sieving of bulk soil samples. Analysis of the pottery is confined to hand-recovered material from the main medieval phases (Periods 1 and 2) and early post-medieval Period 3.

The pottery was sorted by type macroscopically or with the aid of a binocular (x20) microscope, with sherd count and weight recorded for each context. Where this could be determined, vessel form and rim EVEs (Estimated Vessel Equivalents) were recorded. Wares and pottery type nomenclature is adapted from the Bristol pottery type series (BPT) developed by Michael Ponsford and published previously in summary (Ponsford 1988; 1998). The type series housed at Bristol City Museum and Art Gallery, and accompanying descriptions was consulted, and Michael Ponsford was invited to scan the assemblage as part of the analysis. A system of form classification was devised, adapted from the Medieval Pottery Research Group's classification scheme (MPRG 1998), with further recording of other details of rim, base or handle morphology.

The distribution of pottery according to deposit type is shown in Table 4.1. A sizeable proportion of the assemblage was derived from pit and other 'cut' feature fills making it quite untypical among other published Bristol assemblages of the period which typically derive from occupation layers. The proportion of pottery recovered from feature fills is highest in Period 1 (occupation). These groups derive mainly from the backfill of large rectangular features interpreted as possible dyeing pits. Mean sherd weight values are notably higher across Periods 1 (25g) compared to Period 2 (18.7g), where the assemblage is largely made up of material from layers (Table 4.1). The pit groups include some substantially complete vessels (Fig. 4.1; no. 7; Fig. 4.2; nos 18–20) and surface preservation is excellent, helped in some deposits by waterlogging.

Fabrics and assemblage composition (Tables 4.2–4.3)

Bristol C coarseware: BPT 309 (15 sherds; 24g; 0.17 EVEs)
Yellow-brown firing fabric, with inclusions of quartz, carboniferous limestone, calcite and pinkish sandstone (Vince 1984; Ponsford 1991). Characteristic stamped or tooled decoration.
Forms: globular-bodied jar with rolled-out rim and stamped decoration at shoulder (Fig. 4.1; no. 1).

'Motte ditch' type coarseware type: BPT 6 (110 sherds; 1281g; 1.34 EVEs)
Handmade coarseware; typically reduced-fired and with quartz, quartzite and limestone inclusions. The 'motte ditch' association refers to Ponsford's unpublished excavations at Bristol Castle where the type was abundant in the feature believed to be in-filled *c*. 1120. The fabric also occurred at Chepstow (type Ke) and is described by Vince (1991a, 114).
Forms: globular-bodied jars with rolled-out rims (Fig. 4.1; no. 3).

Unsourced Saxo-Norman coarseware 1: BPT 252a (3 sherds; 29g; 0 EVEs)
Handmade coarseware. Dark grey throughout. Hard and sandy feeling. The fabric contains abundant and well-sorted angular, grey-coloured argillaceous inclusions; quartz and sandstone.
Forms: jar with everted rim and basket-pattern circular stamps at shoulder (Fig. 4.1; no. 2).

Unsourced Saxo-Norman coarseware 2: BPT 252b (6 sherds; 226g; 0.37 EVEs)
Grey-firing micaceous fabric. Common well-sorted quartz and common or sparse, ill-sorted angular limestone, sparse angular chert and sparse voids from burnt-out organics. This may be a variant of BPT 4/5 described by Ponsford (1998, 136) and thought to date *c*. 1080–1120.
Forms: handled jar or pitcher with upright rim, untidy rolled-out rim, and fingertipping to rim upper (Fig. 4.1; nos 10–11); jar with upright, rolled-out rim and light fingernail slashing to the rim upper.

Table 4.1 Quantities (sherd count/weight in grams and rim EVEs) by deposit type and period

Period>	1 (construction)			1 (occupation)			2a			2b			2c			3		
Description	Ct.	Wt.	EVE	Ct.	Wt.	EVE	Ct.	Wt.	EVE	Ct.	Wt.	EVE	Ct.	Wt.	EVE	Ct.	Wt.	EVE
construction cut	-	-	-	-	-	-	-	-	-	-	-	-	95	1808	.83	-	-	-
drain	-	-	-	-	-	-	26	245	.19	-	-	-	-	-	-	1	14	-
fill	28	337	.25	1718	48603	25.01	131	2741	1.16	49	958	1.24	142	2253	1.48	84	1883	1.19
furnace	-	-	-	-	-	-	-	-	-	-	-	-	27	265	-	3	26	-
hearth	-	-	-	-	-	-	24	555	.63	-	-	-	14	265	.16	3	26	-
layer	-	-	-	54	775	.28	481	12399	8.57	208	1996	1.80	347	5264	3.00	249	8822	6.66
make-up	-	-	-	-	-	-	43	937	.48	-	-	-	18	310	.51	-	-	-
mixed alluvium	36	426	.52	-	-	-	-	-	-	-	-	-	-	-	-	-	-	-
occupation	-	-	-	-	-	-	247	5121	4.17	-	-	-	-	-	-	-	-	-
occupation layer	-	-	-	-	-	-	94	1798	1.81	-	-	-	-	-	-	-	-	-
postpad	-	-	-	12	290	.18	-	-	-	-	-	-	-	-	-	-	-	-
structure	-	-	-	-	-	-	-	-	-	-	-	-	13	216	-	-	-	-
surface	-	-	-	372	6541	3.55	24	305	.10	37	348	.37	33	558	.55	61	1112	.84
timber	-	-	-	5	176	-	-	-	-	-	-	-	-	-	-	-	-	-
wall	-	-	-	5	65	.10	8	115	.05	8	102	-	82	1395	1.02	1	4	-

Table 4.2 Composition of the pottery assemblages from Periods 1–3 by fabric type

Period	1 (construction)			1 (occupation)			2a			2b			2c			3		
BPT/Description	Ct.	Wt.	EVE	Ct.	Wt.	EVE	Ct.	Wt.	EVE	Ct.	Wt.	EVE	Ct.	Wt.	EVE	Ct.	Wt.	EVE
309: Bristol C coarseware	15	24	.17	-	-	-	-	-	-	-	-	-	-	-	-	-	-	-
252a: Unsourced Saxo-Norman coarseware 1	2	19	-	1	10	-	-	-	-	-	-	-	-	-	-	-	-	-
252b: Unsourced Saxo-Norman coarseware 2	-	-	-	6	226	.37	-	-	-	-	-	-	-	-	-	-	-	-
6: 'Motte ditch' type coarseware	18	230	.15	84	905	.82	4	80	.18	-	-	-	-	-	-	2	20	.04
18c: South-east Wiltshire tripod pitchers	-	-	-	6	108	-	1	36	-	-	-	-	1	10	-	-	-	-
18: Minety type ware (handmade)	3	38	-	143	4175	1.04	140	3884	.42	9	188	.22	13	200	.13	65	1454	.42
114: Pill/'Proto-Ham Green' coarseware	5	59	.07	314	7983	4.09	46	1061	.99	4	72	.12	7	220	.13	4	52	-
26: Ham Green A glazed ware	6	77	-	114	2410	.27	22	503	.15	-	-	-	2	64	-	9	143	.23
27: Ham Green B glazed ware	2	32	-	525	17036	6.34	311	6204	5.72	40	813	.66	53	1231	.80	205	4421	2.09
26/27: Ham Green A or B	-	-	-	11	198	.22	1	4	-	-	-	-	-	-	-	-	-	-
32: Ham Green redware	4	183	.35	430	11868	8.60	197	4944	4.64	12	354	.42	14	323	.38	62	1359	1.03
305: Ham Green redware (large jars)	-	-	-	-	-	-	1	218	.15	-	-	-	-	-	-	-	-	-
46: 'Bath A' type coarseware	4	44	-	423	9136	5.55	135	2783	2.64	16	257	.22	23	356	.44	86	1109	.87
No BPT: Paffrath 'blaugrau' type	-	-	-	4	180	.53	-	-	-	-	-	-	-	-	-	-	-	-
239: Normandy green glazed	-	-	-	29	342	.17	4	31	-	1	44	-	1	10	.10	5	20	.13
366: Misc. north French jugs	-	-	-	1	15	-	4	59	.15	-	-	-	1	14	.08	3	43	.19
192: French jug fabric	-	-	-	3	17	-	10	130	.20	-	-	-	-	-	-	2	11	-
118: Bristol (Redcliffe) glazed jugs	-	-	-	25	444	.37	101	1739	.86	147	730	1.15	64	1018	.60	168	2229	1.29
121: Thornbury type glazed ware	-	-	-	5	252	.05	4	148	.17	-	-	-	2	6	-	17	418	-
134: 'Bath A' glazed	-	-	-	18	401	-	3	54	-	1	6	-	-	-	-	5	276	.32
168: Worcester type glazed ware	-	-	-	2	146	.30	3	65	-	-	-	-	-	-	-	6	161	.22
368: Lacock, Nash Hill glazed ware	-	-	-	1	111	.10	14	158	.14	1	29	.02	4	110	.10	12	197	.08
84: Minety type ware (wheelthrown)	-	-	-	1	8	-	5	154	.05	2	35	-	9	116	.15	32	872	.84
252d: Unclassified medieval glazed	-	-	-	10	230	-	7	147	-	1	10	.07	1	6	-	3	37	-
252e: Unclassified medieval unglazed	-	-	-	15	426	.27	2	49	-	9	61	-	-	-	-	1	19	-
156: South-west French (mottled glaze)	-	-	-	-	-	-	11	86	.05	-	-	-	6	128	-	38	188	.18
157: South-west French (quartz-rich)	-	-	-	-	-	-	-	-	-	-	-	-	-	-	-	1	96	.13
160: South-west French (sparse or no glaze)	-	-	-	-	-	-	1	13	-	7	138	-	35	98	.24	5	77	-
118L: Bristol (Redcliffe) 'late form jugs'	-	-	-	-	-	-	-	-	-	-	-	-	-	-	-	2	26	-

Finds   39

Table 4.2 (cont.) Composition of the pottery assemblages from Periods 1–3 by fabric type

Period	1 (construction)			1 (occupation)			2a			2b			2c			3		
BPT/Description	Ct.	Wt.	EVE	Ct.	Wt.	EVE	Ct.	Wt.	EVE	Ct.	Wt.	EVE	Ct.	Wt.	EVE	Ct.	Wt.	EVE
120: Bristol (Redcliffe) pale glaze/contrast strips	-	-	-	-	-	-	1	7	-	-	-	-	8	95	-	7	55	-
123: Bristol (Redcliffe) soft, pink fabric	-	-	-	-	-	-	-	-	-	-	-	-	1	3	-	5	140	-
126: Bristol (Redcliffe) harder, pink fabric	-	-	-	-	-	-	2	18	-	-	-	-	1	6	-	5	44	-
127: Bristol (Redcliffe) bowls	-	-	-	-	-	-	-	-	-	-	-	-	-	-	-	2	49	.12
128: Bristol (Redcliffe) internally-glazed	-	-	-	-	-	-	-	-	-	-	-	-	8	84	-	7	107	-
85: Bristol (Redcliffe) jars	-	-	-	1	31	.12	1	32	.10	-	-	-	1	8	-	9	276	-
182: 'Tudor Green'	-	-	-	-	-	-	-	-	-	-	-	-	9	19	.16	16	82	.22
197: Malvern Chase redware	-	-	-	-	-	-	3	385	-	-	-	-	11	124	.09	23	576	.37
No BPT: Coarse Border ware	-	-	-	-	-	-	-	-	-	-	-	-	2	24	-	-	-	-
266: Falfield Cistercian type ware	-	-	-	-	-	-	-	-	-	-	-	-	-	-	-	2	5	.03
93: Unsourced Cistercian type ware	-	-	-	1	1	-	-	-	-	-	-	-	-	-	-	4	23	-
282: Algarve micaceous/Merida type ware	-	-	-	-	-	-	-	-	-	-	-	-	-	-	-	3	164	-
285: Unclassified post-medieval glazed	-	-	-	3	115	.17	-	-	-	-	-	-	-	-	-	17	515	.10
96: Wanstrow glazed earthenwares	-	-	-	-	-	-	1	19	-	-	-	-	1	41	-	24	538	.63
286: Frechen stoneware	-	-	-	-	-	-	-	-	-	-	-	-	-	-	-	2	32	-
287: Raeren stoneware	-	-	-	-	-	-	-	-	-	-	-	-	-	-	-	1	11	-
81: Spanish olive jars	-	-	-	-	-	-	-	-	-	-	-	-	-	-	-	1	48	-
108: North Devon gravel-free	-	-	-	-	-	-	-	-	-	-	-	-	-	-	-	1	8	-
112: North Devon gravel-tempered	-	-	-	-	-	-	-	-	-	-	-	-	-	-	-	3	54	-
280: Nether Stowey glazed earthenwares	-	-	-	-	-	-	-	-	-	-	-	-	-	-	-	9	134	-
268: South Somerset glazed earthenware	-	-	-	-	-	-	-	-	-	-	-	-	-	-	-	1	22	.07
Totals	59	706	.74	2176	56774	29.38	1035	23011	16.61	250	2737	2.88	279	4348	3.47	875	16111	9.6

Table 4.3 Composition by fabric type of the larger pottery groups associated with the occupation of Period 1

| Layer/feature no. | 2009 | | 1848 | | 2314 | | 1773 | | 3229 | | 3217 | | 1932 | | 3066 | | 3300 | |
BPT/description	Ct.	EVE	Ct.	EVE	Ct.	EVE	Ct.	EVE	Ct.	EVE	Ct.	EVE	Ct.	EVE	Ct.	EVE	Ct.	EVE
6: 'Motte ditch' type coarseware	3	.12	3	.15	2	.02	-	-	1	.02	-	-	-	-	-	-	-	-
114: 'Pill'/'Proto-Ham Green' coarseware	8	.29	46	.67	10	-	33	.29	1	-	18	.72	-	-	9	.23	2	-
32: Ham Green redware	87	1.18	40	.59	35	.84	29	.65	39	1.93	16	.71	15	.07	3	.23	2	.14
46: 'Bath A' type coarseware	42	.45	32	.29	142	1.06	38	.44	10	.08	14	.53	12	.07	13	.42	9	.06
18: Minety type ware (handmade)	27	-	37	.12	3	.10	9	-	-	-	2	-	7	-	1	-	9	-
18c: South-east Wiltshire tripod pitchers	-	-	-	-	-	-	-	-	-	-	-	-	-	-	1	-	-	-
252d: Unclassified medieval glazed	1	-	4	-	4	-	-	-	-	-	-	-	-	-	-	-	-	-
252e: Unclassified medieval unglazed	2	.17	10	.10	-	-	6	.37	-	-	-	-	-	-	1	-	-	-
26: Ham Green A glazed ware	33	.17	14	-	2	-	7	-	-	-	-	-	1	-	2	-	2	-
27: Ham Green B glazed ware	158	.64	33	.20	38	1.12	52	.34	26	.90	22	.86	22	-	19	.47	33	.24
134: 'Bath A' glazed	-	-	1	-	-	-	-	-	-	-	-	-	-	-	13	-	1	-
192: French jug fabric	2	-	-	-	1	-	-	-	-	-	-	-	-	-	-	-	-	-
239: Normandy green glazed	-	-	2	-	3	.17	-	-	-	-	-	-	-	-	-	-	1	-
366: Misc. north French jugs	-	-	23	-	-	-	-	-	-	-	-	-	-	-	-	-	-	-
118: Bristol (Redcliffe) glazed jugs	-	-	-	-	-	-	-	-	-	-	-	-	6	.07	1	-	-	-
84: Minety type ware (wheelthrown)	-	-	-	-	-	-	-	-	-	-	-	-	1	-	-	-	-	-
168: Worcester type glazed ware	-	-	-	-	-	-	1	0	-	-	-	-	1	-	1	.30	-	-
No BPT: Paffrath 'blaugrau' type	3	.53	-	-	-	-	-	-	-	-	-	-	-	-	-	-	-	-
368: Lacock, Nash Hill glazed ware	-	-	-	-	-	-	-	-	-	-	-	-	-	-	1	.10	-	-
	366	3.55	245	2.12	240	3.31	175	2.09	77	2.93	72	2.82	65	0.21	65	1.75	59	0.44

Finds   41

Unsourced Saxo-Norman 3: BPT 252c (1 sherd; 20g; 0 EVEs)

A type represented as a single sherd from a tripod pitcher with short and well-made foot. The fabric is unlike that of pitcher types BPT 18 and 18c as it contains quartz, and common limestone and fossil shell. A Kennet Valley origin is possible, although an absence of flint argues against this.

Forms: handmade tripod pitcher (not ill.).

Pill/'Proto-Ham Green' coarseware: BPT 114 (381 sherds; 9460g; 5.40 EVEs)

Type BPT 114 represents a similar tradition to Ham Green redware type BPT 32 (below), very likely contemporaneous, and made close by at Pill. The fabric as described by Vince (1991a, 158) differs from type BPT 32 in the size and sorting of its quartz/sandstone inclusions and the presence of limestone (Ponsford 1998, 137).

Forms: straight-sided jars with sagging bases and everted rims, usually with rolled-out rim uppers. Decoration includes scoring; combing and pinched/fingertip decoration to the rim (Fig. 4.2; nos 18 and 20).

Ham Green A glazed ware: BPT 26 (155 sherds; 3239g; 0.65 EVEs)

The fabric(s) characterising Ham Green jugs are described elsewhere (Vince 1984; Ponsford 1991, 101). The main inclusions are quartz and limestone sand and with varying quantities of clay pellet. The differences between 'A' (BPT 26) and 'B' (BPT 27) fabrics described initially by Barton (1963, 96–7) have proved difficult to reproduce subsequently. The chief characteristics which distinguish the 'A' series are typological and relate to form and decoration, in particular the use of roller stamping (Fig. 4.1; nos 4 and 12), and the glaze which typically in the 'A' series is plain and yellowish. Forms are almost entirely jugs, their main characteristics being stepped shoulder and simple, sagging bases. The lid no. 32 appears to be unique; it shows characteristics of 'A' wares (yellowish glaze) and the 'B' series (applied decoration). The 'A' series certainly pre-dates the B wares, production probably beginning soon after *c*. 1120 and continuing to *c*. 1150/60.

Forms: jugs with stepped neck and diamond-pattern roller stamping (Fig. 4.1; no. 12); rod handles with roller stamping (Fig. 4.1; no. 4); lid with incised and applied pellet decoration (Fig. 4.3; no. 32).

Ham Green B glazed ware: BPT 27 (1218 sherds; 31598g; 16.37 EVEs)

As noted above 'B' series jugs are defined principally on the basis of form and decoration. The glaze tends to be darker compared to the 'A' series, and is commonly mottled, possibly due to the addition of copper. Jugs thought transitional between 'A' and 'B' forms are described by Ponsford (1991; fig. 4a/b), including examples from Pill. Standard 'B' jug forms have collared rims, thumbed bases and applied bridge spouts with decoration limited to close-set horizontal grooves to the girth and shoulder. Strap handles are usual, most commonly with a single column of round-sectioned stabbed 'decoration'. Dating for the 'B' series spans the mid 12th to mid 13th centuries. Variations in form and decoration, some of which may be chronologically significant, have been set out by Ponsford (ibid.).

Forms: large, globular-bodied jugs with bridge spouts and applied thumbed bases (Fig. 4.1; nos 7 and 16 and Fig. 4.3; no. 33). There are some examples with 'transitional' traits consisting of applied decoration and roller stamping (Fig. 4.1; nos 5–6; also applied zoomorphic/anthropomorphic (Fig. 4.1; nos 16–17) or 'dimpled' decoration (Fig. 4.2; no. 21).

Ham Green redware: BPT 32 (737 sherds; 19467g; 15.78 EVEs)

Handmade coarsewares known to be produced at Ham Green alongside the glazed jug wares have been fully described elsewhere (Vince 1984). The fabric is characterised by abundant quartz and sparse sandstone; it differs from that used for the jug wares and commonly fires to a yellowish red. Vessel forms are jars with sagging bases and straight-sided profiles. Decoration is common as combing, including wavy designs to the rim interior and/or exterior patterns, or to the body; and single line scoring.

Forms: straight-sided jars with sagging bases and everted rims, usually with rolled-out rim uppers. Decoration includes scoring, combing or applied strips to the body and pinched/fingertip decoration to the rim (Fig. 4.2; nos 22–23).

Ham Green redware (large jars): BPT 305 (1 sherd; 218g; 0.15 EVEs)

Variant type distinguished by jar forms which are significantly larger than standard Ham Green redware vessels. The example illustrated has applied strips, possibly intended to increase robustness. Ponsford (1991) has commented on the propensity of the type to occur on or near waterfront sites and considered it 12th century in date.

Forms: large jar with everted rim (Fig. 4.3; no. 30).

'Bath A' type coarseware: BPT 46 (706 sherds; 13990g; 9.91 EVEs)

The 'Bath A' type coarsewares are ubiquitous in medieval assemblages in Bristol and the type probably extends in use beyond *c*. 1250 and possibly past *c*. 1300. The fabric is distinctive, micaceous and contains calcareous and (more sparsely) flint or chert inclusions. A source to the east of Bath has been suggested for this type (Vince 1991a, 118). The type may have its origins in the 11th century, however the main period of occurrence in Bristol is the 12th and 13th centuries (Ponsford 1998, 137). Forms are mainly rounded-bodied jars with sagging bases; the vessels almost certainly functioned as cooking pots. There are also a significant number of inturned dish/'west country' type vessels (Fig. 4.2; no. 19). The everted rims for these vessels, and those of jars, are 'developed'; commonly with an internal ledge and expanded rim 'lip'.

Forms: rounded-bodied jars with sagging bases and 'developed' everted rims; inturned dishes (Fig. 4.2; no. 19).

South-east Wiltshire tripod pitchers: BPT 18c (8 sherds; 154g; 0 EVEs)

Type BPT 18c is among the first of the regional wares to occur in any quantity. Vince (1984) suggested that importation into the Severn Valley area started as early as *c*. 1100 and the type is present in deposits securely dated to the early or mid 12th century at Dundas Wharf, Bristol (Ponsford 1991, 84). The characteristic pitcher forms are not dissimilar to those of Minety type ware, though the hard, buff or light grey-firing sandy fabric and thin yellowish-green glaze are distinct.

Forms: handmade tripod pitchers. Strap handles with central thumbed strip (Fig. 4.1; no. 9).

Minety type ware (handmade): BPT 18 (383 sherds; 10155g; 2.28 EVEs)

Glazed wares from Minety, north Wiltshire, approximately

40km to the north-east of Bristol, are well known from the city. The later wheelthrown Minety products are identified under type code BPT 84 (below). The handmade type is thought to date before *c.* 1250; the calcareous gravel-tempered fabric and yellowish glaze are easily distinguishable from the contemporary Ham Green and other types. Among the earliest well-dated occurrences are those at Dundas Wharf (Ponsford 1991, 84) from deposits dated to the mid 12th century. The type also occurs in quantity in Dublin, and other Irish ports from earlier 12th-century deposits (McCutcheon 2006, 40). The 12th-century forms at Redcliff Street and elsewhere are all or mostly pitchers which are commonly highly decorated with combed wavy and applied strips. One spouted vessel matches an example from Dublin (ibid., fig. 14.3), although the tubular spout in this instance is not functional. Forms identified at Redcliff Street in Periods 1–2 are mainly tripod pitchers, and include examples with characteristic 'composite' handles using twisted clay rod(s) as the core. Probable jugs with slashed, U-shaped handles are thought to be 13th-century forms.

Forms: handmade tripod pitchers (Fig. 4.3; no. 31); jugs and jars/cooking pots with simple everted rims (not ill.).

Miscellaneous unidentified medieval wares: BPT 252d/e (41 sherds; 934g; 0.34 EVEs)

Catch-all for medieval glazed (BPT 252d) and unglazed (BPT 252e) fabrics of uncertain provenance and date.

Normandy green glazed: BPT 239 (41 sherds; 453g; 0.40 EVEs)

Pottery production across northern France is believed to have been highly localised with many of the larger towns supplied from their own kilns. This grouping may then encompass material from a variety of sources. The fabrics are nevertheless fairly consistent, and share the characteristics of white or pale grey colouring and varying amounts of coarse quartz inclusions with the 'Normandy gritty' coarsewares which are well known from the region. The glaze is typically bright and 'coppery' with abundant darker mottles. Extensive roller-stamped decoration to the body is characteristic (Fig. 4.1; no. 15) and there are comparisons in form and decoration with the 'Miscellaneous French B' group described from Dublin (McCutcheon 2006, fig. 43).

Forms: wheelthrown jugs with bifid or collared rims; some with tooled or roller-stamped decoration (Fig. 4.1; nos 8 and 15).

Miscellaneous north French jugs: BPT 366 (12 sherds; 168g; 0.54 EVEs)

This grouping serves as a catch-all for wheelthrown and white-firing jug fabrics of non-English origin and lacking the coarse quartz of the 'Normandy' fabric, or characteristics of the other French wares (BPT 156, BPT 192). The glaze is typically French: bright and speckled and the forms reflect French styles current to *c.* 1250.

Forms: wheelthrown jugs with bifid or collared rims; some with tooled decoration (Fig. 4.2; no. 27 and 4.3; no. 29).

French jug fabric: BPT 192 (17 sherds; 192g; 0.20 EVEs)

This distinctive type is described previously by Ponsford (1983, 222). Its main characteristics are a light-firing, slightly sandy fabric containing possible haematite lumps and a plain 'emerald' glaze. The decoration is also distinctive, consisting of narrow applied strips which are knife-slashed or roller-stamped. The type is known from Exeter, and also Dublin where it was most common among 'miscellaneous' French wares. The origin, whether northern or south-western French, is uncertain although McCutcheon (2006) notes the similarity with Parthenay-type ware from the northern Poitou-Charente region.

Forms: wheelthrown jugs with collared rim (Fig. 4.3; no. 28); vertical applied strips to body (Fig. 4.1; no. 14).

Paffrath 'blaugrau' type (no BPT) (4 sherds; 180g; 0.53 EVEs)

This type, one of very few Rhenish wares known prior to the late medieval period, is characterised by very hard, semi-vitrified fabric and pimply texture. The characteristic form (Fig. 4.1; no. 13), is previously described as a ladle, although 'pipkin' is more appropriate and the single vessel represented here exhibits heavy sooting from use. The type appears to be moderately common from south coast ports (Allan 1984, 15; Brown 2002, 34), Allan suggesting the vessels were used for a specific purpose or were regarded as 'curiosities'. This is probably the first recorded instance of the type in Bristol, although the wider occurrence in Dublin (McCutcheon 2006) and some vessels from Worcester (L. Griffin, pers. comm.) is probably the result of 'recirculation' via Bristol. Production at Paffrath, near Cologne, is attested as early as the late 9th century, although the main period of importation to southern Britain is the 11th and 12th centuries. Interestingly the date of the context for the illustrated vessel, with sherds spread across Period 1 deposits (drain 1773 and layer 2009) accords with the predominantly late 12th/earlier 13th-century dating for the type from Irish sites.

Forms: handmade ladle/pipkin (Fig. 4.1; no. 13).

Bristol (Redcliffe) glazed wares: BPT 85, 118, 118L, 120, 123, 126, 127, 128 (608 sherds; 7304g; 4.81 EVEs)

The Bristol glazed-ware series including variant types based on fabric and forms are a typically defining feature of 'high' medieval assemblages in Bristol emerging in the city during the mid 13th century. To date no kilns have been identified for the type although various waster deposits make it clear that production was within Bristol or its suburbs, and more than likely in Redcliffe (the closeness of the production sites to Ham Green/Pill and the exploitation of similar Coal Measures clays mean that the types can be difficult to distinguish). The Bristol fabric is similarly light-firing although unlike the Ham Green glazed wares it contains sand inclusions which are not calcareous, and fragments of red sandstone. The glaze with the Bristol wares is also brighter and mottled compared with the Ham Green series, and its products are wheelthrown. The numerous subdivisions identified for the ware type (Table 4.2) are based on variations in firing, glaze or vessel form.

Early production is confined to jugs. The majority from the present site is typical of production up to *c.* 1300/1325, some resembling standard and late style Ham Green B vessels, or with other influences evident in the 'highly decorated' style of vessels. Later 14th-century and later vessel forms are seemingly less-well represented in the assemblage, but include a number of plainer jugs and bottles, as well as some jars and open vessel forms. The divided dish/condiment set from Period 3 layer 1799 (Fig. 4.3; no. 35) probably belongs to the later (14th century or possibly 15th century) phase of production. Its boat-shaped form may reflect the overseas origins of the pepper and spices this vessel may have held; a possibly intentional reference aimed towards the merchants or traders whose tables the condiment set might have adorned. A comparable vessel is illustrated from St Bartholomew's Hospital, Bristol, with references to further examples from Bristol and Cirencester (Ponsford 1998, fig. 61, no. 150). The St Bartholomew's example suggests that the boat depicted has a flat stern end.

Forms: BPT 118: globular-bodied, bridge-spouted jugs, some with applied decoration. BPT 118L: smaller, pulled-spout jugs and bottles. BPT 85: globular-bodied jars with everted rims; BPT 128: divided dish (Fig. 4.3, no. 35).

Minety type ware (wheelthrown): BPT 84 (58 sherds; 1352g; 1.04 EVEs)

The glazed wares from Minety, north Wiltshire have a long production span, the transition from handmade (BPT 18) to wheelthrown vessels occurring by the mid or later 13th century. By this time tripod pitchers are no longer produced, and jugs and jars are the main forms produced. Late medieval production (*c.* 1350–1500+) is characterised by a very much expanded range of vessels, as illustrated from the production site (Musty 1973). Identifiable forms at Redcliff Street are mainly large jars which are similar to published examples (Watts and Rahtz 1985, fig. 80, no. 107; Ponsford 1998, fig. 60, no. 103). A lid from Period 3 furnace feature 1530 (Fig. 4.3; no. 37) is an example of the late production, probably dating to the 15th century.

Forms: jugs with simple, flattened rims and U-shaped or rod handles; jars with everted/some bifid rims; lid (Fig. 4.3; no. 37).

Lacock, Nash Hill glazed ware: BPT 368 (35 sherds; 644g; 0.30 EVEs)

Whilst never abundant, Nash Hill wares occur with some regularity among larger excavated assemblages from the city. Of three fabrics recognised at the manufacturing site (McCarthy 1974), only the glazed jug fabric is represented. This has been described previously by Vince (1984); its main characteristics are abundant quartz sand and 'sandwich' firing, with grey core and orange/buff margins and surfaces. The glaze is typically even, thicker and darker (green) compared with Bristol wares and decoration commonly makes use of underglaze white clay and red-brown coloured strips. The main period of use in Bristol appears to be the mid/later 13th to early 14th centuries as suggested by the by 'highly decorated' style jugs which make use of applied and stamped motifs. A possible baluster jug (Fig. 4.2; no. 25) is of interest; this form is not represented among pottery illustrated from the kiln site.

Forms: jugs with bridge-spouts with rod or U-shaped handles (not ill.); baluster jug with pulled spout (Fig. 4.2; no. 25).

Worcester type glazed ware: BPT 168 (12 sherds; 396g; 0.30 EVEs)

Worcester type wares have been described elsewhere by Bryant (2004, 290–7). The fabric is sandy and the most distinctive characteristic is the use of a white underslip which can extend into the unglazed vessel interior (Fig. 4.2; no. 26), and extensive use of roller-stamped decoration. Although production starts in the late 11th century the type's main floruit is the 13th to early 14th centuries (Bryant 2004, 296) and most incidences from Bristol are of this date. At Redcliff Street occurrences are mainly confined to Period 2a–2c (Table 4.2). The represented forms are all jugs; the sherd illustrated with collared rim, bridge spout and roller-stamped decoration. An unillustrated jug sherd, residual in Period 5 fill 1157, has an applied frilled base comparable to examples from Worcester (ibid., fig. 181).

Forms: globular-bodied, bridge-spouted jugs (Fig. 4.2; no. 26).

Thornbury type glazed ware: BPT 121 (30 sherds; 917g; 0.32 EVEs)

The Thornbury type jug fabric (Ponsford 1998, 137) is characterised by a grey-firing sandy fabric and dark olive-coloured glaze. Decoration is less elaborate compared to other jug types, most often consisting of lightly combed lines. Dating in the first half of the 14th century suggested by Ponsford (in notes accompanying the Bristol pottery type series) would accord with the plain style of the vessels. At the present site the type occurs mainly in Period 2a and later deposits; three sherds in earlier deposits (Period 1) are probably intrusive.

Forms: ?globular-bodied jugs with simple/flattened rims and strap handles (not ill.).

'Bath A' glazed: BPT 134 (27 sherds; 672g; 0.20 EVEs)

The similarity in fabric with this type and coarseware BPT 46 suggests a similar, west Wiltshire source. The glaze is thin and appears dark green over the reduced fabric. Vessel forms (Fig. 4.2; no. 24) consist of jugs with comb and comb-stabbed decoration. Dating in the 13th to early 14th centuries is likely.

Forms: ?globular-bodied jugs with stabbed strap or U-shaped handles (Fig. 4.2; no. 24).

South-west French wares: BPT 156, 157 and 160 (115 sherds; 864g; 0.60 EVEs)

All the types described are characterised by an off-white/pinkish fabric which is usually micaceous. BPT 157, which at the present site occurs as a single sherd from a mortar (Fig. 4.3; no. 36), differs in containing medium coarse quartz. Types BPT 156 and 157 feature an all-over coppery green glaze which is mottled. Unglazed or sparsely glazed type BPT 160 is thought to be a late variant, dating *c.* 1300–1400. South-west French wares, including Saintonge products, are increasingly common on English sites as a consequence of the shift southwards of the wine trade following the loss of Normandy in 1204. In Bristol the main period of use is after *c.* 1250, continuing to *c.* 1350 (Ponsford 1998, 137). This dating is reflected at the present site, where all material (excepting the post-medieval vessel described below) came from Period 2a–2c deposits. Identifiable forms from Redcliff Street are jugs and include examples with the characteristic S-shaped strap handles and splayed-out bases. Saintonge wares continue sporadically into the post-medieval period, probably as 'prestige' or novelty items. The female figurine with low-cut dress and pearl(?) necklace (Fig. 4.3; no. 38) is an example of this. The form represented is a small figurine jug of the type described by Hurst (1974, fig. 2) which is thought to date to the first half of the 17th century.

Forms: BPT 156: jugs with collared or simple/flattened rims; BPT 157: mortar (Fig. 4.3; no. 36); BPT 160: figurine jug (Fig. 4.3; no. 38).

Malvern Chase redware: BPT 197 (75 sherds; 1749g; 1.05 EVEs)

The important pottery industry of the Malvern Chase area in Worcestershire has been described by Vince (1977). The later products are characterised by a bright orange colour, typically sparse inclusions of igneous rock, and a thin clear lead glaze which is speckled with copper. Production of the oxidised glazed wares from this source had commenced by the mid 13th century, although their main period of use in Bristol appears to be the 15th, and particularly, the 16th, century. A very wide array of forms occurs in the type. At Redcliff Street these mainly comprise

open forms, complex-rim jars and bung-hole vessels, all of which appear typical of late (15th or 16th-century) production (Bryant 2004, 300–7).
Forms: jars/pipkins: everted 'complex' rims, some with handles and some with applied, thumbed strip at neck; bowls: flaring, straight-sided vessels with thickened rims; cisterns: large, straight-sided bung-hole vessels.

'Tudor Green': BPT 182 (28 sherds; 121g; 0.23 EVEs)

'Tudor Green' whitewares and coarser 'Border wares' are regularly present, though seldom very numerously, among Bristol assemblages. BPT 182 is a slightly sandy fine white-firing fabric with bright green glaze extending over interior and exterior surfaces. It occurs in Bristol as early as c. 1420 and may be an essentially 15th-century type (Pearce and Vince 1988, 79). The Redcliff Street group is typical of groups from Bristol and the west of England, almost entirely made up of thin-walled (lobed) cups and handle sherds. A probable costrel sherd from Period 2c deposit 1209 is more unusual, but compares to examples known from London (ibid., fig. 126, nos 587–8).
Forms: lobed cups; probable costrel (Fig. 4.3; no. 34).

Cistercian type wares: BPT 93/BPT 266/BPT 275 (12 sherds; 74g; 0.03 EVEs)

Cistercian type wares are distinguished by a very hard-fired red earthenware fabric and black glaze, often with a metallic sheen. There are a number of sources in the midlands and eastern England. Type BPT 266 is fairly local from Falfield, South Gloucestershire. It is distinguished by yellow clay pellet inclusions in a sandy purplish-black fabric. Cistercian type wares date in the range c. 1500–1700. Occurrences at the present site are thin-walled cup sherds and handles primarily from Period 3 deposits.

Wanstrow (East Somerset) glazed earthenwares: BPT 96 (63 sherds; 1471g; 0.85 EVEs)

Probably the most numerous of internally-glazed red earthenwares supplying Bristol between c. 1550 and c. 1750. At Redcliff Street it comes from Period 3 (and later deposits). The glaze is typically dark olive in colour and with an oil on water sheen (M. Ponsford, pers. comm.). The fabric has dull orange surfaces, reddish orange margins and a grey core and with abundant fine quartz sand.
Forms: jars/pipkins and wide bowls/pancheons.

Nether Stowey (West Somerset) glazed earthenwares: BPT 280 (63 sherds; 1471g; 0.85 EVEs)

The coarser red earthenwares associated with Nether Stowey are known from Bristol as early as the mid 16th century, continuing to c. 1700. A distinctive feature of some vessels is a white under-slip. Other vessels feature a clear (appearing brown) glaze. A range of forms is illustrated by Good (1987) from Narrow Quay. At Redcliff Street there are numerous sherds in Period 4 deposit 1470, most of which probably date to the mid 17th century.
Forms: flagons/bottles.

English tin-glazed earthenware: BPT 99 (7 sherds; 136g; 0 EVEs)

Manufacture of tin-glazed wares begun in Brislington and then Bristol in the later 17th century and continued until c. 1770. The small quantities recorded from Redcliff Street come from Period 4 layer 1470. Sherds from a charger with clear lead glaze underside and blue-painted face might date to the mid/later 17th century. Other sherds, including from a posset pot and a vessel with sponged manganese purple decoration are probably of 18th-century date and intrusive.
Forms: bowl/charger with foot-ring; posset pot.

Staffordshire (or Bristol) yellow slipwares: BPT 100 (3 sherds; 44g; 0.05 EVEs)

This ware type is typically dated c. 1660–1800 in Bristol, although the most commonly encountered press-moulded plates with combed or feathered decoration belong to the 18th century. The fabric is typically pale yellow and Bristol/Staffordshire products are indistinguishable based on fabric alone. The few sherds of this type at Redcliff Street are from Periods 3 and 4. A sherd from Period 4 layer 1470 has embossed decoration and is probably a Staffordshire product.
Forms: press-moulded plates.

Staffordshire (or Bristol) mottled brown-glazed earthenwares: BPT 211 (8 sherds; 557g; 0.12 EVEs)

Mottled brown-glazed wares with a pale yellow fabric are typically considered of Staffordshire manufacture, although comparable wares, sometimes referred to as 'Tiger ware' are known from Bristol as wasters. Dating is comparable to yellow slipwares, and as with BPT 100, most material is of the first half of the 18th century. Its sole occurrence at the present site is from Period 4 layer 1470, as sherds from a handled cup or small bowl.

Algarve micaceous/Merida type ware: BPT 282 (5 sherds; 196g; 0.10 EVEs)

This is a highly distinctive red earthenware with abundant gold mica. It occurs in Bristol as early as the 13th century, though is most common from 15th to 17th-century deposits. A shallow bowl in this type with thickened rim occurs from (unphased) deposit 1174.

Spanish amphorae and olive jars: BPT 81 (2 sherds; 92g; 0 EVEs)

Red or buff-firing earthenware fabric with metamorphic inclusions and biotite mica. It occasionally has a white slip or an internal green glaze. Used to transport olives, olive oil and other substances and known from Bristol from c. 1550 to c. 1700. It occurs only as bodysherds from Period 3 and 4 deposits at the present site.

Frechen stoneware: BPT 286 (2 sherds; 32g; 0 EVEs)

This typically is the more common of the Rhenish stonewares encountered in Bristol and dated c. 1550–1700. The archetypal form is the 'bartmann' type drinking jug.

Raeren stoneware: BPT 287 (1 sherds; 11g; 0 EVEs)

Raeren stonewares date as early as c. 1480, continuing to c. 1550. The throwing lines and brown glaze are distinct from Frechen types.

The pottery assemblages by period

Period 1 (construction) (12th century)

It is from the Period 1 construction deposits that material associated with the establishment of the Redcliffe suburb from c. 1120 would be expected to derive. No pottery which certainly pre-dates c. 1120 occurs in this group, although types including 'motte ditch' type BPT 6 and Bristol C wares, which are present in small quantities, would be expected to span the later 11th and 12th centuries.

A total of 59 sherds (706g/0.74 EVEs) relates to the construction of Period 1. The composition of the assemblage is presented in Table 4.2. The largest single context group derives from mixed alluvium deposit 2082 (28 sherds). This is notable in containing 'early' elements including Saxo-Norman 'motte ditch' type BPT 6 and a vessel of Bristol C type with stamped rosette decoration (Fig. 4.1; no. 1). A rod handle from a Ham Green A vessel (Fig. 4.1; no. 4) suggests that constructional activities continued into the middle decades of the 12th century. The presence of further vessels with stamped Saxo-Norman style decoration (Fig. 4.1; no. 2) and an absence of types such as Ham Green B jugs are consistent with activity commencing before c. 1150.

Illustrated vessels from Period 1 (construction) (Fig. 4.1)

1. Layer 2082. Bristol C: BPT 309. Globular jar with upright/expanded rim. Repeated stamped rosette decoration at shoulder.
2. Fill 3070 of posthole 3075. Unsourced Saxo-Norman coarseware: BPT 252a. Jar with everted rim. Repeated stamped 'basket' decoration at shoulder.
3. Fill 3134 of beamslot 3133. 'Motte ditch' type coarseware: BPT 6. Globular jar with upright/expanded rim.
4. Layer 2082. Ham Green A: BPT 26. Jug rod handle with rouletted decoration.

Period 1 (occupation) (early 12th to mid 13th centuries)

The pottery assemblage associated with the occupation of Period 1 is by far the largest compared to the other phased groups at 2,176 sherds (56.8kg/29.38 EVEs). The large bulk of the assemblage derives from the infilling of large rectangular pits possibly associated with dyeing.

Five dendrochronological dates from Period 1 timbers indicate activity on the site in the second half of the 12th century, and in three instances in the final quarter of the 12th century (Chapter 4.13). Wood from pit 3188 gave a felling date of 1288–1313, but this deposit is more likely to have been associated with construction works in Period 2a.

The quantities of pottery deriving from individual pits of similar size and form are very variable, suggesting that only some features served a secondary use for rubbish disposal. Pits 1848, 2314 and 1773 produced large groups of 245, 240 and 175 sherds respectively, with eight features producing moderately-sized groups of between 35 and 77 sherds (Table 4.3). The condition of the pottery from the larger pit groups is good, with several substantially complete vessels present, including a Ham Green B jug (Fig. 4.1; no. 7).

The larger pit groups exhibit a more or less consistent range of fabrics (Table 4.3), one that is typical for the later 12th or earlier 13th centuries. Unglazed cooking wares make up over half of the assemblage (1269 sherds; 58.6%). Almost all comprise jars, although the specialist inturned dish/'west country vessels' are a notable presence (Fig. 4.2; no. 19). In all instances representation of imported wares is low (the 23 sherds of north French BPT 366 from pit 1848 are from the same vessel). Overall there is similar ratio of jugs to coarseware (cooking pot) types, although there is variability in the representation of the common coarseware types (BPT 32, BPT 46 and BPT 114). There is no clear evidence for this coarseware variability reflecting chronological trends, but this may reflect fluctuations in supply/availability across the period represented.

The dating evidence from the pottery associated with the occupation of Period 1 is principally reliant on the Ham Green series. Viewed overall, and in each of the larger context groups (Table 4.3), Ham Green B is strongly dominant over Ham Green A, implying dating after c. 1150/60. The date range for the B series can be broad, with the 'standard' vessel forms thought by Ponsford (1991) to continue to c. 1250. The squat-profiled and poor quality vessels regarded by Ponsford as representing the final Ham Green products which survived until c. 1275, are not obviously present in Period 1 although identification from smaller sherds would be difficult.

Although the overall date range for the Period 1 assemblage is secure, there is little evidence for chronological separation across this phase of activity. It was the personal opinion of Michael Ponsford from an inspection of the assemblage that the clear chronological focus of the Period 1 groups was in the late 12th century. A few Ham Green jugs exhibit mixed characteristics of A and B style vessels (Fig. 4.1; nos 5–6). Similar 'transitional' Ham Green A/B jugs are considered by Ponsford (1991, fig. 4a) to date to after c. 1150. The large and elongated pit 3217, the construction of which is associated with a dendrochronological date of 1152–1177 and thus is one of the earlier features on the site, produced an assemblage of 72 sherds (Table 4.3). This group is indistinguishable in its overall composition from other Period 1 groups and the Ham Green B jugs include at least two vessels with applied anthropomorphic/zoomorphic decoration. Ponsford's (1991, 98) postulated dates for vessels with such decoration are in the range 1175–1225(?), and the comparatively early date from the dendrochronology is considered insufficient grounds for pushing the Ponsford's dating earlier, given the likelihood that the tree was felled some time before the pit was infilled.

The evidence for Period 1 activity extending into the middle decades of the 13th century is slight, and is based on the limited incidence of 'high medieval' types within selected pits (Table 4.3). For the most part, and in particular from the extensive occupation

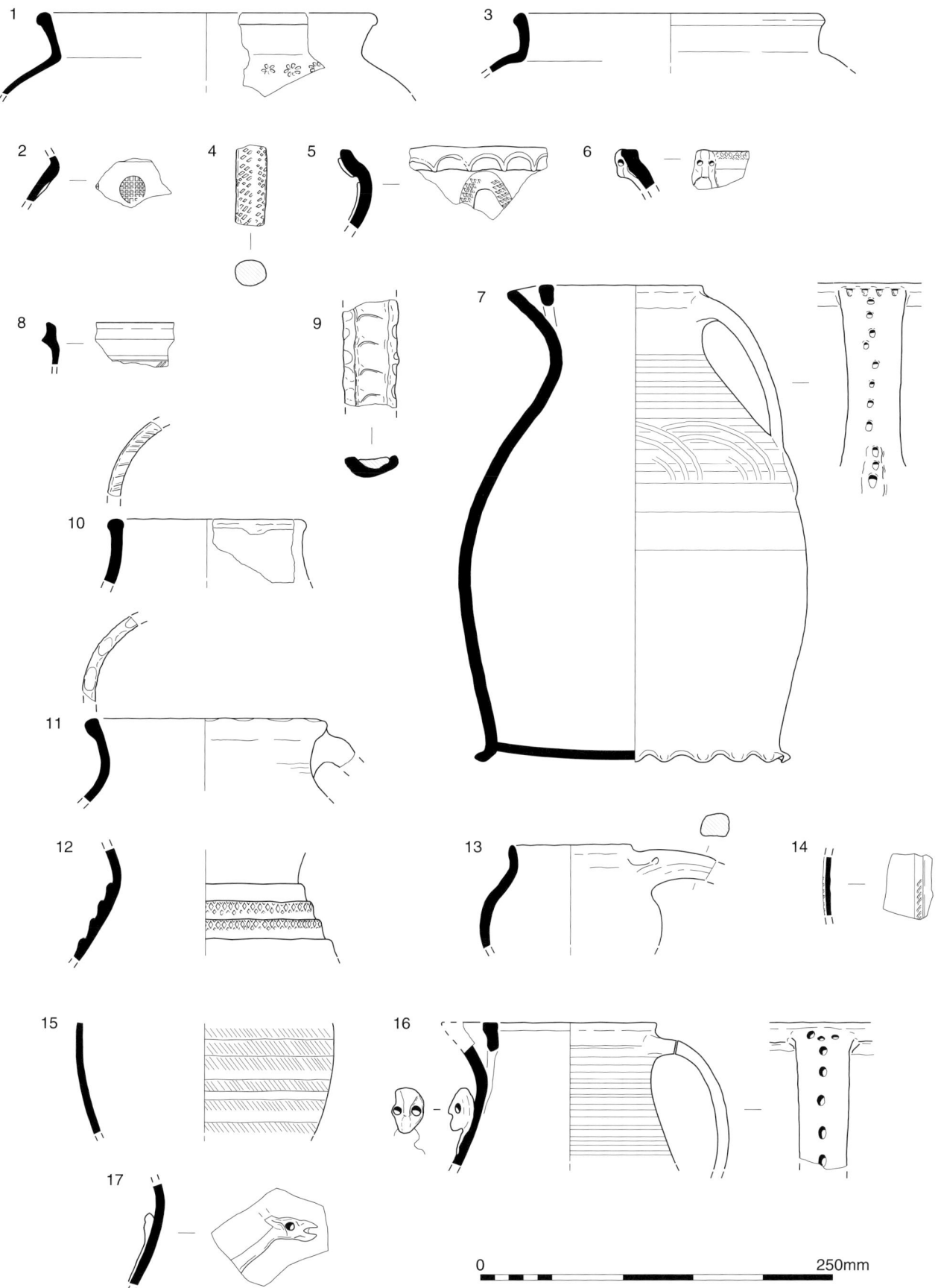

Fig. 4.1   Pottery vessels nos 1–17 from Period 1.   Scale 1:4

surface 2009 and the drain 1773, both open features which might be expected to have received pottery over an extended period of time, the later ware types are entirely absent. The best evidence for continued activity to *c.* 1230/50 comes from pit 3066 (fill 3015), which stratigraphically and morphologically belongs with Period 1 rather than Period 2a. This feature included three vessels, each represented by large or joining sherds in Bristol and non-local jug types (Fig. 4.2; nos 24–5), for which dating after *c.* 1230/50 is probable.

Illustrated vessels from Period 1 (occupation)
(Figs 4.1–4.2)

5. Fill 3187 of pit 3188. Ham Green B: BPT 27. Jug with mixed Ham Green A (rouletting; pulled spout; ridged shoulder) and Ham Green B (applied decoration) form traits. The fabric/glaze is more characteristically Ham Green A.
6. Fill 3203 of pit 3201. Ham Green B: BPT 27. As above, shows mixed Ham Green A/B properties. Applied anthropomorphic decoration and rouletting. Ham Green B-like fabric.
7. Fill 2477 of pit 2479. Ham Green B: BPT 27. Complete 'standard' form Ham Green jug. Scored horizontal and arcing decoration at shoulder.
8. Fill 2476 of pit 2479. Normandy green glazed: BPT 239 jug. Bifid rim; scored decoration at neck.
9. Fill 3147 of pit 3146. South-east Wiltshire tripod pitcher: BPT 18c. Pitcher handle.
10. Fill 1771 of drain 1773. Unsourced Saxo-Norman coarseware: BPT 252b. Globular jar; upright rim with slashed decoration to rim upper.
11. Fill 1771 of drain 1773. Unsourced Saxo-Norman coarseware: BPT 252b. Handled jar/pitcher with U-shaped handle.
12. Fill 3088 of pit 3087. Ham Green A: BPT 26. Jug with stepped shoulder and diamond-pattern roller stamping.
13. Layer 2009. Paffrath 'blaugrau' type (no BPT) pipkin.
14. Layer 2009. French jug fabric: BPT 192. Strip-decorated jug sherds.
15. Fill 1862 of pit 1848. Normandy green glazed fabric: BPT 239. Roller-stamped jug sherds.
16. Fill 3218 of pit 3217. Ham Green B: BPT 27. Jug with thickened rim, bridge spout and strap handle. Applied anthropomorphic decoration below spout.
17. Fill 3218 of pit 3217. Ham Green B: BPT 27. Jug sherd with applied dragonesque decoration.
18. Fill 2121 of pit 2123. Pill/'Proto-Ham Green' coarseware: BPT 114. Jar with everted rim. Combed decoration.
19. Fill 1866 of pit 1839. 'Bath A' coarseware: BPT 46. 'West country vessel'/inturned dish.
20. Fill 1869 of pit 1848. Pill/'Proto-Ham Green' coarseware: BPT 114. Jar with high, everted rim with finger-tipping.
21. Fill 1818 of pit 2134. Ham Green B: BPT 27. Jug. Dimpled decoration.
22. Fill 3218 of pit 3217. Ham Green redware: BPT 32. Jar with simple everted rim. Combed and applied strip decoration.
23. Fill 3218 of pit 3217. Ham Green redware: BPT 32. Jar with simple everted rim. Combed decoration.
24. Fill 3015 of pit 3066. 'Bath A' glazed fabric: BPT 134. Jug with comb-stabbed decoration to handle.
25. Fill 3015 of pit 3066. Lacock, Nash Hill: BPT 368. ?Baluster jug with pulled spout.
26. Fill 3015 of pit 3066. Worcester type glazed ware: BPT 168. Bridge-spouted jug. Roller-stamped decoration.

Period 2a (late 13th to mid 14th centuries)

The major reorganisation and rebuilding which characterises Period 2a is not for the most part marked by major changes in the character or composition of the pottery. A total of 1,035 sherds (23.0kg/16.61 EVEs) relates to Period 2a; the great majority of the material coming from layers (Table 4.2).

There is a single dendrochronological determination relating to Period 2a, from well 1822, a plank from this feature providing a felling date of 1229–54. The latest backfill of Period 1 pit 3188, a feature sealed by floor surfaces relating to the stone-built building at No. 18, produced a dendrochronological date which provides a *terminus post quem* of 1288 for the construction of the Period 2a structure. There are in addition indicators of dating provided by leather shoes, including 13th-century examples from occupation layer 1809/1812, which overlaid surface 2009 at No. 17, and a coin of 1205–1217/18 from make-up 3675 at No. 20. The construction date for Period 2a structures is not greatly elucidated by the pottery. Stone wall 3053 at No. 18 produced just two sherds of pottery (Bristol glazed type BPT 118) suggestive of a date after *c.* 1240/50. Similarly the circular hearths are also poorly dated.

There is no clear chronological separation evident between certain of the large layer groups of Period 2a (make-up 1749 below surface 1732 and occupation layer 1809/1812, both at No. 17), and larger pit and layer groups of Period 1 which are likely to date to the late 12th century. Ham Green wares, 'Bath A' coarsewares and Minety type ware continue to dominate, and this, together with small quantities of north French imports (Fig. 4.2, nos 27–8), suggest that that a significant proportion of the Period 2a assemblage originates before *c.* 1250 and is redeposited.

'High medieval' types, expected to date after *c.* 1220/1250 (BPT 84; BPT 85; BPT 118; BPT 121; BPT 134; BPT 156; BPT 168, BPT 368) are present in Period 2a, although in relatively modest quantities (151 sherds; 14%) and in most instances are sufficient only to provide *termini post quem*. They are most prominent from make-up layer 2031 and drainage features (make-up 1920 and drain 1911) at No. 17; the surfacing of Little Thomas Lane (surfaces 1566 and 1892; not illustrated), and selected other features (hearth 3534 at No. 19 and pit 3614 at No. 20). An aspect of the Period 2a groups which is consistent with a later dating compared with Period 1 is the reduction in the quantities of unglazed coarsewares (38% by count compared to 58.5%), which

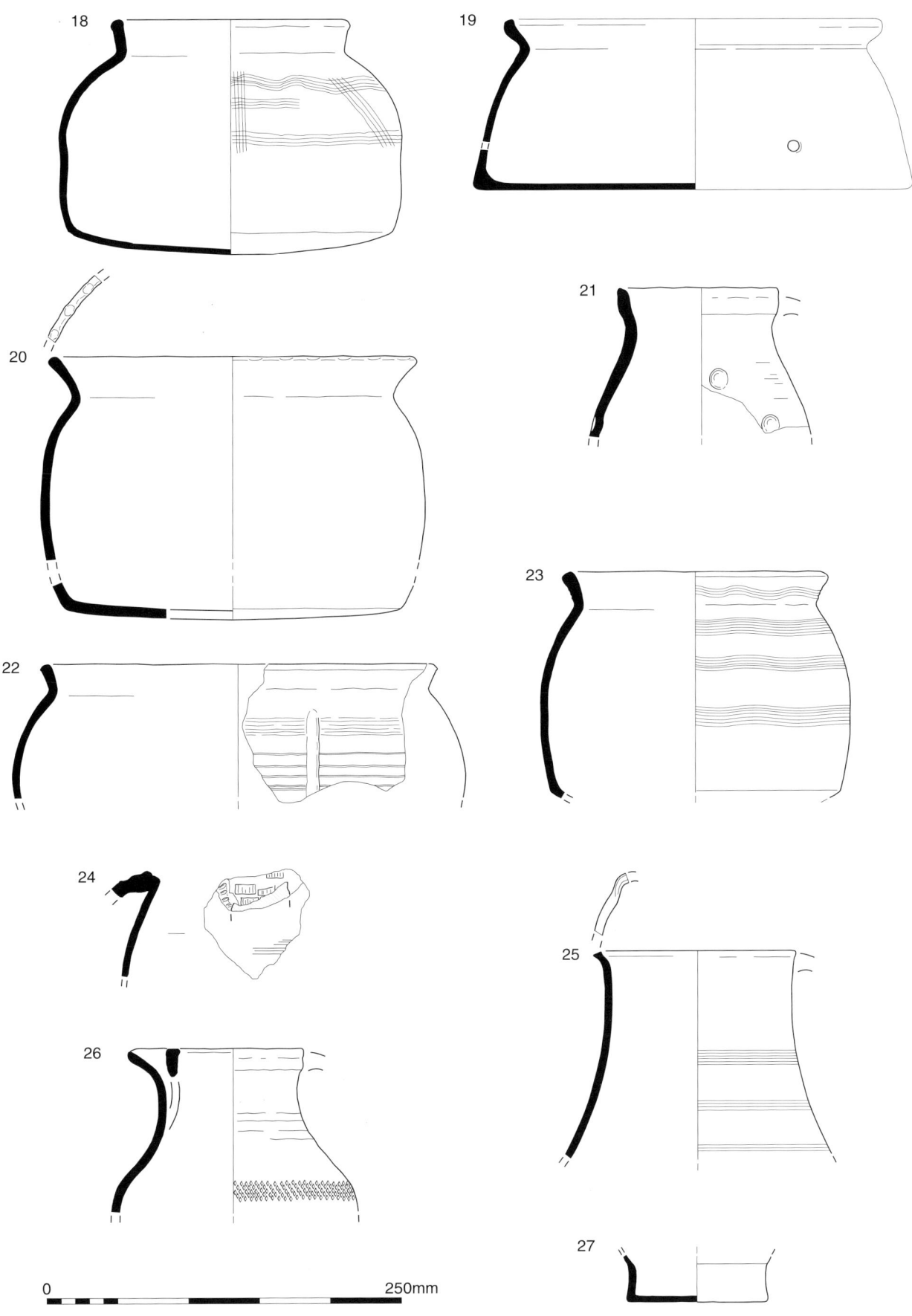

Fig. 4.2   Pottery vessels nos 18–27 from Periods 1 and 2a. Scale 1:4

corresponds to a pattern of decline in the use of ceramic cooking wares in Bristol at this time.

The absence from these groups of late medieval ware types is significant and suggests that Period 2a had closed before *c.* 1350. Dating probably in the second half of the 13th century is suggested by decorated jug sherds in Bristol glazed (BPT 118) and Lacock, Nash Hill (BPT 368) types. Further examples of this 'highly decorated' style thought to pre-date *c.* 1300/25 are present elsewhere in Period 2a.

Illustrated vessels from Period 2a (Figs 4.2–4.3)

27.	Layer 1812. North French jug fabric: BPT 366. Jug base.
28.	Layer 1749. French jug fabric: BPT 192. Jug with collared/bifid rim.
29.	Layer 1958. North French jug fabric: BPT 366. Collared/bifid-rim jug.
30.	Layer 1958. Ham Green redware variant: BPT 305. Large jar. Applied strip decoration.
31.	Layer 1964. Minety type ware (handmade): BPT 18. Pitcher with blocked tubular spout.
32.	Fill 2244 of irregular feature 2249. Layer 1809. Ham Green A/B: BPT 26/27. Lid with applied pellet and incised decoration.
33.	Layer 1809. Ham Green B: BPT 27. Jug with applied 'serpent' decoration. As McCutcheon 2006, fig. 17, no. 17.

Period 2b (mid 14th century)

The Period 2b group is considerably smaller than that of Period 2a, comprising 250 sherds (2.7 kg/2.88 EVEs). It derives from only 15 separate deposits, mainly layers. Context groups are small, none exceeding 42 sherds. The Period 2b group differs significantly in its composition compared to Period 2a, with 'high medieval' ware types now making up over half of the assemblage (by count). Bristol glazed wares dominate (154 sherds; 62%), including the 'late' variant BPT 118L, which suggests dating well into the 14th century. Unglazed cooking pot types (BPT 32; BPT 46; BPT 114) together contribute only 32 sherds (13%) and are very likely all residual. The Bristol glazed and other wares rarely provide specific dating. Exceptions are jugs and bottles from layers 1603 and 1645 at No. 17 which exhibit restricted use of glaze, similar to that noted with south-west French products and probably dating to the middle decades of the 14th century. Overall the plain character of the Bristol and other jugs from Period 2b accords with dating after *c.* 1300/25.

Period 2c (mid 14th to early 15th centuries)

Pottery relating to Period 2c amounts to some 279 sherds (4.3kg/3.47 EVEs) recovered from 36 deposits. The assemblage derives mainly from layers (Table 4.1), relating to a continuance of domestic and dyeing activity, and the construction of furnace structures associated with the production of metal vessels. The high proportion from layers may account for the seeming high rate of redeposition of Anglo-Norman type wares (Table 4.2). Large and sealed pottery groups are largely lacking from Period 2c. Stone tank/cistern 1692 produced only 15 sherds which provide only an inexact date (a date after the mid 13th century is indicated by bodysherds of Bristol glazed ware BPT 118).

Redeposited Anglo-Norman pottery is a sizeable element in Period 2c; however differences compared with the previous phase are apparent in an expanded range of glazed types (Table 4.2). Dating after *c.* 1400/1420 is likely for certain Period 2c deposits based on the occurrence, albeit in limited quantity, of Malvern Chase redware BPT 197 and 'Tudor Green' BPT 182, types which are common in Bristol only after this time. These types are present from make-up layers/dumped deposits 1155, 1291, and 1346, drain 1350 and layer 1814. Excepting the Anglo-Norman elements, the remaining part of the Period 2c group is made up of later Bristol glazed-ware variants, regional glazed wares, and south-west French types.

Pottery associated with furnace 1845 amounted to 54 sherds although the majority would seem to be composed of redeposited material. Elements from the associated structure (1939) consisted of sherds in Bristol glazed variants BPT 126 and 128, south-west French type BPT 156 (2 sherds) and Minety type BPT 84. They provide a *terminus post quem* of *c.* 1300. Other context groups (deposits 1940, 2019 and 2092) associated with furnace 1845 present consistent, though equally broad dating, comprising sherds of types BPT 118, 121 and 128 (6 sherds in total).

Illustrated vessel from Period 2c (Fig. 4.3)

34.	Layer 1291. 'Tudor Green': BPT 182. Costrel.

Period 3 (early 15th to late 17th centuries)

Period 3 is characterised by industrial redevelopment associated with the manufacture of copper-alloy vessels. The Period 3 pottery assemblage is moderately large at 875 sherds (16.1kg/9.60 EVEs), although as with Period 2 much of the assemblage is clearly redeposited (Table 4.2).

The larger part of the pottery assemblage derives from layers; the largest context groups from cobbled surface 3348 and layers 1799 and 1474. Reworking of earlier material continues to be evident, and the extent of residuality can be judged from the two largest context groups, where a substantial majority of sherds comprised Ham Green or other 'Anglo-Norman' types (76 of a total of 89 sherds and 51 out of 86 sherds respectfully). Boat-shaped divided dish (Fig. 4.3; no. 35) and Saintonge mortar (Fig. 4.3; no. 36), both of which probably date to the 14th century, are presumably residual or may be survivals in use.

Period 3 corresponds to a period of ceramic change in Bristol, following from the apparent demise of Bristol glazed wares by *c.* 1450. Relatively small quantities of pottery however relate to Period 3 and much of what

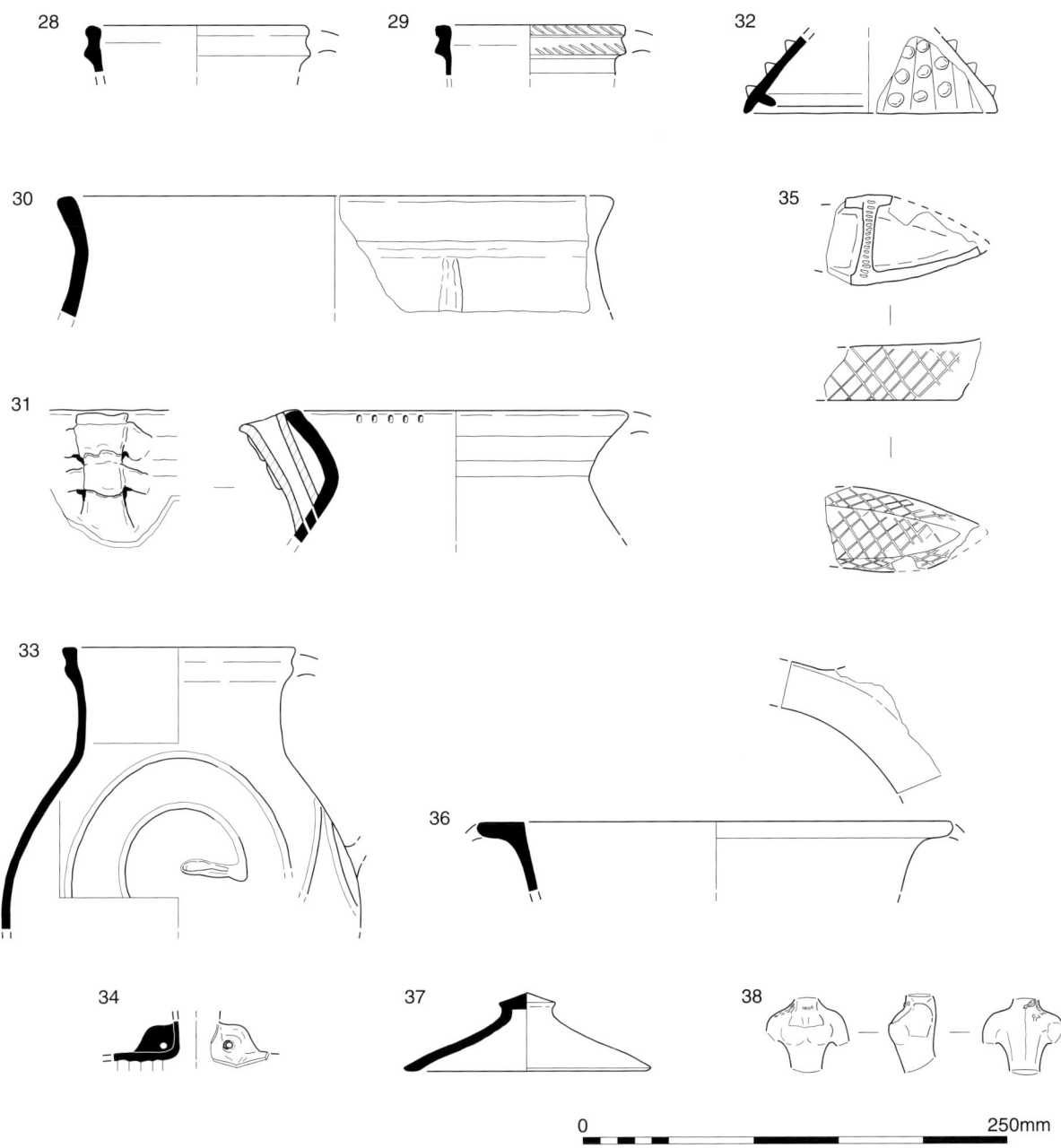

Fig. 4.3 Pottery vessels nos 28–38 from Periods 2a, 2c and 3. Scale 1:4

is deposited continues to be reworked Anglo-Norman and 'high' medieval material (Table 4.2). Period 3 encompasses the period (after *c.* 1580/1600) when use of clay tobacco pipes becomes prevalent with the result that such material is an increasingly important tool for dating. Dating before *c.* 1600 can reasonably be claimed for some deposits based on the presence of certain types (BPT 197, BPT 182, BPT 266; BPT 287) and from an absence of clay tobacco pipe. The relatively small pottery groups from furnace structure 1530, as well as make-up/surfacing deposits 3468, 1270, 1463, 1487, pit fill 1827 (fill of 1828) and hearth deposits 3523 and 3529 probably date before *c.* 1600, and, informed by an absence of certain post-medieval pottery types (below), probably before *c.* 1550. The new pottery types common only after *c.* 1550 are primarily the glazed earthenwares from Somerset and other west country sources (BPT 96; BPT 280; BPT 108; BPT 112). Such types are present in some Period 3 assemblages, in some instances occurring with well-dated groups of clay tobacco pipe; notably make-up 3422 and pit fill 1333 (fill of 1340).

Context groups relating to industrial features include the construction and backfill of furnace structures, ashy deposit 1392 and dumped industrial debris 1463. The backfill of furnace 1530 (fill 1529) included a Minety type ware lid and a 'Tudor Green' cup sherd which would support a 15th or early 16th-century date for its disuse. A single 'Tudor Green' sherd was recovered from the backfill of furnace 1426. Material from a clay deposit (1389) sealing furnace 1426 comprised mainly redeposited medieval sherds and one sherd of post-medieval type BPT 96, dating after *c*. 1550.

Periods 4–5 (late 17th to late 20th centuries)
Detailed analysis was not undertaken for the small quantities of pottery (384 sherds weighing 8kg) from the later post-medieval and modern-dated deposits. A sherd from a Saintonge figurine jug (Fig. 4.3; no. 38) is a residual find of earlier 17th-century date.

Illustrated vessels from Periods 3–4 (Fig. 4.3)
35. Layer 1799. Bristol glazed ware 'internally-glazed': BPT 128. Boat-shaped divided dish. Incised cross-hatch decoration.
36. Period 3 layer 1619. South-west French 'quartz-rich' type: BPT 157. Mortar.
37. Furnace backfill 1529. Minety type ware (wheel-thrown): BPT 84. Knobbed lid.
38. Period 4 fill 3393 of wall construction cut 3392. BPT 160. Female torso from Saintonge figurine jug.

Discussion
The pottery assemblage presents 'asymmetric' evidence for pottery supply and use at the site. It is biased distinctly to Anglo-Norman types with the bulk relating to Period 1 (occupation) and Period 2a. Of most significance are the Period 1 pit groups which provide a good indication of pottery supply and use in this part of the city *c*. 1160/75–1200/25.

The small assemblage associated with the construction of Period 1 can add relatively little to our understanding of pottery supply before *c*. 1150, reflecting the documented date for expansion into the Redcliffe suburb. Typical of this period is the stamp-decorated 'Bristol C' vessel (Fig. 4.1; no. 1), and the assemblage is comparable, for example, with Saxo-Norman material from St Mary le Port (Watts and Rahtz 1985). More unusual are the basket-pattern stamps (Fig. 4.1; no. 2), although similar decoration is known from Melksham, Wiltshire (Crawford 2014, 129, fig. 8, no. 4).

The dendrochronological dates from Period 1 deposits demonstrate a focus for activity in the final quarter of the 12th century (a single late date from a post originally assigned to Period 1 was anomalous and suggests that the post was a pile associated with Period 3 Building 3A). The Period 1 (occupation) groups and associated dendrochronological dates provide further support for the dating established for Ham Green and other types based on material from Dundas Wharf (Ponsford 1991).

In most aspects of its composition the medieval assemblage is broadly reflective of pottery supply in the city as far as can be determined from the major published groups (Ponsford 1988; 1998). The continental wares of Norman French and Rhineland origin, whilst not present in large quantities, are noteworthy as further evidence of the trading links of the town in the later 12th/earlier 13th centuries.

The north French and Paffrath 'blaugrau' type vessels account for 1.7% of the Period 1 (occupation) total by count. The figure is significantly lower than that from the south coast ports, for example from Southampton where continental wares account for 7% of the Anglo-Norman material (Brown 2002, 91, table 3). It accords, however, with the typically low representation of such types noted from Bristol sites (Ponsford 1998, 138). Most common are Normandy/north French glazed jug fabrics (BPT 239/366), the main *floruit* for which, based on evidence from the south coast ports, is the later 12th continuing into the earlier 13th century (Allan 1983 196–8; 1984, 18). The Paffrath 'blaugrau' type vessel (Fig. 4.1; no. 13) is a significant new addition to Bristol assemblages of the period, although perhaps not unexpected given occurrences in Ireland and Worcester.

Pottery imports from Period 2b are proportionally a little higher than for the previous phase, rising to 2.5% by count. Included are a small number of sherds in south-west French type BPT 156, reflective of the forced shift in trade to this region after *c*. 1220/1250. The north French wares present in Period 2a/b may be largely residual, though the increased representation of unsourced type BPT 192 would be consistent with the dating of *c*. 1225–50 thought likely for this type based on an occurrence at Bristol Castle (Ponsford 1983, 222).

The Period 1 (occupation) and Period 2a groups are primarily made up of local or regional ware types, amongst which types Minety type ware (handmade) BPT 18 and 'Bath A' coarsewares BPT 46 are most prominent. Minety type ware occurs as tripod pitchers, a specialised form of large capacity which is not represented in the Ham Green repertoire. Quantities increase proportionally: 6.6% in Period 1 (occupation) rising to a 13.6% in Period 2a. 'Bath A' coarsewares decrease in Period 2a, although seemingly as a more general fall-off in the abundance of unglazed coarsewares probably relating to the increased use of metal cooking vessels. Across Period 1 (occupation) and Period 2a vessel forms amongst the coarsewares are almost exclusively jars (31.18 EVEs; 96%). Evidence for use includes sooting or internal carbonised residues on 701 sherds (*c*. 36%). Despite its rarity the Paffrath ladle (Fig. 4.1; no. 13) exhibits heavy sooting, suggestive of use for cooking or heating of its contents. Other vessel forms among coarseware types are limited to incurved dish/'west country vessels', of which there are eight examples, all of 'Bath A' coarseware BPT 46. These doubtless served a particular function, although what this was remains uncertain (suggestions have included cheese making (Duncan Brown, pers. comm.) and as the bases for bee 'skeps'). Few, if any vessels of this class have been previously published among Bristol groups. It is unclear whether the number of these vessels at Redcliff

Street is unusual and therefore denotes a specialist use in the area. Their seeming prevalence may reflect chronology (all came from Period 1 (occupation) and Period 2a deposits) and the class as a whole is thought to date mainly to the 12th and earlier 13th centuries (McCutcheon 2006, 81).

Pottery use in Bristol in the 'high medieval' period (*c.* 1250/70–1350/1400) is marked by changes in the supply of tablewares and the decreasing use of cooking pot types (BPT 114; 32; 46). Ham Green wares were no longer produced after *c.* 1250/70, the major supply of tablewares passing to the Bristol glazed ware series (BPT 118 *et al.*), and supplemented by a number of regional (BPT 121; 168; 368; 84) and continental wares (BPT 156; 157; 160). This pattern of supply is broadly reflected at Redcliff Street in the Period 2a–2c groups, although this is obscured somewhat by the large quantities of redeposited material. Unglazed coarseware type BPT 46 continued to be manufactured until *c.* 1300 and possibly beyond. There appears to be no attendant increase in this ware type in Period 2a/b in response to the unavailability after *c.* 1250 of Ham Green cooking wares, and neither Bristol glazed jars (BPT 85) or Minety type ware (wheelthrown) jars (BPT 84) would be sufficient to compensate. It seems likely then that cooking wares of all types declined in use during the 13th century, possibly reflecting the wider availability of metal cooking vessels.

Ignoring a sizeable redeposited element, the Period 2c and Period 3 assemblages are illustrative of quite fundamental changes in pottery supply after *c.* 1400/1450, which see a move away from locally-produced types. Production of Bristol glazed wares has ceased by the later 15th century, its place taken largely by regional imports of Malvern Chase redwares (BPT 197); 'Tudor Green' type (BPT 182) wares from the Hampshire/Surrey border, and other earthenwares in the Cistercian ware tradition (BPT 93 and 266). Although the overall size of the group is small, the range of vessel forms represented in Malvern Chase type (BPT 197) is reasonably wide and reflects the greater diversity of form typical of the period *c.* 1450–1600. The latest Minety type ware (BPT 84) products also continue into this period, with production thought to continue into the early 16th century. Importation of German stonewares, first in the form of Raeren ware (BPT 287), had begun by *c.* 1450 and Iberian wares, particularly Algarve micaceous/Merida type wares (BPT 282) were increasing, probably reflecting expanding trade.

Malvern Chase redwares appear to have ceased production by the early 17th century, and before this time their use in Bristol was likely to have been in decline. From *c.* 1550 lead-glazed red earthenwares primarily from Somerset (BPT 96, 280, 285) are increasingly present among Bristol assemblages, as utilitarian and 'display' vessels (Good 1987). Such types are uncommon among Period 3 context groups, only becoming abundant in Period 4.

4.2 Medieval Ceramic Roof Tile
Angus Crawford

A total of 212 fragments of medieval ceramic roof tile, weighing 11.85kg, was recovered. The material was visually examined and, where possible, classified with reference to the Bristol Roof Tile Fabric Series as enlarged and described by Burchill (2006). No complete tiles or roof furniture were present within the assemblage and none have been illustrated.

Composition and character

The roof tile assemblage is dominated by glazed ridge tile fragments, with 191 pieces recorded, accounting for nearly 90% of the assemblage (Table 4.4). Of the remainder, a small quantity comprises unglazed flat roof tile and (post-medieval) pan tile fragments and the group is consistent with an established pattern from medieval sites in Bristol where ridge tiles dominate. This suggests that buildings were roofed with other materials, such as stone or shingles, combined with glazed ceramic ridge caps.

The majority of the roof tile (171 fragments; 81%) conforms to types BRF 1–3 and 5. Previous petrological analysis (Burchill 2006, 133) incorporating types BRF 1, 2 and 5 identified similarities with 'Bristol Redcliffe' pottery type BPT 118 and a local source can be assumed. Twenty-seven tiles are recorded as BRF 3, which has also been identified as locally produced due to the similarity of the fabric to Bristol glazed ware variant BPT 123. The glazes of all the ridge tiles are typically thick and exhibit a range of mottled or streaky green finishes. One fragment in BRF 1 is unusual in its use of a distinctively yellow glaze.

Of the remaining material, 13 fragments (6.1%) originated from the Malvern Chase area (BRF 7). A further ten fragments (4.7%) were identified as pan tiles (BRF 13) and only three further fragments were categorised under miscellaneous types (BRF 14).

Tiles preserving ridge crests occurred in Bristol-made types BRF 1–3 and 5 and feature two distinct types. The most common was a saw-tooth effect formed by cutting away triangular sections of the tile after a ridged-back has been formed. A number of examples of this type also feature knife stabs into or through the crests. In a few instances this resulted in a horizontal slot through the centre of the crest. The majority, however, appeared to have been stabbed fairly haphazardly or rapidly. A number of tiles exhibit stab marks executed using a circular implement.

The second crest type was formed by cutting away, probably with a knife, concave sections from the ridge. The effect created peaks separated by shallow concavities. Comparison between fabric types and the variations in crest heights of this type has been previously considered (Williams and Ponsford 1988). Due to the small number within the assemblage, no association can be suggested between fabrics and ridge crest types.

Table 4.4 Medieval ceramic tile fabrics (Bristol Roof Tile Fabrics; BRF) by period

	Period	<>	1	2a	2b	2c	3	4	5	Total
	BRF									
Furnit.	louvre					1				**1**
	other							1		**1**
Ridge (glazed)	Type 1	14		3		5	7	46	3	**78**
	Type 2	4		5	3	4	11	11	1	**39**
	Type 3	6		8		6	6	1		**27**
	Type 4					1	1	1		**3**
	Type 5	1		4		4	10	5	3	**27**
	Type 7	2		1		1	1	6	2	**13**
	Type 10		3	1						**4**
Other	Type 6 (peg)						4	2		**6**
	Type 13 (pan)							10		**10**
	Type 14 (misc.)	1	1	1						**3**
	Total	28	4	23	3	22	40	83	9	**212**

Roof furniture

Two fragments of roof furniture were identified. This included a dome-shaped knob finial, in a deep green glaze on a pale grey fabric with abundant quartz inclusions. Similar examples from Nash Hill in Wiltshire have been identified as medieval louvre fragments (Dunning 1974, 129–31). A possible base fragment from a louvre with 'p' shaped section was also found. This identification is tentative, however, and the fragment could also have originated from a decorative ridge tile edge. A further fragment of roof furniture appeared to be a fragment of a hollow shaft or finial.

Distribution and phasing

There was a scarcity of roof tiles from Period 1 (occupation) deposits suggesting that, as with previously published tile assemblages, there was little use of ceramic tile in the 12th century. Only four tile fragments were recovered, in 'poorly-mixed' fabric BRF 10 and 'miscellaneous' BRF 14.

The roof tile recorded from Periods 2a to 2b (late 13th to mid 14th centuries) was dominated by the locally produced Bristol fabrics BRF 1, 2, 4 and 5. This is consistent with the mainly 14th-century date previously asserted for Bristol-made ridge tiles. The 23 fragments from Period 2a deposits hint at an earlier start to production, perhaps contemporary with the start of Bristol glazed pottery production in the mid/late 13th century.

Material from Period 2b is poorly represented with only three fragments recorded (BRF 2). This is probably reflective of the insubstantial character of the archaeological deposits associated with this phase. Twenty-two roof tile fragments, predominantly Bristol-types BRF 1–3 and 5 were recovered from Period 2c deposits. A single fragment of Malvern Chase roof tile (BRF 7) was also present; this accorded with previous studies in supporting a 15th to 16th-century date for this type in the Bristol region (Burchill 2006, 132).

4.3 Coins and Tokens
Edward Besly

1. Period 2a make-up 3675: Silver 'Short Cross' penny in the name of Henry. *Obv*: hENR[IC]VS R-EX *Rev*: ILGER . ON . LVN[ ] (Ilger, London). Weight: 1.18g, corroded and incomplete. Ilger was active in classes 5b–6 (*c*. 1205–1217/18) (Spink 2009). Perhaps class 5c, in which case before *c*. 1209, but this is not certain. Registered Artefact 74.
2. Period 2c wall 1494: Copper-alloy jetton (reckoning counter). Probably France or Tournai, early 15th century. *Obv*: Arms of France, with legend V F A V M etc. (a version of *Ave Maria*, etc.). *Rev*: Cross in quatrefoil; [ ] – V – E – [ ] (*Ave*). Diameter 16mm approximately; weight 1.70g (fragment). Registered Artefact 30.

4.4 Objects of Metal and Worked Bone
E.R. McSloy

Over 350 items of iron, copper alloy, lead or lead alloy and worked bone were recovered. The large majority comprised nails and unidentifiable, fragmentary items. The published catalogue is confined to items of interest in terms of dating or relating to crafts or industrial processes. The remaining portion of the assemblage has been recorded in brief for the archive.

The published group is small and restricted in its range. There are very few items from the Period 1 pits, features which were highly productive of pottery and animal bone. The few Period 1 finds comprise personal items including knife or shears blades and a possible harness fitting (cat. no. 9) and nothing is present which would relate directly to dyeing. In contrast, finds from Period 2 include items relating to industry/crafts and probably to activities involving textiles. The presence of writing implements (cat. nos 18 and 19) and possibly the decorative chape (cat. no. 1; Fig. 4.5; no. 7) might reflect changed status by the later medieval period and occupation by members of a literate, mercantile class.

Material from Period 3 includes unfinished copper-alloy items cat. nos 2 and 4. Candlestick cat. no. 2 (Fig. 4.4; no. 5) is good evidence for manufacture of objects other than metal vessels. Both items probably date to the 15th or 16th centuries.

Copper alloy

1. Unstratified. (Dagger?) chape from sheet metal. Sub-triangular four-sided in form. Decoration consists of pierced quatrefoil to front and upper edge as crude 'plumes' separated by punched holes and with details as incised lines. There is also an incised border with perforations, probably for stitching to a leather scabbard. A discoloured band at the toe of the chape suggests a separate terminal was brazed in place. Sheet metal chapes of simpler design are known from Ludgershall, Wiltshire (Robinson and Griffiths 2000, fig. 6.2, nos 7–8) and York (Ottaway and Rogers 2002, 2904), the latter probably of 14th to 15th-century date. Length 38mm; width at top 20.5mm. Registered artefact 38 (Fig. 4.5; no. 7).
2. Period 3 ashy layer 1407 (within furnace 1426). Stem from a 'bunsen type' candlestick. Simple cylindrical form with expanded, cup-like socket and 'decoration' as biconical projection at the mid point of the stem. Unfinished, with no indication that it was ever fixed to its base. It also lacks the incised groove decoration to its socket seen with most known examples. The base is likely to have been of shallow, cylindrical form which would have been manufactured separately and riveted in place (Brownsword 1985, 1). There is a high probability it was cast in the furnace within which it was found. Candlesticks of this form may date as early as *c.* 1400 (ibid., 3), but continue into the post-medieval period. This piece lacks features of later forms which display more elaborate moulded decoration and a 'lipped' socket (ibid.). It therefore probably dates before the late 16th century. Length 124mm; diameter at socket 27mm, and at stem 10mm. Registered artefact 23 (Fig. 4.4; no. 5).
3. Period 3 ashy fill 1392 of pit 1436. Cast single-looped buckle with integral plate. Squared oval frame with knops at the junction with the plate. The plate tapers in width and has two rivet holes and a larger hole for a buckle pin, which is absent. The plate terminates in short, squared branches and with central 'hook'. The hook is rolled with only a small opening for suspension. Buckles of this form are described by Whitehead (1996, 32) as spur buckles and this mode of use is illustrated by a 14th-century find from London (Ellis 1995, 138, fig. 97, no. 330). Other 'specialised' use is also possible (Egan and Pritchard 1991, 78). Dating would seem to be in the 13th and 14th centuries. Length 41mm; width at frame 16mm. Registered artefact 26 (Fig. 4.5; no. 6).
4. Period 3 occupation layer 1349. Heart-shaped drop handle. Unfinished, with casting flash to its inner and outer edges. The outer portion of one lobe is flawed, the probable reason for rejection, presumably for recasting. Cast handles of this form are thought to derive from chafing dishes, probably dating to the late 15th and 16th centuries (Lewis 1973). Examples are known from Acton Court, South Gloucestershire (Courtney 2004, 371, fig. 9.35) and elsewhere in Bristol (McSloy 2013, 240, fig. 4.28, no. 10). This piece and a clay mould from Period 3 pit 1472 (Chapter 4.5), may be the first evidence for English manufacture. Length 46mm; width 60mm; thickness 4mm. Registered artefact 13 (Fig. 4.4; no. 4).
5. Period 4 brick hearth 1215/1197. Pin with looped over terminal. Possibly from an annular brooch of medieval type. Length 59mm; diameter 2mm. Registered artefact 8. Not illustrated.
6. Period 4 make-up 1187. Buckle(?) or strap fitting. From folded strip with round-sectioned rivets; the rearmost with buckle pin set in a cylindrical mounting. Post-medieval. Length 16mm; width 9mm. Not illustrated.
7. Period 5 make-up 3488. Domed thimble from sheet metal with spiral of punched(?) lentoid indentations and border groove. Post-medieval. Height 20mm; weight 4g. Registered artefact 66. Not illustrated.

Iron

8. Period 1 fill 3019 of posthole 3021. Shears blade. It is insufficiently complete for classification, although it lacks the 'moulding' at the junction of blade and handle which is a feature of some late medieval shears (Goodall 1980, 96–7). It was associated with pottery of 12th-century date. Length (surviving) 126mm; width (blade, maximum) 19.5mm (Fig. 4.4; no. 1).
9. Period 1 fill 3088 of pit 3087. Fragment of ring with D-shaped section. X-ray shows silver-wire inlay. Possible uses include part of a horse harness or buckle. Found with 12th-century pottery. Diameter approximately 75mm; thickness approximately 9mm (Fig. 4.4; no. 3).
10. Period 2a occupation layer 2005. Knife or shears blade fragment; straight-backed. Length (surviving) 78mm (Fig. 4.4; no. 2).

Lead/Lead alloy

11. Period 2c occupation layer 1341. Disc-shaped weight with off-centre perforation. 'Pan' weights of lead are common in the medieval period. Many, like this example, are unmarked. Diameter 35mm; thickness 3mm; weight 29g (1oz). Registered artefact 14. Not illustrated.
12. Period 5 make-up 3488. Lead-alloy. Buckle with double oval frame. Pin missing. Such buckles are

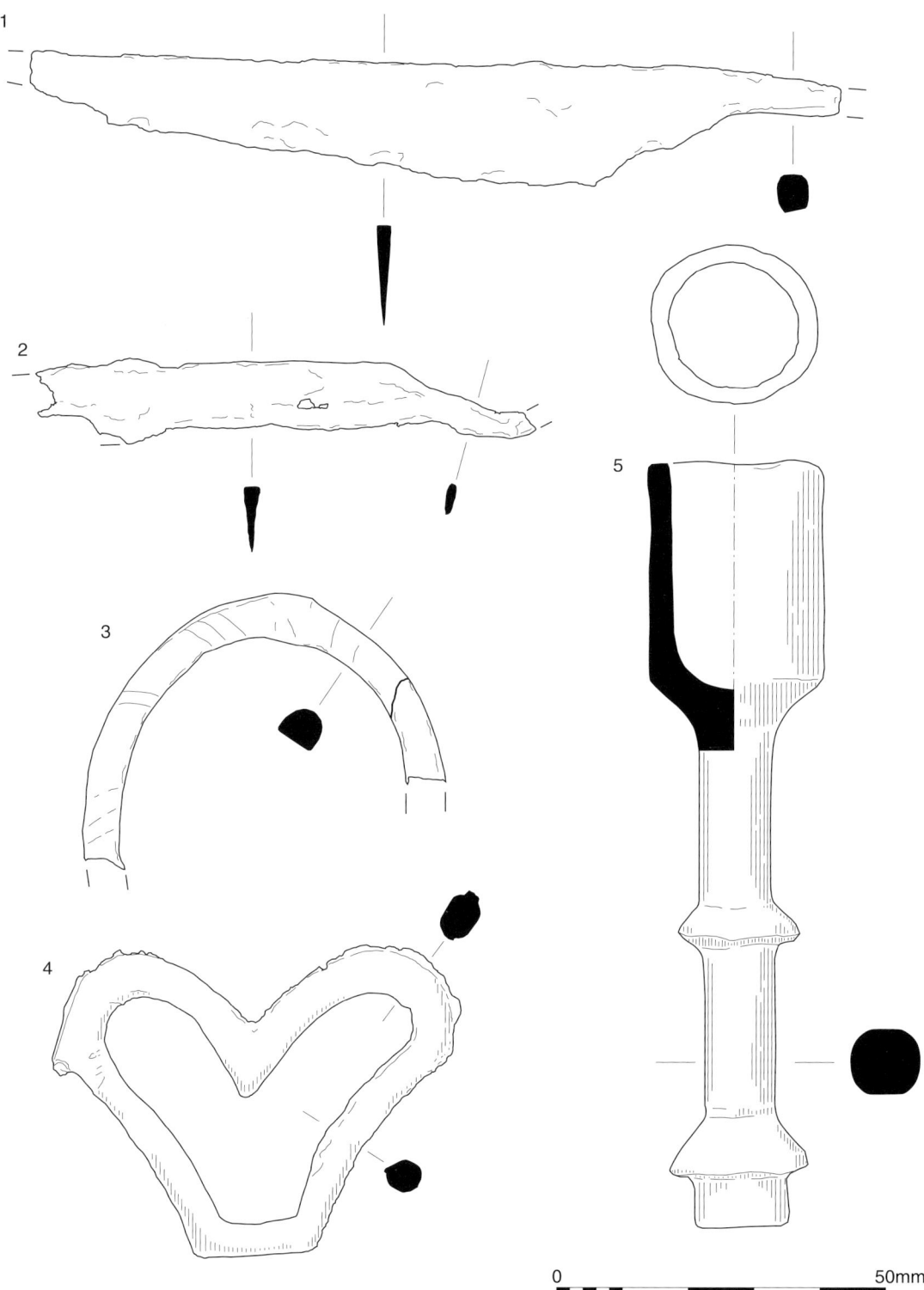

Fig. 4.4 Illustrated objects of metal nos 1–5. Scale 1:1

common from the medieval period and later. Small examples in lead/tin are thought to be shoe buckles (Egan and Pritchard 1991, 86). Dating in the 15th or 16th centuries is suggested by Whitehead (1996, 52). Length 35mm; width 25mm. Registered artefact 68 (Fig. 4.5; no. 8).

Worked bone

13. Period 1 fill 1771 of drain 1773. Handle fragment, plano-convex in section. The narrowing width from its end suggests it is an implement handle, probably from a scale-tanged knife. Single rivet hole, bored

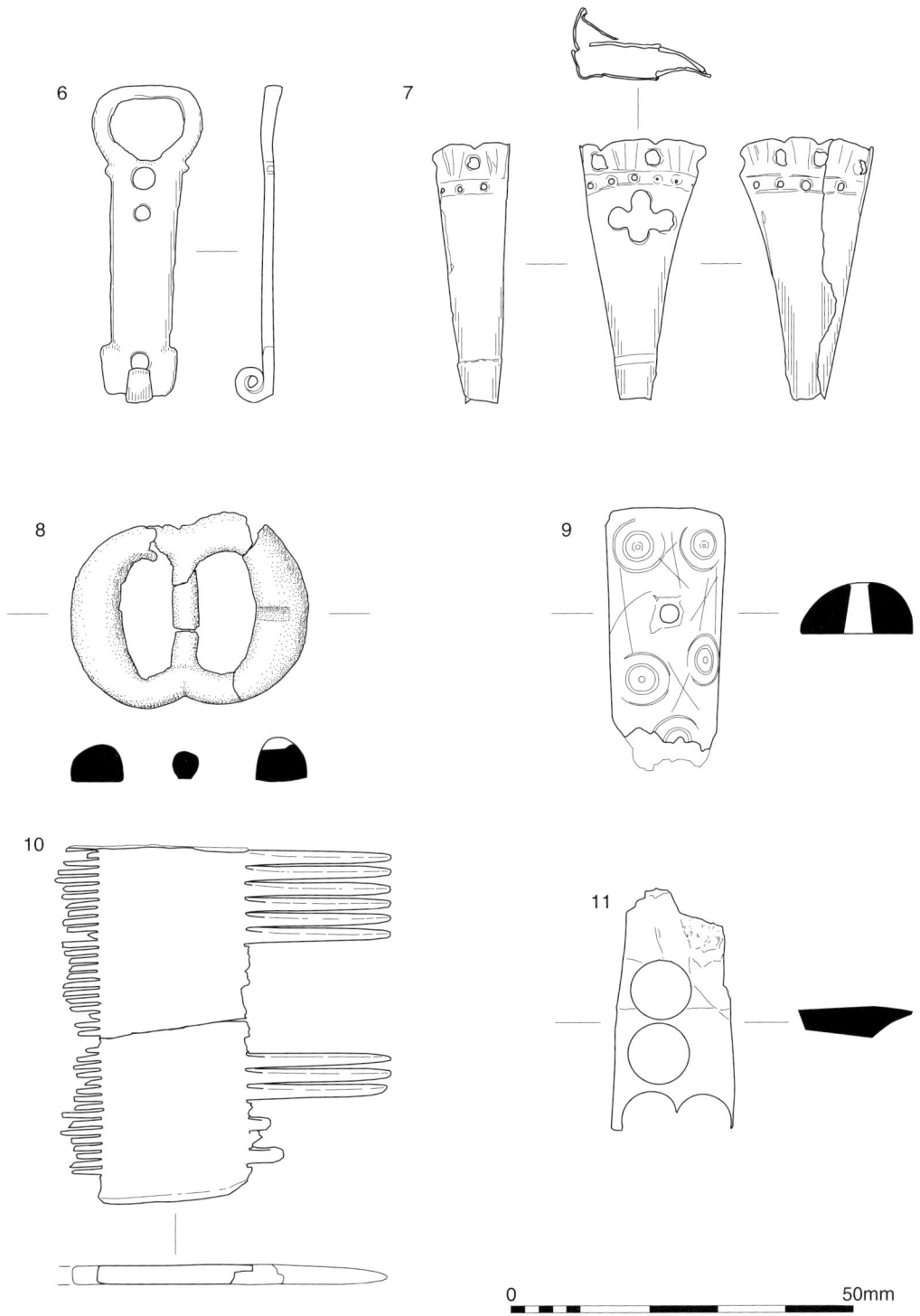

Fig. 4.5 Illustrated objects of metal and worked bone nos 6–11. Scale 1:1

from flat surface. Elaborate decoration consisting of double ring and dot, over design of incised arcs. The evidence from London suggests that one-piece 'whittle' tangs were the norm before the 14th century and so the handle would appear to date to the later part of Period 1. Length (surviving) 39mm; width 17–15mm; thickness 6mm. (Fig. 4.5; no. 9).

14. Period 1 fill 3199 of pit 3229. Pointed bone implement made from a pig fibula. One end of has been roughly trimmed to a point. Possibly an unfinished object or rough piercing tool. Length 125mm. Not illustrated.

15. Period 2a make-up 3760. Pointed bone implement made from a horse canon bone. It exhibits the high polish of tools used with textiles and in particular

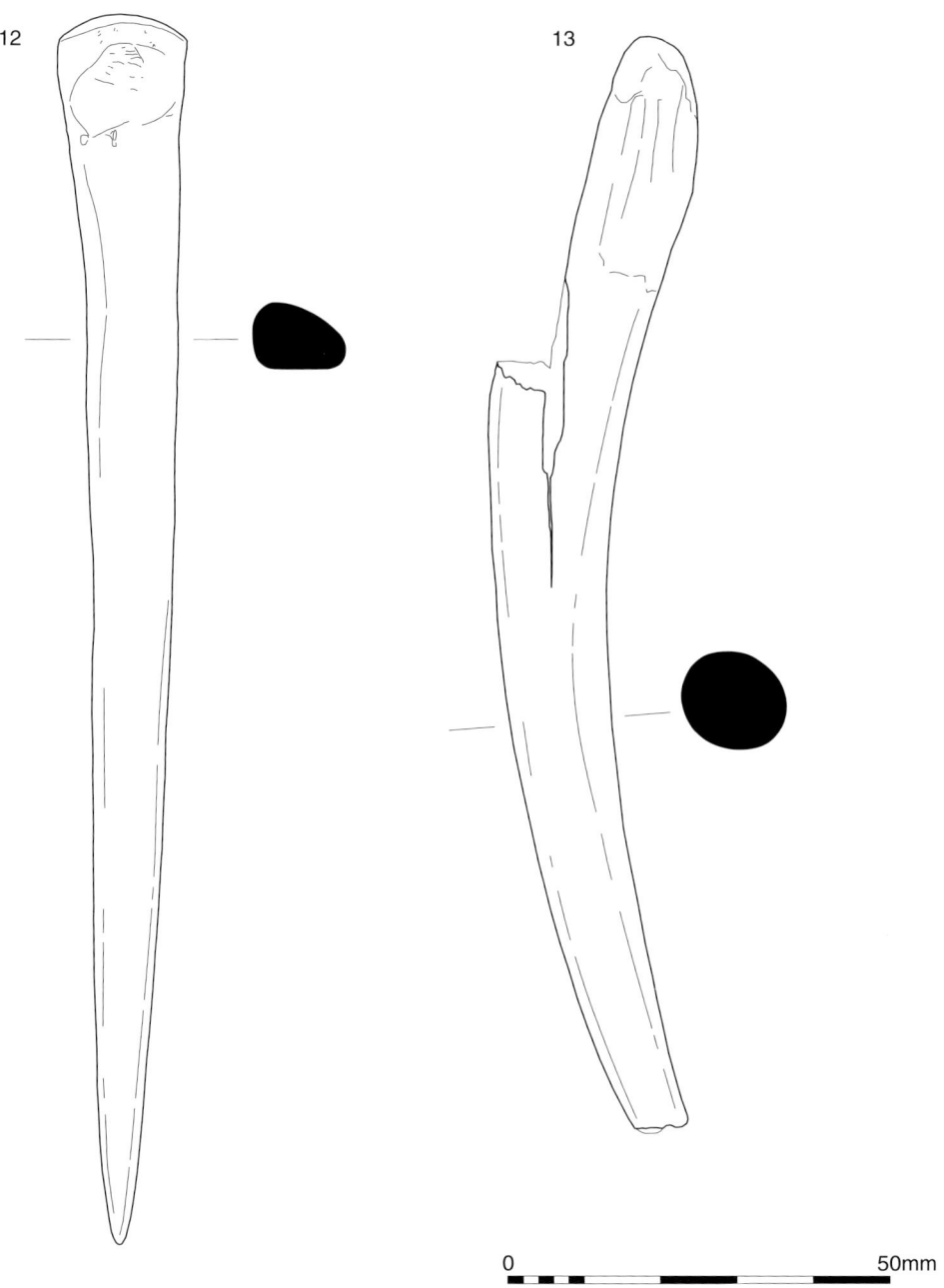

Fig. 4.6 Illustrated objects of worked bone nos 12–13. Scale 1:1

weaving. Single-ended implements made from limb bones in the manner of this piece are reported from Late Saxon or Viking-age contexts (MacGregor 1985, 189). These may be late developments of 'pin-beaters' familiar from Early or Middle Saxon sites and thought to be used as a weaver's tool for releasing knots and tangles. A similar object, described as a weaving tool, is recorded from a 14th-century context from St Bartholomew's Hospital, Bristol (Good 1998, 172, fig. 72, no. 315). Length 162mm. (Fig. 4.6; no. 12).

16. Period 2a make-up 1958. Red deer antler tine with damage to both ends. Roughly worked at wider end and with high surface polish from use. It appears to have been made to fit the hand; the high polish is most pronounced nearer the point. As with cat. no. 15, the high polish could indicate use with textiles. Length 144mm (Fig. 4.6; no. 13).

17. Period 2a make-up 3617. Waste panel fragment, probably made from a mandible of a cow-sized animal. With four circular perforations, each of 9mm diameter. Comparable waste material, thought to relate to the manufacture of beads using a drill, is known from several English towns (MacGregor 1985, 99–102). Dated waste material from London, utilising cattle femurs, metapodials and mandibles, dates to the late 13th to 14th centuries (Egan and Pritchard 1991,

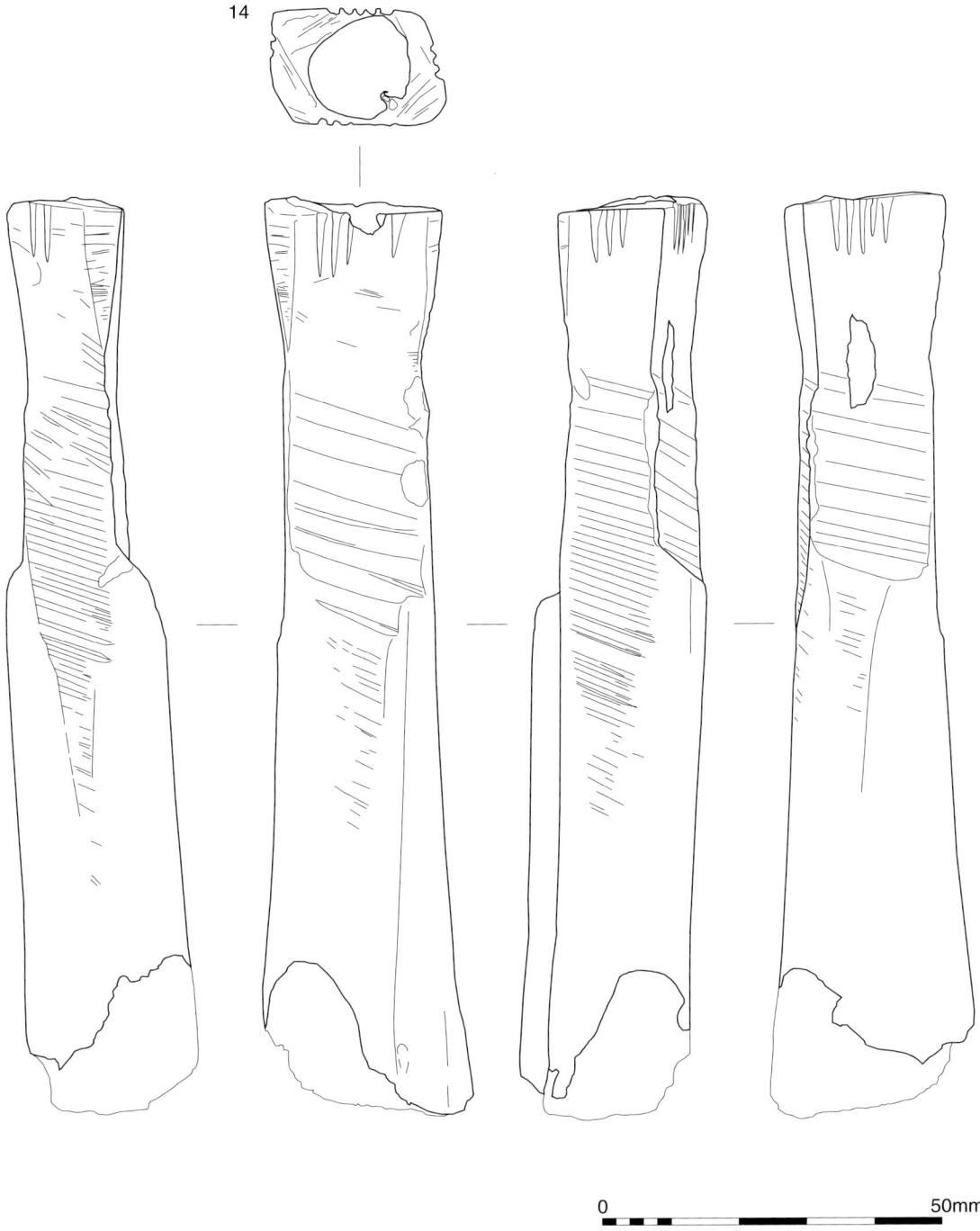

Fig. 4.7 Illustrated object of worked bone no. 14. Scale 1:1

207). Length (surviving) 35mm. Registered artefact 45 (Fig. 4.5; no. 11).

18. Period 2a make-up 1474. 'Pen' made from a goose radius with knife-sharpened 'nib'. The practicality or otherwise of such items for the purposes of writing is discussed by MacGregor (1985, 125–6). In common with examples described by him, this piece exhibits dark staining to its 'nib'-end, supporting a use associated with ink. Margeson (1993, 69) asserts a 14th-century date to such objects and this item was associated with pottery of later 13th to 14th-century date. Length 120mm. Not illustrated.

19. Period 2c occupation layer 2005. Stylus or parchment 'pricker'. Lathe-made with spherical head and double-grooved decoration below. The shaft tapers towards an open tip, which is damaged and misses its metal point. Objects such as this have been identified previously as styli for use with waxed writing tablets. MacGregor (1985, 124–5) prefers an interpretation as parchment prickers, for marking out the margin

and horizontal lines on manuscripts and in use up to the 15th century. Comparable items are mainly from later medieval deposits (Riddler 1998, 272). Length 57mm. Not illustrated.

20. Period 4 fill 1047 of well 1046. 'Pinner's bone' adapted from a cattle metapodial. The proximal end has been squared using a saw and there are grooves in each of the faces. Pinner's bones were used in the manufacture (sharpening/finishing) of copper-alloy wire pins, common from the late medieval and post-medieval periods. They date to before the end of the 18th century when manufacture was fully mechanised (MacGregor 1985, 171). Length 127mm. Registered artefact 2 (Fig. 4.7; no. 14).

Ivory

21. Period 4 fill 1470 of furnace 1535. One-piece comb with coarse and finer teeth. Identification as ivory is based on growth rings visible to the flat surfaces. Simple one-piece bone or ivory combs are known from the 16th and 17th centuries (MacGregor 1985, 81), with examples known locally from Acton Court (Courtney 2004, 385, no. 118 and 395, no. 211). It was found with pottery and clay pipe of mainly mid 17th-century date and is probably of similar date. Length (surviving) 52mm; thickness 3.5mm. Registered artefact 27. (Fig. 4.5; no. 10).

4.5 Clay Mould Debris
E.R. McSloy

A total of 933 fragments of clay mould, weighing 19.2kg was recovered. A system of classification and recording has been adapted from that used for the broadly contemporary, though larger, assemblage from Cowick Street, Exeter (Blaylock 2000). The assemblage was scanned by context and quantified according to fabric, element class (whether cope/core/other), element type/position (location on mould), diameter where measurable, and thickness range. Where they were present, decoration or other marks were also recorded.

The provenance/phasing of the clay mould fragments is shown in Table 4.5. Almost all material was recovered from deposits contained within the boundaries of Nos 16 and 17 Redcliff Street. A small quantity (5 fragments) relates to (late medieval) Period 2c furnace structure 1845/2092. The majority derives from Period 3 contexts (early 15th to late 17th centuries). Of the Period 3 group a proportion derived from the fills of furnace 1426 (at No. 16) and 1530 (at No. 17, with the largest single context group (254 fragments) coming from the backfill of this furnace). The remaining portion comes from dumped deposits and pit fills to the rear of No. 17 which probably relate to the use of furnace 1530.

The assemblage from furnace 1845/2092 and from other Period 2c deposits is small and no comparisons based on the character or dating indications for each group can usefully be made. Similarly material from furnace 1426 at No. 16 is very restricted in quantity and range.

Fabric

The mould fragments are in a soft, friable fabric with common organic inclusions visible as burnt-out voids, possibly present as natural inclusions in the clay. The mould surfaces, where in contact with the metal, are smooth, possibly as the result of the application of fine clay slip, and are harder-fired as a result of the heat. The fabric is visibly similar to that from Mitchell Lane, Redcliffe (Morris 2011, 45), the thin-section analysis for which supported a source from local alluvial clays.

A different fabric distinguished by lighter colour and coarser organic inclusions, probably representing chopped straw or chaff, is employed for the outer layer of clay 'luting', functioning to hold in place the pre-fabricated mould elements (below). The flat open moulds described below also are made from this fabric.

Assemblage composition (Tables 4.5–4.6)

The large majority of mould fragments, other than those too small to be identified, relate to the manufacture of metal cooking vessels. There are in addition a number of fragments identifiable as deriving from the manufacture of chafing dishes and of 'portable objects', mainly (if not exclusively) candlesticks. The assemblage is described below according to object 'class'.

Vessels

The technology for producing large lead-bronze vessels, cast in clay moulds, is thought to have existed in England from the late 12th century and becomes progressively more common throughout the medieval and early post-medieval periods. Casting in clay moulds continues until c. 1690/1700, with sand-casting dominant thereafter.

The complex and highly-skilled process of casting metal vessels in clay moulds has been described by Blaylock (2000) and further explored by Butler and Green (2003, 22–7). This assemblage can add little more to the understanding of this process. The majority of fragments conform to the two main components of the mould forming the body of the vessel, comprising an inner 'core', and an outer 'cope' (Table 4.5). Examples of feet and handle moulds were also identified, and some pieces show how these were made separately and luted in place. Cope and core fragments were usually readily distinguishable from their morphology (whether the casting surface is concave or convex) and also the colouring: generally the core fragments and the inner surfaces of the cope fragments were reduced-fired to grey or black as the result of restricted air circulation. The identification of several cope mould fragments with flat-faced 'mould joins' is further evidence to suggest that the cope was formed from two halves, in order to release the 'pattern', with the cope halves luted back together prior to casting (ibid., 24–5).

Table 4.5 Clay mould fragments by period, context and object 'class'

Form	Element	2c/Furn. 1845/2092	2c/other	3/Furn. 1426	3/Furn. 1530	3/other	4	Unph.	Totals
Cauldron/	cope	3	40	12	151	165	5	4	**380**
Posnet	core	-	20	-	82	58	-	-	**160**
	leg	-	1	-	21	14	-	-	**36**
	leg/handle	-	-	-	-	3	-	-	**3**
Cauldron	handle	-	-	-	-	2	-	-	**2**
Posnet	handle	-	-	-	5	-	-	3	**8**
Chaf. Dish/	drop handle	-	-	-	1	-	-	-	**1**
other	cope	-	-	-	-	2	-	-	**2**
Object	candlestick	-	-	-	-	22	-	-	**22**
	cand. base	-	-	3	4	16	4	-	**27**
	lid	-	-	-	6	3	-	-	**9**
Other	flat	-	-	-	-	1	-	-	**1**
	indet.	2	17	36	65	149	10	3	**282**
Totals		**5**	**78**	**51**	**335**	**435**	**19**	**10**	**933**

Table 4.6 Cauldron/posnet rim diameters derived from cope and core rim mould fragments

	Period			
Diameter (mm)	2c	3	Unph.	Totals
140	-	4	-	4
180	-	1	-	1
220	-	1	-	1
240	1	11	-	12
260	-	16	1	17
280	2	10	-	12
300	2	18	-	20
320	-	6	-	6
340	-	7	-	7
360	-	2	-	2
38	-	1	-	1
400	-	2	-	2
Totals	**5**	**79**	**1**	**85**

Cauldrons/posnets

The large majority of mould fragments relate to the casting of vessels of low-bellied or bag-shaped profiles, sharply everted rims and supported on legs of varying height and form. Such characteristics are common to both cauldron and posnet forms (the term posnet is used here in preference to the more generic 'skillet' to reflect this distinctive profile); the difference being in the type of handle employed.

Indications from vessel rim diameter (Table 4.6) are that cauldrons comprised the majority of vessels represented; the evidence from surviving posnet vessels suggests that these are smaller, roughly equivalent to the medium-size cauldrons and rarely exceeding c. 250mm. Further evidence comes from the doubled 'wire' mouldings, a decorative feature common with surviving cauldron and leg mould fragments, some of which are of the longer form seen on larger cauldrons.

Leg mould fragments are moderately well represented (Table 4.5). These are of variable form. The most common form is flat, with a longitudinal strengthening rib. One detached and substantially intact leg mould for this type is in excess of 160mm long (Fig. 4.8; no. 1). Less common are shorter, sturdier legs with a D-shaped section. The leg terminals are plain or chamfered, without the decorative collar seen on many extant vessels and recorded at Cowick Street, Exeter (Blaylock 2000, 63–4; figs 23–4). Unlike the Cowick Street group, a separately-made leg end cap was luted to the leg terminal (Fig. 4.8; no. 2). Some legs featured external ribs; the evidence for this is a single cope fragment with tapering grooves, seemingly intended to give the impression of the leg ribs extending into the vessel's body (Fig. 4.8; no. 3).

Only two cauldron handles were (tentatively) identified, from small, rounded-section mould fragments. Surviving examples of cauldrons show these to be simple angled or rounded lugs used for suspension. A circular-sectioned rod of clay from fill 1471 (Period 5 pit 1472) is tentatively suggested as part of a clay pattern used when forming the handle mould, although there are indications from elsewhere that wooden patterns were used for this purpose.

Good evidence for the manufacture of posnets, which differ from cauldrons in the use of a straight handle extending from the rim or upper part of the vessel, is present in the form of a number of handle mould fragments (Table 4.5). In only one example from dump cleaning layer 1344 (Fig. 4.9; no. 2) is the terminal section preserved. This is down-turned, a characteristic of earlier vessels of this class (Butler and Green 2003, 9). Most of the remainder are half-rounded in section and all probably represent the lower portions of a two-part mould. Other examples with flattened D or polygonal sections are probably handles rather than legs.

Chafing dishes/other

The evidence for this is limited to a single example of a double-sided 'piece mould' with central locating boss/domed recess on the opposing faces (Fig. 4.8; no. 4). The items moulded were heart-shaped drop handles, an example of which was recovered from the site (Chapter 4.4 cat. no. 4; Fig. 4.4; no. 4). Drop handles of this type are known to derive from metal chafing dishes, long-suspected to be of English manufacture ('Type B': Lewis 1973, 63–4), and probably dating to the 15th or 16th centuries.

Objects (candlesticks)

Evidence for production of candlesticks of English single-stemmed form comes from a number of Period 3 deposits (Table 4.5). Examples occur in association with furnaces 1426 and 1530, though with the largest group from deposit 1367, the fill of pit 1371.

The form of the candlestick stem and socket which is reconstructable from the mould fragments (Fig. 4.9; nos 3–5) is consistent with the unfinished candlestick from layer 1407, associated with the use of furnace 1426 (Chapter 4. 4; cat. no. 2; Fig. 4.4; no. 5). Fragments preserving the central knop moulding show the candlesticks to be of slightly differing size to the unfinished candlestick. The use of circumferential double-grooved decoration, not seen on the unfinished example from this site, occurs on at least two mould fragments (Fig. 4.9; no. 5).

The method of manufacture for the stem/socket part of the candlestick can be determined in part from the mould fragments from deposit 1367. These were made in groups of four (or possibly more), cast in two-piece moulds fixed with a thin layer of luting clay and with the casting 'gate' at the terminal end and entering at angle (Fig. 4.9; no. 4). The 'piece' moulds were aligned centrally using a row of locating tenons/mortices (Fig. 4.9; no. 3). It is supposed that a plug of clay was the means by which the sockets were kept open, although no evidence for this was recorded.

Several examples of moulds for candlestick bases were identified (Fig. 4.9; no. 6), including cope and core elements. The illustrated upper cope fragment no. 6 and several smaller unillustrated fragments preserve the round tenon moulding required to keep open the stem of the setting candlestick. The stepped form of the base is an elaboration compared to the earlier shallow cylindrical bases typical of Brownsword's Type 2 'Bunsen' types (Brownsword 1985). They are closer to the succeeding types of deep, conical form (ibid., nos 8–10), considered by Brownsword to be of 16th-century date.

Other material

A disc-like object, 80mm in diameter from Period 3 deposit 1830 may represent a cover for the 'sprue cup', into which the molten metal was poured. Similar items are described from Cowick Street, Exeter (Blaylock 2000, 71, fig. 28. no. 142). Squared, plate-like fragments from Period 3 deposit 1529 in the same fabric as the moulds are almost certainly equivalent to objects described as flat open moulds from Cowick Street, Exeter (ibid.). None of the Redcliff Street fragments feature the bossed projections seen with the (much larger) Exeter group.

Marks

Scratched marks of the kind seen on cope fragments from Exeter (Blaylock 2000, 53, fig. 18) and visible as date marks or signatures on some surviving vessels (Butler and Green 2003, appendix B), were not recorded. It should be stressed that the Redcliff Street group represents less than 3% of the total recovered from the Exeter site and that scratched marks might be more common than supposed. A scratched mark similar in style to extant examples was recorded to the outer clay surface (and thus not visible on the casting) of a cope fragment from Period 3 deposit 1463 (Fig. 4.9; no. 1). This somewhat counter intuitive positioning is unusual (Butler, pers. comm.) and may have identified the 'products' of individual mould makers, perhaps at the drying stage prior to casting.

Linear knife-cut marks visible to the outer surface of a number of leg or handle mould fragments possibly represent positional guides when assembling the mould.

An incised cross was also recorded on the lid from Period 3 pit fill 1830 (Fig. 4.8; no. 5), though the significance of this is unclear. Post-firing marks noted to the outside of some vessels probably result from breaking open the mould after casting using an edged metal implement.

Discussion and dating

The identity of the founder(s) operating at Nos 16 and 17 Redcliff Street is not known. There are hints from documentary sources for metalworking activity in the area as early as the 1450s when two 'brasiers' (brass workers), Thomas Elyot and William Tanner, are recorded as living somewhere within Nos 1–32 Redcliff Street (Chapter 2.1). Dating on typological grounds for the cauldron/posnet vessel profiles is in the range *c.* 1400–1580/1600 and thus sufficiently broad to accommodate mid/later 15th century activity. The few more specific dating indications from the metal vessels and the candlesticks, however, favour a 16th-century date (at least) for the most substantive Period 3 activity. Most significant (in terms of dating) among the vessel mould pieces is the posnet handle from layer 1344 (Fig. 4.9; no. 2); its down-turned form probably dates to the 16th century (Butler, pers. comm.). Dating in the 15th or 16th century is probable for the chafing dish handle mould from pit 1472 (Fig. 4.8; no. 4).

Support for a 16th-century date for the assemblage is strongest from the candlestick moulds, and the base forms in particular which appear to be a variant of the conical forms dated to this period (Brownsword 1985, 1). Few comparable groups of candlestick-related waste are known and the Redcliff Street group may be the earliest. An assemblage which also includes moulds for multiple castings is that from the Guildhall, London (Egan 2007, 351–2), in this instance thought to date to the later 16th century. A group which included metal vessel and a small number of candlestick mould fragments is known from Worcester (Taylor 1996).

Photographed fragments (Fig. 4.8)

1. Period 3 pit fill 1919 (fill of 1927). Cauldron?; leg mould with central rib. Knife marks to rear.
2. Period 3 wall 1814. Cauldron/posnet; leg mould end cap.
3. Period 3 dumped layer 1463. Cauldron/posnet; cope with splayed grooves (extension from leg ribs).
4. Period 3 pit fill 1471 (fill of 1472). Double-sided piece mould for heart-shaped drop handle for chafing dish; central locating boss.
5. Period 3 pit fill 1830 (fill of 1815). Lid? with incised cross. Diameter 140mm.

Drawn fragments (Fig. 4.9)

1. Period 3 layer 1463. Cauldron/posnet?; cope with scratched mark to outside.

Fig. 4.8 Photographs of clay mould fragments. Scale 1:2

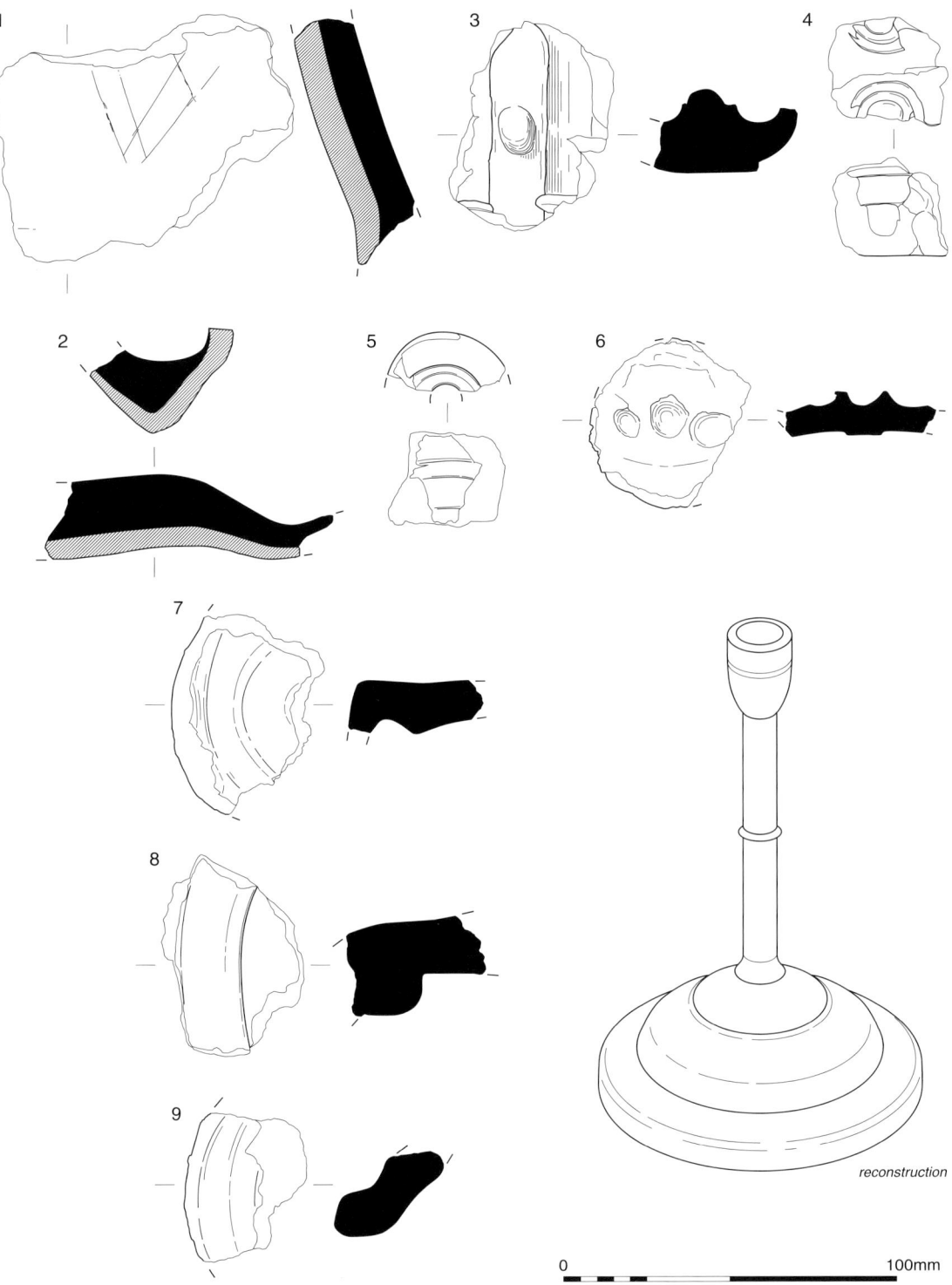

Fig. 4.9 Drawn fragments of clay mould. Scale 1:2

2. Unphased cleaning layer 1344. Posnet handle with down-turned terminal.
3. Period 3 pit fill 1367 (fill of 1371). Candlestick double mould: stems and knop moulding.
4. Period 3 pit fill 1367 (fill of 1371). Candlestick double mould: rebated terminals.
5. Period 3 pit fill 1367 (fill of 1371). Candlestick mould: socket/stem junction with grooved decoration.
6. Period 3 pit fill 1471 (fill of 1472). Candlestick base mould (upper) with setting for stem rebate.
7. Period 3 layer 1463. Candlestick base mould (lower). Diameter 100mm.
8. Period 3 pit fill 1367 (fill of 1371). Cope mould for candlestick base of stepped form.
9. Period 3 pit fill 1367 (fill of 1371). Candlestick base core mould: lower 'rim'.

Table 4.7 Weights of different metallurgical materials examined by period (kg)

Period	Crucible	Mould	Copper spillage	Copper slag	Iron slag	Other	Total
1	0	0	0	0	0.025	0.256	0.281
2a	0.066	0	0	0	1.365	0.179	1.610
2b	0	0	0	0	0.112	0.132	0.244
2c	0	0.014	0	0.021	0.536	0.081	0.652
3	0.736	2.014	0.331	4.637	0.287	5.989	13.994
4	0	0	0.214	0	0.068	2.700	2.982
5	0	0	0	0.002	0.097	0.202	0.301
unphased	0	0	0	0	0	0.010	0.010
Total	0.802	2.028	0.545	4.660	2.490	9.549	20.074

4.6 Copper-Alloy Working Debris
David Dungworth

Visual examination

Methodology

All of the material submitted for examination was examined visually following standard procedures (e.g. Bayley *et al.* 2001). Material was assessed based on directly observable characteristics such as colour, density, surface morphology, porosity, etc. Material from each context was examined, weighed and assigned to one of several categories (Table 4.7). Half of the material submitted for examination comprised material of limited industrial significance (baked clay, stone, iron concretions, etc.). The remaining categories of material are described below.

Crucibles

These fragments (Table 4.8) comprise highly fired ceramic vessels in which copper alloys were melted prior to casting in moulds (Bayley 1996; Bayley and Rehren 2007). The manufacture of crucibles would normally have involved firing to temperatures comparable to those required during their use (for melting copper alloys typically 1000–1200°C). Prolonged use would tend to vitrify the ceramic fabric of the crucibles and encourage chemical reactions between the ceramic fabric and the metallic contents of the crucible. Following the breakage of the crucibles, some fragments might be lost within a furnace where they would undergo further heating and even vitrification over time. The ways in which crucibles were used and lost can therefore lead to apparent variations in fabric which are not representative of the ways in which they were originally manufactured. Several Redcliff Street crucible fragments show at least partially oxidised fabrics (beige) but it is assumed that this colour reflects post-use alteration.

Small spots of green produced by the corrosion of copper were visible on many of the crucible sherds (Fig. 4.10; no. 1). The qualitative EDXRF analysis of the crucible sherds detected copper and associated metals (including tin, zinc, lead, antimony, arsenic and nickel). Zinc was often the most abundant element from such analyses, however, it is not a good indicator of the nature of the alloy that was melted.

The crucibles have been divided into two main fabrics. Fabric 1 is characterised by small (<1mm) fragments of a carbon-rich black material (Fig. 4.10; no. 1). Fabric 2 contains abundant grog particles (1–3mm, Fig. 4.10; no. 2). Fabric 2 has been divided into two sub-groups: 2a has clear grog inclusions while 2b appears to be the same fabric but it has been exposed to higher temperature during use, which has largely obscured the difference between the paste and the grog inclusions (cf. Freestone and Tite 1986, fig. 15).

The crucible fragments are all 12–22mm thick and most have parallel sides 18–22mm thick. The crucible fragments all have curvatures which indicate vertical walls and external diameters in the region of 150mm (Table 4.8). None of the fragments were sufficiently large to reconstruct the original heights but these were clearly in excess of 100mm (Fig. 4.10; no. 1). The only base fragment shows a curving rather than flat base. The size and shape of the crucibles are similar to other medieval and early post-medieval crucibles (Bayley 1992; 1996; Taylor 2004; White and Kearns 2010). It is likely that the crucibles would have had an effective capacity of approximately 1 litre (i.e. about 10kg of copper alloy).

Table 4.8 Crucible fragments

Context	Period	Part	Fabric	Wt (g)	Th (mm)	Ø (mm)
2114	2a	Body	1	66	18	
1484	3	Body	1	65	19–22	
1463	3	Body	1	189	12–20	150
1404	3	Body	2a	80	18–20	150
1404	3	Body	2a	91	18–20	150
1392	3	Base	2b	152	18–19	150
1405	3	Body	2b	159	17–19	150

Fig. 4.10 Photographs of crucible fragments (nos 1–2) and clay mould fragments (nos 3–5) subjected to metallurgical analysis. Scales 1:2 for nos 1–2 and 1:3 for nos 3–5

Moulds

Very few fragments of mould from the excavations at Redcliff Street were submitted for examination (most of the mould fragments are reported on separately in Chapter 4.5). The mould material submitted for examination mostly comprised medium-sized (<50mm) fragments of mould within a matrix of much smaller fragments of mould from Period 3 occupation layer 1375. A selection of the larger fragments of mould was gently cleaned to reveal original surfaces. The mould fragments are all made from clay loam with abundant fine organic temper. The fragments are all extremely friable indicating that they were baked rather than fired. Most of the fabric of the moulds is black due to the organic temper; the exterior surface is red or orange due to more oxidising conditions, while the interior surfaces have a pale very fine clay surface (cf. Blaylock 2000).

The interior surfaces of all of the mould fragments examined have convex surfaces: the surfaces all curve in two planes, i.e. the moulds were used to produce spherical rather than cylindrical objects. In addition it is clear that all of these fragments came from the core mould (i.e. within the spherical object). The size, fabric and shape of the mould fragments are entirely consistent with the manufacture of cauldrons and similar domestic cooking vessels. A few mould fragments were also preserved in contact with metallic copper-alloy casting debris (see below).

Slag

Slags are produced during a variety of different metallurgical operations. The slags recovered from Redcliff Street comprise small lumps of dark grey slag with occasional spots of green caused by the corrosion of

Fig. 4.11 Photographs of copper-working debris nos 6–7. Scale 1:2

copper-alloy droplets trapped within the slag (Fig. 4.11; no. 6). The presence of copper-alloy droplets leaves little doubt that these slags were produced during the working of copper alloys rather than iron alloys.

Slags can be formed during the smelting of copper ores to produce metallic copper. In this case, slags are a vital part of the process of separating the metallic copper from the various impurities in the ore. Very little is known about the morphology of medieval copper smelting slags in England as none have yet been identified (Bayley *et al.* 2008). It is presumed that copper smelting slags of this period are likely to resemble iron smelting slags, and in particular tap slags. By the 18th century copper smelting slags were often cast into moulds to form bricks (Dungworth and White 2007; Spry 2003).

Slags can also be produced during the melting of copper alloys. Molten copper will quickly react with atmospheric oxygen and any earthy materials it is in contact with to form a surface dross or slag. This dross or slag is usually scraped off the surface of the molten copper just before teaming or casting takes place. Such slags will tend to be rather small in size and be rather amorphous. The Redcliff Street slags lack a distinctive morphology and it is therefore most likely that they result from copper melting rather than copper smelting. This identification is further strengthened by the chemical analysis of the slags which shows the presence of a wide range of alloying elements in addition to copper (see below).

Metal waste

During the melting and casting of metal it is inevitable that some spillages will occur. Most of the metallic copper-alloy waste submitted for examination comprises small amorphous lumps which are most likely to have formed as spillages during casting. The Redcliff Street metal waste also includes several sprue cups, that is, the funnel of metal which formed at the top of the mould (Fig. 4.11; no. 7). The copper-alloy casting waste also included a fragment of a curved, thick-walled vessel which is likely to be a fragment of a cauldron.

Scientific examination

Methods

In order to provide more information about the nature of the copper-alloy casting industry which operated at Redcliff Street a series of samples was selected for scientific examination. The samples included crucibles, slag, metal and mould from Period 3 deposits (Table 4.9). The samples were prepared using standard metallographic techniques (Vander Voort 1999). Where necessary the samples were cut with a water-cooled,

Table 4.9 Samples selected for scientific examination

#	Context	Period	Description
1	1484	3	Crucible
2	1502	3	Slag-ceramic?
3	1503	3	Cast vessel fragment (failed casting?)
4	1463	3	Crucible
5	1529	3	Slag
6	1529	3	Slag
7	1463	3	Mould-metal
8	1392	3	Crucible
9	1405	3	Crucible
10	1739	3	Slag
11	1404	3	Spillage?
12	1405	3	Sprue
13	1405	3	Sprue

low-speed saw, embedded in a low-viscosity epoxy resin and ground and polished to a 1-micron finish. The prepared samples were carbon coated and then examined using a scanning electron microscope (SEM). Where suitable, back-scattered electron images were obtained and chemical analysis carried out using an energy dispersive x-ray spectrometer (EDS) attached to the electron microscope. The chemical compositions reported here represent the average of multiple analyses of several different areas within each sample (the size and number of areas varying depending on the nature of the samples). The results showed a range of analysed totals which were usually less than 100wt% due to varying degrees of porosity. In addition, the fabric 1 crucibles displayed even lower totals as the carbon content of the inclusions could not be measured (the polished samples were coated in carbon). In order to facilitate comparisons between different samples all the results have been normalised to 100wt%.

The crucibles and mould

The examination of four crucibles with the SEM confirms the visual assessment of their fabrics: the fabric 1 crucibles contain carbon-rich inclusions (Fig. 4.12 A) while the fabric 2 crucibles contain highly fired ceramic inclusions. The SEM images were formed using a back-scattered electron detector which produces atomic number contrast images, the higher the average atomic number, the brighter the image. Carbon-rich inclusions were absent from the fabric 2a and 2b crucibles (Fig. 4.12 B). The exact nature of the carbon-rich temper remains uncertain. It is known that clay naturally containing graphite was exploited in Bavaria from at least the 16th century for the manufacture of metalworking crucibles (Martinón-Torres and Rehren 2009). It is not certain, however, that the carbon-rich temper in the Redcliff Street crucibles is graphite. The Bavarian graphite-tempered crucibles usually contain long thin flakes of graphite (ibid., fig. 6) while the Redcliff Street carbon-rich inclusions tend to equiaxed (axes of approximately equal length). The carbon-rich temper in the Redcliff Street crucibles may be coal dust, however the use of coal dust as a temper in crucible manufacture is usually thought of as a 19th-century development (Ure 1844, 381).

The chemical analysis of the crucibles (SEM-EDS) provides information on the chemical composition of the ceramic fabric of the crucibles, vitrified/slag surface layers and (where present) metallic droplets trapped in surface layers. Unfortunately it was not possible to determine the carbon content of the graphite crucibles. In order to allow SEM examination and analysis it is necessary to earth the samples using a coating of carbon; this coating precludes the determination of carbon content. The SEM images suggest that the crucible contained approximately 15vol% (or 25wt%) graphite. The chemical compositions of the crucibles reported in Table 4.10 represent data which exclude carbon and which has been normalised to 100wt%. Despite the differences in the temper used for the two types of crucible, it is striking that the ceramic fabrics share almost identical chemical compositions. The crucibles are rich in silica and alumina and would have been capable of withstanding the temperatures required to melt copper alloys. There are very few other analyses of English medieval crucibles that the Redcliff Street samples could be compared with. A range of medieval

 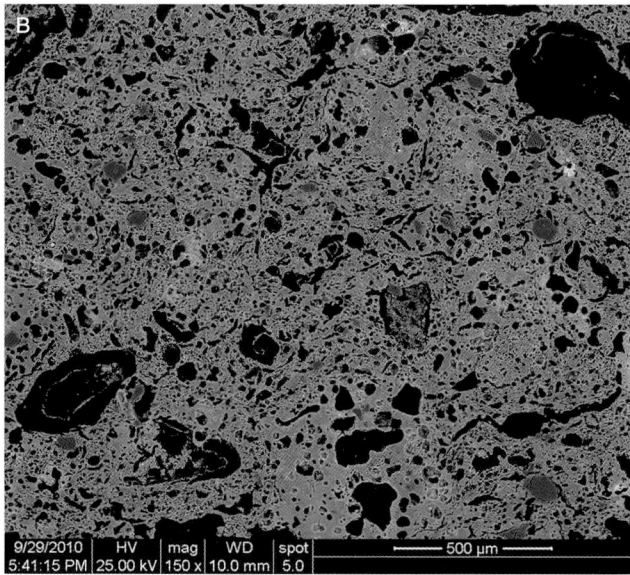

Fig. 4.12 A (left): Scanning Electron Microscope (SEM) image (back-scattered electron detector) of crucible from context 1463 (fabric 1, sample 4). An example of the carbon-rich temper is indicated with a white arrow. B (right): SEM image (back-scattered electron detector) of crucible from context 1392 (fabric 2b, sample 8)

Table 4.10 Chemical composition of the crucibles, mould and slag

#	Description	Na$_2$O	MgO	Al$_2$O$_3$	SiO$_2$	P$_2$O$_5$	SO$_3$	K$_2$O	CaO	TiO$_2$	MnO	Fe$_2$O$_3$	NiO	CuO	ZnO	As$_2$O$_3$	SnO$_2$	Sb$_2$O$_5$	BaO	PbO
1	Crucible fabric	0.6	1.1	24.3	61.8	0.3	0.2	4.8	1.4	1.0	<0.1	2.9	<0.1	0.9	0.3	<0.2	<0.2	<0.2	<0.2	<0.2
1	Vitrified surface	<0.8	2.4	13.2	51.9	0.8	<0.2	3.6	7.3	0.6	0.2	9.4	<0.1	1.1	7.6	0.3	0.3	<0.2	<0.2	0.8
2	Ceramic	1.0	1.8	9.0	74.1	0.9	<0.2	3.4	5.2	0.5	0.1	3.2	<0.1	0.2	<0.1	<0.2	<0.2	<0.2	<0.2	0.2
2	Vitrified ceramic	1.0	2.6	10.6	59.4	0.8	<0.2	3.7	9.0	0.7	0.2	7.1	<0.1	0.4	0.6	<0.2	1.1	<0.2	<0.2	1.7
4	Crucible fabric	0.5	1.1	23.7	62.0	0.2	0.2	4.8	1.4	1.0	<0.1	2.9	<0.1	1.0	0.5	<0.2	0.2	<0.2	<0.2	0.2
4	Vitrified surface	<0.6	2.4	13.2	48.2	0.8	<0.2	1.7	9.9	0.8	0.2	7.4	0.1	5.4	5.5	<0.2	0.8	0.6	<0.2	2.9
5	Slag	0.6	5.2	10.2	49.7	0.6	<0.2	3.6	11.1	0.5	0.2	12.2	0.1	1.1	0.2	<0.2	1.2	0.5	<0.2	2.6
6	Slag	0.5	4.5	8.0	42.9	1.1	<0.2	2.5	13.5	0.4	0.3	20.3	<0.1	0.6	0.4	<0.2	1.7	0.4	0.3	2.5
7	Mould	0.6	2.5	11.0	65.9	1.4	<0.2	3.9	6.9	0.7	0.1	4.2	<0.1	1.5	<0.1	<0.2	0.2	<0.2	0.3	1.0
8	Crucible fabric	0.7	1.2	24.1	60.0	<0.2	<0.2	5.1	1.6	1.0	<0.1	2.6	<0.1	1.7	1.1	<0.2	0.2	<0.2	<0.2	0.2
8	Vitrified surface	<0.5	1.4	18.1	40.6	2.2	<0.2	4.1	4.7	0.7	<0.1	6.1	0.2	13.2	1.7	<0.2	4.7	0.8	<0.2	1.2
9	Crucible fabric	0.7	1.2	25.4	59.9	0.3	<0.2	5.4	1.5	1.0	<0.1	3.0	<0.1	0.7	0.4	<0.2	<0.2	<0.2	<0.2	<0.2
9	Vitrified surface	<0.8	2.0	5.6	28.0	0.9	<0.2	1.5	8.8	0.3	0.2	9.3	0.3	0.9	8.2	0.9	14.2	1.1	<0.2	17.5
14	Crucible fabric	0.7	1.2	24.7	58.4	0.3	<0.2	5.4	1.7	1.0	<0.1	2.8	<0.1	1.7	1.3	<0.2	0.3	<0.2	<0.2	<0.2

and late medieval crucibles from London has been analysed by Freestone and Tite (1986) and White and Kearns (2010). The London crucibles from both studies could be divided into quartz-tempered and grog-tempered fabrics; the former have higher silica content and lower alumina content. The Redcliff Street crucibles show some compositional similarities with the London grog-tempered crucibles although they have significantly higher potassium.

Sample 2 was initially assumed to be slag, but the microstructure and chemical composition both suggest that this sample is a highly vitrified ceramic. The composition of the ceramic, however, is sufficiently different from the crucibles (very low Al:Si ratio) to suggest that it is not a crucible. It is possible that this sample represents a fragment of a furnace wall. Sample 7 is a fragment of mould from a failed casting. The mould fabric contains abundant fine quartz inclusions as well as feldspars and calcite. The range of minerals present confirms that the mould was not fired to a high temperature. The overall composition of the mould also differs from the crucibles but shares some similarities with the possible furnace wall fragment (sample 2).

The vitrified surfaces of the crucibles are generally glassy with few crystalline phases present. These vitrified surfaces contain elevated levels of metallic elements including copper, zinc, tin and lead. These metallic elements derive from the copper alloys that were melted in the crucibles, however, the concentrations of these elements vary significantly from crucible to crucible. In some crucibles copper is the most abundant alloy element, while in others it is zinc, and in another it is tin and lead. It is noticeable that zinc is generally often found at higher concentrations in the vitrified surfaces of the crucibles compared to the metallic droplets trapped within these surfaces (see below). The copper slags have compositions which share many similarities with the vitrified surfaces of the crucibles, however, they usually contain lower concentrations of metallic elements.

The metal waste and metallic droplets within crucibles and slag

The metal waste comprises sprues, spillages and failed castings. These samples all share very similar compositional characteristics: they are copper alloys that contain a wide range of alloying elements including lead, tin, antimony, zinc, arsenic, and nickel (Table 4.11). The presence of relatively high concentrations of antimony and arsenic (on average 2.5wt% and 1.2wt%, respectively) is of particular importance. These elements are, however, found at high levels in medieval and early post-medieval domestic cooking vessels (Dungworth and Nicholas 2004).

The metallic droplets within crucibles and slag have chemical compositions which resemble the metal waste in many respects, although on the whole, the metallic droplets contain less zinc and lead but more arsenic, antimony, nickel and tin. In addition, the droplets display considerable variation, while the metal waste shows greater consistency. The metal waste was poured from a crucible and quickly solidified: as such its present composition should be a good indicator of the nature of the alloys cast at Redcliff Street. The metallic droplets, however, will have become trapped in vitrified material and exposed to further heating. This will have encouraged some elements to migrate from the droplets, be oxidised and be incorporated into the vitrified material. The degree to which elements will remain in such trapped metallic droplets or will migrate into the surrounding vitrified material will depend on the temperature and duration of any subsequent heating episode, as well as the chemical and physical properties of the different elements (Dungworth 2000). The depletion of zinc and lead from the metal droplets is complemented by the enhancement of these elements in the surrounding vitrified material. This migration of zinc and lead from the trapped metal droplets is likely to result from the volatility of these metals and the relative ease with which they are oxidised.

Table 4.11 Composition of copper alloy (including droplets within crucibles)

#	S	Fe	Co	Ni	Cu	Zn	As	Sn	Sb	Pb
2	<0.1	0.2	0.2	1.2	71.2	<0.1	3.0	14.7	7.2	2.1
3	0.7	0.2	<0.1	0.5	73.6	0.1	1.4	6.6	3.7	13.1
5	0.1	0.7	0.2	4.3	64.4	<0.1	2.8	6.6	15.7	5.0
6	<0.1	0.2	0.1	3.8	63.5	<0.1	2.3	13.7	13.8	2.2
7	0.6	<0.1	<0.1	0.6	77.8	0.1	1.8	6.5	4.0	8.3
8	0.0	<0.1	<0.1	0.2	94.7	<0.1	1.1	1.8	1.9	<0.2
10	0.1	<0.1	<0.1	0.6	68.0	<0.1	2.7	7.4	9.0	11.9
11	0.2	0.5	<0.1	0.2	81.9	4.2	0.8	5.7	0.7	5.6
12	0.3	0.2	<0.1	0.2	67.2	1.2	1.2	5.5	2.0	22.0
13	0.3	0.3	<0.1	0.2	65.2	1.4	1.1	5.9	1.9	23.4

Discussion

The visual examination and scientific analysis of the copper-alloy working debris shows that the main activity comprised the melting of copper alloy, and casting this to make large domestic cooking vessels. The alloy used to make cauldrons was a highly distinctive copper alloy which was rich in lead as well as tin, antimony, arsenic, zinc and nickel (often referred to as leaded antimony bronze for the sake of simplicity). This alloy has been identified as a waste material leftover from the extraction of silver from copper (Dungworth and Nicholas 2004). Once the silver had been extracted the remaining copper alloy could either be used directly for casting items such as cauldrons or could be refined to form pure copper. The scale of this silver extraction industry is attested by the abundance of domestic cooking vessels made using this alloy. There is unfortunately insufficient evidence available at present to indicate whether this industry was based in Britain or continental Europe.

The size and shape of the Redcliff Street crucibles are broadly similar to late medieval and early post-medieval crucibles from elsewhere in Britain (Bayley 1992; 1996; Taylor 2004; White and Kearns 2010). There are still minor differences between the Redcliff Street crucibles and the few contemporary crucibles which have been published. Some of the crucibles have grog-tempered fabrics which can be paralleled among examples from London (Freestone and Tite 1986; White and Kearns 2010). The fabric 1 crucibles represent something of a puzzle: they contain a small proportion of a fine organic material. SEM-EDS examination shows that this material is rich in carbon, however, it is unlikely that this is graphite. The use of coal dust as a temper for metal-melting crucibles is known, but none appear to be as early as those from Redcliff Street.

The Legge's Mount crucibles from London include some with curved bases (White and Kearns 2010) but these are usually somewhat larger than the Redcliff crucibles. The Deansway, Worcester, crucibles are a little smaller, were generally cylindrical or with slightly flaring walls, and have flat bases. The Deansway examples were up to 100mm high and had rim diameters up to 100mm (Taylor 1996; 2004). Taylor suggests that these crucibles were used to melt brasses rather than leaded antimony bronze (Taylor 1996; 2004) on the basis of qualitative analysis of the crucibles (Bayley 1989). However, the chemical and physical properties of zinc inevitably lead to its enrichment in crucible fabrics (Dungworth 2000); as a result, crucibles which contain zinc were not necessarily used to melt brasses. The detailed analysis of the Redcliff Street crucibles demonstrates that these were used for melting leaded antimony bronze but that the crucibles often contain high concentrations of zinc.

The analysis of the metallic waste, crucibles, the vitrified surfaces of crucibles and the metallic droplets trapped within these vitrified surfaces provides important information. The metallic droplets within the vitrified surfaces of the crucibles and the metallic waste share almost identical chemical compositions which indicates that the same alloy was used to produce cauldrons as was melted in the crucibles. The vitrified surfaces of the crucibles, however, are of more variable chemical composition and show some enrichment of volatile and easily oxidised elements, in particular zinc. This confirms that the ratio of metallic elements which can be detected in a crucible are a poor indication of the nature of the alloy melted (Dungworth 2000). The suggestion that the Deansway crucibles were used to melt brass and that they were not associated with the cauldron casting industry (Bayley 1989; Blades 2004; Taylor 1996; 2002) may not be correct.

The crucible fragments recovered were clearly used to cast the same metal that was used in the manufacture of the cauldrons, however, there is some doubt as to whether the crucibles would have been used to melt the metal needed for cauldrons. Most cauldrons would have required more metal than could be melted in a single crucible. While it is possible that the casting could have been achieved by pouring metal from several crucibles at the same time, it is striking that other cauldron manufacturing sites have yielded few or no crucible fragments (Blaylock 1996; 2000; McDonnell and Dungworth 2006; Taylor 1996; 2004). It is generally assumed that the metal for cauldrons was melted in simple furnaces rather than crucibles (Blaylock 1996; 2000). The crucible fragments could have been used for casting smaller objects such as candlesticks and perhaps even posnets.

The copper-alloy casting evidence was recovered primarily from Periods 2c and 3 with some residual material recovered from later post-medieval contexts. There are few significant differences in the nature of the evidence recovered from different periods. The nature of the alloy used appears to undergo no significant change. The size and shape of the crucibles appears to remain constant, although the fabrics do show some change. It is likely that essentially the same casting industry was carried out from the mid 14th century to the 17th century. This time span falls within the main period of cast copper-alloy cauldron manufacture (Dungworth and Nicholas 2004, fig. 3). Before the 11th century most cauldrons were made from sheet metal, and after the end of the 17th century cauldrons continued to be cast but usually from cast iron.

The reverberatory furnaces

Three furnaces were identified from Period 3 (Fig. 3.17): 1426 at No. 16 (Fig. 3.18) and furnaces 1530 and 1535 at No. 17. The furnaces at No. 17 replaced an earlier circular Period 2c furnace (Fig. 3.16). In all cases the furnaces are associated with melting copper alloys.

Furnace 1530 was stone-built and was at least 3m long and 1.6m wide (0.8–1m internal width). It survived to a height of 0.8m but appears to have been truncated. Furnace 1535 was more severely truncated, surviving only as a partial construction cut and preparatory mortar floor. Furnace 1426 was a complex structure (2m long and 1m wide) with one end divided by a central partition wall (Fig. 3.18). The eastern part of the structure was 0.35m wide and 1.5m long, the western one 0.25m wide and perhaps 1.2m long (the partition wall was only present/survived at the northern end). To the east of the partition wall the superstructure of the furnace at the north end incorporated a stone-built cylinder (0.75m high and 0.35m diameter) which resembled a simple chimney. The provision of a partition wall and a possible chimney suggest that this was a reverberatory furnace.

A reverberatory furnace is a complex structure which includes three key elements. Foremost of these is a low roof which reflects heat onto the material which is to be melted or smelted. Secondly, the fuel and the charge to be melted or smelted are separated by a low wall. Thirdly, the furnace is provided with a chimney, at the opposite end to the fire. Thus the fire-box contains the fuel and an air inlet to provide the heat required. The presence of the chimney at the other end of the furnace encourages flames and heat to pass over the top of the charge whilst the low ceiling helps to ensure the efficient heating of the charge in the central portion of the furnace.

The presence of a reverberatory furnace for melting copper alloys in Bristol in a 15th, 16th or 17th-century context is of considerable importance. Reverberatory furnaces appear to have been developed in the late Middle Ages for melting the large quantities of copper alloy needed for casting large artefacts such as cauldrons, bells and canons (Jenkins 1934). The reverberatory furnace became important from the end of the 17th century because it allowed the use of coal instead of wood fuel. Normally it was not possible to melt or smelt metals in direct contact with coal since this contains sulphur which would contaminate the metal.

There are indications that reverberatory furnaces using wood fuel were in use for some time prior to their use with coal. Jenkins (1934) reports the use of what might be reverberatory furnaces (in this case using wood fuel and without the aid of bellows) for the melting and smelting of copper in the 16th century in Germany, although he does not refer to, or illustrate any furnace which could properly be described as a reverberatory furnace. In Britain the earliest references to what appear to be reverberatory furnaces are found in patents and publications early in the second decade of the 17th century. Both Sturtevant and Rovenson claim to have developed furnaces for the smelting of metals using coal fuel. The published descriptions are far from complete but do specify that the furnaces contained a division to separate the fuel and the metal. The furnaces are not described as reverberatory but the term 'wind-furnace' is often used to distinguish it from those in which air was introduced using bellows. Much of the documentary evidence for the use of reverberatory furnaces in the 17th century comes from patents, many of which were concerned primarily with the (unsuccessful) attempts to smelt iron with coal rather than charcoal. It is not until the late 17th century that the reverberatory furnace was successfully used to smelt first lead and then copper. Bristol was an early centre for the smelting of copper using coal in reverberatory furnaces (Day 1991, 144). Any evaluation of the early historical references to the possible application of reverberatory furnaces is constrained by the nature of the sources and in particular the limited descriptions and absence of illustrations. While the reverberatory furnace of the 19th century and later is well known, it is by no means certain that all of the elements (the dividing wall, the low ceiling and the separate chimney) were all developed and introduced at the same time. It is perfectly possible that the separate elements were developed separately.

Archaeological evidence for the possible use of reverberatory furnaces for melting copper alloys has been recovered from a few sites in Britain. Reverberatory furnaces have been reported from early post-medieval contexts in Exeter (Blaylock 1996; 2000) and Keynsham Abbey (Lowe 1987, 147–9). The superstructure of these furnaces never survives completely and there is some doubt about their overall form and function.

Conclusions

The scientific examination of a range of industrial debris from Redcliff Street has provided a variety of information on the nature of medieval and early post-medieval metal industry. The presence of substantial quantities of ceramic mould from the site (Chapter 4.5) shows that cooking vessels and candlesticks were produced. The examination of metal spillages, sprues and failed castings has confirmed that the alloy used was a complex alloy distinguished by significant amounts of antimony and high levels of lead. This alloy is known to have been used in the manufacture of cauldrons and other domestic cooking vessels from the 11th to the 17th century. This alloy (leaded antimony bronze or *caldarium*, Dungworth and Nicholas 2004) was a waste product arising from the extraction of silver from some copper ores.

Photographed fragments of crucibles, clay mould and fragments of copper working debris (Figs 4.10–4.11)

1. Crucible from Period 3 context 1463 (sample 4, fabric 1).
2. Composite photograph of crucible from Period 3 context 1405 (sample 9, fabric 2b) showing interior surface, profile and exterior surface (left to right).
3. Two views of mould fragments from Period 3 context 1375.
4. Interior surfaces of individual mould fragments from Period 3 context 1375.
5. Exterior surfaces of individual mould fragments from Period 3 context 1375.
6. Copper melting slag from Period 3 context 1529.
7. Copper-alloy sprue from Period 3 context 1405.

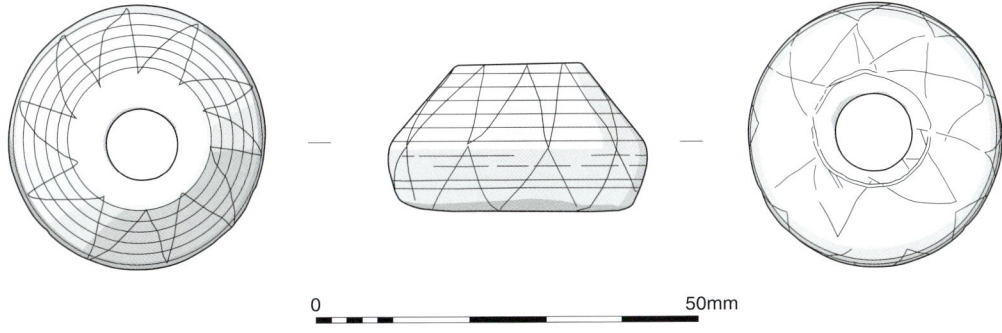

Fig. 4.13 Stone spindlewhorl cat. no. 4. Scale 1:1

4.7 Objects of Worked Stone
E.R. McSloy and Victoria Taylor

Spindlewhorls cat. nos 1–4 are typical of the lathe-made objects made from softer, easily-worked stone which are common in the medieval period. Finds from London suggest use from the Anglo-Norman period onwards (Pritchard 1991, 165, 259, nos 170–4; Egan 1998, 258, fig. 202–3). The examples from Periods 4 and 5 (cat. nos 3 and 4) are almost certainly redeposited medieval items. Cat. no. 1 could be an unfinished whorl although its internal diameter is untypically large and the object may have served a different function.

Spindlewhorls

1. Period 2a make-up 2043. Roughly made or unfinished spindlewhorl/weight of coarse mudstone. Drilled centre with chiseled exterior. Diameter 74mm; thickness 13mm. Registered artefact 48. Not illustrated.
2. Period 3 make-up 1619. Lathe-made plano-convex/domed spindlewhorl of lias or mudstone. Undecorated. Diameter 33mm; thickness 19mm. Not illustrated.
3. Period 4 brick hearth 1101. Lathe-made, 'bun-shaped' spindlewhorl of lias(?). Undecorated. Diameter 39mm; thickness 21mm. Registered artefact 3. Not illustrated.
4. Period 5 wall 1177. Lathe-made, 'bun-shaped' spindle-whorl of lias (?) with incised chevron decoration over turned banding. Diameter 36mm; thickness 20mm. Registered artefact 6. Fig. 4.13.

Hone

5. Period 2a occupation layer 1749. Well worn-down hone fragment, broken at both ends. Dense, silver-grey stone, probably Norwegian schist. Length (surviving) 56mm. Not illustrated.

Jetton mould

6. Period 1 fill 2107 of pit 3201. One half of 'piece' mould for casting multiple (lead?) jettons, each approximately 15mm in diameter. Fine-grained pale grey stone, probably lias. The jettons are of differing design, two with a cross formed from double lines and with pellets to each quadrant and one with double-lined cross only. The dating and use of lead tokens is poorly understood, although the similarity of this piece and other examples to long-cross silver coinage suggests a medieval origin. Pottery from this pit dates to the 12th to mid 13th centuries. Similar examples occur from St James' Priory, Bristol (Jackson 2006a, 162). Length 46mm; width 43mm; thickness: 9.5mm. Registered artefact 60. Fig. 4.14.

Fig. 4.14 Stone jetton mould. Scale 1:1

4.8 Clay Tobacco Pipe and Pipe Kiln Assemblage
Reg Jackson

There were 548 clay pipe fragments from 28 deposits. Of these, 171 derived from pipe bowls, although 20 were too small to be dated. There were no decorated or marked pipe stems. The clay pipes date mainly from the early 17th century to the early to mid 18th century with only two from the 19th century. A full catalogue of the clay pipe fragments is available in the archive.

Bristol was a major centre for the manufacture of clay tobacco pipes and it is not surprising that the identifiable pipes were produced in the city. All the unmarked bowls are typical of the forms produced in Bristol. Marked pipes made by the following Bristol pipe makers are represented in the assemblage: John Abbott, Richard Berryman, Flower Hunt, John Hunt I, John Macey I and John Squibb.

The identity of the maker of two spurred bowls with the initials 'IW' in a circle in relief on the side of the bowl cannot be determined with certainty as there were three makers working in Bristol with these initials during the early to mid 18th century: John Wilson, Joel Williams and John Wickham.

One heeled bowl is marked in relief on the heel with an unusual eight-pointed star, perhaps with a flower at the centre (from Period 3 dumped layer 1470). The bowl form is typical of those made in Bristol during the third quarter of the 17th century, but the maker cannot be identified. This deposit contained a large number of clay tobacco pipes, including a fragment from the base of a bowl which does not have a heel or a spur. This form is unusual in mid 17th-century Bristol pipes and generally does not occur until the later 18th century.

Kiln material

Period 4 contexts 1532, 1533, and 1470 produced clay tobacco pipe kiln material and waste from a 17th-century pipe factory, together with examples of pipes produced in that factory. The majority of the kiln material, which mainly comprises fragments of a muffle kiln (or kilns), came from context 1470. Clay tobacco pipe kilns have been extensively researched by Peacey (1996) and muffles appear to have been adopted as a means of firing pipes from as early as 1612.

The kiln muffle from Redcliff Street is hard and brittle and varies in colour from cream through to a light grey. The fabric is coarse and appears to include grog, in the form of clay pellets. All the muffle fragments are reinforced with rows of pipe stems and in the larger examples these rows of stems can be seen to be laid alternately at right angles to each other. A large number of over-fired and warped pipe stems, some with fragments of muffle adhering, had obviously come from the broken muffle. Over-fired clay pipe bowls, with fragments of muffle adhering, were probably used to strengthen the junction between the base and wall of the muffle.

Most of the fragments are from the core of the muffle wall, displaying broken surfaces from every aspect. However, a few are parts of the inside lining of the muffle being smooth on one surface to which layers of white slip had been applied, a process known as luting. The fragments are too small for an estimate to be made of the internal diameter of the muffle. One fragment of fired refractory clay had a 'fin' on one side and may have been part of a buttress supporting the muffle within the outer furnace (1532). One strip of fired pipe clay with thumb impressions along one face may have been used to support pipes within the muffle (1470). Fragments of dried pipe clay containing pipe stems and bowls and pieces of cinder and clinker were probably general debris from the workshop floor (contexts 1470 and 1532).

Products of the pipe factory and its probable period of operation

Waste pipes which had been used within the fabric of the kiln muffle bore the pipe makers' initials 'FH' and 'IH' and had a distinctive bowl typology: forward projecting and heeled and with some of the bowls having a burnished finish. This bowl typology dates from the middle and through the third quarter of the 17th century and is often typical of pipes made by members of the Hunt family in Bristol, Somerset and Wiltshire.

In addition to pipe bowls used within the kiln muffle, the kiln waste groups also produced pipes made in the factory and having the following marks (Fig. 4.15):

1. The three line mark 'FLO/WER H/VNT' incuse on the heel (two examples from 1470). Fig. 4.15; no. 1.
2. The initials 'FH' with decoration above and below all incuse on the heel (two examples from 1470 and 1533). Fig. 4.15; no. 2.
3. The three line mark 'IOH/N.HV/NT' incuse on the heel (eight examples from 1470 and 1532). Fig. 4.15; no. 3.
4. The initials 'IH' in a decorated panel all in relief on the heel (49 examples from 1470, 1532 and 1533). Fig. 4.15; no. 4.
5. The three line mark 'IOH/N.HV/NT', with a small star after the T, all incuse on the heel (27 examples from 1470, 1532 and 1533). Fig. 4.15; no. 5.

A close examination of the bowls showed that a different pipe mould had been used for the production of each of the pipes illustrated.

The pipes bearing the marks 'FH' and 'FLO/WER H/VNT' were certainly made by the Bristol pipe maker Flower Hunt who took his freedom to work in the city in 1651 and died in 1672 (Jackson and Price 1974; Price and Jackson 1979). Those marked with 'IH' and 'IOH/N.HV/NT' were made by the pipe maker John Hunt who first worked in Norton St Philip/Woolverton in Somerset from about 1644 (Marek Lewcun pers. comm.), obtained his freedom to work in Bristol in 1651 and was still working in the city in 1653, but had moved back to Woolverton by 1655 and worked there until 1680. A second John Hunt obtained his freedom to work as a pipe maker in Bristol in 1689 but it seems unlikely that he made the pipes from this kiln group as the typology of the pipe bowls is certainly not late 17th century in date.

The occurrence of both Flower Hunt and John Hunt pipes in the kiln assemblage suggests that they were working together or sharing a kiln. The fact that John

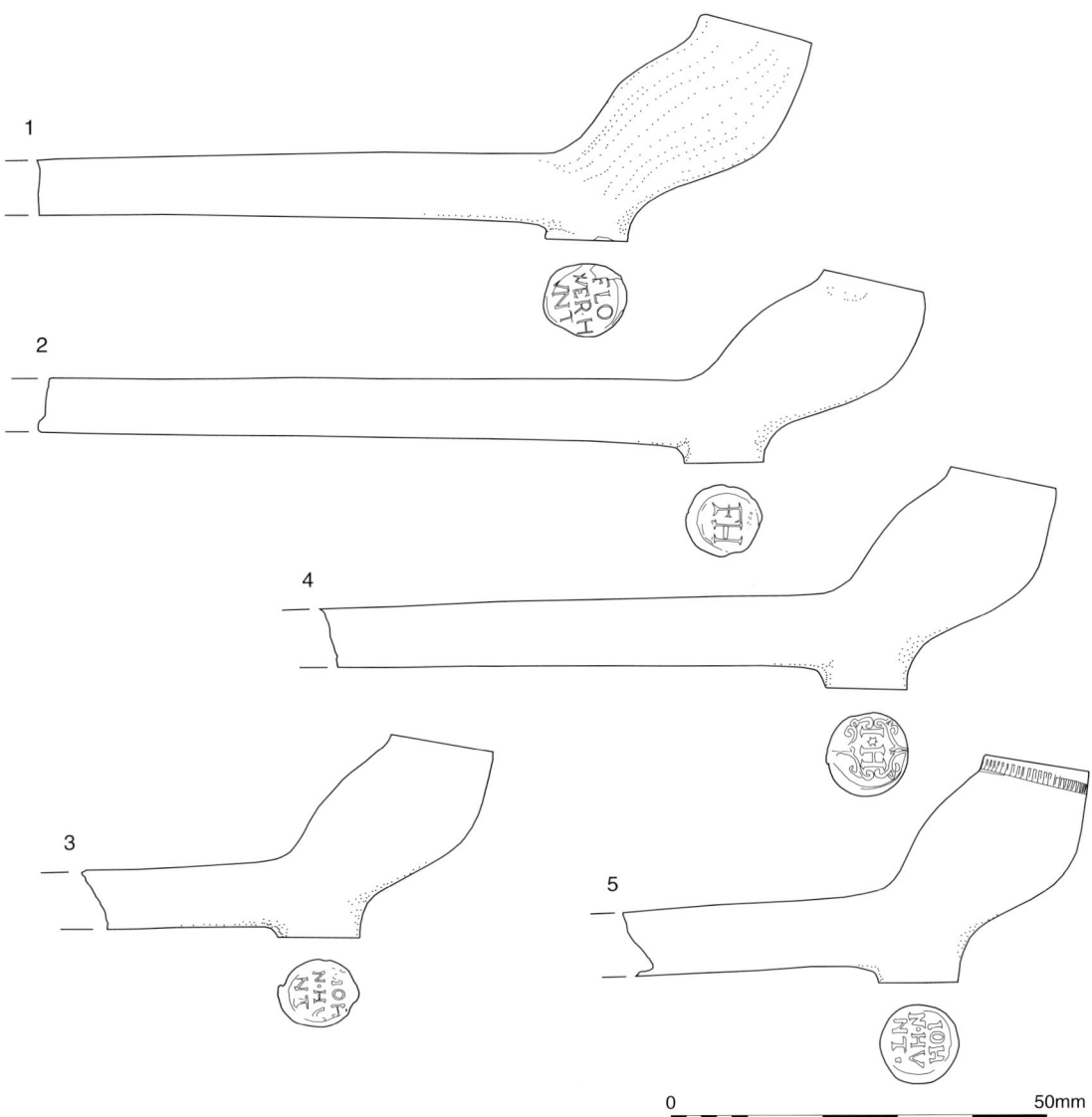

Fig. 4.15 Clay pipes nos 1–5. Scale 1:1

Hunt's pipes form the larger proportion of the assemblage may simply be due to the relatively small sample size of the assemblage and may not be representative of the output of the factory.

We do not know where John Hunt's pipe factory was located, it may have been on the site or the waste may simply have been disposed onto the site from elsewhere. The disposal of waste from pipe and pottery kilns was always a problem in an urban environment and it was frequently used as hard core or for filling in holes during building or street construction. We know from documents that Flower Hunt had property 'scituate in the Castle of Bristoll' (on the opposite side of the River Avon from Redcliff Street) in 1656, was recorded as living in the Castle Precincts in 1667 and, following his death in 1672, was referred to as 'Flower Hunt of the Castle' in 1673. However, it is not clear whether, in addition to being his home, this was also the site of his pipe factory. He may have worked elsewhere. While Flower Hunt worked in Bristol from 1651 until 1672, John Hunt was only in the city from 1651 until, at the latest, 1654, and so the pipe waste must date to the period 1651 to 1654.

Context 1470, which contained pottery of a later date, also produced one example each of pipes marked with the initials 'IA' and 'RB' and neither appear to be wasters. These are presumably incidental to the waste material (that is, they were not produced in the factory from which the waste derived) but the working dates of their makers, John Abbott 1651 to 1681 and Richard Berryman 1619 to 1652, overlap with, and provide further evidence for, the suggested production date of the pipe waste.

4.9 Glass and Glass Waste
E.R. McSloy

A small assemblage of 67 fragments of glass (1271g), including vessel and window categories, was hand-recovered. Further small quantities (five fragments weighing 4g) were retrieved from soil samples. The assemblage relates to 27 separate deposits, primarily layers and pit fills relating to Periods 3–5. Fragments of glass found in Period 1 and 2 contexts are probably intrusive. Full details of the assemblage are contained in the archive.

Vessel glass

The majority of the vessel glass consists of thick-walled fragments from wine or spirits bottles. The 'dirty' dark green colouring of this material is consistent with 'high lime low alkali' type glasses which typify bottle glass manufacture from the mid 17th to the later 19th centuries (Dungworth 2005). The larger part of this material consists of body and base fragments for which close dating is not possible. A base fragment from Period 1 deposit 1779 derived from broad-based bottles with a high internal 'kick', typical for the period to c. 1750, and is almost certainly intrusive.

In addition to thick-walled bottle glass, a small number of fragments deriving from pharmaceutical phials were recovered from Period 3 and 4 deposits. Notable from Period 3 fill 1333 (pit 1340) is the base of a hexagonal phial, characteristic of the early 17th century (Noël Hume 1969, 73). The remainder are 'bottle-shaped' and cylindrical forms, typically of the later 17th and 18th centuries.

Window glass

Small quantities of window glass were recovered from Period 3 and 4 deposits. Small fragments of greenish glass, for example from Period 3 fill 1333 (pit 1340), might derive from diamond leaded lights of 16th or 17th-century date. The majority consist of natural green or clear window glass of later 18th or 19th-century date.

Glass bead

A single small bead in an opaque, pale blue-coloured glass was recovered from a sample taken from Period 2b fill 1608 (stone cistern 1604). The bead, half of which is present, measures 4mm in diameter and is typical of the small beads known from the early post-medieval period and particularly from the 17th century (Noël Hume 1969, 54). The occurrence of this bead in a medieval context may be due to animal burrowing.

Glass waste

In addition to the vessel and window glass, quantities of waste material relating to glass manufacture and glass crucible fragments was hand-recovered. This material is typical of glassworking waste of the type encountered during investigations at glasshouses in Bristol and other areas, and is likely to be associated with bottle manufacture between the later 17th and 19th centuries.

4.10 Architectural Stone Fragments
Peter Davenport

A total of 40 fragments was recovered and catalogued under 32 catalogue entries. The items were all reused within Period 4 wall 1254 (late 17th to late 19th century). All are probably from ecclesiastical buildings and the obvious source would be the demolition of St Thomas's Church in the 1790s (Bettey 2001, 43). Some pieces (for example cat. nos 13, 15, 21, 28, 30 and 31) could have come from high-status domestic buildings. Taken as a whole however, the group is more likely to come from a church. This is especially true of the large fragments of traceried window (cat. nos 2, 5, 9, 22 and 23) from which the mullions and bar tracery pieces (cat. no. 6) could well be subsidiary parts. The stop on the hood moulding (cat. no. 9) seems to indicate that the window was quite low-arched but not four-centred. A close parallel to the re-entrant quirk moulding on the internal face of these can be found in the windows of the choir and south transept of St Mary Redcliffe, probably of later 14th-century date (though sometimes dated a little earlier). The battlemented piece (cat. no. 4) is from the top of a screen or tomb and this also applies to the canopy head (cat. no. 12).

The date range of the fragments is predominantly late 14th to early 16th century, in Perpendicular style and the less closely dateable pieces could lie within this date range. This would imply significant alterations and additions to St Thomas's, probably in the 15th century, and may even be evidence for a rebuilding. The present tower is the late medieval one and certainly its upper stages, and stair turret, which have escaped major refacing and alteration, seem to be late 15th to early 16th century in date.

Catalogue (none illustrated)

Dimensions are generally given with depth running back from the observer, width as left and right from the observer. Where possible the stone is described as if *in situ*, but the original orientation is not always known.

1. A narrow ashlar block with a curved chamfered corbel on one end. The remains of orange stripes over a white ground occur on the corbel and there is red plaster at the opposite end. The long sides have been thinned down roughly, after the plastering, so that the full width only survives at the back. This appears to be some sort of bracket at the top of a moulded wall panel, but is difficult to categorise. The white and orange paint is probably original. 475mm deep x 150mm wide x 255mm high. Probably 15th to early 16th century.

2. A very damaged section of window mullion, reworked. It was probably reused at least once before ending up in its find spot. White paint survives on the secondary faces, which indicate it to have been used in a wall 275mm thick. From the same design of window as cat. nos 5 and 23; the dimensions of the front square moulding suggest it was part of a jamb. 480mm deep x 275mm wide x 210mm high (no complete dimension). Probably late 14th to 15th century.
3. Three fragments of one stone. The profile suggests a coping stone, with a re-entrant roll moulding at the base of the top slope. One block has a recess as if a drip-stop channel in the bottom face, but this may be secondary, as it is too far back from the face to function as such. 375mm deep (calculated) x 230mm wide x 305mm high. Later medieval.
4. Ashlar block (in two joining parts) with 'battlemented' cornice on one face. This has white paint on the well-finished, battlemented front. It would have been part of a cornice or string course inside a building. 325mm deep x 350mm wide x 177mm high. Later 15th to 16th century.
5. Springing block of two arches from a mullioned window, straight-chamfered profile with angle recess or quirk. Internal central moulding is a square section. White paint on the surviving mouldings. Only the internal face survives; from same design of window as cat. nos 2 and 23. 235mm deep (approximately 50% present) x 380mm wide (maximum, reconstituted) x 315mm high. Probably late 14th to 15th century.
6. Three pieces: a slightly curved piece of bar-tracery with a plain chamfer externally and sharply re-entrant quirk in the internal chamfer, producing a squared internal moulding; central glazing slots. 280mm deep x 120mm wide x 400mm long (across the chord, orientation unclear); another piece of straight mullion, 480mm high; another piece with identical half profile, thus a jamb, 230mm high. Probably late 14th to 15th century.
7. Three identical sections of mullion, blunt chamfer each side with a hexagonal nose moulding created by a simple quirk in the chamfer. A V-shaped slot on each side may represent glazing but is not a proper channel. 310mm deep x 160mm wide x 260mm to 270mm high (all broken both ends). Later 14th to later 15th century.
8. Fragment of symmetrical ovolo moulding framing a sunken panel. Moulding 10mm wide, projects 50mm from wall face, sunken panel recessed by further 30mm. White painted. Later 15th to 16th century.
9. Stopped end of hood moulding for window of same dimensions and profile as cat. nos 22 and 23. It appears to be part of a four-centred arch. The label is missing, probably damaged. 190mm deep (max surviving) x 470mm wide x 375mm high. 15th to 16th century.
10. Ashlar block with shallow chamfer to upper face, possible shallow coping block. >380mm deep x >215mm high, width not recorded, profile only. Undateable.
11. Ashlar block with true ogee corner moulding. Probably a door or window jamb. 155mm deep x >300mm wide x 110mm high. Moulding and shallow course suggests 13th to 14th century.
12. A squared block with deep relief carved detail. 220mm deep x 350mm wide x 310mm high. This is a block from a tomb or screen and shows the upper part of a tall, pinnacle-style canopy, which would have framed or capped a recess or niche. The carving is as much as 130mm deep. Above the cross finial are the remains of a vegetal or floral boss. Most of this is damaged but elements of buds or grapes are visible both sides, which may be elements of a linking foliate frieze and the general ovoid shape of the boss is evident. 15th to 16th century.
13. Two identical halves of four-centred heads of cinquefoil window lights. A glazing slot was placed about two-thirds of the way in from the outside edge (based on weathering). 210mm deep x 330mm wide x 275mm high. Window block width would be 660mm, internal opening 460mm. Very shallow rebate on jamb edge, function unknown. 15th to 16th century.
14. A very similar block to cat. no. 10 but with a shallower angle and 235mm wide. Undateable.
15. Two simple, chamfered and rebated jambs, 200m deep x 250mm wide x 240mm and 300mm high. The larger block has a stub of a chamfered window sill at the base, indicating these are window jambs with rebates for shutters. No sign of glazing. Medieval.
16. A rebated and moulded jamb. The moulding is a simple, fairly flat, wave (i.e. double ogee) moulding. Block is complete in plan, 270mm deep x 285mm wide x 350mm high. One joint surface has been cut at an angle, probably secondarily. 15th to 16th century.
17. Complete coping stone with quadrant cut-out in lower front corner 320mm deep x 380mm wide x 150mm high.
18. Tall, isosceles triangle-shaped block, 175mm deep at the base x 350mm wide x 220mm high. Smoothly finished except for base which is neatly scored longitudinally at *c.* 19mm spacing.
19. Fragment of a deeply-moulded voussoir, wave moulding on one corner but adjacent face roughly cut back. A deep and undercut cavetto moulding survives in the cut face, suggesting a series of deep mouldings removed by the cut-back. >420mm deep x >310mm wide x >215mm high. 15th to 16th century.
20. Simple shallow-chamfered block, plinth or coping (complete) and another fragment. Same angle as, but different dimensions from, cat. no. 14. 230mm deep x 382mm wide x 150mm high. Undateable.
21. Two small, chamfered and rebated door or window jamb fragments. The side away from the opening has a large hollow moulding, which is probably from an earlier phase of use. The rebate has white paint surviving. 185mm deep x 130mm wide. Height not recorded. Medieval.
22. Two moulded voussoirs of a window head. The moulding matched that of cat. nos 2, 5, 9 and 23. Probably 460mm wide but one projecting fillet has been reduced by 25mm. The intrados moulding has been smashed off one but the other was intact and the same as cat. no. 23. Thickness 180mm. The voussoirs were 350mm and 260mm wide (measured across the

inside chord). The very slight curvature can be used to calculate the radius at about 3.8m. Later 14th to 16th century.

23. Curved fragment of bar tracery, similar to cat. nos 2, 5, 9 and 22. White paint survived on the mouldings on one side and a possible glazing slot on the intrados (all faces on the other blocks potentially with this slot were damaged or abraded). Radius similar to cat. no. 22.

24. Cornice or string course block, simple scotia, plain fillet above and shallow rebate below. >310mm deep (>225m into wall and 85mm projecting) x 310mm wide x 210mm high. White paint on mouldings, over ochre paint. Late or post-medieval.

25. Finely finished and painted ashlar block of uncertain function. One lateral face and a small chamfer have white paint very evenly and thinly applied over well-finished stone faces. A rebate is cut on the opposite corner from the chamfer. One lateral face is concave, well-finished but a little abraded and has several geometric marks cut into it. These appear to be masons' marks, but their significance in this position is uncertain. 295mm deep x 280mm wide x 490mm high. Undated.

26. Elongated hexagonal-section mullion with traces of projecting square-section nose moulding. Similar to cat. no. 7 but dumpier proportions. 1600mm wide x 225mm deep x unrecorded height.

27. Fragment of the head of a cusped, traceried window with a hexagonal nose moulding. Very similar to cat. no. 7 with slight dimensional differences. Bar is 215mm deep x >255m high. 180mm length survives.

28. This is the base or cill of the left-hand light (seen from outside) of a multi-light mullioned window. It has a slot for glazing and a central, diagonally-set, square hole for a vertical iron bar, set inside the glazing slot line. Cat. no. 29 seems to fit it well, with the nose moulding external. The block is 580mm long x 210mm deep x 295mm thick. The light would have been 390mm wide. Early 16th to 17th century.

29. Fragment (just more than half the profile) of a hexagonal mullion with a hexagonal nose moulding. Similar in style, but not size, to cat no. 7. Probably part of a mullion for cat. no. 28. 195mm deep x 230mm thick (reconstituted). Height not recorded but short fragment. Later medieval.

30. Plain hexagonal mullion, no glazing slot. 185mm deep x 195mm wide. Height not recorded but short fragment. Medieval to post-medieval.

31. Small block with semi-octagonal fillet running diagonally across it. Part of hood-moulding? The moulding measured 47.5mm diagonally from face to face. Medieval.

32. Large chamfered and rebated door jamb, 610mm wide x 705mm deep x 450mm high. The chamfered and adjacent faces are finely finished. The rebate has vertical combing. An iron pin or nail has been fixed into a drilled hole in the corner of the rebate. Secondary use has deposited green and grey paint and soot on the vertical surfaces, and a neat, very shallow (3mm) rebate 190mm wide has been worked on joint face opposite the shaped faces, postdating the paint and soot. Almost certainly medieval.

4.11 Leather
Quita Mould

Approximately 362 leather items were examined (currently in 459 fragments). The majority of the leather (87%) came from Period 1 and was recovered principally from pits in the rear parts of the tenement plots. A further 10% came from Period 2a, with the remainder from Periods 2b and 3. Consequently Period 1 will be the focus of this report. The small amount of leather from the later periods showed no significant difference from that from Period 1 and was probably residual. A full description of the whole assemblage is contained in the archive.

The majority of the leather recovered was footwear. While the shoes were chiefly represented by unassociated shoe parts, 13 shoes were relatively well preserved with a significant proportion of their shoe components present. It is estimated that the shoe parts recovered represent a minimum of 51 shoes, with 82% coming from Period 1 contexts. Fourteen pieces of leather derived from five other objects and a small amount of waste leather (dry weight 427g) was also present. The leather finds provide evidence of the work of the cobbler who bought old shoes and refurbished them for resale.

Small groups of leather of this date (late 12th/early 13th century) have been found previously in a number of locations in the centre of Bristol on both sides of the river (Mould 2001; 2008a; 2008b; 2013) with a larger group of leather dating slightly earlier (first part of the 12th century) and to the same period recovered from Finzel's Reach, Redcliffe (Mould 2010a). These sites provide evidence that the cobbling trade was well established in the city at this time.

The nature and provenance of the material

Cobbling waste was present in at least 16 of the 25 features attributed to Period 1 that contained leather. The cobbling waste principally occurred in the backfills of pits located across much of the excavation and does not appear to be concentrated in any one plot. It is possible that the leather was a part of general rubbish that was used to backfill the series of large pits when they fell out of use. The recovery of a very small group of cobbling waste comprising worn-out shoe parts, some cut up to salvage reusable leather, and a small amount of waste leather from Period 1 surface 2009 at No. 17 Redcliff Street, and a small group of similar material from fill 1771 of an associated drain (1773), potentially indicates that a cobbler's workshop was located close by (Table 4.12). A larger group of the same composition was found within occupation layer 1809/1812 which directly overlaid surface 2009 but belonged on stratigraphic grounds to Period 2a, although the leather itself includes shoe parts that are stylistically similar to those from the drain/surface. If a cobbler was working at No. 17, then sweepings from

Table 4.12 Leather from a Period 1 floor and associated drain, and Period 2a occupation layer, at No. 17 Redcliff Street

	2009 Floor	1771 Drain	1809=1812 Occupation layer
Sole	2	0	7
Sole fragments	1	4	9
Rand	0	0	3
Clump	0	2	2
Upper, drawstring thro' thong slots	0	0	1
Upper, drawstring thro' vertical thong	1	1	0
Upper, fastening unknown	0	0	1
Upper insert	0	0	3
Heel stiffener	0	0	1
Drawstring fragment	0	0	1
Waste, secondary	9 (16g)	1 (1g)	18 (37g)
Waste, primary	0	1 (8g)	13 (55g)

a workshop floor might easily have been thrown out into the yard behind and subsequently incorporated into the material that accumulated on the surface when the structure was abandoned. Should this be the case, Redcliff Street marks one of the very few locations in this country where a medieval cobbler's workshop has been identified.

Period 1

Shoe parts dominated the leather from Period 1 contexts and at least 42 shoes are represented although, as many are fragmentary, this may well be an underestimate. While some appears to be the result of discarded domestic rubbish, a significant proportion is certainly cobbling waste. Some 19% of the shoe parts had been cut up to salvage reusable leather and the discarded seams and fastenings were all that remained of an item of sheep/goatskin, the greater part of it having been recycled (Fig. 4.17; no. 8). Approximately a quarter (25%) of all the shoe sole fragments had been repaired at least once before they had been thrown away. Seventeen patches, known as clumps, used to repair worn-out shoe soles were also noted, including two (Archive cat. nos 19 (fill 1925 of pit 3300 at No. 17 Redcliff Street) and 26 (fill 2474 of pit 2475 at Nos 12–15 Redcliff Street)) that had been cut out of old shoe parts, but discarded before they could be used. One shoe (Fig. 4.16; no. 1) had an unusually pieced sole made of two parts sewn together that is more likely to be the result of the cobbler's art rather than an act of extreme frugality on behalf of the shoemaker.

All the shoes recovered during the excavations were of turnshoe construction. The wide soles had oval or short pointed toes and distinct waists. Several examples had a rand sewn between the sole and the upper seam. Most of the rands were narrow and flat, with at least nine examples measuring between 4–6mm wide, with no rand more than 10mm wide. The shoe uppers were made of one piece of leather that wrapped around the foot and joined with a single seam at the side. This side seam was located closer to the heel in some examples. Small additional pieces, known as inserts, were added where necessary to lengthen the upper or raise its height. Occasionally heel stiffeners and top bands were added but they were not a common feature of this assemblage.

The shoes were of ankleshoe style varying in height from just below the ankle (e.g. Fig. 4.16; nos 1–2) to well above the ankle at 'below calf' height, what we would term 'ankle boots' today. They fastened with a drawstring. While at least 20 one-piece uppers have no evidence of their method of fastening remaining (e.g. Fig. 4.16; no. 1), nine had paired thong slots or holes through which the drawstring passed and was held in place. The shorter examples had the drawstring passing through a single row of paired thong slots (e.g. Fig. 4.16; nos 2–3), those with taller legs had the drawstring passing through multiple pairs of slots or holes, examples with two rows (Archive cat. no. 30), four rows (Archive cat. no. 31) and seven rows (Fig. 4.16; no. 4) were found. The presence of differing numbers of rows of paired slots in the same upper seen on some examples (e.g. Archive cat. no. 31 and Fig. 4.16; no. 4) indicated that one long drawstring had been spirally wound around the leg. Other examples may have fastened with a number of shorter drawstrings each wrapped once around the leg and tied at the front. The type of drawstring was also found to vary. Two narrow, round-sectioned drawstrings, similar to modern shoelaces, survived *in situ* (Fig. 4.16; nos 3–4), while another ankleshoe (Archive cat. no. 30) had fastened with a drawstring of flat thong, a fragment of which remained.

A further four ankleshoes (Archive cat. nos 5, 21, 30 and Fig. 4.17; no. 5) differed in having the drawstring passing not through paired slits or holes but through a series of separate looped 'keepers' created by a thong threaded vertically through the upper (drawstring type 3, Grew and de Neergaard 1988, 17, tables 1 and 2; Goubitz type 10 variant II, Goubitz *et al.* 2001, 136).

The drawstring fastening ankleshoe was the principal shoe style worn during the second half of the 12th century and the first half of the 13th century, both those with the drawstring passing through paired thong slots or holes and those with the drawstring passing through vertical loops of leather thong are commonly found both in this country and the Continent. In the closely dated deposits in the city of London the variant with looped 'keepers' of thonging was common in later 12th and early/mid 13th-century contexts (Grew and de Neergaard 1988, 14–15). Three examples were found at Finzel's Reach in Redcliffe, two came from contexts of similar date (mid–later 12th century and late 12th/early

13th century) while one came from a pit dated earlier to the early/mid 12th century (Mould 2010a). On the Continent this variant is said to have had an even longer 'lifespan' of *c.* 1100–1300 (Goubitz *et al.* 2001, 136) though, to date, there appears to be no evidence for this being the case in Britain.

Only one example was found of a shoe with a different style of fastening. An upper insert with a row of five lace holes (Fig. 4.17; no. 6) from a heavily worn shoe of sheep/goatskin that laced up the side of the foot was found in upper fill 2476 of pit 2479 at Nos 12–15 Redcliff Street. The end of the shoe lace is knotted through the lowest hole suggesting that it fastened with a single lace threaded in a 'zig-zag' fashion alternately through the holes in one side and then the other and knotted at the top as seen preserved on an example from London (Grew and de Neergaard 1988, 19, fig. 27). Side-lacing footwear appears for the first time amongst the closely dated shoe assemblages from the waterfront sites in the city of London in the early/mid 13th century (ibid., 18). The style also becomes popular in the Netherlands from *c.* 1200 onward (Goubitz type 50 variant I, Goubitz *et al.* 2001, 175).

A significant proportion (39%) of the shoe uppers that were identifiable (36) were made of sheep/goatskin, the remainder being of bovine leathers with nearly half being of calfskin. The increased use of fine skins, in particular sheep/goatskin, is feature of shoe assemblages of 12th and early 13th-century date. The proportion of sheep/goatskin here is notably lower than that found at Finzel's Reach (69%; Mould 2010a) and in the Oxford Castle motte assemblage (62%; Mould 2010b). While in each instance the numbers identifiable are too low to be statistically significant it may point to the group from Redcliff Street dating slightly later than the other two groups. Other characteristics exhibited by the Redcliff Street shoes (sole shape, rand profile and width, upper cutting pattern and method of fastening) suggest that shoes dating to the second half of the 12th and first part of the 13th centuries are present in the group. It may be that this material was deposited at the very end of the 12th and the early part of the 13th century.

Other objects

Straps

Pieces torn from two folded straps of bovine leathers were found. One piece (Fig. 4.17; no. 7) from fill 3200 of pit 3229 at No. 18 Redcliff Street has a butted back seam and has been torn from a heavy strap 40mm wide. The second piece (Archive cat. no. 42) from fill 3150 of pit 3155 at No. 18a Redcliff Street is of smaller size, being just 16mm in width, with a line of widely spaced grain/flesh stitching running along each folded edge. The narrow size might suggest it came from a bridle.

Unidentified objects

The fragmentary remains of an unidentified object made of sheep/goatskin (Fig. 4.17; no. 8) were found in fill 2474 of pit 2475 at Nos 12–15 Redcliff Street. The object had two large fastening latchets and whip stitching on the latchets indicate it had been lined. The seams and the latchets had been cut off and discarded while the rest of the leather had been salvaged for reuse elsewhere.

A heavily worn panel of sheep/goatskin (Fig. 4.18; no. 9) was part of the group recovered from fill 2476 of pit 2479 at Nos 12–15 Redcliff Street. It has been cut and torn from a larger item, possibly a garment, originally internally lined and with stitching marking the former position of a tongue-shaped tab along one edge.

The waste leather

A relatively small amount of waste leather was found (Table 4.13). The primary waste comprised edges trimmed from hides and unusable areas of skin such as that from under the legs (axillae) and belly. The secondary waste was produced when cutting out pattern pieces and trimming them to size. Much of this appears to have been produced when resoling and repairing old shoes, though three pieces of secondary waste characteristic of shoemaking were also present. Only two contexts contained noticeably larger amounts of waste leather than the rest, upper fill 3218 of pit 3217 at No. 18 Redcliff Street and fill 2474 of pit 2475 at Nos 12–15 Redcliff Street. These two contexts both contained old, worn shoes, some with secondary cuts, along with the waste leather, supporting the interpretation of the material as cobbling waste.

Catalogue of illustrated leather objects from Period 1 deposits (Figs 4.16–4.18)

1. Turnshoe ankleshoe, left foot. Sole with oval toe, medium waist and seat, the left side of the waist and upper seat area has an elliptical section added. Edge/flesh seam, stitch length 5mm. A line of three closely

Table 4.13 Waste leather by count and dry weight

Waste	Period 1 count	Period 1 weight	Period 2a count	Period 2a weight	Period 2b count	Period 3 count	Period 3 weight
Primary	54	189g	13	55g	0	2	14g
Secondary	167	132g	18	37g	0	0	
Total	221	321g	31	92g	0	2	14g

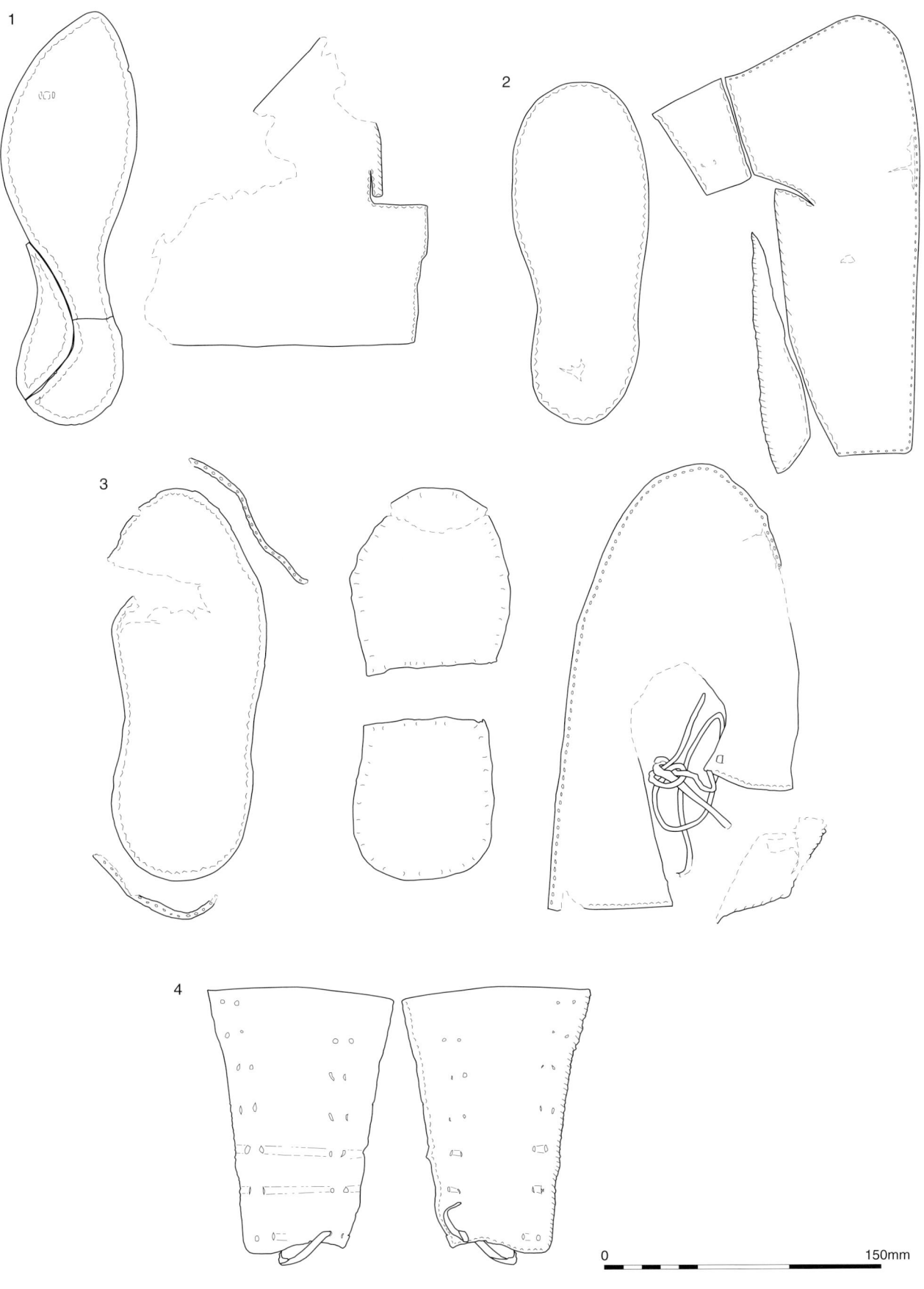

Fig. 4.16   Objects of leather nos 1–4. Scale 1:3

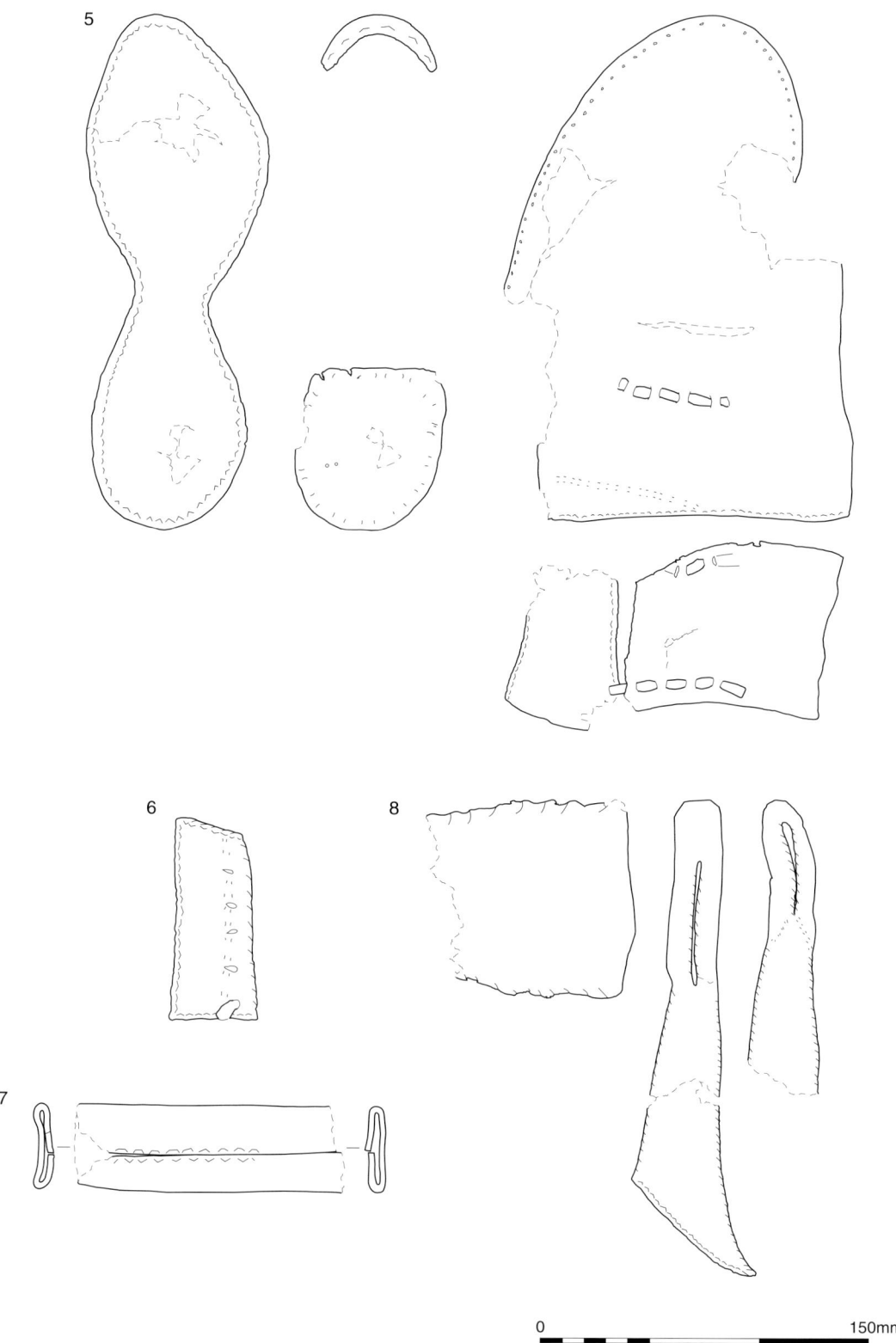

Fig. 4.17   Objects of leather nos 5–8. Scale 1:3

spaced thong holes is present at the tread. Forepart area of upper, toe and much of the left side torn away, with a butted edge/flesh side seam, stitch length 2.5mm, and similar seaming at the front opening with part of the right front opening with whip stitching surviving. Upper leather worn bovine 2.07mm thick. Sole length 223mm (dry). Adult size 2(34). Fill 3215 of pit 3300 at No. 17 Redcliff Street (Archive cat. no. 59).

Fig. 4.18   Object of leather no. 9. Scale 1:3

2. Turnshoe ankleshoe, drawstring fastening, right foot. Sole with oval toe, wide tread, slight waist and wide seat, with a hole worn through at the seat. Edge/flesh seam, stitch length 6mm. One-piece upper with rectangular insert with a small pair of thong slots on the outside of the foot joined with edge/flesh butted seams, stitch length 2.5mm. Tapering triangular piece whip stitched and edge/flesh stitched to the top edge to raise the height on the outer edge. Height centre back 75mm. Leather heavily worn sheep/goatskin 1mm thick. Sole length 215mm. Adult 1(33). Fill 3182 of pit 3177 at No. 17 Redcliff Street (Archive cat. no. 48).

3. Turnshoe ankleshoe, drawstring fastening, right foot. Sole with oval toe, wide tread, waist and seat, hole worn at the great toe joint. Edge/flesh seam, stitch length 5mm. Repair clumps to tread and seat. Narrow, flat rand, 4mm wide. One-piece upper, the lasting margin worn and cut away along the left side, with a butted edge/flesh seam, stitch length 4mm, close to the back (heel area) of the shoe. The high throat has whip stitching but much of the top edge is now broken away. A single pair of thong slots is present at the junction of the throat and the side seam with a long, narrow, knotted drawstring, 3mm wide, surviving. The remains of a small heel stiffener are also present. Upper height *c.* 70mm. Upper leather worn sheepskin 1.40mm thick. Sole length 250mm. Adult 5(38). Fill 3200 of pit 3229 at No. 18 Redcliff Street (Archive cat. no. 55).

4. Insert from a tall drawstring fastening ankleshoe, adult size. Insert from the left front opening of a tall drawstring fastening ankleshoe with butted edge/flesh seams, stitch length 4mm, a whip stitched front opening and a plain cut top edge. Two columns of paired fastening holes are present 6mm apart, with six rows in one column and seven rows in the other. The impression of the drawstring is visible in the holes and on the grain side of the insert. A fragment of the drawstring, 4mm wide, survives, knotted through the lowest pair of fastening holes. Leather sheep/goatskin 2.05mm thick. Height 143mm, maximum width 101mm. Fill 3218 of pit 3217 at No. 18 Redcliff Street (Archive cat. no. 72).

5. Turnshoe ankleshoe, drawstring fastening, right foot, adult size. Sole with oval toe, distinct waist and wide seat, holes worn at the tread and seat. Edge/flesh seam, stitch length 6mm. Stitching from repair to tread and seat. Seat clump worn through at the centre. Toe area of rand, 9mm wide, with stitching to attach a repair. One-piece upper with plain cut front opening and top edge, broken at toe joints to each side. The stitching for a narrow but tall heel stiffener is present (stiffener missing). Two upper inserts joining to the vertical seam located close to centre back. A vertical line of thong, 5mm wide, forming drawstring keepers

6. Upper insert with lace holes, adult size. Rectangular insert piece with five lace holes. The insert has three butted edge/flesh seams and stitching from a lapped seam with whip stitching to attach a lace hole lining. Leather worn sheep/goatskin 1.67mm thick. Height 95mm, width 43mm. Fill 2476 of pit 2479 at Nos 12–15 Redcliff Street (Archive cat. no. 34).

7. Folded strap. Fragment of straight strap, torn at each end, with central back seam with butted edge/flesh stitching visible for 68mm along its length. Leather cattle hide 3mm thick. Length 122mm, width 40mm. Fill 3200 of pit 3299 at No. 18 Redcliff Street (Archive cat. no. 53).

8. Cut down unidentified item. A strap latchet with a blunt end with cropped corners and a central slot 55mm long. The latchet has an oblique butted edge/flesh seam, stitch length 3mm, and whip stitching around the sides and slot. A second latchet with a rounded end with whip stitched sides and central slot 43mm long has been torn off. A rectangular piece with a cut and a torn end and whip stitched sides, stitch length 10mm, and a fragment with similar whip stitched edges and six pieces of cut down whip stitched seam (not illustrated) also survive. Leather sheep/goatskin 1.2mm thick. Complete latchet length 230mm, maximum width 45mm. Fill 2474 of pit 2475 at Nos 12–15 Redcliff Street (Archive cat. no. 28).

9. Panel from a ?garment. A rectangular panel with a short length of closed seam with grain/flesh stitching, stitch length 3mm, surviving on one side, the other edges are cut with two concave areas torn away. Whip stitching from a lapped seam marks the position of a tongue-shaped tab, 56mm x 40mm, along one edge and a large lining that extended nearly halfway across the panel sewn to the flesh side (interior). The grain side is heavily worn and the surface is cracked. Leather sheep/goatskin 1.8mm thick. Length 390mm, width 285mm. Fill 2476 of pit 2479 at Nos 12–15 Redcliff Street (Archive cat. no. 29).

4.12 Worked Wood
D.M. Goodburn

Methodology

The structural woodwork was planned and photographed on site, with each timber given a unique number and recorded on pro-forma sheets by the fieldwork team. All items were provided with a measured sketch and 20 were drawn in detail to scale. Selected woodworking features were also photographed off-site. The finer wattlework was recorded under one number, although for heavier roundwood structures, each stake was given a number. The recovered wood was polythene wrapped or stored in wet tubs.

The author's involvement began during the post-excavation process and included a re-examination of the items during which the primary records were updated with information such as species, type of conversion tool marks and evidence for previous use etc. Some were drawn to scale and photographed and tree-ring samples were taken where appropriate (in this case viable items comprised oak and beech timbers with over 45 annual rings; Chapter 4.13). Species identification was made visually for mature items with clear diagnostic features whilst small immature roundwood and less diagnostic material was sampled for microscopic species identification (Chapter 5.3). Some items displayed recent damage by machine and as a result of infestation of some wrappings with decay organisms. The resulting archive is in line with the standards set out by Historic England (Brunning 1996).

The quantity and range of the worked wood

In total 149 individual worked timbers and sections of wattle work and roundwood stakes were recorded. In addition, 49 deposits were noted as containing small fragments of worked wood. A total of 19 tree-ring samples and 43 wood species identification (Sp ID) and age samples was taken. Nationally this assemblage would qualify as a medium-sized assemblage but is large in terms of published material from Bristol (Jones 1991). This writer was able to examine about half of the material in person, mostly the more elaborately worked items.

The surviving woodwork included a wide range of material. The most substantial timbers were the bases of sub-rectangular building posts from the western part of the site (the side nearest to the street frontage). Some of these timbers had features apparently remaining from hauling out of the woodlands they were made in. Lighter building posts and wattle stakes were also found along with wattle and 'plank and pile' revetments for drains and pit linings. Some items included redundant fastening holes or joints, showing that they were reused weather boarding, boat planking or building posts. The vast majority of the timber derived from native oak whilst the roundwood was mainly of hazel, with some holly and other species.

Historical background: 'treewrighting' versus carpentry; revolutionary changes in structural woodworking at the end of the 12th century

In the period c. 1180–1200 a radically new woodworking technology, hereafter referred to as carpentry, arrived in the south-east of England (Milne 1992). Prior to this the woodworking technology utilised a technique referred to here as treewrighting (the Old English term for structural woodworker, 'treewright' has been adopted here for the woodworkers and 'treewrighting' for the overall repertoire of techniques and approaches used in England in Saxon and Norman times). The bulk of the excavated evidence of pre-carpentry structural woodwork comes from waterlogged urban sites in London, with smaller assemblages from York and more isolated rural sites (Hall 1984; Goodburn 1992; 1997; 1999; 2007). Typical treewrights' techniques include the widespread use of controlled splitting or cleaving, the limited use of relatively simple, largely axe-cut, joints, and the absence of the use of saws to cross-cut timber or convert it into planks. Timbers of the Saxon and Norman period were not generally cut to regular square sections nor is there evidence of extensive pre-fabrication (as in later medieval timber frame carpentry). However, it is also clear that there was a tendency towards the hewing of straighter and squarer timber from the mid 12th century onward (Milne 1992, 60).

Wattlework was used very extensively and most styles of building were based on earth-fast timbers resulting in timber buildings having short lives, with the partial exception of some of middling or high-status structures built with raised sill beams used with stave work or forms of hewn-log construction. Some timber buildings of the 11th and 12th centuries used substantial earth-fast posts combined with slightly raised sills set between supporting vertically planked 'stave' walls (Herrnbrodt 1958; Milne 1992, 132; Goodburn 1997) (Fig. 4.19) and other middling and higher status structures used a 'bulwark' technique in which the posts were set c. 1m to 2.5m apart with wall boards, set on edge, in opposed grooved post edges (Jorgensen 1986, 51; Goodburn 1997; 2007). Both the latter two techniques may be relevant to understanding the large post bases found at this site. Bulwark and stave construction with cleft timbers used for building walls died out in England during the early 13th century (Milne 1992, 73). Recent woodworking finds within Bristol have been made at the Cabot Circus and Finzel's Reach, Redcliffe, sites (Goodburn 2013; 2008). Both sites included treewright-

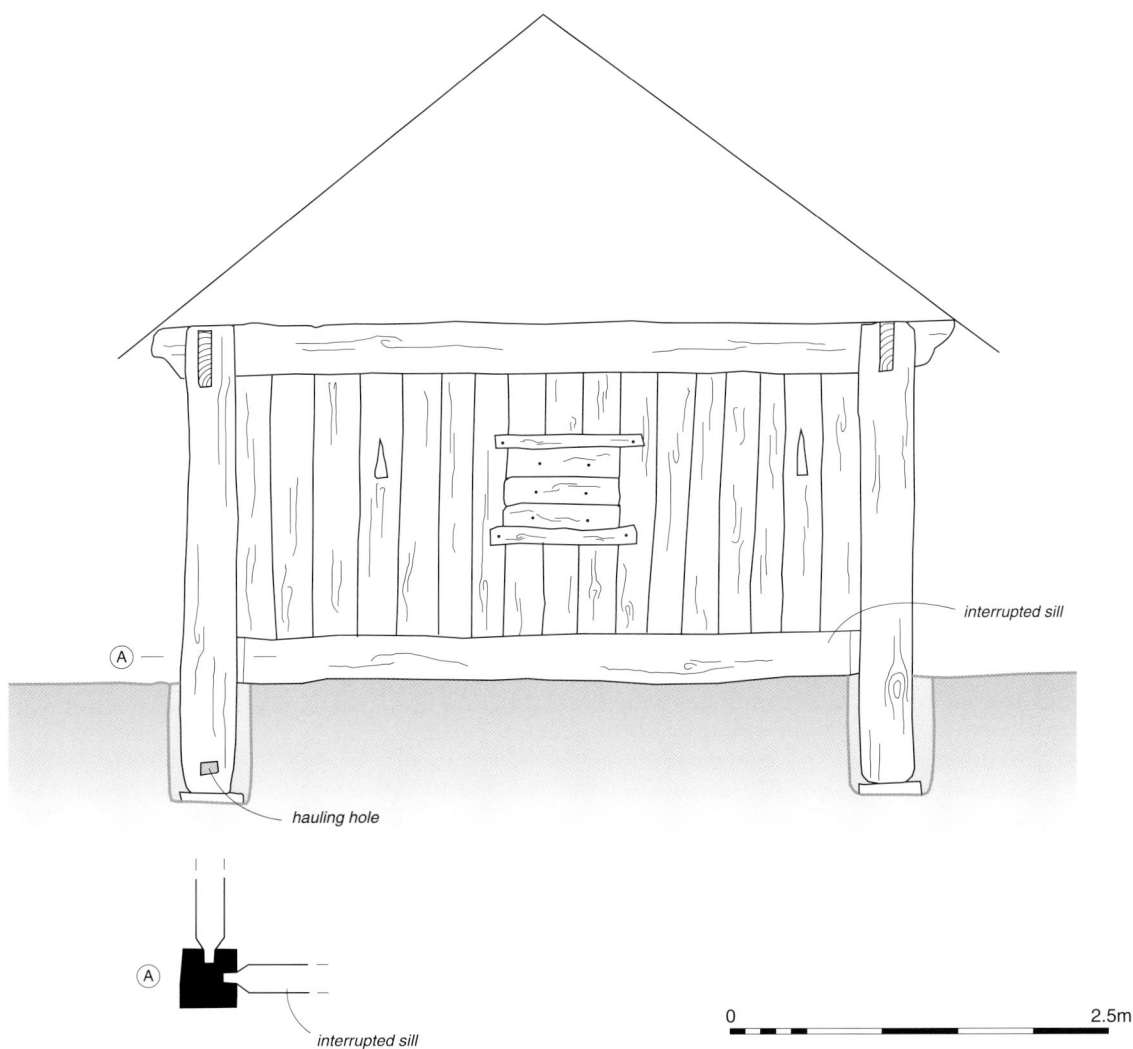

Fig. 4.19 Interpretation of a 12th-century style stave wall construction based on interrupted sill beams (end wall). Scale 1:50

type woodwork that was broadly contemporary with that found at Redcliff Street.

The majority of the items recovered from Redcliff Street date stylistically to the later part of the treewrighting period, namely the 12th to early 13th centuries. This dating has been confirmed and tightened by tree-ring analysis (Chapter 4.13).

Period 1

The stratified nature of the deposits encountered makes it difficult to assess the groundplan of the fragmentary structures that survived. Only the rear walls of timber buildings were preserved, their frontages lying beyond the western limit of the excavations.

Nos 16/17 Redcliff Street
Post pit 3124 contained decayed stake 3126 and small, radially-cleft pale fragment 3127, possibly the remains of a lightly built wall whilst posthole 3084 included a stone slab postpad sitting on a thin board 280mm long, 180mm wide and 4mm thick. The post that had occupied the hole was absent but must have had a joint or joints cut in it which required fairly careful levelling and this implies some degree of prefabrication.

The later alterations or additions to Building 1A included posthole 3021, which contained two fragmentary thin cleft-oak boards, 3020, presumably either a 'shim' to adjust the height of a post (not extant) or to spread the load of the foot of the post. Similarly, posthole 2183 contained the rotted base of a timber post sitting on a pad stone. The finding of several stone and timber pads set in postholes on this site probably indicates that levelling the axe cut tops of the major uprights was crucial to the building system in the absence of large cross cut saws which might be used today.

No. 18 Redcliff Street
Postholes 2076 and 2078 may be the corner posts for a modest rear wall of a building fronting on to Redcliff Street. The postholes were just *c.* 5m apart, a plausible building width for the period. It is possible that the gap was filled with a raised grooved sill beam for a vertically planked stave wall, although the postholes may be a little too small for such implied posts and instead the wall may have been of light wattle and daub construction, not founded deep enough to have left a trace.

Rebuilding at Nos 17, 18 and 18a Redcliff Street
Postpads 2049 and 2055 have centres *c.* 4.5m apart and clearly once held substantial posts (not extant) which in this period would probably be linked by a raised sill beam supporting some form of stave wall (Fig. 4.19) (Milne 1992, 66; Herrnbrodt 1958). Any doors to the rear may have been in the side wall since posthole 2070 is potentially a relict of a door jamb, being less than 1m west of postpad 2049. The posthole still contained two vertically set oak timbers, 2072 and 3055, both worked in typical 12th-century style to roughly rectangular cross sections (Fig. 4.20). The larger timber, 2072, was *c.* 200mm wide, 140mm thick and survived to a length of 480mm. It had been box-quartered by cleaving and hewing and the axe-cut base was sloped on one side, possibly a relict of a felling cut or 'gob'. This timber may have been the main post and possible door jamb with timber 3055, a typical box-halved timber *c.* 160mm wide, 70mm thick and surviving to 400mm long, made by cleaving and hewing, being post-packing or a repair. Both timbers were made from fast-grown oak with barely 45 annual rings and so were not tree-ring sampled.

Drain 1773 at the rear of No. 17 Redcliff Street was revetted with roundwood but included at least one other phase of revetting with timber boards (Fig. 3.5). Most of the stakes were of small roundwood with bark on and the weave used was a simple plain in and out of single rods at a time. Many samples of the stakes were taken and found to have been of hazel, holly and fruitwood (Chapter 5.3) which are likely to be of local hedgerows and gardens and may reflect *ad hoc* collection by the tenant. This spread of species is typical of wattlework in medieval London, particularly in wattlework woven *in situ* such as most cess pit linings, fences and revetments (Goodburn 1998b, 136). In contrast very fine, regular wattlework, particularly portable hurdle panels, are often made of one or two species with similar sized rods of the same age (see below for pit 3175).

Fragments of an earlier board revetment survived behind the wattling stakes. Two were recovered (3001 and 3002) and were found to have been radially split oak boards 20mm to 30mm thick. Board 3001 was pierced by two redundant peg holes and was probably a piece of reused weather boarding. Fragments of similar boards were recovered under number 1772, all of which had been cleft out of a straight-grained, narrow-ringed parent tree of wildwood type. Some of the stakes used in this revetting were larger than those for the wattlework and of the two recovered items, both were small sections of cleft oak just over 50mm thick (stakes 3012 and 3013).

Small flat-bottomed post 3035 was found within the drain. It was hewn from a narrow-ringed 1/16th split section of oak and survived to 300mm length, 180mm width and 110mm thickness. Traces of an old peg hole could be seen on the axe-cut bottom. This timber is typical of posts used in earth-fast, post and wattle buildings of the Saxon period to the early 13th century (Goodburn 2007, 312). Posthole 3137, also within the drain, included stakes made of cleft quarter poles of maple (3161) and a small, tangentially-cleft pale of beech (3160).

Further timber was recovered from other drains. Drain 3057 fed into drain 1773 and comprised two parallel lines of radially-cleft oak boards, set on edge. Of these, board 3057 included several features indicating

Fig. 4.20 Period 1 post base 2072 (left) and 3055 (right). Scale 0.3m

that it originated as a plank on a clinker boat. One edge included six holes, probably originally to hold iron rivets or wooden pegs to fasten its edge to an adjacent boat board. The reuse of boards from medieval clinker-built vessels in port towns is widely recorded (Goodburn 1991; Marsden 1996; McGrail 1993). Drain 3044 was of similar construction and also fed into drain 1773. It survived as fragments of radially-cleft oak boards set on edge and held upright by stakes made of cleft quarter poles of oak. The boards were *c.* 20mm thick and survived up to 180mm wide and 1.84m long. Drain 2137 fed into drain 1773 from the north and contained small fragments of cleft oak board lining 2136 and a cleft oak batten, 2135, 430mm long, 110mm wide and 40mm thick, pierced by two peg holes *c.* 23mm in diameter. This timber may have originally been part of a door ledge or window shutter.

A line of three posts were found to the rear of the building at No. 17 Redcliff Street (posts 1874, 1876 and 1877). Post 1874 was hewn to a wedge-shaped cross section with an axe-cut flat base. It had been made from a 1/8th log section of fairly slow-grown oak and survived to 400mm length, 230mm width and 110mm thickness and is typical of earth-fast building posts of the Saxo-Norman period (Goodburn 2007, 311). The same details apply to cleft oak post 1876 which survived to 310mm length, 190mm width and 115mm thickness. One of its wider faces had a carved groove which could have held wattle or board ends in the simple jointing of the treewrighting period (Fig. 4.21). Together these timbers provided a felling date range of *c.* 1174–1201.

Two building-sized postholes, 2103 and 2106, were found along the boundary between Nos 18 and 18a Redcliff Street. Posthole 2106 contained a typical mid to later 12th-century earth-fast post, 2104. This was axe-hewn to a rectangular boxed heart section and the original end was cross-cut with an axe rather than sawn. It survived to a 410mm length and a width of 305mm by 200mm. Although weathered and split, clear axe marks and a hole near the base survived (Fig. 4.22). The sapwood survived on the edges of the timber enabling a tree-ring felling date range of 1150–1160 to be determined. The hole through the base was *c.* 100mm by 70mm and was clearly roughly cut with a narrow-

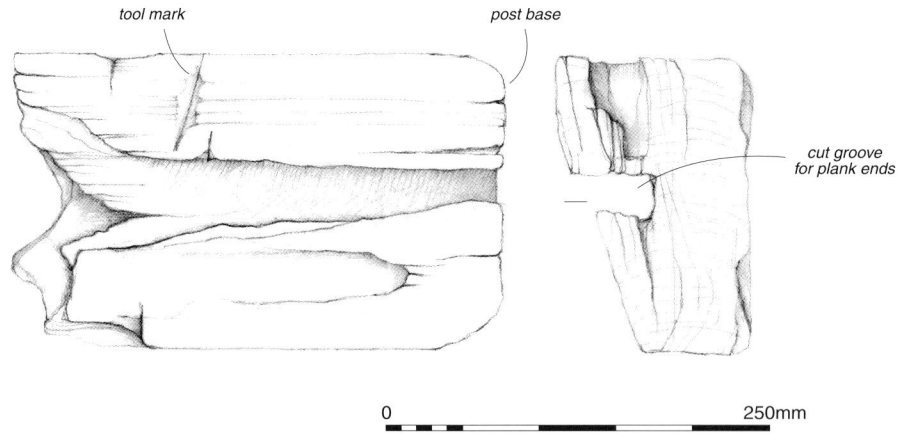

Fig. 4.21 Period 1 grooved oak building timber 1876 with felling date of 1176–1201. Scale 1:5

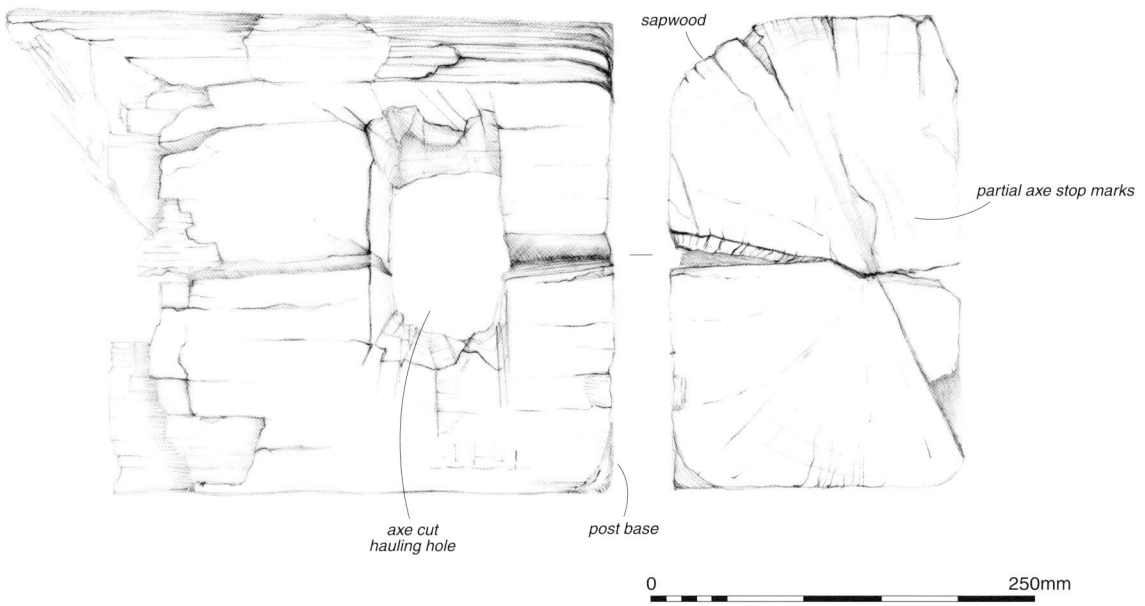

Fig. 4.22 Period 1 oak post base 2104 with axe-cut end and hauling hole. Felled 1150–60. Scale 1:5

bladed axe, probably to accommodate a rope during haulage from the felling site (Fig. 4.23).

Pits

Many of the pits contained fragments of wattle work or thin cleft oak boards. Part of the lining of pit 2130 at Nos 12–15 Redcliff Street survived as a radially-cleft oak board (2125) retained on edge by small cleft oak and oak roundwood stakes. The stakes survived as axe cut tips only, but the board was comparatively intact, surviving to 1.64m length, 260mm width and 15mm thickness, and was clearly reused. It was pierced by two small iron nails and had a square cut-out in one end and probably originated as a building weather board. The board was a fine cleft section, either a 1/32nd or even 1/64th from a distinctive slow-grown, straight-grained oak, the parent tree of which would have been at least 0.8m in diameter and probably around 200 years old. Such timber derives from the high dark woodland remnants of the last wildwood.

Fill 3175 of pit 3173 at No. 17 Redcliff Street included an unusual wattlework and post structure (Fig. 3.6) comprising two wattle lines, joined at right angles around post 3273, dividing the pit into two. The post survived to 790mm long, 120mm width and 95mm thickness and was hewn from a cleft quarter section oak which was fast grown with insufficient annual rings for tree-ring dating. The wattlework was very fine, comprising small rods with weavers of 15–20mm diameter, and probably derived from intensively

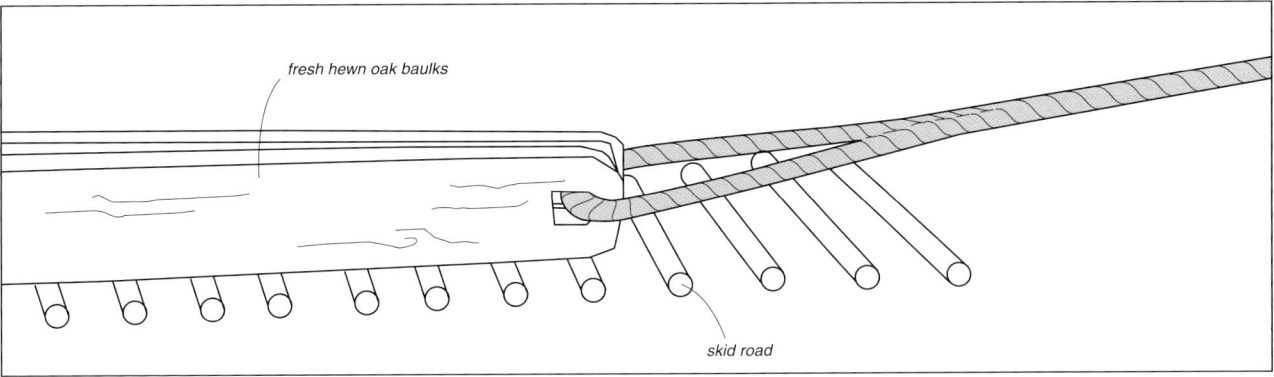

Fig. 4.23 Interpretation of hauling timbers using oxen

managed coppiced woodland. Microscopic study of sub samples of the wattlework showed that it was mostly hazel with a little ash and maple (Chapter 5.3). Tree-ring counting confirmed that the hazel had been cut at three seasons' growth and this is common in ancient wattlework whereas the recent tradition commonly uses much older hazel rods (Goodburn 2007, 303). The ash and maple weavers were a little older at five to seven years. The uprights or stakes were also mainly hazel, with some ash and maple ranging in age from c. 6–12 years and being 20mm to 30mm in diameter. The ends of nearly all the weavers and stakes were cut to 'chisel' points with a bill hook or small axe.

Pit 1860, also at No. 17, contained wooden lining 1904 comprising small, radially-cleft boards held on edge by closely set stakes that were a mixture of roundwood and cleft oak. The best-preserved section of lining board was in several fragments but when rejoined had the proportions of a roof shingle, 380mm long, 100mm wide and 10mm thick. The thinning of the ends also suggested a roof shingle origin. Pit 1848 at No. 17 contained fragments of thin oak boards and a roughly-trimmed half pole of ash full of woodworm, showing that it derived from an above-ground location.

Pit 3188 at No. 18 Redcliff Street contained an oak board fragment within its lower fill (3187) which provided a felling date range of 1288–1313. Also at No. 18 part of a coopered vessel was recovered from fill 3219 of pit 3217; it returned a tree-ring felling date of 1152–77. Pit 3157 at No. 18a was apparently wattle lined and included the remains of two radially-cleft oak stakes, 3231 and 3232, at the base, the former straight with a square cross section, the latter rather crooked.

Two fragmentary sections of wattlework were found within pit fills 3038 and 3128 (pits 3066 and 3149 respectively), both at No. 17 Redcliff Street (Fig. 3.3). As the wattlework was horizontal it was probably not part of the pit linings but may have been used to cover recent backfills. Wattlework 3128 was finely made and probably part of a portable, professionally made hurdle, although not sufficiently well preserved to determine species.

Some smaller wooden objects were also found within the pit fills. Pit 2123 at No. 16 Redcliff Street contained a small section of neatly shaved yew roundwood within fill 2141, part of a handle or staff. Pit 1932 at No. 17 included fill 3215 which contained a beech container and lid (Fig. 4.24).

Catalogue of illustrated wooden object (Fig. 4.24)

1. Lathe-turned beechwood container and lid. The fragmentary body of the vessel (now distorted: Fig.4.24 B) was cylindrical with deep rebate for lid. Diameter of lid 64–68mm; depth (lid) 24mm. Period 1 pit 1932 (fill 3215).

Period 2a

Timber 2113 was recovered from fill 1821 of well 1822 at No. 17 Redcliff Street (Fig. 4.25) and comprised a radially-cleft and hewn plank 0.86m long, 180mm wide and 60mm thick, probably made from a 1/16th section. It was solid enough for structural use but has no obvious function. One end was axe-cut at roughly 90°, the other was formed into a point and pierced by three 20mm holes. It was made from slow-grown oak, with a tree-ring felling date range of 1229–54.

Period 2b

Timber 1741 was built into the masonry wall of cistern 1604 at No. 17 Redcliff Street. The timber was hewn to a rectangular cross section from half a log and survived to 650mm length, 245mm width and 110mm thickness. The timber would appear to have been reused given its felling date of 1178–1203 and is typical of larger earth-fast posts used in Saxo-Norman buildings. Timber 1726 was found within backfill 1711 of cistern 1604 and was the tenoned end of an 80mm-wide oak beam, which had been crudely cut off with an axe, leaving axe marks 75mm wide. It may well be debris from the demolition of local timber buildings. The form of the tenon with its neat shoulder is typical of the mortise and tenon jointing of later medieval carpentry.

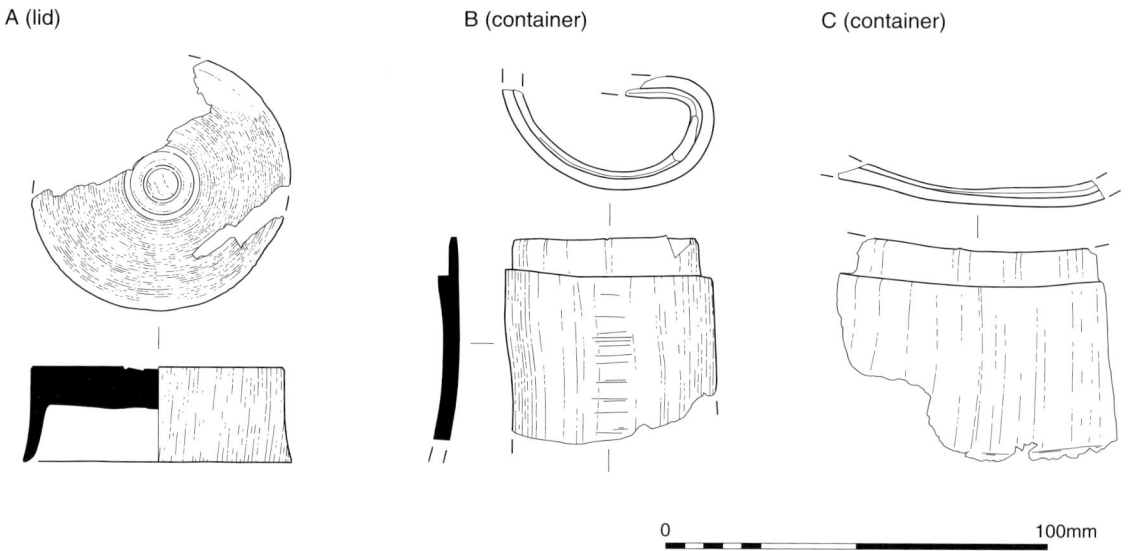

Fig. 4.24 Beechwood lidded container from Period 1 pit 1932. Scale 1:2

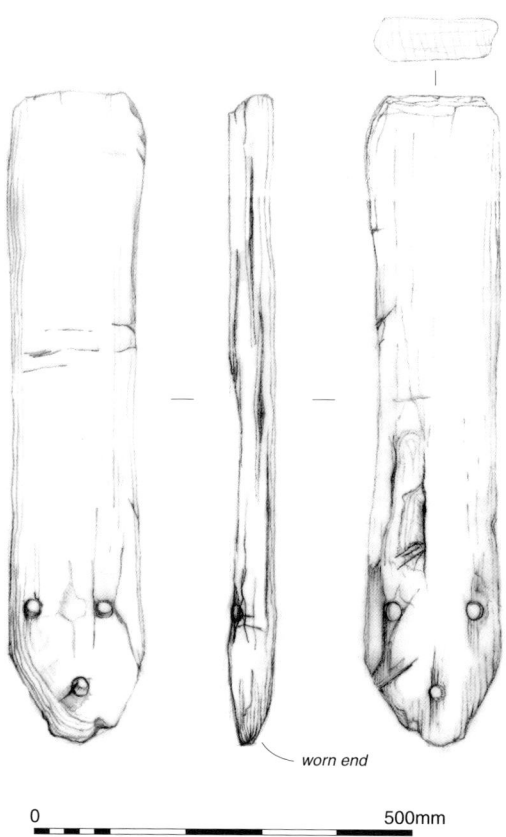

Fig. 4.25 Timber 2113, felled 1229–54, from Period 2a well 1822. Scale 1:10

Period 3

Timber 1537 was a radially-cleft oak plank reused in the floor of furnace 1530 at No. 17 Redcliff Street. It survived to 610mm long, 170mm wide and 24mm thick and was hewn from a 1/32nd cleft section of oak. Both ends were axe-cut and it had several relict features, comprising three nail holes, a 32mm-diameter peg hole and an irregular lap joint. It was probably reused more than once and its original function is unclear. The timber used was moderately slow grown and was tree-ring matched to a felling date range of 1268–93, and would seem to be a rare example of the very long term reuse of material, possibly boarding from a demolished medieval timber building.

In the party wall of Building 3A at No. 18a Redcliff Street two wooden posts were found beneath wall 1517. Of these, post 2101 overlaid a horizontal, beam off-cut of oak 2100 which presumably acted as a postpad. The axe used on post 2101 gave its clear negative blade imprint in the oak end grain 140mm wide and slightly curved. Post 2101 survived to 570mm long, and was 330mm by 250mm. This timber was tree-ring sampled and gave a felling date range of 1510–1535. Beam off-cut 2100 was 0.62m long by 280mm by 150mm with one end rather roughly axe cross-cut. It was very fast grown with barely 45 annual rings, so was not tree-ring sampled.

At No. 16 Redcliff Street a small lap-jointed piece of oak (1406) was recovered from ashy layer 1429 within furnace 1426. It included a halving joint cut on one face and faint traces of red pigment, and may have been part of a small piece of furniture or machinery.

Assorted small woodwork fragments of note

Small non-structural items of worked wood were found and retained from 49 deposits. Most of this material dates to Period 1 or later and was typically eroded and residual. Brief notes were made on relevant context sheets which are part of the site archive, but here only a few comments are relevant. Typical material included small abraded oak (occasionally beech) chips, one or two roundwood cut ends, twig fragments and small fragments of cleft oak boards.

Discussion

The waterlogged woodwork has provided evidence of the general forms of two types of structures built on the site, buildings and pit linings. The work has also added to the dated corpus of treewright's work during the 12th-century expansion of Bristol. There are two areas which have had the greatest light shed on them, the logistics of timber supply, briefly drawn together here and the closely linked subject of woodland management ('woodmanship').

For any solid structural work the species chosen was predominantly the two native oaks and their hybrids, here simply 'oak', and a little ash and beech. The great weight of the fresh oak is compensated for by its ease of working when green and both factors and a need for timely use of the material resulted in a tendency to work logs of any size where they were felled. Once a tree was felled it was then debranched ('snedded') and cross cut ('bucked') into logs of the desired length and shape.

The evidence from Redcliff Street demonstrates that some of the largest logs, weighing as much as 1 tonne per metre, were divided lengthways by cleaving into boards. The heavier structural timbers were often hewn to roughly rectangular beam sections from whole or cleft half logs. The largest of these might have weighed as much as a tonne and even the more moderate timbers were many hundreds of kilograms. Holes cut through the ends of the beams may have been to facilitate the moving of these heavy timbers (Figs 4.22–4.23). The rectangular cross section of most of the beams may suggest that they were moved in pairs or more, so as to prevent them toppling over (Fig. 4.23). They would probably have been hauled using animals to barges for delivery to the port with the minimum use of expensive road transport.

The axe-cut notch in post timber 2104 of Period 1 is exactly matched in similar oak post bases and beam timbers of mid to late 12th-century date found at two other recent Bristol excavations at Cabot Circus and Finzel's Reach (Goodburn 2013; 2008). A similar approach to hauling timber but using axe-cut notches through the corners has also been seen in the ends of some heavy Roman oak baulks excavated in London at Regis House and other sites (Goodburn 1998b). Despite the larger corpus of woodworking evidence this feature has not been found in 12th-century woodwork in London. Therefore, it seems likely that the occurrence of this feature on a number of sites in Bristol suggests that an organised, large-scale, timber-supply technology was in operation in the mid to late 12th century.

Evidence for the use of wildwood resources and managed woodland

The 12th and 13th centuries have been highlighted as the period of most dramatic change in treeland types with the last of the wildwood being converted into managed woodland of various forms (Rackham 1976, 49). From the late 1980s detailed archaeological work in London has continued to shed new light on the nature of the wildwood and various forms of managed treeland in the London hinterland of this period (Goodburn 1992; 1998a; 2007, 302). The evidence from Redcliff Street and other recent excavations in Bristol will contribute to the less well-advanced study of this subject in the South West.

Many small fragments of oak boards and pales of narrow-ringed, straight-grained oak together with a few larger sections of radially split boards, e.g. 2125, and cleft building posts such as 1876 have narrow rings (2mm wide or less), a straight grain and implied large diameter (*c.* 0.8–1.2m) that are typical features of mature wildwood-type timber from temperate zones (Peterken 1996). This suggests areas where large, narrow-ringed oaks over *c.* 180 years old, grew in the hinterland of the port (Fig. 4.26). This material was a key commodity of later medieval trade and could be transported over long distances, and the Redcliff Street timbers may have been sourced further afield, such as Ireland.

The rectangular section building posts such as 2104 seem to have predominantly come from smaller diameter oaks growing for less than *c.* 90 years before felling. The ring widths varied but were generally moderate (average width *c.* 2.5mm–*c.* 4mm), and a parent tree for a post like 2104 would have been *c.* 0.4m diameter at breast height and fairly straight. Such parent trees would be typical of either managed woodland using coppice with standard timber trees or possibly regrowth in areas of felled wildwood (Fig. 4.26).

Finally, the small roundwood found as the remains of stakes and weavers of wattlework in pit and drain linings provides evidence of very different treeland, most probably very close to Bristol itself due to the bulkiness and lower value of small roundwood. Here it suffices to note that intensively managed hazel coppice was clearly harvested regularly in the hinterland. Also, it was cut at the young age of three years for some purposes, e.g. the lining for Period 1 pit 3173 (Fig. 3.6). However, much of the other wattlework found and sampled was made of more mixed species including holly, ash, hazel, fruitwoods and a little maple. These species might well derive from hedgerows, branch loppings from larger trees and even orchard prunings. The holly typically grows as understorey in oak woodland on acid soils and may have been cut for stakes as it has surprising strength and durability outdoors (author's personal observations).

In sum, the evidence recorded at Redcliff Street shows that from the mid 12th to 13th centuries wildwood-type

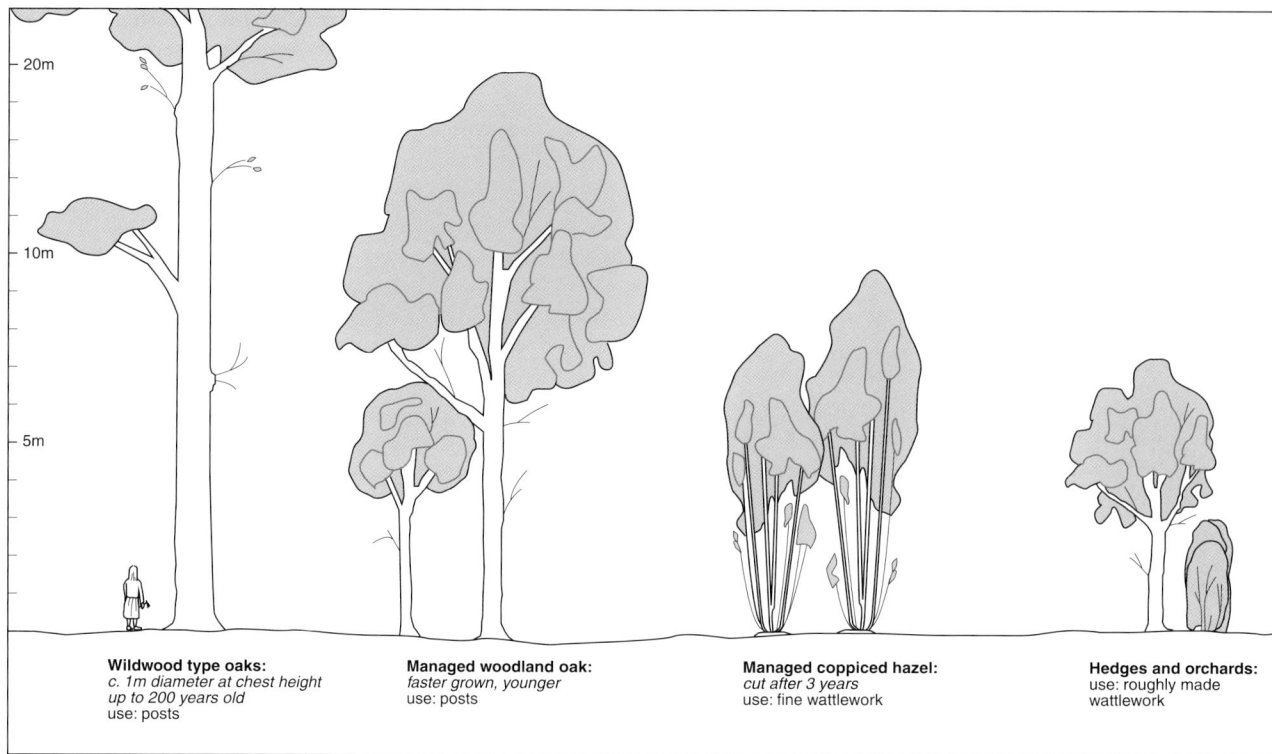

Fig. 4.26 Woodscape of parent trees for 11th to 13th-century timbers and roundwood

woodland was harvested in the hinterland, alongside timber and roundwood from more open settings such as managed coppiced woodland and hedgerows. The wildwood-type oaks are likely to have been growing in areas like the Forest of Dean and some might even have been Irish. Some of the coppice was managed on much shorter rotations than is typical today of only three years. This is broadly in keeping with the evidence from two other recent Bristol excavations at Cabot Circus and Finzel's Reach (Goodburn 2013; 2008). The evidence from this site has helped to provide extra details extending initial information recorded for the presence of the last of the wildwood in the South West in Gloucester Priory roof (Rackham 1976, 65).

4.13 Tree-Ring Analysis of Timbers
A.J. Arnold and R.E. Howard

A total of 19 separate samples of slices or sections of wet or waterlogged timbers was submitted to the Nottingham Tree-ring Dating Laboratory. Of these, 17 samples were of oak, and two of other tree species. The latter two were considered too unreliable for tree-ring dating and were not subject to further analysis.

Tree-ring dating

Trees grow by adding one, and only one, growth-ring to their circumference each, and every, year. Each new annual growth-ring is added to the outside of the previous year's growth just below the bark. The width of this annual growth-ring is largely, though not exclusively, determined by the weather conditions during the growth period (roughly March–September). In general, good conditions produce wider rings and poor conditions produce narrower rings. Thus, over the lifetime of a tree, the annual growth-rings display a climatically influenced pattern. Furthermore, and importantly, all trees growing in the same area at the same time will be influenced by the same growing conditions and the annual growth-rings of all of them will respond in a similar, though not identical, way.

The pattern of a short period of growth, 20, 30 or even 40 consecutive years, might conceivably be repeated two or even three times in the last one thousand years. A short pattern might also be repeated at different time periods in different parts of the country because of differences in regional micro-climates. It is less likely, however, that such problems would occur with the pattern of a longer period of growth, that is, anything in excess of 54 years or so. In essence, a short period of growth, anything less than 54 rings, is not reliable, and the longer the period of time under comparison the better.

Methodology

All samples sent to the Laboratory were frozen to consolidate them. The larger sections were reduced to multiple smaller cross-sectional radii samples. All the samples were either surformed, planed, or scalped to clearly show the ring sequences. The widths of the annual growth-rings of the 17 samples were measured to a tolerance of 1/100 of a millimetre. The growth patterns of these samples were then compared with a series of reference patterns or chronologies, the date of each ring of which is known. When the growth-ring sequence of a sample 'cross-matched' repeatedly at the same date span against a series of different relevant reference chronologies the sample could be dated. The degree of cross-matching, that is the measure of similarity between sample and reference, is denoted by a 't-value'; the higher the value the greater the similarity. The greater the similarity the greater is the probability that the patterns of samples and references have been produced by growing under the same conditions at the same time. The statistically accepted fully reliable minimum t-value is 3.5.

When samples derived from the same archaeological period cross-matched with each other, they were combined at their matching positions to form a 'site chronology'. This had the effect of reducing the anomalies of any one individual (brought about in the case of tree-rings by some non-climatic influence) and enhanced the overall climatic signal. The greater the number of samples in a site chronology the greater is the climatic signal of the group and the weaker is the non-climatic input of any one individual. Combining samples in this way to make a site chronology usually has the effect of increasing the time-span that is under comparison; the longer the period of growth under consideration, the greater the certainty of the cross-match.

Having obtained a date for the site chronology as a whole, the date spans of the constituent individual samples were found, and from this the felling date of the trees represented was calculated. Where a sample retained the outermost ring produced by the tree before it was cut (i.e. complete sapwood), the felling date of the tree was calculated. Where the sapwood was not complete the likely felling date of the tree was estimated. Such an estimate could be made with a high degree of reliability because oak trees generally have between 15 to 40 sapwood rings.

Analysis

The annual growth-ring widths of the 17 samples were measured, multiple readings of different radii often being made. Details of the samples are given in Table 4.14. For one reason or another, it was not always possible to measure all the rings present on a sample and where this occurs some estimation of the number of unmeasured rings is given (this may be seen with sample 2125 where the first or inner-most 150 rings are measured but a section of outer rings are too compacted to distinguish one ring from another and are un-measurable). Where the ring sequence of a sample was dated the first and last measured ring dates are given, along with the date of the heartwood/sapwood boundary ring if this was included within the measured portion of the sample. The table also shows an estimation of the likely felling date range of the timber.

The data analysis produced two separate groups of cross-matching samples comprising four samples (1741, 1874, 3035, and 3219) and two samples (1876 and 2104). The samples of each group were combined at their indicated offset positions to form site chronologies SQ01 and SQ02, with combined overall lengths of 107 and 96 rings respectively. Each site chronology was compared to an extensive corpus of reference data for oak. This indicated consistent and repeated cross-matches against a high number of these when the dates of the first and last ring of each site chronology are 1057–1163 and 1066–1161 respectively. The evidence for this dating is given in the t-values of Tables 4.15–4.16 where a small selection of the best cross-matches is given.

The two site chronologies SQ01 and SQ02 were compared against the remaining 11 measured but ungrouped samples, but there was no further satisfactory cross-matching. Each of the 11 measured but ungrouped samples was compared individually against the full corpus of reference data, this indicated cross-matches and dates for five of these 11 samples, 1537, 2010, 2101, 2113, and 3187. The evidence for the dating of these five individual samples is given in the t-values of Tables 4.17–4.21. Six of the 17 measured samples remain both ungrouped and undated.

Interpretation

Amongst the 11 grouped and dated samples shown in Table 4.14 the earliest material probably dates to the middle part of the 12th century, with a further group of timbers being felled in the later 12th or possibly the very early 13th century. A few other timbers appear to have different felling dates ranging from the early to mid 13th century to the late 13th century, and possibly into the early 14th century. Another timber has a felling date in the earlier part of the 16th century, and a final timber from the later 16th century onwards. As such the tree-ring dates obtained here appear to correspond closely with the other archaeological evidence from the site.

Six samples remain ungrouped and undated (1770, 2125, 2135, 2136, 3002, 3232). All but 3232 (which has only 52 rings) have sufficient rings for reliable analysis and none show any particular problems such as compaction or distortion in their measured ring sections, which might hinder analysis. As more data is accumulated from Bristol and the surrounding area (the likely source of the undated timbers), further matches could be achieved with the undated material from this site.

It may be of interest to note that, although the exact location of the woodland sources of the trees utilised for the timbers found at Redcliff Street cannot be determined precisely through tree-ring analysis, they

Table 4.14 Dated tree-ring samples listed in potential felling date order

Sample no.	Sample type and context	Sapwood rings	Last ring date	Comments
2010	Post. Not found *in situ*	none	1551	Unlikely to be felled before 1576
2101	Post pile for Building 3A	3	1498	Felled 1510–35 (this is assumed to be an intrusive pile post associated with Period 3 construction)
3187	1st fill pit 3188	h/s	1273	Felled 1288–1313
1537	Beaten earth floor of furnace 1530	possible h/s	1253	Possibly felled 1268–93
2113	Plank/post within fill 1821 of well 1822	h/s	1214	Felled 1229–54
1741	Wooden stake built into side of stone tank/cistern 1604	h/s	1163	Felled 1178–1203
1876	Wooden lining of pit 1860	possible h/s	1161	Possibly felled 1176–1201
1874	Wooden lining pit 1848	possible h/s	1159	Possibly felled 1174–99
3035	Part of wooden lining of drain 1773	none	1160	Unlikely to be felled before 1175
3219	Possible wooden lining of tanning/dye pit 3217	h/s	1137	Felled 1152–77
2104	Post within Period 1 posthole 2106	15	1145	Sapwood near complete. Felled 1150–60?

* h/s = heartwood/sapwood boundary

are likely to have been of at least regional origin. As may be seen from Tables 4.15–4.21, which list the reference chronologies with which the two site chronologies and the various individual samples from Redcliff Street have been matched, some high *t*-values (i.e. the greatest degrees of similarity) are found with material made up of data from other western or south-west sites. It would appear, however, that although some of the timbers do have overlapping date spans, none of the trees represented by this analysis were growing close to each other in the same wood, or, indeed, appear even to have been growing in adjacent woodlands.

Table 4.15 Results of the cross-matching of site sequence BRCASQ01 when first ring date is 1057 and last ring date is 1163

Reference chronology	Span of chronology	*t*-value	*t*-value
East Midlands Master Chronology	882–1981	8.4	Laxton and Litton 1988
Gloucester Blackfriars, Gloucester	1024–1237	8.4	Howard *et al.* 2002
Chapter House & Deanery, Brecon Cathedral	996–1227	6.6	Howard *et al.* 1994
Stokesay Castle, Shrops.	1046–1289	6.5	Miles and Worthington 1997
Bristol, Dundas Wharf	770–1202	6.4	Nicholson and Hillam 1987
Hansacre Hall, Staffs	965–1279	6.0	Esling *et al.* 1990

Table 4.16 Results of the cross-matching of site sequence BRCASQ02 when first ring date is 1066 and last ring date is 1161

Reference chronology	Span of chronology	*t*-value	*t*-value
Gloucester Blackfriars, Gloucester	1024–1237	5.8	Howard *et al.* 2002
Medbourne Manor, Leics	1068–1287	5.8	Howard *et al.* 1999
Chapter House & Deanery, Brecon Cathedral	996–1227	4.8	Howard *et al.* 1994
Sandwell Priory, West Midlands	1002–1209	4.5	Howard *et al.* 1986
England Master Chronology	401–1981	4.4	Baillie and Pilcher 1982
Bristol, Dundas Wharf	770–1202	4.0	Nicholson and Hillam 1987

Table 4.17 Results of the cross-matching of sample BRCA2113 when first ring date is 1129 and last ring date is 1214

Reference chronology	Span of chronology	t-value	t-value
Naas House, Lydney, Glos	1127–1229	6.5	Howard *et al.* 1998
Bristol Bridge, Bristol	1032–1239	5.9	Hillam 1984
Hansacre Hall, Staffs	965–1279	5.8	Esling *et al.* 1990
St John's Hospital, Cirencester, Glos	1091–1201	5.3	Arnold and Howard 2007
Salisbury Cathedral, Wilts	1119–1241	5.2	Howard *et al.* 1996a
Chapter House & Deanery, Brecon Cathedral	996–1227	4.8	Howard *et al.* 1994

Table 4.18 Results of the cross-matching of sample BRCA1537 when first ring date is 1168 and last ring date is 1253

Reference chronology	Span of chronology	t-value	t-value
Stokesay Castle, Shrops	1046–1289	6.0	Miles and Worthington 1997
Quaintree House, Braunston, Leics	1165–1305	5.4	Alcock *et al.* 1991b
Southern England Master Chronology	1083–1981	5.3	Bridge 1988
186/7 Horniglow St, Burton upon Trent, Staffs	1101–1345	5.2	Howard *et al.* 1995
Medbourne Manor, Leics	1068–1287	5.0	Howard *et al.* 1999
East Midlands Master Chronology	882–1981	5.0	Laxton and Litton 1988

Table 4.19 Results of the cross-matching of sample BRCA3187 when first ring date is 1169 and last ring date is 1273

Reference chronology	Span of chronology	t-value	t-value
Salisbury Cathedral, Wilts	1119–1241	5.9	Howard *et al.* 1996a
7–9 Stourport Road, Bewdley, Worcs	1060–1301	5.5	Arnold *et al.* 2005
Naas House, Lydney, Glos	1127–1229	5.3	Howard *et al.* 1998
Exeter Cathedral, Devon	1132–1337	5.1	Arnold *et al.* 2003
Gloucester Blackfriars, Gloucester	1024–1237	4.8	Howard *et al.* 2002
Southern England Master Chronology	1083–1981	4.5	Bridge 1988

Table 4.20 Results of the cross-matching of sample BRCA2101 when first ring date is 1424 and last ring date is 1498

Reference chronology	Span of chronology	t-value	t-value
Isaac Lord, Ipswich, Suffolk	1420–1635	5.4	Bridge 1999
St Andrew's Church, Ford, W. Sussex	1286–1511	4.9	Bridge 2000
Barbican/Gatehouse, Warwick Castle	1310–1503	4.9	Howard 1995
Broughton Hall, Northants	1355–1509	4.6	Meirion-Jones *et al.* 1987
Gloucester Blackfriars, Gloucester	1412–1520	4.4	Howard *et al.* 2002
England, London	413–1728	4.3	Tyers and Groves 1999

Table 4.21 Results of the cross-matching of sample BRCA2010 when first ring date is 1479 and last ring date is 1551

Reference chronology	Span of chronology	t-value	t-value
Lodge Farm, Hollington, Derbys	1468–1600	6.0	Howard *et al.* 1996b
Walton-on-Wolds, Leics	1400–1580	5.6	Howard *et al.* 1992
Gotham Manor, Notts	1391–1590	5.4	Howard *et al.* 1991
Coates' Barn, Cosby, Leics	1473–1556	5.0	Alcock *et al.* 1991a
East Midlands Master Chronology	882–1981	4.9	Laxton and Litton 1988
Keyworth barn, Notts	1465–1628	4.5	Laxton *et al.* 1984

Chapter 5
Biological Evidence

5.1 Animal Bone
Sylvia Warman

Animal bone totalling 5910 fragments from 5679 bones weighing 114kg was hand recovered. An additional 4237 bone fragments from 4096 bones weighing 1.6kg were recovered from processed samples. The animal bone assemblage was derived from 384 excavated deposits ranging in date from medieval to modern. The entire assemblage was assessed for its significance and potential for future analysis (Warman 2010). The assessment concluded that much of the material from Periods 3 and 4 (early 15th to late 19th centuries) derived from make-up layers and features cutting earlier deposits, and therefore a high level of residuality can be assumed. Consequently full analysis of this material was not undertaken as the results could not be reliably linked to contemporaneous activity. The following analysis focuses on the assemblage from early 12th to early 15th-century deposits (Periods 1–2c) which comprised 1581 fragments from 1456 bones weighing 50kg. A summary of the assemblage from Periods 3 and 4 is provided. Data on these groups and the modern material, which was also assessed, can be found in the archive.

Methodology

Period 1 and 2 assemblages
The animal bone data recorded included weight; species; element; parts present (using Dobney and Rielly 1988); size; sex; fusion of long bones for ageing estimates (following Silver 1969); tooth wear for age estimates (following Grant 1982); pathology; butchery; burning and weathering (following Behrensmeyer 1978). Whole long bones were measured following the dimensions defined by von den Driesch (1976) to enable the calculation of withers heights in cattle and sheep, using the factors of Fock (1966) and Teichert (1975). The numbers of animals of each species represented by the assemblage were estimated using MNI (minimum number of individuals) calculations. The NISP (number of identified specimens) was calculated, and used to aid comparison with other published assemblages. Sheep and goat were distinguished wherever possible using the criteria of Boessneck (1969).

Period 3 and 4 assemblages
Information recorded for the purposes of the assessment was utilised for the summary sections. Bone was recorded at context level, including number of bones; number of fragments; weight of bones in grams; number of bones identifiable to species; fragmentation and preservation; numbers of mandibles, epiphyses and whole bones; species and body parts present; age and state (including modifications such as butchery, burning, gnawing, etc.).

Results

Period 1 (early 12th to mid 13th centuries) (Table 5.1)
Deposits dated to Period 1 produced over 1,000 identifiable specimens of mammal and bird bone from a range of species. The main domestic species, namely cattle (*Bos taurus*), ovicaprids (sheep and/or goat) (*Ovis aries et/siva Capra hircus*) and pig (*Sus* sp.) were present in large quantities, reflected in the NISP values and weight of bones. Horse (*Equus caballus*), dog (*Canis familiaris*), cat (*Felis catus*), rabbit (*Oryctolagus cuniculus*) and rat (*Rattus* sp.) were present in much smaller quantities. Domestic fowl (*Gallus gallus*) and domestic goose (*Anser anser*) were also present. A small quantity of duck bones (*Anas platyrhynchos*) was present, their small size suggesting these were from wild rather than domestic birds. Three other wild species were identified: fallow deer (*Dama dama*), as metacarpals from fill 1925 of pit 3300, and from fill 3018 of posthole 3021, both deposits at No. 17; part of a wing of a common buzzard (*Buteo buteo*), and 13 bones identified as crow (*Corvus* sp.).

The animal bones were very well preserved, often stained mid to dark brown in colour, smooth and rarely weathered. Damage by dog gnawing and burning was

Table 5.1 Animal bone from Period 1 deposits by species

Species	Number of fragments	Weight in grams	Number of bones (NISP)	Minimum number of individuals (MNI)
horse	3	369.00	3	1
cattle	403	27302.25	391	46
sheep	91	2552.00	83	9
goat	13	717.00	12	10
sheep/goat	342	5348.10	325	n/a
pig	106	2398.90	95	8
fallow deer	1	50.00	1	1
dog	3	59.00	3	1
cat	6	10.90	5	2
rabbit	1	2.00	1	1
rat	5	1.40	5	1
goose	59	281.20	53	5
duck	5	8.80	5	2
chicken	46	94.50	46	4
crow	13	12.88	12	1
buzzard	2	3.70	2	1
Totals	**1099**	**39211.63**	**1042**	

rare. The assemblage was, it seems, deposited rapidly and remained in a stable environment until excavation. A fragment of cattle horn sheath was recovered from fill 3235 of pit 3236. Horn does not usually survive in archaeological deposits unless desiccated or waterlogged; in this case, it was the latter.

The assemblage was recovered from a range of features including pits, postholes, beam slots and occupation layers. The animal bone appears to be waste from a variety of activities including butchery, domestic waste and the processing of animal products for bone and horn working.

The main domestic mammals (cattle, ovicaprids and pigs) present in larger quantities include a range of body parts, and this pattern is seen across feature types. Cattle, goat and sheep show a bias towards skull and horncore fragments, which, taken with the butchery marks on these elements, is consistent with their use for hornering. Other activities which could produce similar assemblages include tanning, however the low numbers of foot bones from these species seem to preclude that interpretation. Meat-bearing limb bones from cattle ovicaprids and pig are also present within the assemblage. Some show evidence for butchery, including the vertical splitting of long bones facilitating the removal of marrow.

Age at death
Ageing of the main domestic species was carried out using both epiphyseal fusion of long bones following Silver (1969), and the eruption and wear of the mandibular teeth following Grant (1982). The cattle fusion data indicate that around three quarters survived past 2.5 years but only half survived to full skeletal maturity past 3.5 years. The information supplied by the fusion data can be supplemented by ageing data derived from the eruption and wear of the mandibular teeth which involves the calculation of mandible wear scores (MWS). The MWS scores recorded from well-preserved mandibles were: 18, 24, 24, 41, 43 and 47. This double peak of 18–24 and 41–43 suggests that the cattle comprised a group of juveniles/subadults and another group of fully mature animals which is consistent with the fusion data.

The fusion data for ovicaprids indicate that half survived beyond 2.5 years but only 10% reached full skeletal materiality. This suggests a focus on lamb rather than mutton, which could be taken as an indication of relative wealth/higher status in terms of foods consumed by the residents. The tooth wear data present a slightly different picture; a much wider range of ages is indicated by MWS scores ranging from 3 to 44. A possible explanation for this, taking into account the large numbers of skull and mandibles present, is that hides with heads and feet still attached were being imported into the city rather than just live animals of a suitable age for slaughter to provide meat. If, as the butchery evidence suggests, there was a specialism in hornering at the site, or in the waste material that found its way on to the site during the early medieval period, this would explain the bias.

The fusion data for pigs indicate that around three

quarters made it past a year old, but only 6% passed two years of age, and none reached full skeletal maturity. This is not at all unusual given that pigs were raised solely to provide meat products. The MWS for pig ranged from 11 to 31, which is generally consistent with the fusion evidence. The upper end of the range suggests that a small number of fully adult animals were present, although the majority were juvenile or subadult.

Amongst the other species present, the horse, deer, dog and rabbit were all adult specimens, whilst the cat and rat included adult, subadult and juvenile specimens. The goose, fowl and duck specimens were all adult. However the presence amongst the identified species of bird bones of juvenile specimens raises the possibility that fowl and goose were raised on site or locally. The buzzard is adult and its large size and morphology are consistent with it being a female (J. Cooper pers. comm.).

Pathology
The level of pathology in the assemblage is between 1% and 2% of the total fragment count. This is comparable to other medieval assemblages and suggests the animals represented here derived from healthy herds and flocks.

Four cattle skull fragments from Period 1 deposits show a number of small irregular perforations on the occipital bone. These anomalies, which are not uncommon in archaeological bone material, have been interpreted as a result of congenital or yoking pressure (Brothwell *et al*. 1996). More recent research has further argued that these are benign anomalies with a genetic origin (Fabiš and Thomas 2009). It is unlikely to have caused the animal pain, and may suggest that these skulls were from animals within the same population or herd.

Pathologies were also noted in ovicaprid specimens. Two mandibles exhibit dental calculus on the cheek teeth, resulting from mineralised dental plaque (Hillson 1986). Another mandible shows the early stages of periodontal disease, where the bone around the tooth sockets becomes more open in texture. This animal also shows signs of inflammation between the fourth premolar and first molar, a condition occurring when gingivitis (gum disease) becomes severe and spreads into the bone (Miles and Grigson 1990). Possible pathologies are also seen on limb bones; a radius from fill 3116 of pit 3114 at No. 18 Redcliff Street shows additional bone growth around the articulation with the ulna and humerus. This could be the result of the animal bumping the joint against a hard surface leading to a condition referred to as 'penning elbow', which occurs when sheep are kept in small enclosures. A metatarsal from pit 3087 at No. 16 exhibits enthesophytic bone growth at the proximal end of the medial side, and indicates soft tissue trauma involving the muscle attachment. This condition may develop in very active animals, possibly driven some distance to the city for slaughter.

A single pathological pig specimen was noted in the Period 1 assemblage; a tibia from the fill of drain 1773 at No. 17 had a section of the distal fibula shaft fused to it (in the pig these are two separate bones). The fusion may be the result of healing following trauma earlier in the animal's life.

A single bird bone exhibited pathology. A fowl tibia from the fill of pit 3229 at No. 18 had an area of new bone growth on the distal shaft which reflects ossification of a tendon.

Long bone measurements and wither heights calculations
A cattle metatarsal from pit 2314 at No. 17 had a length of 195mm, which gives a withers height of 1.06m. Two sheep long bones provided length measurements for use in calculating animal size; a metatarsal of 119.9mm giving a withers height of 0.54m, and a radius of 147mm giving a withers height of 0.59m. These are similar to those recorded for sheep at the Friary North area at Cabot Circus (Warman 2013, 281). A fallow deer metacarpal had a maximum length of 1.82m. Deer are not common in assemblages from Bristol and there are no published factors available for withers height calculation in this species.

Butchery
Both long bones and skulls from the main meat-producing domesticates have damage consistent with being chopped vertically. In the case of skulls, this is part of the butchery process facilitating brain removal. The long bones, including both meat-bearing elements such as the tibiae, radii and metapodials, are more likely to result from the extraction of marrow. A further possibility is the splitting up of bones into suitable blanks as raw material for bone working.

Many of the cattle skulls had been split vertically and almost all ovicaprid skulls had also been treated in this manner. A cattle frontal bone found in pit 1797 at Nos 16/17 displayed damage to the vault consistent with the animal having been pole-axed, a method of immobilisation prior to slaughter.

Evidence for hornering
The butchery process for cattle and ovicaprids included the removal, and presumably later utilisation, of the horn sheaths. For ovicaprids, this appears to have been achieved by cutting or chopping the base of the horn which leaves cut and chop marks on the horncore where it protrudes from the skull. A different method appears to have been employed for the cattle horns as a number of cores had been completely sawn through around 50–100mm along from the base. The use of a saw is interesting as they were not widely used by butchers at this time, being the preserve of craftsmen such as the horners (Serjeantson 1989). Also present in the assemblage were numerous horncore tips, comprising just the top 50mm. The recovery of these two parts

of the horncore, and the lack of the middle part, is of interest. The central section of horn sheath, the part most likely to be favoured by the horn worker, encased the section of horncore that is consistently missing from the assemblage. The reason for this is not obvious, but may suggest the waste material found on site represents only the initial stages of preparation, or that the central core was traded on for secondary use elsewhere.

Worked bone

Finished worked bone artefacts are considered in Chapter 4.4. In addition a number of sheep and ovicaprid metapodia from Period 1 deposits had small circular holes drilled in the proximal articulation. The holes are positioned centrally. One specimen found within the wood-lined drain 3044 at No. 17 additionally shows a very polished smoothed surface to the bone of the shaft, as if it has been repeatedly handled. It is not clear what item or artefact these were destined to become, but it does appear that bone working was occurring on, or near, the site.

Period 2 (late 13th to early 15th centuries) (Table 5.2)

Deposits dated to Period 2 produced over 400 identifiable specimens of mammal and bird bone from a range of species. Cattle, ovicaprids and pig were present in large quantities, reflected in the NISP values and weight of bones. Horse, dog, rabbit, unidentified leporids (hare/rabbit) (*Leporidae* sp.), and rat were present in much smaller quantities. The main domestic species showed a similar range of elements as were found in Period 1, again with a large number of skull and mandibles from cattle, sheep and goat. Pig bones also included a large number of these bones, although meat-bearing limb elements were also present. As with the bones from Period 1 contexts, this material was very well preserved, and is likely to have been deposited rapidly once it had become refuse.

The assemblage was recovered from a similar range of features as the Period 1 assemblage, although less material was recovered from occupation layers, and many of the bones were associated with waste from dyeing activities. The animal bone appears to be waste from a variety of activities including butchery, domestic waste and the processing of animal products for bone and horn working.

Butchery

Vertical chopping of long bones of domestic species was noted, including from the fill of dye vat hearth 3534 at No. 19 Redcliff Street. This results from the requirement to split the bone open for the extraction of marrow. Many skulls (cattle, sheep and goat) had also been split vertically, presumably to extract the brain. There were also many long bone shafts which had been chopped through transversely. This is likely to have resulted from the jointing process within butchery and suggests that the material includes domestic as well as primary butchery waste. Cattle limb bones were the most heavily chopped-up. This was seen to a lesser extent in ovicaprids and was all but absent in pig, suggesting the latter was subject to a very different butchery process. Cattle bones included axis and atlas which frequently showed butchery marks and may have still been attached to the skull when the carcass was divided. Cut and chop marks were rarely observed on cattle phalanges and very few complete metapodials were found. The latter appear to have been chopped in half

Table 5.2 Animal bone from Period 2 deposits by species

Species	Number of fragments	Weight in grams	Number of bones (NISP)	Minimum number of individuals (MNI)
horse	1	532.00	1	1
cattle	184	5662.20	137	4
sheep	49	897.50	46	4
goat	2	103.00	2	2
sheep/goat	125	2142.27	118	n/a
pig	64	734.60	53	4
dog	1	0.60	1	1
rabbit/hare	1	1.10	1	1
rabbit	1	4.00	1	1
rat	1	0.10	1	1
goose	37	218.70	37	4
duck	1	1.60	1	1
chicken	15	42.70	15	3
Totals	**482**	**10340.37**	**414**	

transversely to remove the non meat-bearing from meat-bearing part of the carcass. Finer cut marks, made by the use of a knife, were rare on cattle bones but were visible on ovicaprid, goose and fowl bones. Goose may also well have been a source of additional non-food products such as down, feathers and quills.

Age at death
Understanding of the fusion and tooth eruption and wear evidence for the main domestic species is hampered by the smaller assemblage size from Period 2 compared with Period 1. The epiphyseal fusion data for cattle indicate that most survived beyond two years, but few (15%) exceeded 3.5 years in age. This gives a slightly younger age profile compared to that of Period 1. Only one mandible was suitable for dental ageing and had a MWS of 40 which is consistent with a fully adult specimen. The fusion data for ovicaprids reveal that most survived their first and second years, and almost half (42%) survived to full skeletal maturity. This shows a notable shift towards the culling of older animals compared with Period 1. Dental data for ovicaprids gives a range of MWS from 23 to 43, which suggests a similar age range as that provided by the fusion data. The fusion data for pigs indicate that half survived their first year, and a quarter their second, but none reached full skeletal maturity. No mandibles suitable for dental ageing were present.

Evidence for hornering
The treatment of the cattle horncores was the same as with the Period 1 assemblage. The Period 2 assemblage, however, contrasts with that from Period 1 in that it lacked evidence for bone working within the mammal bone. A single goose sternum appeared to have small rectangular sections cut from it, possibly for the manufacture of decorative inlays.

Metrics
The maximum lengths of three sheep metacarpals range from 112mm to 115mm. Using Teichert's factor (1975), this gives a range of withers heights from 0.54m to 0.56m. These are within the range of those from deposits of similar date at Cabot Circus (Warman 2013, 281).

Pathology
A cattle metatarsal from the fill of the flue of furnace 1845 at No. 17 exhibited nodules of additional bone on its ventral surface of shaft, possibly a reaction to trauma affecting the lower limb, or from an infection. Of the 23 ovicaprid mandibles present, four exhibited dental calculus on the buccal surfaces of the cheek teeth. Another specimen showed a more serious dental pathological condition with an abscess in the jaw between the fourth premolar and the first molar, which would have caused the animal discomfort. A pig mandible from make-up layer 1749 at No. 17 also showed signs of periodontal inflammation in the bone along the gum line on the buccal (exterior) surface between the second and third premolar.

Period 3 (early 15th to late 17th centuries)

Animal bone totalling 1360 fragments from 1312 bones weighing 9.8kg was recovered from 55 deposits including make-up layers, surfaces, layers, drains, dumps and pits. A total of 188 bones was identifiable to species which comprised horse, cattle, sheep, ovicaprids, pig, rabbit, goose and fowl. Horse appears more numerous than in the Period 1 and 2 assemblages. A single deer tooth was present but could not be identified to species. The domestic mammal bones were heavily butchered and staining from contact with copper items is common, as waste from the Periods 2 and 3 metalworking furnaces was mixed with domestic waste. Adult and sub-adult specimens dominated the material, which also occasionally included some juvenile remains.

Period 4 (late 17th to late 19th centuries)

A total of 509 fragments from 498 bones weighing 7.2kg was recovered from 32 deposits in contexts which included wells, cellars, walls, make-up layers and pits. Of these, 139 bones could be identified to species, which included cattle, sheep, ovicaprid, pig, rabbit, rat, goose and fowl. The mammal remains showed high levels of butchery and copper staining was noted in some specimens, indicating the presence of residual animal bone that had been in contact with casting waste from earlier periods. Adult and sub-adult specimens predominated with occasional juveniles also being present.

Discussion

The animal bones from Periods 1 and 2 provide information on many aspects of the medieval economy and environment. Cattle and ovicaprids were the most numerous domestic mammals, and reflect the primary species used for consumption. Cattle in particular showed very heavy primary butchery of the meat-bearing bones, secondary butchery from domestic food preparation, and the processing of carcasses for bone working. During Period 1, there was a focus on younger ovicaprids. This may reflect a preference for lamb which could be a sign of the higher status of the inhabitants, with this product being selected over cheaper mutton. Pigs were present in smaller numbers than cattle and ovicaprids, and appear to have been butchered in a different manner with less intensive chopping-up of the bones. The reason for this is unclear, but may relate to different processes used for the preparation of pork. Another explanation is that pig bones are likely to have been considered less useful for bone working, as they are smaller than cattle bones, more curved than ovicaprid bones, and significantly more porous than both due to the younger age of slaughter. Pig is also a species that is relatively easy to raise in an urban environment although the lack of bones from foetal and newborn specimens, as well as shed deciduous teeth, inhibits any firm conclusion that pigs were reared at the site during this period.

Domestic birds (goose in particular) also made a contribution to the diet. Although the number of individuals represented is not large, each goose would have provided a substantial quantity of meat compared to fowl. It is not clear whether the geese consumed at Redcliff Street were brought into the city for slaughter or raised more locally. Geese have traditionally been valued as effective guards, loudly raising the alarm when disturbed (Albarella 2005), and it would have been sensible to have some security given the level of craft and industrial work taking place at the site. Equally, geese raised in rural areas were also commonly driven to cities for market (ibid.). To establish if the geese were imported or raised on site would require evidence of young individuals and goose egg shell at Redcliff Street, which were not identified in this assemblage.

The assemblage from both Periods 1 and 2 reveals aspects of the use of animal products other than meat, in particular horn working. There are disproportionally more skulls and horncores of cattle than the number of postcranial bones, which suggests that the material may include horner's waste. This is further supported by the evidential use of a saw to remove the horn. Butchers would have favoured cleavers and knives at this time, which are reflected in the very heavily chopped-up long bones. The skull and horncores of the cattle, and possibly those of the sheep and goat, appear to be the waste product from which the keratinous material of the horn sheath had been removed. The middle section of the cattle horncore, which was largely missing from the Period 1 and 2 assemblages, would have been the most useful part being larger and smoother than either the base or the tip. Horn, along with bone and antler, would have provided a suitable raw material for a variety of objects. Once soaked, heated and rolled out flat, a reasonably large area of workable material would be obtained. Items for which a larger area of horn was required include, for example, combs (MacGregor 1985). The absence of the middle section of horncore could be because only the first stage of horn preparation took place on the site, or because the horncore was sold, or passed on, for reuse elsewhere.

The assemblage also includes sheep skulls with horncores attached, and goat skulls and horncores. Apart from the skull and the feet, these two closely related species are difficult to separate. Bones identified as ovicaprids will of course include both sheep and goat. However, judging by the numbers of bones positively identified as sheep, it is likely the bulk of the remains were sheep rather than goat. If this is indeed the case, then the presence of such a restricted range of bones from a single species could reflect the import into the site of something other than whole animals or carcasses. A similar situation has been noted at Cabot Circus (Warman 2013, 281), and from other sites across medieval England, and one explanation proposed is that the horns and feet came in attached to skins imported from as far afield as the Continent (Albarella 2003).

Very little use was made of wild species of mammal and bird at the site in the medieval period, although the ducks present are small and likely to be wild rather than domestic specimens. It has been observed that goose was more popular as a domestic bird in the medieval period, whilst duck was more often wild in origin (Albarella 2005). While the hare remains were of wild animals, the rabbit bones present could have been from both wild and domestic animals. The only evidence for larger wild mammals is the single deer metapodial. This lack of wild mammals, especially of deer, is a common factor in assemblages from medieval Bristol, and the large assemblage from Cabot Circus also included very few specimens. Deer are in general rare in medieval assemblages from urban and ecclesiastical sites but more common in rural and higher status communities (see Soderberg 2003).

Two species which are not representative of human consumption, but whose presence is of interest, were crow and buzzard. Crows as scavengers on carrion would have been attracted to waste from butchery and other processing of animal carcasses. The fact that dog gnawing and weathering were so rare in the assemblage suggests that not much was left out to attract scavengers but was instead rapidly buried. The crow bones were recovered from a pit used for disposal of cess and could represent just a single individual killed on site and discarded into the pit. If, as has been suggested above, geese were being raised on site, species such as crow, jay and magpie would have been attracted by the presence of eggs. The most unusual species identified in the assemblage was buzzard. Today, birds of prey are not common in cities unless they have been introduced deliberately to control feral pigeons. In medieval towns however, raptors were more common, scavenging as well as hunting. Birds of prey are present in many medieval assemblages across England, albeit in small numbers (Mulkeen and O'Connor 1997).

5.2 Fish Bones
Philip L. Armitage

Fish bones were recovered by hand collection during the excavation and from sieved samples. Examination of this material has resulted in the identification of 786 bone elements representing the remains of 20 species (Table 5.3). This report provides a summary of the analysis of the fish remains. Spreadsheets showing the complete data sets of recorded anatomies for each species present in the hand-collected and sieved samples by period and

Table 5.3 Summary counts (NISP) of the identified fish bones by period and taxa. H = hand collected S = sieved samples

Period	1 H	1 S	2a H	2a S	2b H	2b S	2c H	2c S	3 H	3 S	4 H	Totals
cod *Gadus morhua*	-	-	1	-	-	2	1	-	-	-	-	4
hake *Merluccius merluccius*	4	3	4	-	2	3	-	1	2	-	1	20
ling *Molva molva*	-	-	-	-	-	-	-	-	1	-	-	1
whiting *Merlangius merlangus*	-	3	-	4	-	3	-	-	-	4	-	14
haddock *Melanogrammus aeglefinus*	-	1	1	-	-	1	-	-	-	-	-	3
pollack *Pollachius pollachius*	1	-	-	-	-	-	-	-	-	-	-	1
Gadoids (codfishes) *Gadidae*	1	1	1	7	2	6	-	5	-	1	-	24
herring *Clupea harengus*	-	18	-	247	8	124	-	31	3	25	-	456
mackerel *Scomber scombrus*	-	1	-	-	-	2	-	3	-	1	-	7
plaice *Pleuronectes platessa*	4	1	1	-	-	9	-	2	-	-	1	18
flounder *Platichthys flesus*	-	1	-	-	-	-	-	-	-	-	-	1
turbot *Scophthalamus maximus*	1	-	-	-	-	-	-	-	-	-	-	1
sole *Solea solea*	-	-	-	-	-	-	-	1	-	-	-	1
flatfish (plaice/flounder/sole)	2	1	-	5	-	9	1	2	1	3	-	24
conger eel *Conger conger*	15	1	10	7	-	6	2	-	1	-	2	44
gurnards *Triglidae*	-	-	1	-	-	-	-	2	-	-	-	3
thornback ray (or roker) *Raja clavata*	4	-	-	2	-	1	-	1	-	-	-	8
Elasmobranch (sharks & rays)	-	-	-	-	-	1	-	1	-	-	-	2
salmon *Salmo salar*	-	-	-	-	-	3	-	-	-	-	-	3
freshwater eel *Anguilla anguilla*	-	11	-	64	4	26	-	19	3	19	3	149
roach *Rutilus rutilus*	-	-	-	1	-	-	-	-	-	-	-	1
twaite shad *Alosa fallax*	-	-	-	-	-	-	-	1	-	-	-	1
TOTALS	32	42	19	337	16	196	4	69	11	53	7	786

context are contained in the archive, together with the metrical data collected from selected bone elements of freshwater eel and conger eel and the single roach dentary from fill 3629 of Period 2a hearth 3651 at No. 19 Redcliff Street. Sizes (Total Lengths) in the freshwater eel were back-calculated from the collected measurements using the regression formulae of Libois *et al.* (1987). Omitted from the analysis were unidentified fin rays, spines and ribs (details in the site archive).

Results

Preservation
The overall preservation of the fish bone is good with the exception of five abraded/eroded vertebrae: three from Period 1 fill 1853 of pit 1838, and two from fill 1313 of Period 2c pit 1352, both at No. 17. No burnt bone is present, even in specimens from hearth rakings, although several bones from such contexts do exhibit adhering concretions of ashy material. A single bone (a caudal vertebra of a large plaice) from Period 1 pit 3151 at No. 18 exhibits evidence of butchery, in the form of a knife cut mark across the centrum (cranial aspect). Partially crushed vertebrae centra of herring and freshwater eel were recovered from five separate Periods 1 and 2a deposits. They derive from fish that had been masticated (chewed/ingested) and their bones voided in human faeces, indicating the presence of cess. Contact with copper (?post deposition) is evidenced by green-stained fish bones from a number of Periods 2c and 3 contexts.

Period 1 (early 12th to mid 13th centuries)
The fills of a number of pits, a wattle drain and a posthole yielded 74 fish bones, with the first category the main source (74% total NISP). Some 24% of the fish bones (all from sieved samples) are identified as herring, 21.6% as conger eel, 14.9% as freshwater eel (all from sieved samples) and 13.5% as flatfish (plaice/flounder/turbot/sole), 9.4% as hake, 5.4% as thornback ray (all dermal denticles), and whiting 4%, with haddock, pollack, and mackerel also represented. The turbot maxilla from

Period 1 pit 3189 at No. 18 is the only record of this prime commercial flatfish found at the site. A ceratohyal (cranial bone) from Period 1 pit 1838 at No. 17 comes from a freshwater eel with an estimated total length of 319mm.

Period 2a (late 13th to mid 14th centuries)
A range of deposits yielded a total of 356 fish bones. Concentrations of herring bones from sieved samples (247 in total), all of which were potentially associated with hearth 3651 at No. 19, form the greatest proportion (69.2% of the total NISP) with freshwater eel contributing 17.9% (all eel bones from sieved samples). Conger eel bones comprise 4.8% of the assemblage, gadoids (hake, whiting, cod and haddock combined) make up 5% of the total and flatfish (plaice) 1.7% (notably less than in the Period 1 deposits). Freshwater fish (other than eel) is represented by a solitary roach dentary from hearth 3651 at No. 19. The size of the cod ceratohyal from occupation layer 1809, which overlaid Period 1 surface 2009 at No. 17 compares with a modern specimen of total length 1.09m; just falling into the lowest range of the 'extra-large' category (over 1m), using the system of Nicholson (2004, 47). A cleithrum (bone from the pectoral girdle) from occupation layer 3590 at No. 19 comes from a freshwater eel with an estimated total length of 283mm.

Period 2b (mid 14th century)
Of the total 212 fish bones from Period 2b, 106 (50%) specimens came from ashy layer 1577 (which was probably associated with a number of hearths at No. 17), 84 (39.6%) from fills associated with stone cistern 1604, (also at No. 17), 21 (9.9%) came from the backfill of the construction cut of the same cistern (1692) and a single bone (0.5%) from make-up layer 1635. Apart from salmon (see below) there is a striking similarity with the Period 2a assemblage in respect of the overall range of species present but with some variations in their frequencies. In rank order of representation/frequency, herring again predominates (62.3% of the total NISP) with freshwater eel second (14.1%). Gadoids (hake, cod, whiting and haddock) form 9% of the total and flatfish 8.5%; both of these groups of fish have a slightly higher frequency than in the Period 2a assemblage, whilst conger eel is of lower frequency at 2.8%. Mackerel, thornback ray and salmon make up the balance (3.3%). Period 2b produced the only evidence of salmon consumption at the site, indicated by three vertebrae (possibly the same fish) recovered from occupation layer 1577 overlying surface 1634 at No. 17.

Period 2c (mid 14th to early 15th centuries)
Some 73 fish bones were recovered from Period 2c pit fills, occupational/trample and make-up layers, and a wall. In respect of the range of the major species represented there is similarity with Periods 2a and 2b: 42.5% of the bones are identified as herring (all from sieved samples), 26% as freshwater eel (also all from sieved samples), 9.6% as gadoids (cod and hake), 6.8% as flatfish (plaice and sole) and 2.7% as conger eel. There are also a few gurnard, thornback ray bones, and notably, a twaite shad caudal vertebra from fill 1313 of pit 1352 at No. 17.

Period 3 (early 15th to late 17th centuries)
Make-up layers, floor and occupation surfaces, hearth/ashy deposits and a demolition layer yielded a total of 64 fish bone specimens predominated by herring (43.7%) and freshwater eel (34.4%). Gadoids (hake, whiting and ling) form 12.5% of the assemblage, flatfish (plaice/flounder) 6.2%, with only minor representation by mackerel (one vertebra) and conger eel (one premaxilla from a small fish). A cleithrum (bone from the pectoral girdle) from pit 1340 at No. 17 derives from a small freshwater eel with an estimated total length of 250mm. Occupation layer 3556 (overlying surface 3589) at No. 19 yielded a dentary from a much larger freshwater eel of estimated total length 594mm; probably an adult female. A freshwater eel articular from pit 1927 at No. 17 derives from a fish with an estimated total length of 579mm, probably an adult female.

Period 4 (late 17th to late 19th centuries)
The very small fish bone assemblage from Period 4 is limited to seven specimens (all hand collected): one hake precaudal vertebra and one conger eel precaudal vertebra; one plaice maxilla and three freshwater eel bones (two dentaries and one articular), and one small conger eel premaxilla. The freshwater eel articular derives from a small fish with an estimated total length of 191mm. Owing to the very small size of this assemblage no firm conclusions can be drawn from these particular excavated fish bones.

Discussion

From the evidence provided by the assemblages from Periods 1 to 3 it is possible to explore the diet and status of the inhabitants of the Redcliffe area during the medieval and early post-medieval periods, and also consider wider aspects of the trade connections linked to fish supplies to the city.

Analysis of the Redcliff Street bone assemblages provides evidence of the great variety of marine/estuarine fish species consumed by the local inhabitants throughout the medieval period. Based on the available evidence, freshwater fish (apart from the ubiquitous freshwater eel) apparently did not feature to any significant degree in the local diet. Other Bristol sites, including 30–38 St Thomas Street (Nicholson 2004), 55–61 Victoria Street (Locker 2008) and Cabot Circus (Armitage 2013) have revealed a very similar fish-consumption pattern, characterised by a predominance of marine/estuarine species. Of particular note in the

Table 5.4 Frequency of conger eel bones from Periods 1–2c in comparison with other medieval sites in Bristol

Site	% frequency conger eel	Total no. fish bones	Data source
1–2 Redcliff Street	5.7%	716	Armitage this report
30–38 St Thomas Street	3.2%	94	Nicholson 2004
55–61 Victoria Street	2.0%	441	Locker 2008
Cabot Circus	1.4%	1198	Armitage 2013

Redcliff Street medieval assemblages, however, is the much higher component of conger eel compared with the other documented Bristol sites (Table 5.4). Conger eels, both fresh and preserved (salted), were considered in the medieval period a highly prized delicacy and although abundant in South-West waters their presence in quantity in the food debris at the Redcliff Street site suggests the inhabitants may have been relatively well off, especially as the majority of the conger eels represented were of large size and would therefore have been a relatively expensive food item at that period. The popularity of conger eels in high-status diets is illustrated by entries in the household records kept by Bishop Swinfield of Hereford showing he purchased a total of 72 conger eels (70 salted and 2 fresh) at Bristol in November and December 1289 (Woolgar 2000, 42). Two other of the more expensive fish in medieval times (Serjeantson and Woolgar 2006) are also identified in the Redcliff Street deposits, namely large-sized plaice and large, female freshwater eels, and their presence probably further reflects the spending power of the local inhabitants. Although the larger and choicer freshwater fish in the medieval period were generally expensive luxury foods (especially pike), the presence of roach among the Redcliff Street food deposits is probably not indicative of status as these fish supplied to Bristol from the River Severn fisheries were as cheap as herring, at 1/4d each (Dyer 2000, 108) and therefore were within the purchasing power of even the less wealthy. The twaite shad, an anadromous fish (ascending rivers from the sea for breeding), may also have been relatively inexpensive, as the River Severn was renowned for the abundance of these fish (Wright 1891, 598). Fisheries operating in the Severn estuary and Irish waters probably supplied the herring, which were apparently eaten in quantity but its presence at Redcliff Street provides no clear information on the status of the inhabitants as this fish, although more generally associated with the food of the poorer classes, also often featured as a breakfast dish in well-to-do households in medieval and later times. Line-caught hake was an important commercial fish in the South West of England and its relatively high frequency in the medieval deposits at Redcliff Street is therefore to be expected. This fish, in processed form (i.e. headed, gutted and salted and/or dried), would have been especially abundant in the Bristol fish market from the 14th century onwards, as by that period the city had become the chief entrepôt for the Irish fisheries and considerable quantities of such preserved hake, as well as dried whiting ('Buckhorn') and preserved salmon, were being shipped to the city (Kowaleski 2000, 27). Again, as in the case of herring, the presence of hake at the site offers little insight into the status of the Redcliff Street inhabitants, as this fish was eaten by poor and wealthy alike. In 1342, six dried hake could be purchased in the West Country for 1d (Serjeantson and Woolgar 2006, 120).

In summary, the balance of the evidence offered by the fish remains from the medieval deposits points to the presence in the area of inhabitants who were able to afford a wide variety of fish including some of the choicer species. Applying the classification system of Ervynk *et al.* (2003, 429) the fish consumption pattern revealed by the analysis suggests they enjoyed a level 3 diet, i.e. one beyond basic subsistence, approaching affluence but not reaching level 4, a truly luxurious diet. Although the comparatively smaller size of the fish bone assemblage from the Period 3 early post-medieval deposits (Table 5.3) prevents similar detailed assessment, the noticeable reduction in the range of species consumed and absence of prime food fish perhaps suggests the inhabitants by this time were of lower socio-economic status than their medieval predecessors. The Period 4 assemblage was too small to be meaningfully compared with assemblages from earlier periods.

5.3 Plant Macrofossil and Charcoal Remains
Sarah Cobain

A total of 94 bulk soil samples was processed and assessed for plant macrofossil and charcoal remains. These samples were taken from a variety of features from Periods 1–4 including postholes, possible dyeing pits, hearths, occupational layers, industrial furnaces and drains. Following assessment (Jones 2010) 23 samples were selected for detailed plant macrofossil analysis and six samples for charcoal analysis in order to provide additional information regarding the function of features sampled, socio-economic activities and to infer the composition of the local woodlands and flora.

Methodology

Where waterlogged plant macrofossil material was identified the samples were processed by wet sieving (minimum 0.5mm mesh) from which the seeds were identified. Samples which did not contain waterlogged material were processed by standard flotation procedures using a 250 micron sieve to collect the flot and 1mm mesh to retain the residue. The residue was dried and sorted by eye, and the floated material scanned. The seeds were identified using a low power stereomicroscope (Brunel MX1) at magnifications of x10 to x40. Identifications were carried out with reference to images and descriptions by Bekker *et al.* (2006), Berggren (1981) and Anderberg (1994). Nomenclature follows Stace (1997).

Up to 100 charcoal fragments of the >2mm sieve fraction were fractured by hand to reveal the wood anatomy on radial, tangential and transverse planes. The pieces were identified under an epi-illuminating microscope (Brunel SP400) at magnifications from x40 to x400 with reference to images and descriptions by Cutler and Gale (2000); Heller *et al.* (2004) and Baas *et al.* (1989). Nomenclature of species follows Stace (1997).

Results

The 23 samples analysed contained a very well-preserved plant macrofossil assemblage with 112 individual species identified. This level of preservation is unusual in archaeological plant macrofossil assemblages, as biological material usually succumbs to decay over time and has therefore provided a rare opportunity to investigate in detail the biological waste from a range of activities. Details of the plant macrofossils recovered are presented in Tables 5.5–5.6 and the charcoal analysis in Table 5.7.

Period 1

No. 12 Redcliff Street
Sample 89 was retrieved from fill 2474 of pit 2475. The plant macrofossils identified were dominated by species from arable and disturbed environments such as corncockle (*Agrostemma githago*), stinking chamomile (*Anthemis cotula*), fat hen (*Chenopodium album*) and bramble species (*Rubus* spp), as well as grasslands/pasture (such as self heal (*Prunella vulgaris*) and thistle (*Cirsium* spp/*Carduus* spp)). It also included some species of economic value such as oat (*Avena* spp), occasional flax (*Linum usitatissimum*) seeds and occasional weld (*Reseda luteola*) (a dye plant). Foodstuff plants were also relatively abundant and included hazelnut (*Corylus avellana*), crab apple (*Malus sylvestris*), and cherry (*Prunus* spp). Also present were mineralised concretions and fragments of bran and egg shell.

Nos 13–15 Redcliff Street
Detailed analysis of plant macrofossils was undertaken from three pits to the rear of these properties: sample 80 from pit 2130, sample 91 from pit 2471 and sample 92 from pit 2479. A sample was also taken from the contents 2477 of a pot found in pit 2479. The plant macrofossils from these samples were dominated by species from disturbed and arable environments such as stinking chamomile, corncockle, corn marigold (*Glebionis segetum*), bramble and fat hen. There was also evidence for economic plants including cereals (oat, barley, wheat (*Triticum* spp), cereal chaff) and flax, and dye plants (for example relatively small numbers of woad pods (*Isatis tinctoria*), dyer's greenweed tissue/seeds (*Genista tinctoria*) and larger counts of weld seeds and madder tissue/seeds (*Rubia tinctorum*)). Foodstuff plants include large numbers of crab apple, wild strawberry and fig (*Ficus carica*) seeds. There was also evidence for species from heathland, grassland, marshland and hedgerow/scrub/woodland environments. These samples also included mineralised and buff-coloured concretions, bran and possible blue dye residue. The sample taken from the contents of the pot found in pit 2479 contained similar species to the fill within the pit, and therefore did not appear to be directly related to the use of the pot.

No. 17 Redcliff Street
Six samples were analysed for plant macrofossils. Sample 39 from pit 1838, sample 43 from pit 1851, sample 47 from the cessy organic fill of pit 1848, sample 52 from pit 3066, sample 71 from pit 1932 and sample 73 from wattle lining of pit 3173. The plant macrofossils from these samples were again dominated by plants from an arable or disturbed environment. Of the plants indicating economic activity, there is no evidence for the use of madder within this plot, but larger numbers of woad pods were identified than at Nos 13–15. Dyer's greenweed and weld was also present but in smaller quantities. There was also evidence for the use of foodstuff plants such as hazelnut, wild strawberry (*Fragaria vesca*), crab apple, wild and sour cherry, pear and fig. Species indicative of heathland, grassland/pasture, hedgerow/scrub/woodland and marshland environments were also present. There were also mineralised concretions, moss, bone, bran, snails and oyster in these samples.

No. 18 Redcliff Street
Four samples were analysed for plant macrofossils. Samples 67 and 68 from two fills of pit 3229, sample 84 from pit 2143 and sample 85 from pit 2145. As with the other tenements, species indicative of arable and disturbed environments were in the majority. Flax seeds and capsules dominated the economic plants with relatively high numbers of madder, woad and weld present. Hazelnut, wild and sour cherry, grape and apple pips were also recovered. Species indicative of grassland/pasture, hedgerow/scrub/woodland and marshland environments were also present, the most notable of the grassland species being hemlock (*Conium maculatum*). Mineralised concretions, moss, bone, egg shell, bran, oyster and buff concretions (limestone) were found in these samples.

Table 5.5 Plant macrofossils from Period 1 deposits at Nos 12, 13–15 and 17 Redcliff Street

Key: Occ = 1–5 fragments; Mod = 6–20 fragments; Freq = 21–40 fragments; Abun = 41+ fragments. Code refers to the habitat of the plant and uses the following abbreviations: HSW = Hedge/scrub/woodland species; A = Arable/crop species; E = Economic species; He = Heathland species; D = Disturbed ground species; DC = Disturbed ground species, may have been consumed; P = Pasture/grassland species; WL = Marshland species; IM = Imported species

Code	Family	Species	Common Name	Context Number											
				2474	2129	2477	2477	2480	3215	1885	1853	3174	3065	1852	
			Feature Number	2475	2130	2479	N/A	2471	1932	1848	1838	3173	3066	1851	
			Sample Number	89	80	92	N/A	91	71	47	39	73	52	43	
			Flot Volume (ml)	860	1230	610	500	810	1295	1035	385	1095	615	1560	
			Tenement	12	13/15	13/15	13/15	13/15	17	17	17	17	17	17	
HSW	Adoxaceae	Sambucus nigra	Elder							1					
DC	Amaranthaceae	Atriplex patula	Common orache			1			1	1	5				
DC		Chenopodium album	Fat hen	17	23	25	7	11	29	110	11	18	67	42	
D		Chenopodium polyspermum	Many-seeded goosefoot	8	4				2					15	
D		Chenopodium rubrum	Red goosefoot	4				5	1				1		
WL	Apiaceae	Apium nodiflorum	Fool's-water-cress		2	4									
D		Aethusa cynapium	Fool's parsley		4			1		1	1		1	1	
A		Bupleurum rotundifolium	Thorow-wax	2	2	1	1		4						
DC		Foeniculum vulgare	Fennel		2		4					3	2		
P		Torilis arvensis	Spreading hedge parsley		3	2	1	1	1	10		2	2	2	
HSW	Aquifoliaceae	Ilex aquifolium	Holly		1										
P	Asteraceae	Bellis perennis	Common daisy		1										
P		Cirsium spp/Carduus spp	Thistle spp	3	3	3	1		5	7	2		4		
A		Centaurea cyanus	Cornflower		2	1			5						
A		Anthemis cotula	Stinking chamomile	10	51	2	19	8	51		3		13	2	
A		Glebionis segetum	Corn marigold	3	2	3	9	4	7	32		2			
D		Hieracium spp	Hawkweeds				1		1			1			
D		Lapsana communis	Nipplewort	3	1			1		2					
D		Leontodon spp	Hawkbit						1	2					
D		Senecio jacobaea	Common ragwort		10	3	3	3		8					
A		Sonchus asper	Prickly sow-thistle		1				2	9			1		
A		Sonchus spp	Sow thistle										1		
WL	Balsaminaceae	Impatiens parviflora	Small balsam	1	4	43	4			18	5				
HSW	Betulaceae	Betula spp	Birch spp						2						

Context Number				2474	2129	2477	2477	2480	3215	1885	1853	3174	3065	1852
Feature Number				2475	2130	2479	N/A	2471	1932	1848	1838	3173	3066	1851
Sample Number				89	80	92	N/A	91	71	47	39	73	52	43
Tenement				12	13/15	13/15	13/15	13/15	17	17	17	17	17	17
Code	Family	Species	Common Name											
HSW		*Corylus avellana*	Hazelnut	12	63	7	10	5	3	11	43	17	17	19
HSW		*Corylus avellana*	Hazelnut (carbonised)		2				2		20		1	
A	*Boraginaceae*	*Lithospermum arvense*	Field gromwell	1										1
DC	*Brassicaceae*	*Brassica/Sinapsis* spp	Mustard/Cabbage/Charlock	16	10	2	11	3	3	2	6	1	1	
DC		*Brassica/Sinapsis* spp	Mustard/Cabbage/Charlock (carbonised)		1									
E		*Isatis tinctoria*	Woad perianth (pod)					2	11					
A/D		*Raphanus raphanistrum*	Wild radish (perianth)	1	1		5			1				
A	*Caryophyllaceae*	*Agrostemma githago*	Corncockle (whole)	5	4	2			22	4		1	3	
A		*Agrostemma githago*	Corncockle (fragments)	43	Mod	Mod	Abun		Abun	Occ	Occ	Abun	Abun	Occ
DC		*Stellaria media*	Common chickweed	1	4	5	8	14	5	13	1	9	3	3
A		*Spergula arvensis*	Corn spurrey		1		6		1	8		1		
HSW	*Celastraceae*	*Euonymus europaeus*	Spindle tree		1									
WL	*Chenopodiaceae*	*Beta vulgaris* spp *maritima*	Sea-beet			2			2					
WL	*Cyperaceae*	*Carex* spp	Sedge	7	3	3	4		5	9			2	
WL		*Carex dioica*	Dioecious sedge		1				2					1
WL		*Carex flacca*	Glaucous sedge					1						9
WL		*Carex limosa*	Mud sedge									1		
WL		*Carex remota*	Remote sedge			2								
WL		*Eleocharis uniglumis*	Slender spike-rush		12		3		3	2		4		19
WL		*Eleocharis palustris*	Common spike-rush	2	8	1	3	1	5	4		1		18
He	*Ericaceae*	*Calluna vulgaris*	Heather											Abun
He		*Erica* spp	Heather species											Abun
D	*Euphorbiaceae*	*Euphorbia* spp	Spurges		7		2			6				
E	*Fabaceae*	*Genista tinctoria*	Dyer's greenweed		2				3					
E		*Genista tinctoria*	Dyer's greenweed (tissue)		1			3						
A/P/D		*Lathyrus* spp	Vetchlings (carbonised)			2					3			
P		*Medicago lupulina*	Black medick	4	4			1						
D	*Fumariaceae*	*Fumaria officinalis*	Common fumitory				1							

Table 5.5 (cont.) Plant macrofossils from Period 1 deposits at Nos 12, 13–15 and 17 Redcliff Street

Code	Family	Species	Common Name	2474 / 2475 / 89 / 12	2129 / 2130 / 80 / 13/15	2477 / 2479 / 92 / 13/15	2477 / N/A / N/A / 13/15	2480 / 2471 / 91 / 13/15	3215 / 1932 / 71 / 17	1885 / 1848 / 47 / 17	1853 / 1838 / 39 / 17	3174 / 3173 / 73 / 17	3065 / 3066 / 52 / 17	1852 / 1851 / 43 / 17
D	Lamiaceae	*Galeopsis tetrahit*	Common hemp-nettle											
D		*Lamium purpureum*	Red dead-nettle					1						
P		*Prunella vulgaris*	Self heal	9	1	1	1		1					
P		*Prunella vulgaris*	Self heal (carbonised)									1		
D	Linaceae	*Linum catharticum*	Fairy flax						6		2			
E		*Linum usitatissimum*	Flax seed	2		1	1		8	11	1	2	2	
E		*Linum usitatissimum*	Flax seed (crushed)										1	
E		*Linum usitatissimum*	Flax (perianth)	4	1			1				1		
D	Malvaceae	*Malva* spp	Mallow							1				
IM	Moraceae	*Ficus carica*	Fig			74			16		6		1	
WL	Myricaceae	*Myrica gale*	Bog-myrtle			4								
WL	Nymphaceae	*Nuphar lutea*	Yellow water-lily						1					
A	Papaveraceae	*Papaver argemone*	Long pricklyhead poppy	3	1	2	3		1				2	
A		*Papaver dubium*	Long-headed poppy	1			1							
E	Poaceae	*Avena* spp	Oat (carbonised)	1	5	63	1		1	1	25	2		
E		*Hordeum vulgare*	Barley (carbonised)		3	7	3		2		25		2	
E		*Hordeum vulgare*	Barley 6-row hulled (carbonised)								1			
E		*Hordeum vulgare*	Barley 2-row hulled (carbonised)		2									
E		*Hordeum vulgare*	Cereal chaff - rachis		1									
E		*Triticum* spp	Wheat (carbonised)				1					1		
E		*Triticum aestivum/turgidum/durum*	Free-threshing wheat (carbonised)	1	2	4	1				15			
E		*Triticum aestivum type/spelta*	Free-threshing wheat/spelt (carbonised)								3			
E		Poaceae	Indeterminate cereal grain (carbonised)			2					30			
E		Poaceae	Cereal remains - Caryopses	Occ					Abun					
E		Poaceae	Cereal chaff - culm node		9	1	2	1	4	1	1			1

Context Number				2474	2129	2477	2477	2480	3215	1885	1853	3174	3065	1852
Feature Number				2475	2130	2479	N/A	2471	1932	1848	1838	3173	3066	1851
Sample Number				89	80	92	N/A	91	71	47	39	73	52	43
Tenement				12	13/15	13/15	13/15	13/15	17	17	17	17	17	17
Code	Family	Species	Common Name											
E		Poaceae	Cereal chaff - culm node (carbonised)								4			
E		Poaceae	Cereal chaff - Rachis										1	
E		Poaceae	Cereal chaff - Straw	1			1							1
D	Polygonaceae	Fallopia convolvulus	Black-bindweed		11		3							
WL		Persicaria hydropiper	Water pepper		3	1		5		15				
D		Persicaria lapathifolia	Pale persicaria	21	3	41	2		1				2	
D		Persicaria maculosa	Redshank	1	5			14		10		1	1	
D		Polygonum aviculare	Knotgrass	1	4					6			2	
DC		Rumex spp	Dock				3							
DC		Rumex acetosa	Common sorrel	7	4	33	4		6	30	3		6	
DC		Rumex acetosa	Common sorrel (perianth)									2		
DC		Rumex acetosella	Sheep's sorrel		5		3	4	2	31				4
WL		Rumex congolmeratus	Clustered dock				1							
DC		Rumex crispus	Curled dock	13	2	40						2	3	
P	Ranunculaceae	Ranunculus repens	Buttercup	3	2	1	1	1	8	17	2		2	10
E	Resedaceae	Reseda luteola	Weld	8	44		3		12					12
HSW	Rosaceae	Crataegus monogyna/Prunus spinosa	Hawthorn/blackthorn/sloe thorn						2					
HSW		Crataegus monogyna	Hawthorn		1									
HSW		Fragaria vesca	Wild strawberry	23	5	11	26	2	21			4	47	
HSW		Malus sylvestris	Crab apple	16	6	6	73		20			20		
HSW		Malus sylvestris	Crab apple (carbonised)				2							
HSW		Prunus spp	Cherry spp			1					8			
HSW		Prunus avium	Wild cherry		1	4	2		2				1	
HSW		Prunus cerasus	Sour cherry	27	9	4	8		3		2	23	17	
HSW		Prunus cerasus	Sour cherry (cut in half)				1							
HSW		Prunus domestica	Wild plum						6		1		3	
HSW		Prunus domestica	Wild plum (cut in half)										1	
HSW		Prunus padus	Bird cherry	3	1							1		

Table 5.5 (cont.) Plant macrofossils from Period 1 deposits at Nos 12, 13–15 and 17 Redcliff Street

Context Number				2474	2129	2477	2477	2480	3215	1885	1853	3174	3065	1852
Feature Number				2475	2130	2479	N/A	2471	1932	1848	1838	3173	3066	1851
Sample Number				89	80	92	N/A	91	71	47	39	73	52	43
Tenement				12	13/15	13/15	13/15	13/15	17	17	17	17	17	17
Code	Family	Species	Common Name											
HSW		*Prunus spinosa*	Blackthorn/sloe	1			1							
HSW		*Pyrus communis*	Pear		1		2							
HSW		*Rubus fruticosus*	Blackberry		1	1	7	2	4	4	4	3		
HSW		*Rubus ideaus*	Raspberry						2		1		1	
HSW		*Rubus saxatilis* sect *Glandulosus*	Stone bramble	128	22	203	249		58	6	614	61	63	
HSW		*Sorbus aria*	Common whitebeam						3					
A	Rosoideae	*Aphanes arvensis*	Parsley-piert	27		11	108		19		23	2		
D	Rubiaceae	*Galium aparine*	Cleavers		1			1				4		
E		*Rubia tinctorum*	Common madder					1						
E		*Rubia tinctorum*	Common madder (tissue)		Occ			Freq						
D	Solanaceae	*Solanum nigrum*	Black nightshade	54	20	3	38	2	5			1		
HSW	Taxaceae	*Taxus baccata*	Yew		5			4						
D	Urticaceae	*Urtica dioica*	Common nettle					3	3	3		1	1	
D		*Urtica urens*	Small nettle											
IM	Vitaceae	*Vitis vinifera*	Grape	3		2	1				1	1		
IM		*Vitis vinifera*	Grape (charred)				1							3
E			Mineralised concretions	Abun					Abun		Abun	Abun	Freq	
E			Buff concretions		Mod		Mod	Abun						
E			Bran	Abun	Abun				Abun	Abun		Abun		
E			Dye residue - blue (possible)			Mod			Mod					
E			Moss					Abun						Abun
			Snails											Mod
			Oyster			Occ	Occ	Occ	Occ	Occ			Occ	
			Bone	Occ		Occ	Mod	Mod	Occ				Occ	
			Egg shell	Occ	Occ									
			Total macrofossils identified	504	412	638	653	92	395	402	876	174	280	163

Code	Family	Species	Common Name	3199	3200	2142	2144	3700	3779	1812	1643	1647	1313	1530	1934
		Context Number		3199	3200	2142	2144	3700	3779	1812	1643	1647	1313	1530	1934
		Feature Number		3229	3229	2143	2145	3672	3778		1604	1604	1352		1927
		Sample Number		67	68	84	85	100	102	34	27	29	3	36	48
		Flot Volume (ml)		685	670	1020	1125	575	745	1085	735	835	83	55	175
		Period		1	1	1	1	1	1	2a	2b	2b	2c	3	3
		Plot		18	18	17	17	19	19	17	17	17	17	17	17
HSW	Adoxaceae	*Sambucus nigra*	Elder	1	2		1	2	1	1	1		3		2
DC	Amaranthaceae	*Atriplex patula*	Common orache		1										
DC		*Chenopodium album*	Fat hen	4	19	8	28	34	33	5	3	6		3	158
D		*Chenopodium glaucum*	Oak-leaved goosefoot								1				
D		*Chenopodium polyspermum*	Many-seeded goosefoot				2								
D		*Chenopodium rubrum*	Red goosefoot		4										6
WL	Apiaceae	*Apium nodiflorum*	Fool's-water-cress				1				1	1			1
D		*Aethusa cynapium*	Fool's parsley			1									5
A		*Bupleurum rotundifolium*	Thorow-wax			1	6					1			
D/P		*Conium maculatum*	Hemlock			2									
D		*Foeniculum vulgare*	Fennel			6	3	1	1		1			1	
P		*Torilis arvensis*	Spreading hedge parsley				4	1	1	1		1			
HSW	Araliaceae	*Hedera helix*	Ivy				1								
P	Asteraceae	*Bellis perennis*	Common daisy		1										
P		*Cirsium* spp/ *Carduus* spp	Thistle spp				7	1	1			1			
A		*Centaurea cyanus*	Cornflower	1	3		1	1				1			
A		*Anthemis cotula*	Stinking chamomile	10	74	4	10	3		5	3	8			
A		*Glebionis segetum*	Corn marigold		9	1	9	4							
D		*Hieracium* spp	Hawkweeds		6	1	1	2			1				
D		*Lapsana communis*	Nipplewort			1			1			1			
D		*Senecio jacobaea*	Common ragwort			6			5						
A		*Sonchus asper*	Prickly sow-thistle	3	1						1				
A		*Sonchus* spp	Sow thistle	1	5										
WL	Balsaminaceae	*Impatiens parviflora*	Small balsam		3		1	17	8						
HSW	Betulaceae	*Betula pendula*	Silver birch (bract)			1	2								
HSW		*Betula pubescens*	Downy birch (fruit)			1									

Table 5.6 (cont.) Plant macrofossils from Periods 1, 2 and 3 deposits at Nos 17, 18 and 19 Redcliff Street. See Table 5.5 for the key to the abbreviations

				Context Number	3199	3200	2142	2144	3700	3779	1812	1643	1647	1313	1530	1934
				Feature Number	3229	3229	2143	2145	3672	3778		1604	1604	1352		1927
				Sample Number	67	68	84	85	100	102	34	27	29	3	36	48
				Period	1	1	1	1	1	1	2a	2b	2b	2c	3	3
				Plot	18	18	17	17	19	19	17	17	17	17	17	17
Code	Family	Species	Common Name													
HSW		*Corylus avellana*	Hazelnut			27	5	7	14		12					11
HSW		*Corylus avellana*	Hazelnut (carbonised)			1										
A	Boraginaceae	*Lithospermum arvense*	Field gromwell						1							
DC	Brassicaceae	*Brassica/Sinapsis* spp	Mustard/Cabbage/Charlock			3	5	7		1	4		8			4
DC		*Brassica/Sinapsis* spp	Mustard/Cabbage/Charlock (carbonised)					6						4		
D		*Capsella bursa-pastoris*	Shepherd's-purse			1										
E		*Isatis tinctoria*	Woad perianth (pod)		16											
A/D		*Raphanus raphanistrum*	Wild radish (perianth)			2		2					1			
A	Caryophyllaceae	*Agrostemma githago*	Corncockle (whole)		1		15	8	1	3			3			
A		*Agrostemma githago*	Corncockle (fragments)		Occ	Occ	Freq	Abun	Occ	Abun	Occ	Occ	Abun			
G		*Lychnis flos-cuculi*	Ragged-robin			3		1			2	1				
DC		*Stellaria media*	Common chickweed		12	11	1	4	4	1		2	1		29	
A		*Spergula arvensis*	Corn spurrey			1	1	5	7							
HSW	Celastraceae	*Euonymus europaeus*	Spindle tree					1								
WL	Chenopodiaceae	*Beta vulgaris* spp *maritima*	Sea-beet					3								
WL	Cyperaceae	*Carex* spp	Sedge		6	15	2	3	1			2	6		2	97
WL		*Carex dioica*	Dioecious sedge			1										
WL		*Carex flacca*	Glaucous sedge							1		1				
WL		*Carex limosa*	Mud sedge			3		1								
WL		*Carex panicea*	Carnation sedge							2	3					
WL		*Carex pendula*	Pendulous sedge					4						4		
WL		*Carex remota*	Remote sedge			6					8					
WL		*Eleocharis uniglumis*	Slender spike-rush					2			3					
WL		*Eleocharis palustris*	Common spike-rush				2									
He	Ericaceae	*Calluna vulgaris*	Heather			3										
D	Euphorbiaceae	*Euphorbia* spp	Spurges			6		1								1

Biological Evidence   113

Context Number																3199	3200	2142	2144	3700	3779	1812	1643	1647	1313	1530	1934
Feature Number																3229	3229	2143	2145	3672	3778		1604	1604	1352		1927
Sample Number																67	68	84	85	100	102	34	27	29	3	36	48
Period																1	1	1	1	1	1	2a	2b	2b	2c	3	3
Plot																18	18	17	17	19	19	17	17	17	17	17	17
Code	Family	Species	Common Name																								
E	Fabaceae	*Genista tinctoria*	Dyer's greenweed													1											
E		*Lens culinaris*	Pulse													1		1									
P		*Medicago lupulina*	Black medick															2			3						
P		*Trifolium* spp	Clover																4					2			
P		*Vicia* spp	Vetches															1									
D	Fumariaceae	*Fumaria officinalis*	Common fumitory														1		1								
D	Lamiaceae	*Lamium purpureum*	Red dead-nettle																	1							
P		*Prunella vulgaris*	Self heal															1				2	1	3			
D	Linaceae	*Linum catharticum*	Fairy flax													2											
E		*Linum usitatissimum*	Flax seed													4	78	5	5	5				1			
E		*Linum usitatissimum*	Flax seed (crushed)														82	1	1								
E		*Linum usitatissimum*	Flax (perianth)													27	519							1				
D	Malvaceae	*Malva* spp	Mallow														1										
WL	Menyanthaceae	*Menyanthes trifoliata*	Bogbean																1								
IM	Moraceae	*Ficus carica*	Fig																				5	20		9	
A	Papaveraceae	*Papaver argemone*	Long pricklyhead poppy															2	1				2	33			
E	Poaceae	*Avena* spp	Oat (carbonised)															2	2	3							8
E		*Hordeum vulgare*	Barley (carbonised)																1			1					16
E		*Hordeum vulgare*	Cereal chaff - rachis															1									
E		*Secale cereale*	Rye (carbonised)														1										
E		*Triticum* spp	Wheat (carbonised)													1											
E		*Triticum aestivum/turgidum/durum*	Free-threshing wheat (carbonised)															1		3						4
E		*Triticum*	Wheat - glume base (carbonised)																	2							11
E		Poaceae	Indeterminate cereal grain (carbonised)																1								3
E		Poaceae	Cereal remains - Caryopses															Mod									
E		Poaceae	Cereal chaff - culm node														1	9	1	3							

Table 5.6 (cont.) Plant macrofossils from Periods 1, 2 and 3 deposits at Nos 17, 18 and 19 Redcliff Street. See Table 5.5 for the key to the abbreviations

Context Number			3199	3200	2142	2144	3700	3779	1812	1643	1647	1313	1934
Feature Number			3229	3229	2143	2145	3672	3778		1604	1604	1352	1927
Sample Number			67	68	84	85	100	102	34	27	29	3	48
Period			1	1	1	1	1	1	2a	2b	2b	2c	3
Plot			18	18	17	17	19	19	17	17	17	17	17
Code	Family	Species	Common Name										
E		Poaceae	Cereal chaff - culm node (carbonised)										1
E		Poaceae	Cereal chaff - spikelet fork				1							
E		Poaceae	Cereal chaff - Straw			5		2	2					
E		Poaceae	Cereal chaff - Straw (mineralised)										1	
D	Polygonaceae	Fallopia convolvulus	Black-bindweed	1	6		1							
WL		Persicaria hydropiper	Water pepper	26	10		3		2					
D		Persicaria lapathifolia	Pale persicaria	1	15	5	5	2	2					
D		Persicaria maculosa	Redshank				1	10				2		
D		Polygonum aviculare	Knotgrass				3		1					
DC		Rumex spp	Dock	2			1							
DC		Rumex acetosa	Common sorrel	1	32		15	4	11	19				
DC		Rumex acetosa	Common sorrel (perianth)					3	1					
DC		Rumex acetosella	Sheep's sorrel		3		2							
WL		Rumex congolmeratus	Clustered dock				1							
DC		Rumex crispus	Curled dock		41	1	15	15	11	3				
DC		Rumex crispus	Curled dock (perianth)		6			6	1					
D		Rumex sanguineus	Wood dock		3									
P	Ranunculaceae	Ranunculus repens	Buttercup		28	1	2		1	1				1
E	Resedaceae	Reseda luteola	Weld		2	4	15					8		80
HSW	Rosaceae	Fragaria vesca	Wild strawberry		3	5	11	5	1		2	1047		66
HSW		Malus sylvestris	Crab apple			41	4	3	2			52		
HSW		Malus sylvestris	Crab apple (fragments)			19	1							
HSW		Prunus spp	Cherry spp			4						4		
HSW		Prunus avium	Wild cherry			6	2					5		
HSW		Prunus avium	Wild cherry (cut in half)			1								

Context Number			3199	3200	2142	2144	3700	3779	1812	1643	1647	1313	1530	1934
Feature Number			3229	3229	2143	2145	3672	3778		1604	1604	1352		1927
Sample Number			67	68	84	85	100	102	34	27	29	3	36	48
Period			1	1	1	1	1	1	2a	2b	2b	2c	3	3
Plot			18	18	17	17	19	19	17	17	17	17	17	17
Code	Family	Species												
		Common Name												
HSW		*Prunus cerasus* — Sour cherry			20	6	1	2			18			1
HSW		*Prunus cerasus* — Sour cherry (cut in half)			2	2								
HSW		*Prunus domestica* — Wild plum			2	2								
HSW		*Prunus spinosa* — Blackthorn/sloe			1	1				1				
HSW		*Rosa* spp — Rose						1						
HSW		*Rubus fruticosus* — Blackberry		1				4			16			
HSW		*Rubus ideaus* — Raspberry				1					2			
HSW		*Rubus saxatilis* sect *Glandulosus* — Stone bramble	1	4	142	53	35	62	5	2	66			33
HSW		*Sorbus aria* — Common whitebeam				4								
A	Rosoideae	*Aphanes arvensis* — Parsley-piert			7	5								3
E	Rubiaceae	*Rubia tinctorum* — Common madder	1											
E		*Rubia tinctorum* — Common madder (tissue)	Abun	Abun					Abun					
D	Solanaceae	*Solanum nigrum* — Black nightshade		2	15	1				2	120		4	4
D	Urticaceae	*Urtica dioica* — Common nettle			2					1				1
D		*Urtica urens* — Small nettle	2			1	2				5			
IM	Vitaceae	*Vitis vinifera* — Grape			1		1							
IM		*Vitis vinifera* — Grape (charred)				1								
IM		*Vitis vinifera* — Grape (mineralised)									1		2	
E		Mineralised concretions	Freq		Occ	Abun	Abun	Abun			Abun	Mod		
E		Buff concretions		Freq										
E		Bran			Abun	Abun	Abun	Abun			Abun		Mod	
E		Dye residue - red (possible)					Occ			Occ				
E		Moss		Mod	Abun									
		Molluscs										Occ		
		Oyster				Occ								
		Bone		Occ			Occ					Occ		
		Egg shell												Occ
		Total macrofossils identified	126	1049	370	290	201	162	70	33	1653	7	25	548

Table 5.7 Charcoal species. Key: rw = roundwood; hw = heartwood; sw = sapwood

Sample Number			31	8	3	42	97	12
Context Number			1776	1381	1313	1842	3629	1429
Cut Number					1352	1845	3651	1426
Period			2a	2b	2c	2c	2a	3
Flot Volume			37	49	83	36	30	20
Tenement			17	17	17	17	19	16
Family	**Species**	**Common Name**						
Aquifoliaceae	*Ilex aquifolium*	Holly	1	-	-	-	-	-
Betulaceae	*Alnus glutinosa*	Alder	-	-	-	1	2	2
	Alnus glutinosa/Corylus avellana	Alder/hazel	2	2	5	9 rw 1	2 rw 2	1
	Betula spp	Birch	1	-	-	1	-	-
	Corylus avellana	Hazel	-	-	2	-	2	-
Fagaceae	*Fagus sylvatica*	Beech	5	52	17	35	54	-
	Quercus robur/petraea	Sessile/pedunculate oak	32	21	12	2	8	40
	Quercus robur/petraea	Sessile/pedunculate oak hw	30	2	-	-	4	14
	Quercus robur/petraea	Sessile/pedunculate oak sw	7	6	-	4	19	19
Oleaceae	*Fraxinus excelsior*	Ash	-	3	4	10 rw 2	-	2
Rosaceae	*Crataegus monogyna/Sorbus spp/Malus sylvestris)*	Hawthorn/rowan/crab apple	4	8 rw 5	2	1 rw 3	4	1
	Prunus avium/padus	Wild/bird cherry	1	-	1	-	-	1
	Prunus spinosa	Blackthorn/sloe	-	-	2	-	-	-
Salicaceae	*Salix* spp/*Populus* spp	Willow/poplar	1	1	6	-	3 rw	2 rw
		Indeterminate	1	2	5	8	2	8
		Total Fragments Identified:	85	100	51	69	100	82

No. 19 Redcliff Street

Two samples were analysed for plant macrofossils. Sample 100 from pit 3672 and sample 102 from pit 3778. As with all other samples the number of species indicative of arable and disturbed environments remained high. There were also small numbers of wild strawberry, crab apple, sour cherry and grape (*Vitis vinifera*) present as foodstuff remains. There were no plant macrofossils indicative of dyeing activities, although a small number of flax seeds was recovered. Species indicative of grassland/pasture, hedgerow/scrub/woodland and marshland environments were also present. There was also possible red dye residue, bone and bran found in these samples.

Period 2

No. 17 Redcliff Street

Four samples were analysed for plant macrofossils. Sample 34 from Period 2a occupation layer 1812, samples 27 and 29 from Period 2b stone cistern 1604 and sample 3 from fill 1313 of Period 2c pit 1352. These samples contained plant macrofossils indicative of an arable environment and disturbed ground. Most notable foodstuff species included fig, grape, hazelnut, wild strawberry, crab apple and wild and sour cherry. Plants with economic value included a single barley grain, and dye plants dominated by madder with smaller quantities of weld. Flax was also present in small quantities. Other species present included those from a wetland environment. There were also mineralised concretions, possible red dye residue, bran, molluscs and bone in these samples.

Four samples were taken for charcoal analysis from No. 17. Sample 31 from charcoal-rich fill of hearth 1776; sample 8 from Period 2b burnt layer 1381 over the pitched surface 1421 associated with hearths 1417 and 1419; sample 42 from burnt residue 1842 on Period 2c metal-casting furnace 1845 and sample 3 from fill 1313 of water butt 1352. These samples were dominated by beech (*Fagus sylvatica*) and oak (*Quercus robur/petraea*) with smaller quantities of alder/hazel (*Alnus glutinosa/Corylus avellana*), hawthorn/rowan/crab apple (*Crateagus monogyna/Sorbus* spp/*Malus sylvestris*) and willow/poplar (*Salix* spp/*Populus* spp). In addition hearth 1776 included holly (*Ilex aquifolium*), birch (*Betula* spp) and wild/bird cherry (*Prunus avium/Prunus padus*), burnt layer 1381 also contained ash (*Fraxinus excelsior*); water butt 1352 included ash, wild/bird cherry, blackthorn/sloe (*Prunus spinosa*) and furnace 1845 also included birch and ash.

No. 19 Redcliff Street
Sample 97 was taken from the flue fill of Period 2a hearth 3651 for charcoal analysis. This context contained a similar assemblage to that from No. 17 and was dominated by beech with smaller quantities of oak, alder/hazel, willow/poplar and hawthorn/rowan/crab apple fragments.

Period 3

No. 16 Redcliff Street
One sample was taken for charcoal analysis. The charcoal remains recovered from burnt area 1429 (sample 12) in furnace 1426 were dominated by oak with smaller quantities of alder/hazel, ash, wild/bird cherry and poplar/willow.

No. 17 Redcliff Street
Two samples were taken for plant macrofossil analysis: sample 36 from the beaten floor of furnace 1530 and sample 48 from black organic fill of pit 1927. There was a slight change in assemblage composition for these samples with species indicative of disturbed ground dominating. There were fewer seeds indicative of arable weeds and grassland/pasture species. There were also fewer hedgerow/scrub/woodland environment species, but those present included elder (*Sambucus nigra*), hazelnut, wild strawberry and bramble. Wetland species were also represented. A small number of plants with economic value included cereals (oat, wheat, barley), dye plants (weld) and flax. There was also egg shell and bran recovered from this sample.

Discussion

The plant macrofossil remains included an assemblage of dye plants, and those which would have been utilised for dye processing. Evidence for flax-processing may also relate to the cloth industry. There was also a large assemblage of seeds from foodstuff plants as well as plants possibly used for medicinal purposes. The assemblage also provided evidence for plants within the local environment. The charcoal remains provide insights into the trade in timbers and fuel in Bristol.

Dye plants

The use of plants to produce dyes for cloth and wool has its origins back in the late prehistoric period, however widespread commercial use of dyes did not develop until the early medieval period. London, Southampton and Bristol were the three principal ports for importing dye plants during the medieval period (Edmonds 2003, 35). Dye plants identified at Redcliff Street consisted of weld, dyer's greenweed, madder and woad.

Weld is a plant characteristic of disturbed ground, but it is also known to have been cultivated and used as a yellow dye plant. The plant would have been gathered locally and dye would have been extracted by boiling the leaves, stems and flowers of the plant with alum and tartaric acid. Dyer's greenweed is a small shrub that produces a yellow dye (Cutler and Gale 2000, 124) extracted by the same method as for weld. Madder was introduced into Britain in the 10th century and was used as a red dye plant. Madder is native to southern European countries where the drier climate produced a high quality dye but was also grown in northern Europe (ibid., 226). Medieval customs accounts record that it was imported from Flanders, but also southern France and Lisbon (Carus-Wilson 1937). The best quality woad was imported from Picardy, France, due to a drier climate (Edmonds 2006, 16). The roots were harvested, dried and crushed into a powder (Cutler and Gale 2000, 226). Woad was the only source of blue dye in North-West Europe and was cultivated since the Iron Age until the introduction of imported indigo in the 16th century. It was widely cultivated in the southern counties of England (Somerset, Dorset and Hampshire). The process used to produce blue dye was more complicated than other dye plants. The leaves were harvested, shredded and left to dry and then ground down into a powder which was added to a small amount of water and left to ferment. The dried woad was then placed into a vat with lime/potash and boiled, at which point the solution produced could be used to dye cloth (ibid., 33).

There were a variety of recipes and techniques employed in processing dye plants with mordants and acid/alkali mixes used to ensure the highest quality colours on fabrics. Urine and alum were used to prepare cloth and wool before dyeing. The urine removed oily residues from cloth/wool and the alum improved the colour fastness of the dye. The shade and intensity of individual dyes was affected by the pH of the dye solutions. Potash or quicklime were used to make alkaline solutions and saltpetre or tartar made acidic solutions (Hall 1996, 636; Edmonds 2003, 62–4). For example, madder produced several different shades depending on the recipe used. If the madder powder was boiled a yellow dye was released in addition to the red, which results in an orange/brown dye. If an acid solution was used a bright orange colour was produced and if an alkali was added the cloth turned a bright brick red colour (Edmonds 2003, 57). Bran was used to encourage the fermenting process in blue dye production from woad (ibid., 65). The use of these products in the dyeing process at Redcliff Street is suggested by the presence of bran, mineralised seeds/concretions (indicative of cess) and buff concretions possibly representing the use of alkaline solutions. Possible dye residues in the form of red and blue coloured concretions were also visible in some of the samples. These residues give further evidence to confirm a dyeing industry on the site.

The dyeing industry was established during Period 1 with pits all containing waste material from this process, and evidence for the industry continued into Period 2 with further hearths built possibly for cloth-dyeing. Evidence for dyeing diminishes sharply in Period 3. Due to the destructive nature of dye-plant processing, the only identifiable remains are those discarded as waste. It is therefore difficult to pinpoint where the dyeing was undertaken, especially as the remains from all dye plants are positively identified in all plots across the site. The high number of samples analysed from Period 1 allows for some limited spatial analysis of the dyeing waste. The highest frequency of dyer's greenweed, weld and madder occurred to the rear of Nos 13–15, madder was abundant at No. 18 and woad at No. 17. However this may reflect patterns of discard rather than any specialisation between plots. From the smaller number of samples taken from Period 2, it appears that madder was being used at No. 17. This is supported by mineralised concretions, buff concretions and red dye residues being present within the samples. By Period 3 the only dye plant recovered is weld. It is possible that weld was not being utilised, however, since no other dye-processing residues were observed other than bran, and as it is a species which cultivates rapidly in disturbed environments, it may represent species from the local environment rather than dyeing activities.

These results are consistent with dye plant identifications at other medieval sites in Bristol such as Bridge Parade (Cox 1998, 24) and various excavations in Redcliffe (Dundas Wharf (Fig. 2.1, no. 3), Bristol Bridge (Fig. 2.1, no. 2) and Canynges House (Fig. 2.1, no. 6; Jones and Watson 1987, 135, 154)). The results from the present site compared with those from other sites in Redcliffe show that Redcliff Street and its vicinity was a key area for cloth finishing in Bristol (Good 1991, 40).

Linseed oil

Flax was cultivated during the medieval period and linen and rope were produced from the plant fibres and linseed oil from the seeds (Cutler and Gale 2000, 152–3). A large number of flax seeds which had been visibly crushed, possibly to extract the linseed oil, were recovered from the excavations. Linseed oil was used in cooking and in dye production. Edmonds (2003, 44) outlines a recipe using burnt peach shells boiled with linseed oil to produce black dye. Whilst no peach stones were recovered from the present site, some have been identified from other excavations in Redcliffe (Jones and Watson 1987, 152) and thus it is possible that black dye was being produced in this way.

Flax seeds and pods were identified from Period 1 deposits at Nos 13–15, 18 and 19 Redcliff Street and Period 2 contexts at No. 17, but no evidence of flax stems was identified which suggests it is unlikely linen production was taking place on site. The flax remains were only present in small numbers with the exception of the Period 1 assemblage at No. 18, where there are sufficient remains to suggest linseed processing was taking place.

Foodstuff plants

Plants utilised for consumption included cereal remains, fruit, nuts and herbaceous taxa. There was a relatively small occurrence of carbonised oat, free-threshing wheat (*Triticum aestivum/durum/turgidum*), emmer and spelt (*Triticum dicoccum/Triticum spelta*) wheat, rye and barley cereal grains, and carbonised/uncarbonised cereal chaff within the samples. These cereals would have been typically consumed, used to produce beer or used for fodder during the medieval period (Stone 2006, 12). Analysis of assemblages from other Bristol sites has concluded that cereals were brought into town already processed for consumption (Cox 1998, 21; Jones 2011, 49). Given this assumption, the cereal chaff within the Redcliff Street samples is more likely to have originated from bran and straw being brought into the site as animal feed, or to use as a floor surface to soak up water. This waste may subsequently have been swept up, burnt and disposed of in pits on site. Small assemblages of cereal remains have been reported on at Bridge Parade and Dundas Wharf (Cox 1998, 21; Jones and Watson 1987, 154) where a similar conclusion has been proposed.

The cereal remains were recovered in small quantities from Period 1 activity, and only a single carbonised barley grain was recovered from Period 2 samples. A slightly larger cereal assemblage was recovered from pit 1927 (Period 3). All the remains from this pit were carbonised. In addition to the proposal that the plant remains originated from waste straw and hay, it is also possible they might have been discarded waste from a nearby tenement building containing bread ovens, as observed elsewhere in Redcliffe (Jones and Watson 1987, 147).

Hazelnut, elder, cherry species, wild strawberry, crab apple, plum (*Prunus domestica*), pear (*Pyrus communis*), blackberry (*Rubus fruticosus*), raspberry (*Rubus ideaus*) and sloe (*Prunus spinosa*) together with grape (possibly cultivated or imported) and fig (imported) were present in the samples. All these species could have been eaten raw or used to make juices, wine, cider, puddings, tarts and sauces (Atkinson and Atkinson 2002, 916; Pearson 1997, 14). Some of the cherry and plum stones had sharp cuts in them, suggesting the fruit was removed in preparation for processing. Herbs found in the Redcliff

Street samples such as sea beet (*Beta vulgaris* spp *maritima*), common chickweed (*Stellaria media*), dock/sorrel (*Rumex* spp), fat hen, common orache (*Atriplex patula*) and cabbage/mustard/charlock (*Brassica* spp/ *Sinapsis* spp) were all consumed in the medieval period. These were eaten raw as salad, boiled down and used as pottage in stews and soups, and as vegetables similar to spinach (Crackles 1986, 4; Defelice 2004, 195–6; Pearson 1997, 11; Williams, 1963, 716; Behre 2008, 67–8). Water pepper (*Persicaria hydropiper*) has an acrid taste and its seeds were used for spices in food (Timson 1966, 817). Fennel (*Foeniculum vulgare*) seeds were used as a herb/spice to flavour food, and the bulb at the base was eaten raw or boiled as a vegetable (Harvey 1984, 92). Poppy (*Papaver* spp) and flax seeds were used to produce oil used for cooking food (Dickson 1996, 26; Duke 1973, 390). Poppy seeds have also been recorded as being ground down and used to make porridges and glazes for bread/cakes (Duke 1973, 390). All these species would have established within the vicinity of the site and may have been hand collected for consumption.

These species were all found in broadly similar quantities in samples from both Period 1 and 2. Although there appears to be higher amounts of some remains at Nos 13–15, 16 and 17 Redcliff Street, it has to be taken into consideration that there were a larger number of samples analysed from these areas. It can be assumed that fruits, nuts and herbaceous taxa were utilised for food production in buildings associated with the individual tenement plots as well as consumed as snacks by people working in the trades and industries in these tenements, although specific food production activities within each plot cannot be concluded. The range of foodstuff remains decreased in Period 3 samples. In general archaeobotanical remains survive in lower abundance in furnace/hearth features, but this may also reflect increasing industrialisation of the excavated area at the expense of domestic activity. The presence of some wild strawberry, hazelnut, fig and grape seeds does however suggest some continuation of food production and consumption. This assemblage of foodstuff remains is similar to that found at other excavations in Redcliffe such as Dundas Wharf, Bristol Bridge and Canynges House (Jones and Watson 1987).

Herbalism

Herbalism was an important part of society during the medieval period. Typical plants thought to have been used include elder where the flowers, leaves and berries would have been used to treat inflammation, bruises and wounds (Atkinson and Atkinson 2002, 916–17). Cleavers (*Galium aparine*) juices were used to clean the lymphatic system, cleanse wounds and protect against eczema (Press 2002, 62). Mustard/cabbage/charlock has a 'hot and dry' flavour which was thought to be good for removing phlegm from the body, and sorrel was considered a good cure for coughs (Crellin *et al.* 1997, 394). The leaves of common fumitory (*Fumaria officinalis*) are known to have been distilled and juices used to make potions/cures for arthritis, eczema, scabies, liver disorders and gallstones (Mitich 1997, 843).

There is evidence for all these species within Periods 1, 2 and 3 at Redcliff Street. But as these species all establish in areas of disturbed soil, and since no individual plant is represented in high enough numbers to assume deliberate cultivation, they may simply represent vegetation growing within the site area. However with the hazardous nature of dye production and metallurgical activities, any remedy for cuts, abrasions and lung problems would be sought, and any of these plants may have been exploited.

Fuel

The charcoal obtained from Period 2a hearths 1776 and 3651, Period 2b dye-vat hearth 1381, Period 2c water butt 1352 and furnace 1845 was dominated by beech and oak with smaller quantities of ash, hawthorn/rowan/ crab apple, willow/poplar, holly, alder, hazel, birch, wild/ bird cherry and blackthorn/sloe. The charcoal identified from Period 3 furnace 1426 was dominated by oak with smaller quantities of ash, alder/hazel, hawthorn/rowan/ crab apple, willow/poplar and wild/bird cherry. Beech and oak would have been chosen as the main fuel woods as they both have dense heartwood and if dried properly would burn slowly and maintain an even temperature (Cutler and Gale 2000, 110, 120). This would be ideal for fuel in a dye-vat hearth or furnace for metallurgical activity which would require a constant heat for long periods of time. The remaining charcoal recorded from the site (some identifiable as roundwood lateral branches) would most likely have been used within brushwood bundles as kindling for the fire.

Timber utilised on site would have been brought in from outside Bristol. The location of the Redcliff Street site next to the River Avon provides easy access for fuel wood to be transported to it. The Royal Forest of Kingswood lay to the east of the city (Moore 1982), and there were established fuel and timber trading links between Bristol and the Forest of Dean during the medieval period (Rackham 1986). The mature woodland in the Forest of Dean consisted of oak, and in the nearby Wye Valley the woodland was beech and oak. It is most likely that these sources of timber were used on most industrial sites in the area, for example oak and beech dominated assemblages identified from dye vats at the nearby former Courage Brewery site (Fig. 2.1, no. 1; Jackson 2006b, 47).

The additional species of fuel wood identified may have been sourced from local coppices or collected locally to the site (hedgerows/scrub areas). The identification of hazelnut shells, crab apple seeds, cherry pips, blackthorn/sloe stones in the plant macrofossil assemblage is another indicator that these species may have been local to the site. This interpretation of locally collected species must be viewed with caution due to the extent of trade and supply from many external areas. As a result it is not possible to use this assemblage to interpret trees within the local environment. As the fuel wood assemblages remained similar throughout Periods 2 and 3, this suggests that fuel wood was sought from the same locations.

Reconstruction of the local environment

Plant macrofossil remains were identified from a wide range of habitats including woodland/hedgerow/scrub, arable weeds, disturbed environment, disturbed environments, grassland and pasture, wetland and heathland as well as species of economic value that would have been deliberately cultivated and those that would have been imported.

A range of plant macrofossils indicative of a woodland/hedgerow/scrub environment such as hazel, cherry, crab apple, plum, pear, sloe, birch (*Betula* spp), elder, holly (*Ilex aquifolium*), ivy (*Hedera helix*), spindle tree (*Euonymus europaeus*), hawthorn, blackberry, raspberry, bramble, common whitebeam (*Sorbus aria*), yew (*Taxus baccata*), wild strawberry and rose (*Rosa* spp) was identified. These all potentially could have been found growing in hedgerows and scrub areas close to the site, or in the case of cherries, apples and plums in orchards within or just outside the city. Arable weed species such as thorow-wax (*Bupleurum rotundifolium*), charlock/cabbage/mustard, stinking chamomile, field gromwell (*Lithospermum arvense*), corncockle and corn spurrey (*Spergula arvensis*), and poppy are also present and most likely arrived on site with straw and bran. The use of hay as well as straw on site would provide an explanation for grassland/pasture species such as spreading hedge parsley (*Torilis arvensis*), thistle (*Cirsium* spp/*Carduus* spp), parsley-piert (*Aphanes arvensis*), ragged-robin (*Lychnis flos-cuculi*), black medick (*Medicago lupulina*) and self heal being present within the assemblage (Rose 2006). The widest assemblage of species identified is those indicative of a disturbed environment such as fat hen, common chickweed, dock species and black nightshade (*Solanum nigrum*). These are all common species found in town areas as trampling along pathways allows for fresh ground to be disturbed and these opportunistic species to establish. Species such as elder, nettles (*Urtica* spp), common chickweed and black nightshade tolerate a nitrogen-rich environment which would have existed within a medieval town environment. A small assemblage of species indicative of marshland areas was identified. These included clustered dock (*Rumex congolmeratus*), fool's-water-cress (*Apium nodiflorum*), sedge, bog bean (*Menyanthes trifoliata*), spikerushes (*Eleocharis* spp), yellow water lily (*Nuphar lutea*), small balsam (*Impatiens parviflora*) and water pepper. All would have flourished on marshy ground in the River Avon floodplain area (Rose 2006). These species would most likely have been brought in on the shoes of workers collecting water and disposing of waste into the river. This plant macrofossil assemblage is typical of that also found in other excavations in Redcliffe (Jones and Watson 1987, 146–7) and in other areas in Bristol such as Cabot Circus (Giorgi 2013).

The plant macrofossil assemblage was of broadly similar composition in Periods 1 and 2 representing a continuation of activities and similar conditions surrounding the site area. There are local spikes in seed numbers (for example 110 fat hen seeds within pit 1848; sample 47) which may be attributed to a fat hen plant growing on the edge of the pit. The change in activities on site between Periods 2 and 3 has an impact on the plant macrofossil assemblage observed. There are still large numbers of weeds from disturbed environments such as fat hen and common chickweed, and wetland environments such as sedge and fool's-water-cress. However, there are fewer from arable and grassland/pasture indicating a lessening in the use of hay and straw. As discussed above this is most likely due to differing preservation levels within the furnaces or increasing industrialisation of the site.

Conclusion

The samples retrieved from the excavations have provided a rich assemblage of plant macrofossil and charcoal material allowing an interesting insight into socio-economic and industrial activities, as well as the diet of the occupants, throughout the medieval period. A substantial cloth-dyeing industry appears to have been established during Period 1 and it continued into Period 2. Evidence was provided through the identification of seeds/seed pods from plants including madder, woad, dyer's greenweed and weld which would have used for dyeing activities on site. Flax seeds were also identified which raises the possibility of linseed oil extraction or possible black dye production. The cloth industry appears to have ceased by Period 3 when metal-casting activities took over.

There were a large number of remains from foodstuff plants from Periods 1 and 2 including fig, grape, apple, pear, plum, cherry species, blackberry and raspberry. There were also remains from herbaceous taxa such as sea beet, common chickweed, fat hen and dock/sorrel which may have been consumed. Foodstuff plants were less well represented in Period 3 which may indicate a diminishing of food preparation and consumption on site, or less preferential preservation conditions. A small assemblage of cereal remains including wheat, barley, rye and oat cereal grains and chaff was recovered. It is unlikely these remains represent foodstuffs, and with abundant weeds indicative of arable crops and pasture, it is more likely that they accumulated from straw and bran brought onto site. There were also a selection of plants that may have been used for medicinal purposes such as elder, cleavers, mustard/cabbage, drug fumitory and dock/sorrel.

The remaining species identified came from a selection of hedgerow/scrub/woodland, arable, grassland, disturbed ground and wetland habitats. The arable and grassland species, for example stinking chamomile, corn marigold, corncockle, spreading hedge parsley and thistle, most likely originate from straw and hay brought in from arable areas outside the town. Hedgerow/scrub/woodland species such as hazel, crab apple, bramble and elder would have existed in hedgerows and scrub areas close to the site or orchards within the city. Species such as fat hen, common chickweed and dock/sorrel would have quickly established on disturbed ground around the site. Wetland species including sedges, spike-rushes and water pepper would have existed on floodplain areas of the River Avon. These species were all recovered in varying quantities during Periods 1, 2 and 3 indicating a similar background environment throughout.

Charcoal recovered from dye vats and hearths in Period 2, and industrial hearths/furnaces in Period 3, consisted predominantly of beech and oak, which could have been obtained through trade from the Forest of Dean, or more locally from the Royal Forest of Kingswood. The additional species identified such as alder, hazel, birch, ash, hawthorn/rowan/crab apple and willow/poplar were most likely gathered more locally.

5.4 Insect Remains
David Smith

Nine sediment samples were presented for insect analysis. These came from the backfills of Period 1 pits with the exception of sample 29 from the infill of Period 2b cistern 1604. The insect faunas were examined in order to see if they provided information as to the past use of these pits and the nature of any materials that might have been present in them. The assemblage was compared with the insect faunas from the same date at the nearby Finzel's Reach site (Smith 2010; Fig. 2.1, no. 12) and other sites of similar date.

Methodology

The waterlogged samples were processed using the standard method of paraffin flotation as outlined in Kenward *et al.* (1980). The insect remains were sorted from the flots and stored in ethanol.

The Coleoptera (beetles) were identified by direct comparison to the Gorham and Girling Collections of British Coleoptera held at Birmingham University, using a Meiji EMZ microscope at magnifications between x7–x45. The various taxa of insects recovered from each sample are presented in Table 5.8. The taxonomy for the Coleoptera (beetles) follows that of Lucht (1987).

Where applicable each species of Coleoptera has been assigned to one, or more, ecological groupings and these are indicated in the second column of Table 5.8. These groupings are derived from the preliminary classifications outlined by Kenward (1978). The classification used here replicates that used in Kenward and Hall (1995). The groupings themselves are described in Table 5.9. The various proportions of these groups, expressed as percentages of the total Coleoptera present in the faunas, are shown in Table 5.9 and Fig. 5.1. Not all taxa are assigned to a particular ecological group and some taxa occur in more than one group. As a result percentages do not equal 100%.

Some of the Coleoptera have also been assigned ecological codes based upon their extent of synanthropy (dependence on human settlement) (Table 5.8). These codes are derived from those used by Kenward (1997). The author is grateful to Kenward for supplying him with a listing of the species in each grouping. The proportions of these synanthropic groupings, expressed as a percentage of the total fauna, is presented in Table 5.10 and Fig. 5.2.

Table 5.8 lists the plants with which the various phytophage (plant eating) species of beetles are associated. This information comes mainly from Koch (1992) and the plant nomenclature used is based on that of Stace (2010).

The dipterous (fly) pupae were identified using the drawings in K.G.V. Smith (1973; 1989) and, where possible, by direct comparison to modern specimens identified by Peter Skidmore (1999). The various taxa of insects recovered from these samples are presented in Table 5.8. The taxonomy used follows that of Smith (1989) for the Diptera.

Results from Period 1

Nos 13–15 Redcliff Street

Only one insect fauna was recovered from the pits at Nos 13–15. This is sample 80 from the fill of pit 2130. The insect fauna is dominated by a range of species that are normally associated with decaying waste and domestic rubbish around archaeological settlements. The sample included a range of species such as the hydrophilids *Cercyon impressus, C. haemorrhoidalis, C. melanocephalus* and *C. atricapillus* and a range of staphylinids (rove beetles) such as *Omalium* spp, *Oxytelus sculptus*, and *O. rugosus*, which are all associated with decaying waste and rubbish (Hansen 1986; Tottenham 1954). Several other species, for example *Trogophloeus bilineatus* and *Platystethus arenarius*, are today associated with wet watersides, but appear to be common in archaeological settlements where yards and paths have become muddy (Tottenham 1954; Carrott and Kenward 2001). Similarly a number of species of 'dung beetles' such as *Aphodius fossor, A. sphacelatus, A. granarius* and the staphylinid *Platystethus arenarius* were recovered. Today, these are normally associated with field dung and cow pats but are thought to have been capable of breeding in wet decaying settlement waste in the past (Carrott and Kenward 2001; Kenward *et al.* 2004).

Synanthropic taxa (groups 'st' and 'sf' in Table 5.10 and Fig. 5.2) account for 40.3% of the insect fauna from

Table 5.8 The insect remains

Sample no.	Ecological	Synanthropic	80	71	52	73	84	85	67	102	29	Phytophage host plant association (from Koch 1992)
Period			1	1	1	1	1	1	1	1	2b	
Tenement			13–15	17	17	17	18	18	18	19	17	
Feature			2130	1932	3066	3173	2143	2145	3229	3778	1604	
Context			2129	3215	3065	3174	2142	2144	3199	3779	1647	
Description			pit	pit	pit w. wattle lining	pit	dyeing pit	pit	pit	pit	stone tank or cistern	
DERMAPTERA												
Forficulidae												
Forficula auricularia (L.)	-	-	-	-	-	-	-	-	1	-	-	-
COLEOPTERA												
Carabidae												
Carabus ?granulatus L.	oa	-	-	-	-	-	-	-	1	-	-	-
Clivina fossor (L.)	oa	-	2	-	-	-	-	-	-	-	1	-
Trechus rubens (F.)	oa	-	-	-	-	-	1	1	-	-	-	-
T. quadristriatus (Schrk)/ T. obtusus Er.	oa	-	1	-	1	-	1	-	1	-	-	-
Bembidion doris (Panz.)	oa	-	-	1	-	-	-	-	-	-	-	-
Bembidion obtusum Serv.	oa	-	-	-	-	-	-	-	1	-	-	-
Bembidion spp	oa	-	-	-	1	1	2	2	-	-	-	-
Harpalus rufipes (Geer)	oa	-	-	-	-	-	-	1	-	-	-	-
Harpalus spp	oa	-	-	-	-	-	-	-	1	-	-	-
Pterostichus melanarius (Ill.)	oa	-	1	-	-	-	1	-	-	1	-	-
Pterostichus spp	oa	-	-	-	1	-	1	-	-	-	-	-
Calathus melanocephalus (L.)	oa	-	-	-	-	-	-	-	-	2	-	-
Pristonychus terricola (Hbst.)	-	ss	-	1	-	1	-	-	-	-	1	-
Agonum sp.	oa	-	-	-	-	-	-	-	1	-	1	-
Hydraenidae												
Hydraena spp	oa-w	-	-	-	-	-	1	-	-	-	-	-
Ochthebius spp	oa-w	-	1	-	-	1	2	1	-	-	2	-
Helophorus spp	oa-w	-	1	-	2	1	2	2	5	-	1	-
Hydrophilidae												
Sphaeridium scarabaeoides (L.)	rf	-	-	-	-	-	-	-	1	-	-	-
Sphaeridium lunatum F.	rf	-	-	-	-	-	-	-	-	1	-	-
Cercyon depressus Steph.	c	-	1	1	2	5	2	-	-	-	1	-
Cercyon impressus (Sturm)	rf	sf	2	-	-	1	-	-	3	1	-	-

Table 5.8 (cont.) The insect remains

Sample no.	Ecological	Synanthropic	80	71	52	73	84	85	67	102	29	Phytophage host plant association (from Koch 1992)
Period			1	1	1	1	1	1	1	1	2b	
Cercyon haemorrhoidalis (F.)	rf	sf	1	1	-	6	-	3	-	-	-	-
Cercyon melanocephalus (L.)	rf	sf	1	-	1	2	1	-	-	-	-	-
Cercyon unipunctatus (L.)	rf	st	-	-	1	2	1	-	-	-	-	-
Cercyon atricapillus (Marsh.)	rf	st	2	-	1	1	-	-	1	-	-	-
Cercyon analis (Payk.)	rt	sf	5	3	3	1	3	5	8	1	8	-
Megasternum boletophagum (Marsh.)	rt	-	-	-	-	1	1	-	-	-	1	-
Cryptopleurum minutum (F.)	rf	st	-	-	1	-	-	-	3	-	-	-
Hydrobius fuscipes (L.)	oa-w	-	1	-	-	-	-	-	1	-	-	-
Histeridae												
Acritus nigricornis (Hoffm.)	rt	st	-	-	-	-	-	1	-	-	-	-
Dendrophilus punctatus (Hbst.)	rt	sf	-	-	-	-	-	-	1	1	-	-
Hister striola Sahlb.	rt	sf	-	2	-	1	1	-	-	-	2	-
Catopidae												
Catops spp	oa	-	-	1	-	-	-	-	-	-	1	-
Choleva sp.	oa	-	-	-	-	1	-	-	-	-	-	-
Scydmaenidae												
Scydmaenidae Gen. & spp indet.	-	-	1	-	-	-	-	-	-	-	-	-
Ptiliidae												
Ptiliidae Genus & spp indet.	rt	-	-	-	-	-	-	1	-	-	-	-
Staphylinidae												
Micropeplus staphylinoides (Marsh.)	rt	-	-	-	-	1	-	-	-	-	-	-
Metopsia gallica (Koch)	-	-	-	-	-	-	-	1	-	-	-	-
Megarthrus sp.	-	sf	-	-	1	-	-	-	-	-	-	-
Phyllodrepa floralis (Payk.)	rt	-	-	-	-	-	1	1	-	1	2	-
Omalium septentrionis Thoms.	rt	-	-	-	-	-	-	-	-	-	4	-
O. ?caesum Grav.	rt	st	-	1	-	-	-	-	-	-	-	-
O. caesum Grav.	rt	st	-	-	5	-	1	1	-	-	-	-
Omalium spp	rt	-	2	3	-	1	2	2	-	2	-	-
Xylodromus concinnus (Marsh.)	rt-h	-	1	1	2	-	-	1	3	1	2	-
Acidota crenata (F.)	oa	-	1	-	-	-	-	-	-	-	-	-
Lesteva longelytrata (Goeze)	oa-d	st	1	-	-	-	-	-	-	-	2	-

Table 5.8 (cont.) The insect remains

Sample no. Period	Ecological	Synanthropic	80 1	71 1	52 1	73 1	84 1	85 1	67 1	102 1	29 2b	Phytophage host plant association (from Koch 1992)
Lesteva spp	oa-d	sf	-	1	2	-	1	-	-	-	-	-
Coprophilus striatulus (F.)	rt	st	-	-	-	-	-	-	-	1	-	-
Trogophloeus bilineatus (Steph.)	rt	sf	3	-	2	-	1	-	-	1	-	-
Trogophloeus spp	-	-	3	-	1	-	1	-	1	-	-	-
Oxytelus sculptus Grav.	rt	-	2	-	2	-	-	-	-	1	-	-
Oxytelus rugosus (F.)	rt	-	3	-	-	-	2	1	2	-	-	-
Oxytelus sculpturatus Grav.	rt	sf	-	-	-	1	-	-	2	-	-	-
Oxytelus nitidulus Grav.	rt-d	-	2	-	3	1	3	1	14	-	-	-
Platystethus arenarius (Fourc.)	rf	-	1	-	-	1	-	-	-	-	-	-
Platystethus cornutus (Grav.)	oa-d	-	3	-	-	1	1	1	1	-	-	-
Platystethus nodifrons (Man.)	oa-d	-	-	-	-	-	1	-	-	-	-	-
Platystethus nitens (Sahlb.)	oa	-	-	-	3	-	-	-	-	-	-	-
Stenus spp	-	-	1	-	1	1	1	-	2	-	1	-
Stilicus orbiculatus (Payk.)	-	-	-	-	-	-	1	-	-	-	-	-
Lathrobium spp	oa	st	-	-	-	-	-	1	1	-	-	-
Leptacinus spp	rt	st	2	-	-	-	-	-	2	1	-	-
Gyrohypnus fracticornis (Müll.)	rt	st	-	-	-	-	2	-	2	2	2	-
Xantholinus spp	-	-	1	2	-	1	2	2	-	-	-	-
Neobisnius spp	rt	-	2	-	2	-	-	-	-	-	-	-
Philonthus spp	-	-	-	-	4	4	-	5	-	-	-	-
Quedius spp	-	-	-	-	-	-	-	-	-	-	4	-
Staphylinus sp.	-	-	-	1	-	-	1	1	2	1	5	-
Philonthus spp	-	-	4	9	-	-	3	-	4	6	1	-
Tachyporus spp	-	-	-	-	-	-	-	-	-	1	-	-
Tachinus rufipes (Geer.)	-	st	-	-	-	-	1	-	-	-	-	-
Tachinus spp	-	sf	-	-	1	-	-	-	-	-	-	-
Drusilla canaliculata (F.)	rt	-	-	-	-	-	-	-	1	-	-	-
Aleocharinidae Genus & spp indet.	-	-	4	-	2	-	-	3	4	3	5	-
Helodidae												
Helodidae Gen. & spp indet.	oa-w	-	-	-	-	-	-	1	-	-	-	-
Dermestidae												
Dermestes sp.	rd-h	ss	-	-	-	-	-	-	-	1	-	-
Nitidulidae												
Meligethes spp	oa	-	-	-	-	-	-	1	1	-	-	-
O. colon (L.)	rt	sf	2	-	-	-	-	1	-	-	-	-

Table 5.8 (cont.) The insect remains

Sample no. Period	Ecological	Synanthropic	80 1	71 1	52 1	73 1	84 1	85 1	67 1	102 1	29 2b	Phytophage host plant association (from Koch 1992)
Rhizophagidae												
Rhizophagus spp	rt	sf	-	-	2	1	2	-	1	-	-	-
Cucujidae												
Monotoma picipes Hbst.	rt	st	-	-	-	1	-	-	3	-	-	-
M. testacea Motsch.	rt	st	-	-	1	-	-	-	-	-	-	-
Monotoma spp	rt	sf	-	-	-	-	-	-	-	1	-	-
Oryzaephilus surinamensis (L.)	g	ss	-	6	6	14	5	-	4	-	18	-
Cryptophagidae												
Cryptophagus spp	rd-h	sf	-	2	9	1	2	2	12	2	6	-
Atomaria spp	rd-h	st	-	3	-	-	1	1	6	1	2	-
Lathridiidae												
Enicmus minutus (Group)	rd-h	st	6	3	10	5	7	6	30	3	18	-
Cartodere ruficollis (Marsh.)	rd	sf	-	-	-	-	-	-	5	-	-	-
Corticaria/ corticarina spp	rt	sf	-	-	-	-	1	-	4	-	1	-
Mycetophagidae												
Typhaea stercorea (L.)	rd	ss	-	-	-	-	1	-	3	-	-	-
Colydiidae												
Aglenus brunneus (Gyll.)	rt-h	ss	-	2	3	-	-	-	9	-	1	-
Endomychidae												
Mycetaea hirta (Marsh.)	rd-h	ss	-	4	12	2	3	-	6	5	7	-
Coccinellidae												
Coccidula rufa (Hbst.)	oa	-	-	-	1	-	-	-	-	-	-	-
Lyctidae												
Lyctus linearis (Goeze)	l-h	sf	-	-	-	-	-	-	-	-	1	-
Anobiidae												
Stegobium paniceum (L.)	g	ss	-	-	-	-	-	1	-	-	-	-
Anobium punctatum (Geer)	l-h	sf	4	4	13	12	13	12	3	3	26	-
Ptinidae												
Tipnus unicolor (Pill. Mitt.)	rd-h	st	1	4	-	2	1	-	1	1	2	-
Ptinus fur (L.)	rd-h	sf	1	1	1	1	1	-	-	-	5	-
Anthicidae												
Anthicus spp	rt	-	-	1	1	-	1	1	2	-	1	-
Tenebionidae												
Blaps mucronata Latr.	rt	ss	-	1	-	-	-	-	-	-	1	-
Tenebrio obscurus F.	rf	ss	-	-	1	1	-	-	-	-	1	-
Scarabaeidae												
Trox scaber (L.)	rt	sf	1	-	-	-	-	-	-	-	1	-

Table 5.8 (cont.) The insect remains

Sample no. Period	Ecological	Synanthropic	80 1	71 1	52 1	73 1	84 1	85 1	67 1	102 1	29 2b	Phytophage host plant association (from Koch 1992)
Oxyomus silvestris (Scop.)	rt	st	1	-	-	-	-	-	-	-	-	-
Aphodius fossor (L.)	oa-rf	-	1	-	-	-	-	-	-	-	-	-
Aphodius rufipes (L.)	oa-rf	-	-	-	-	1	-	-	-	-	-	-
Aphodius contaminatus (Hbst.)	oa-rf	-	-	-	-	-	1	-	-	-	-	-
Aphodius sphacelatus (Panz.) or *A. prodromus* (Brahm)	oa-rf	-	1	-	-	1	-	2	-	1	-	-
Aphodius fimetarius (L.)	oa-rf	-	-	-	-	-	-	-	-	-	1	-
Aphodius granarius (L.)	oa-rf	-	1	1	1	1	3	3	1	1	1	-
Chyrsomelidae												
Gastroidea spp	oa-p	-	-	-	-	-	1	-	-	-	-	On *Polygonum* spp (knot weed) and *Rumex* spp (dock)
Phyllotreta spp	oa	-	-	-	-	2	-	1	7	1	-	-
Chaetocnema concinna (Marsh.)	oa	-	-	-	-	-	-	-	1	-	-	-
Chaetocnema spp	oa	-	-	-	-	1	-	-	1	-	-	-
Psylliodes sp.	oa-p	-	-	-	1	-	1	-	-	-	-	-
Bruchidae												
Bruchus pisorum (L.)	oa-pu	-	1	3	3	6	5	7	-	8	4	-
Scolytidae												
Leperisinus varius (F.)	oa-l	-	-	-	-	1	1	1	-	-	-	Mainly on *Fraxinus* (Ash)
Dryocoetes villosus (F.)	oa-l	-	-	-	-	1	-	-	-	-	-	under bark on range of hardwood trees
Curculionidae												
Rhynchites spp	oa-l	-	1	-	-	-	-	-	-	-	-	Mainly on Rosacae shrubs
Apion aeneum (F.)	oa	-	1	-	-	-	-	-	-	-	-	Common mallow (*Malva sylvestris* L.)
Apion spp	oa-p	-	-	-	-	1	-	-	1	2	-	-
Sitona lineatus (L.)	oa-p	-	-	-	-	-	-	-	1	-	-	*Trifolium* species (Clover)
Sitona suturalis Steph.	oa	-	-	-	-	1	-	-	-	-	-	
Sitona flavescens (Marsh.)	oa-p	-	1	2	-	-	-	-	1	-	-	*Trifolium* species (Clover)
Sitona humeralis Steph.	oa-p	-	1	-	-	-	-	-	1	-	-	Often on medicks (*Medicago*) and clover (*Trifolium*)
Sitona spp	oa	-	-	-	2	1	-	-	6	-	1	

Table 5.8 (cont.) The insect remains

Sample no. Period	Ecological	Synanthropic	80 1	71 1	52 1	73 1	84 1	85 1	67 1	102 1	29 2b	Phytophage host plant association (from Koch 1992)
Sitophilus granarius (L.)	g	ss	-	2	1	5	4	1	3	-	3	
Ceutorhynchus erysimi (F.)	oa-p	-	2	-	-	1	-	-	-	-	-	On *Capsella bursa-pastoris* (L.) Medik. (Shepherd's purse)
Ceutorhynchus spp	oa-p	-	-	-	-	-	1	-	5	-	-	
Gymnetron spp	oa-p	-	-	-	-	-	-	1	1	-	-	*Plantago lanceolata* L. (plantain)

DIPTERA

SUBORDER NEMATOCERA

Scatopsidae

Scatopse notata L.	-	-	-	4	9	1	2	6	1	-	-	-

SUBORDER CYCLORRHAPHA

Family, genus & spp indet.	-	-	1	9	7	-	-	-	16	10	9	-

Sepsidae

Sepsis spp	-	-	4	-	5	35	22	6	-	-	-	-

Sphaeroceridae

Copromyzinae Genus and spp indet.	-	-	-	1	-	1	-	-	150+	-	-	-
cf. *Telomerina flavipes* (Meigen)	-	-	-	36	-	100+	14	-	-	-	50+	-
Thoracochaeta zosterae (Hal.)	-	-	5	400+	47	150+	37	38	-	100+	100+	-

Calliphoridae

Calliphora vicina Rob.-Des.	-	-	-	-	-	-	-	-	-	-	-	-
Calliphora spp	-	-	1	-	1	1	-	-	-	-	-	-

Muscinae

Musca domestica L.	-	-	-	1	3	10	3	-	-	2	-	-
Muscina stabulans (Fall.)	-	-	-	-	-	10	5	1	-	-	-	-

Hippoboscidae

Melophagus ovinus L.	-	-	1	-	-	5	-	-	-	-	-	-

HYMENOPTERA

Formicoidea Family Genus and spp indet.	-	-	2	-	-	-	-	2	-	-	-	-

Table 5.9 The proportions of the ecological groupings of Coleoptera

Sample number	80	71	52	73	84	85	67	102	29
Context number	2129	3215	3065	3174	2142	2144	3199	3779	1647
Total number individuals	82	67	114	100	101	80	189	55	149
Total number of taxa	46	29	42	46	52	38	55	27	42
oa	26.8%	13.4%	15.8%	23.0%	27.7%	31.3%	21.2%	29.1%	10.1%
w	3.7%	0.0%	1.8%	2.0%	5.0%	5.0%	3.2%	0.0%	2.0%
d	7.3%	1.5%	7.0%	2.0%	5.9%	2.5%	7.9%	0.0%	1.3%
c	1.2%	1.5%	1.8%	5.0%	2.0%	0.0%	0.0%	0.0%	0.7%
oa-p	4.9%	3.0%	0.9%	2.0%	3.0%	1.3%	5.3%	3.6%	0.0%
l	6.1%	6.0%	11.4%	14.0%	13.9%	16.3%	1.6%	5.5%	18.1%
rd	9.8%	25.4%	28.1%	11.0%	15.8%	11.3%	33.9%	21.8%	26.8%
rf	12.2%	3.0%	5.3%	17.0%	5.9%	11.3%	4.2%	7.3%	2.0%
rt	31.7%	20.9%	23.7%	9.0%	20.8%	18.8%	29.1%	20.0%	18.1%
pu	1.2%	4.5%	2.6%	6.0%	5.0%	8.8%	0.0%	14.5%	2.7%
g	0.0%	11.9%	6.1%	19.0%	8.9%	2.5%	3.7%	0.0%	14.1%

Ecological coding (Kenward and Hall 1995)

oa (& ob) - species which will not breed in human housing   w - aquatic species
c - species associated with salt water and coastal areas   d - species associated with damp watersides and river banks
rd - species primarily associated with drier organic matter   rf - species primarily associated with foul organic matter often dung
rt - insects associated with decaying organic matter but not belonging to either the rd or rf groups
g - species associated with grain   l - species associated with timber
p - phytophage species often associated with waste areas or grassland and pasture
pu - species associated with pulses (peas and beans)

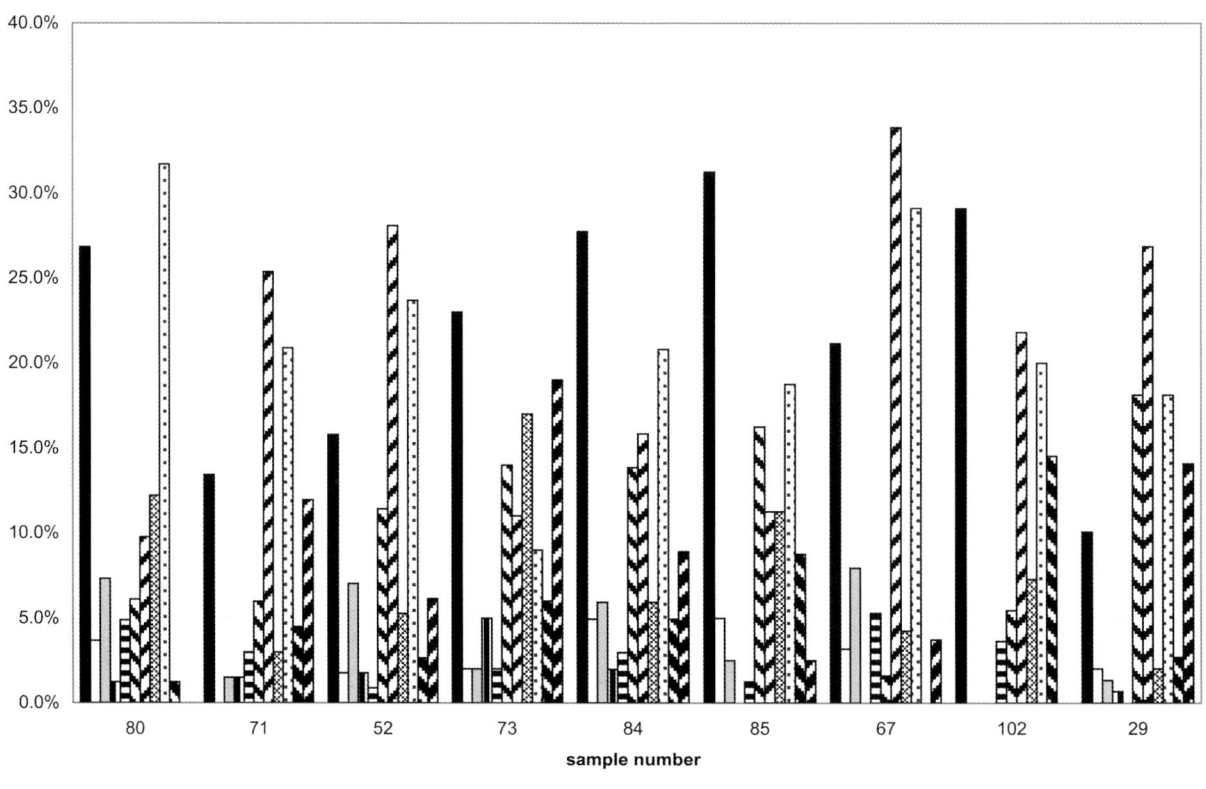

Fig. 5.1 The proportions of the ecological groupings of Coleoptera

Table 5.10 *The proportions of the synanthropic groupings of Coleoptera*

Sample Number	80	71	52	73	84	85	67	102	29
Context number	2129	3215	3065	3174	2142	2144	3199	3779	1647
st	15.9%	16.4%	16.7%	11.0%	13.9%	12.5%	25.9%	14.5%	18.1%
sf	24.4%	20.9%	30.7%	27.0%	25.7%	28.8%	20.6%	16.4%	34.2%
ss	0.0%	23.9%	20.2%	23.0%	12.9%	2.5%	13.8%	9.1%	21.5%
h	15.9%	35.8%	43.9%	23.0%	27.7%	27.5%	37.6%	29.1%	47.0%

sf - facultative synanthropes - common in 'natural' habitats but clearly favoured by artificial ones
st - typically synanthropes - particularly favoured by artificial habitats but believed to be able to survive in nature in the long term
ss - strong synanthropes - essentially dependant on human activity for survival
h - members of the 'house fauna' this is a very arbitrary group based on archaeological associations (Hall and Kenward 1990)

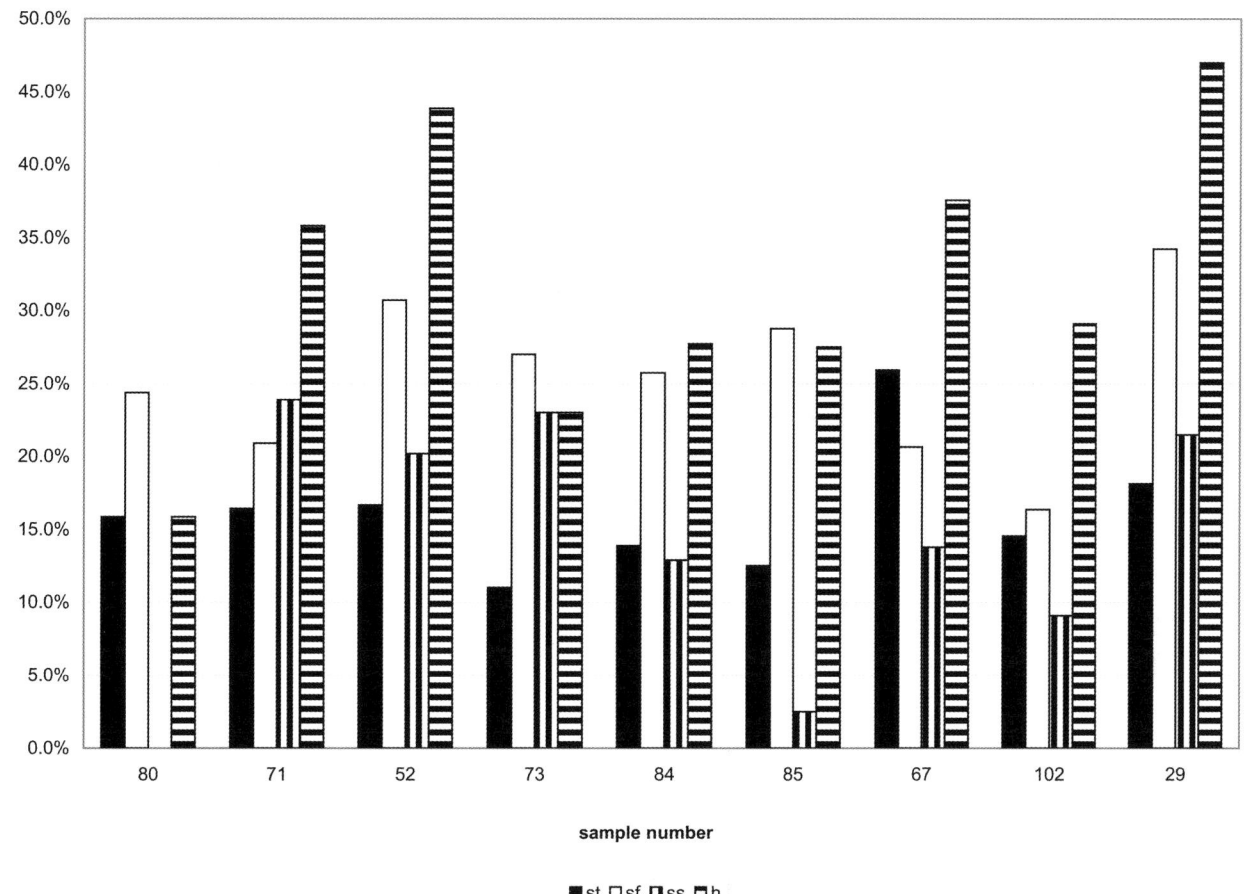

Fig. 5.2 *The proportions of the synanthropic groupings of Coleoptera*

this context. A number of insects, such as *Xylodromus concinnus, Enicmus minutus* and the spider beetles *Ptinus fur* and *Tipnus unicolor* are associated with dry straw, hay and other settlement material. These species, along with the 'woodworm' *Anobium punctatum* account for the relatively high proportion (15.9%) of Kenward's 'house fauna' recovered in this sample.

There also are a number of indications that cess also may have become incorporated into this deposit. The *Sepsis* spp and *Thoracochaeta zosterae* flies are usually associated with faecal material (Smith 1989; Belshaw 1989; Skidmore 1999). Though the 'pea weevil' *Bruchus pisorum* can enter deposits in spoilt pulses, it is usually thought to have been consumed by accident in food and then subsequently becoming incorporated directly into cess (Osborne 1983).

There are hints that hide processing and wool or dyeing wastes also entered this deposit. A single individual of *Trox scaber* was recovered. The presence of large numbers of this species in archaeological pits has been specifically linked to tanning waste (Hall and Kenward 2003). Similarly, a single puparia of the 'sheep ked' *Melophagus ovinus* was also recovered. This species has been linked directly to wool processing and dyeing (Hall and Kenward 2003; Buckland and Perry 1989).

Lastly, a small number of species may indicate the nature of the vegetation in the yards around these pits. Both *Sitona flavescens* and *S. humeralis* are associated with clover (*Trifolium* spp), and the small weevil *Ceutorhynchus erysimi* is associated with shepherd's purse (*Capsella bursa-pastoris* (L.) Medik.) (Koch 1992).

No. 17 Redcliff Street

Three insect faunas (sample 71 from pit 1932, sample 52 from pit 3066 and sample 73 from pit 3173) were recovered from No. 17. The insect fauna are dominated by species associated with settlement waste and cess, but taxa associated with cess are particularly abundant in the insect fauna. More than 400 puparia of the small fly *Thoracochaeta zosterae* were recovered from pit 1932 and more than 150 from pit 3173. Today, *T. zosterae* is associated with seaweed but is frequently recovered from archaeological cess pits (Belshaw 1989; Webb *et al.* 1989). It has been suggested that archaeological pits which contained a mix of decayed plant materials, saturated in urine and faecal matter, may have produced an environment similar to that found in seashore debris along the tide line. This species of fly also prefers a wet saline environment as larvae but drier material when it pupates (Webb *et al.* 1989). This may suggest that the material in the pits at Redcliff Street were seasonally, or periodically, dry and then wet. Saline conditions also are suggested by the presence of a number of individuals of *Cercyon depressus*. Today, this beetle is associated with seaweed and the coast (Hansen 1986), but is sometimes recovered from archaeological cess and rubbish pit deposits. Large numbers of the larvae of the flies c.f. *Telomerina flavipes* and *Sepsis* were recovered. Both taxa are typically associated with cess, as is the 'filter fly' *Scatopse notata* (Smith 1989). The grain pests *Sitophilus granarius* (the granary weevil) and *Oryzaephilus surinamensis* (the sawtoothed grain beetle) and *Bruchus pisorum* (the pea weevil) can be associated with spoilt stored products and food, but they also can occur in cess pits as a result of the consumption by humans of rough pottage and 'horse bread' which contained infested grain and peas (Osborne 1983).

There is also evidence that a range of domestic rubbish and settlement waste entered these pits. This is clearly suggested by the relatively large numbers of Kenward's 'house fauna' and other synanthropic species of beetle recovered (Table 5.10 and Fig. 5.2). This includes a range of species commonly associated with dry materials around human settlements such as *Xylodromus concinnus*, the lathridiids, the cryptophagids, *Mycetaea hirta*, the spider beetles *Ptinus fur* and *Tipnus unicolor,* and the 'woodworm' *Anobium punctatum*. In addition, the 'ground beetle' *Pristonychus terricola*, the 'churchyard beetle' *Blaps mucronata* and the 'darkling beetle' *Tenebrio obscurus* are all particularly associated with human settlement and are regarded as strongly synanthropic (Harde 1984; Kenward 1997). Similarly, many of the species of *Cercyon* and staphylinid beetles, discussed above (see sample 80 from pit 2130), which were indicative of decaying settlement waste were also recovered here. Also present were a number of individuals of *Hister striola*, a species of 'pill beetle' which is associated with decaying food waste and predates on small fly larvae (Halstead 1963). *Aglenus bruneus*, *Rhizophagus* spp, *Monotoma picipes* and *Monotoma testacea* are also associated with similar materials, but in the archaeological record these beetles are thought to indicate material which has been redeposited or buried (Carrott and Kenward 2001).

There is limited evidence that wool processing or dyeing occurred in the area. This is suggested by the recovery of the puparia of five sheep keds, *Melophagus ovinus*, in pit 3173. This species is thought to have a clear association with wool processing waste in the archaeological record (Buckland and Perry 1989; Hall and Kenward 2003).

Finally, a very small number of phytophages, such as *Sitona* spp and *Ceutorhynchus erysimi* may suggest that clover (*Trifolium* spp), and shepherd's purse (*Capsella bursa-pastoris* (L.) Medik.) grew in the yards surrounding these features.

No. 18 Redcliff Street

Three insect faunas (sample 84 from pit 2143, sample 85 from pit 2145 and sample 67 from pit 3229) derived from pits at No. 18. The majority of the insects recovered are clearly associated with a range of decaying settlement waste (ecological groups 'rt' and 'rd' in Table 5.9 and Fig. 5.1). The *Cercyon* species, many of the staphylinids 'rove beetles' and the puparia of both the 'common housefly' *Musca domestica* and the 'lesser stable fly' *Muscina stabulans* are typical of this type of settlement rubbish. There is also clear evidence that drier settlement material and waste was incorporated into these deposits. This is indicated by the relatively large proportions of taxa from Kenward's 'house fauna' and other synanthropes recovered (Table 5.10 and Fig. 5.2). The range of taxa from this grouping includes *Xylodromus concinnus,* lathridiids, cryptophagids, *Typhaea stercorea, Mycetaea hirta, Anobium punctatum* and the 'spider beetles' *Ptinus fur* and *Tipnus unicolor*.

As with the other pits, there is good evidence for the presence of cess from the fly puparia such as *Scatopse notata, Sepsis* spp, *Thoracochaeta zosterae* and the Copromyzinae (with over 150 individuals of the latter recovered in sample 67). Various pests of stored products were also recovered from these pits; for example, the 'sawtoothed grain beetle' *Oryzaephilus surinamensis*, the 'granary weevil' *Sitophilus granarius*, the 'pea weevil' *Bruchus pisorum* and the 'biscuit beetle' *Stegobium paniceum*. As with the other pits from this area of Bristol it is possible that the presence of these species indicates that spoilt stored goods were dumped here, but it is as likely that these insects entered these pits in cess after being consumed in infested foodstuffs.

Very few individuals were recovered which indicate the nature of the surrounding landscape. This consists of a narrow range of 'ground beetles' such as *Pterostichus melanarius* and *Harpalus rufipes* and weevils such as the different species of *Sitona* and the *Gymnetron* spp recovered. The former are associated with clover (*Trifolium* spp), and the later with plantain (*Plantago* spp) (Koch 1992), and together they suggest that rough ground and weedy areas were present.

No. 19 Redcliff Street

Only one insect fauna was recovered from No. 19 (sample 102 from pit 3778). This produced an insect fauna which is essentially similar to those recovered from the other pits with many of the beetles associated with a range of decaying settlement and housing waste. There is also evidence for the inclusions of cess into these deposits, since over a hundred pupae of the fly *Thoracochaeta zosterae* were recovered. This species of fly seems to be particularly associated with cess pits in the archaeological record (Osborne 1983; Skidmore 1999).

Results from Period 2b

One insect fauna was recovered from a Period 2b deposit, sample 29 from the fill of cistern 1604 at No. 17 Redcliff Street. The insect fauna is essentially similar in the nature to those from the Period 1 pits, with many indicators that settlement waste and cess were incorporated into this deposit. This is particularly suggested by the many hundreds of puparia of flies that were recovered. Both the larval and pupae stages of the flies *Thoracochaeta zosterae* and c.f. *Telomerina flavipes* are often associated with cess pits in the archaeological record (Osborne 1983; Skidmore 1999).

Conclusions

The insect faunas were all very similar with the majority of the insects being synanthropic and often part of Kenward's 'house fauna' (Kenward and Hall 1995), suggesting an origin in settlement and domestic waste. This includes a range of species such as *Xylodromus concinnus*, lathridiids, cryptophagids, *Typhaea stercorea*, *Mycetaea hirta*, the 'woodworm' *Anobium punctatum* and the 'spider beetles' *Tipnus unicolor* and *Ptinus fir*. Other species, particularly the range of hydrophilid *Cercyon* and staphylinid 'rove beetles' recovered, are normally associated with wet decaying rubbish and waste (Hansen 1986; Tottenham 1954). Many of the flies puparia recovered, such as *Thoracochaeta zosterae*, *Scatopse notata*, *Sepsis* spp and c.f. *Telomerina flavipes* are associated with cess in both the archaeological record and the present (Belshaw 1989; Skidmore 1999; Smith 1973 and 1989). A range of pests of stored products were also recovered, including the 'granary weevil', *Sitophilus granarius,* and the 'pea weevil', *Bruchus pisorum*. These may have been included into these deposits in dumped spoilt grain and pulses. However, it seems more likely that they represent the inclusion of cess since they have probably been consumed in low quality food such as 'horse bread' and rough pottage (Osborne 1983).

This type of insect fauna, often recovered from sub-rectangular pits or latrine pits, is very common in many medieval sites of this period, for example Worcester (Osborne 1983); Leicester (Skidmore 1999); St Mary's Spital, London (Smith 1997); The Charterhouse, London (Smith 2002a); Winchester Palace, London (Smith 2006); Edgbaston and Parks Street, Birmingham (Smith 2009) and the Guildhall site, London (Smith and Morris 2007). In terms of Bristol itself, 5–7 Welsh Back also produced a set of insect faunas very similar to those recovered at the present site (Smith 2001). The insect fauna is also very similar in its nature to many of those retrieved from the pits and well/latrine shafts of an equivalent date at Finzel's Reach (Smith 2010). Where there is a clear difference is that some of the insect faunas in the ditches and pits at Finzel's Reach clearly suggested that they contained distinct dumps of stabling waste (Kenward and Hall 1997). The insects recovered from the fills of a 13th to 14th-century pond at the Cathedral School/College Square site in Bristol also appeared to indicate the dumping of stabling material (Smith 2002b).

Unfortunately, there is little evidence for either tanning or dyeing in the insect remains. Both crafts appear to have sets of distinctive insects and plants associated with them (Hall and Kenward 2003). With the exception of the limited number of sheep keds which have been associated with wool preparation, very few taxa of these 'indicator groups' were recovered from the present site. Therefore, it is more likely that the material recovered was later infilling of these features with domestic industry settlement waste and rubbish after their primary use. The possible tanning pits at Edgbaston and Park Streets, Birmingham (Smith 2009) appear to have been infilled in the same way. More relevantly, many of the pits at Finzel's Reach also appeared to contain a similar mix of settlement waste and cess to that recovered from here, which may suggest a general abandonment of this part of Redcliffe by the dyeing/tanning industry in the 12th/13th centuries.

5.5 Geoarchaeology
Keith Wilkinson

In July 2007 ARCA drilled three geoarchaeological boreholes as part of the excavation. The archaeological and palaeoenvironmental evidence of the stratigraphy recorded in the boreholes was examined together with that reported in an earlier geotechnical survey (C.J. Associates 2007). Detailed lithological descriptions of the borehole stratigraphy are available in the archive.

Previous geoarchaeological borehole surveys have been undertaken in a number of localities in the vicinity of the site. Wilkinson (2004) examined cores collected by Soil Mechanics Ltd at Redcliff Backs, a study that revealed a stratigraphy comprising fluvial gravels interbedded with estuarine and alluvial silts overlying the Mercia Mudstone bedrock. ARCA undertook a geoarchaeological borehole survey at 55–61 Victoria Street in 2006 (Wilkinson 2007a). The stratigraphy at 55–61 Victoria Street comprised a 6–7m thick sequence of laminated alluvial sands, alluvial/intertidal silts and clays overlying bedrock. A further borehole survey was undertaken by ARCA at 32–6 Victoria Street in July 2007. The stratigraphy at this site comprises a 9m thick complex of laminated sand and silt overlying a palaeosol dating from 5320–5070 cal BC (Beta 245646, 6280±40 BP; Wilkinson 2008a). Finally a geoarchaeological and geotechnical survey has also been carried out at 55–60 St Thomas Street. This revealed a sequence comprising 9.5m of sands, silts and clays and 3m of made ground overlying 2m of Pleistocene gravels and the Mercia Mudstone bedrock (Wilkinson 2008b; 2011b).

The objectives of the geoarchaeological study were to accurately record the Holocene and Late Pleistocene stratigraphy at the site; to determine how the Quaternary stratigraphy from this site correlates with that from elsewhere in central Bristol (lithologically, chronologically and biostratigraphically), to determine whether deposits suitable for microbiological analysis exist within the sequence, and if so, to provide a picture of palaeoenvironments at the site, and to determine the impact of people on past environments in the Redcliffe/central Bristol area.

Methodology

The three boreholes were drilled in the locations shown on Figure 5.3 through the base of the excavation trenches. Therefore the borehole cores sample the base of the archaeological sequence (in the case of BH 3) and the underlying alluvial and intertidal strata. Drilling was carried out using Eijelkamp drilling equipment. This comprises an Atlas Cobra petrol-powered pneumatic hammer, gouge augers with diameters of 40mm, 50mm and 60mm, a 53mm diameter by 1000mm long core-sampler and 1000mm extension rods (see van Walt 2005 for details). Gouge auger heads were used to drill through the 'made ground' (i.e. archaeological sediments), while the core sampler was used to sample the underlying alluvial/intertidal succession. The boreholes were drilled to a depth of between 9 and 10m. The Atlas Cobra drilling equipment is extremely time consuming and labour intensive to use at depths below 10m, while gravels of the (Pleistocene) Avon Formation were reached at 9.95m below ground surface in Borehole BH 2. For these reasons the decision was taken to discontinue the boreholes on reaching a depth of 10m (9m in BH 3). In addition to BH 2, several of the geotechnical boreholes provide information on the Pleistocene and earlier stratigraphy that underlies the site. Cores were labelled and sealed on site and transported to the laboratory for further study.

In the laboratory the plastic tubes containing the cores were sliced open using an angle grinder. The sediments revealed were carefully hand-cleaned and described using standard geological criteria (Tucker 1982; Jones *et al.* 1999a; Munsell Color 2000). Each core was then individually photographed. Sediment retention was excellent in all cores and drilling operations appear to have caused minimal damage to the sampled stratigraphy.

A single sub-sample of 10mm thickness was extracted from an organic lamina at the base of BH 1 for AMS radiocarbon dating. It was submitted to the Beta Radiocarbon facility, Miami, Florida for measurement (Table 5.11).

Lithological descriptions were combined with positional information within a RockWorks database (Rock Ware 2008). Lithological data obtained by the C.J. Associates (2007) geotechnical survey was then added to the database to augment the stratigraphic record. The RockWorks software was then used to combine lithological units into higher-level groupings (informal and formal 'formations') corresponding to geological/geographic and archaeological events. The RockWorks database was used to plot the cross section shown in Fig. 5.4.

The archive resulting from boreholes comprises a paper

Table 5.11 AMS radiocarbon dating results. The radiocarbon date was calibrated using the IntCal04 curve (Reimer et al. 2004) and OxCal 4 software (Bronk Ramsey 2008).

Lab. No.	BH	Depth interval	14C age	Calibrated age
Beta-245645	1	9.87–9.88m	4720±40 BP	3630–3580 cal BC (15.0%), 3540–3360 cal BC (80.4%)

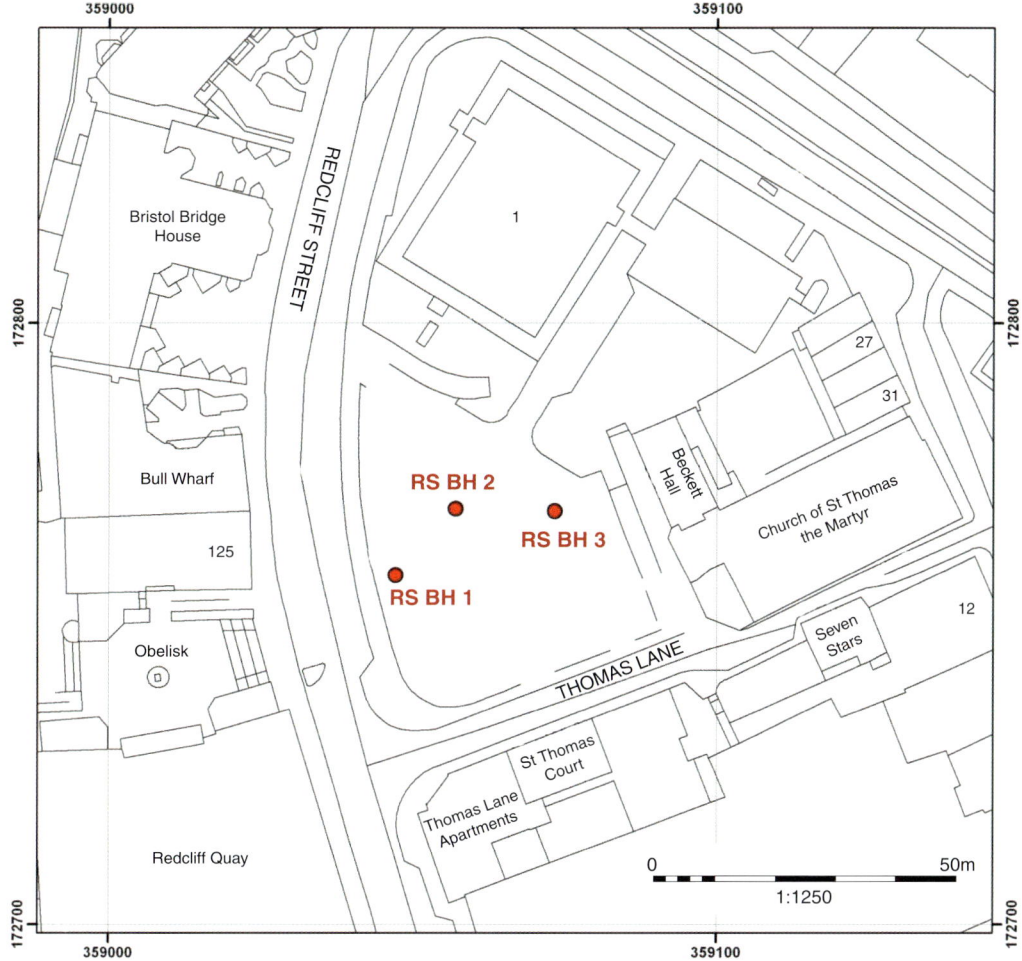

Fig. 5.3   Location of the geoarchaeological boreholes. Scale 1:1250

and digital record (a copy of the written component forms part of the site archive). The cores have been retained in storage at the University of Winchester.

Stratigraphy

Four major stratigraphic units ('formations') are present (one of which, i.e. strata of the Mercia Mudstone Group, was only found in the geotechnical boreholes). The stratigraphy is reviewed below in chronological order and is presented as a composite cross section in Fig. 5.4.

Mercia Mudstone Group

ARCA's drilling operations stopped after drilling through 9–10m of deposits of the Wentlooge formation. Deposits of the Mercia Mudstone Group (MMG: previously and now informally known as Redcliff Sandstone) were not encountered in the ARCA boreholes. However, the MMG was found in two C.J. Associates boreholes at 13.8m below ground surface. The C.J. Associates driller's logs suggest that the MMG comprises alternating beds of mudstone and conglomerates.

Avon Formation

According to the geotechnical boreholes, fluvial gravels attributable to the Avon Formation (Pleistocene) (*sensu* Campbell *et al.* 1999), unconformably overlie the MMG across the whole site (the lower contact of the Avon Formation was not reached in the ARCA boreholes and the upper contact only in BH 2). The gravel beds are between 1.3m and 2.6m in thickness and according to the C.J. Associates driller's logs comprise rounded pebbles and cobbles of limestone and calcareous mudstone in a sand matrix. The fluvial gravels outcrop in excess of 10m below the ground surface.

As with other sites in central Bristol where fluvial gravels of the Avon Formation have been noted, the gravels probably represent a former bed of the River Avon forming in braided channels. Braided rivers only existed in southern Britain during cold stages of the Pleistocene and therefore the relatively low elevation of the gravel outcrop at the present site suggests a date in the latest part of the Late Pleistocene, i.e. the Devensian Late Glacial (Bates 2003).

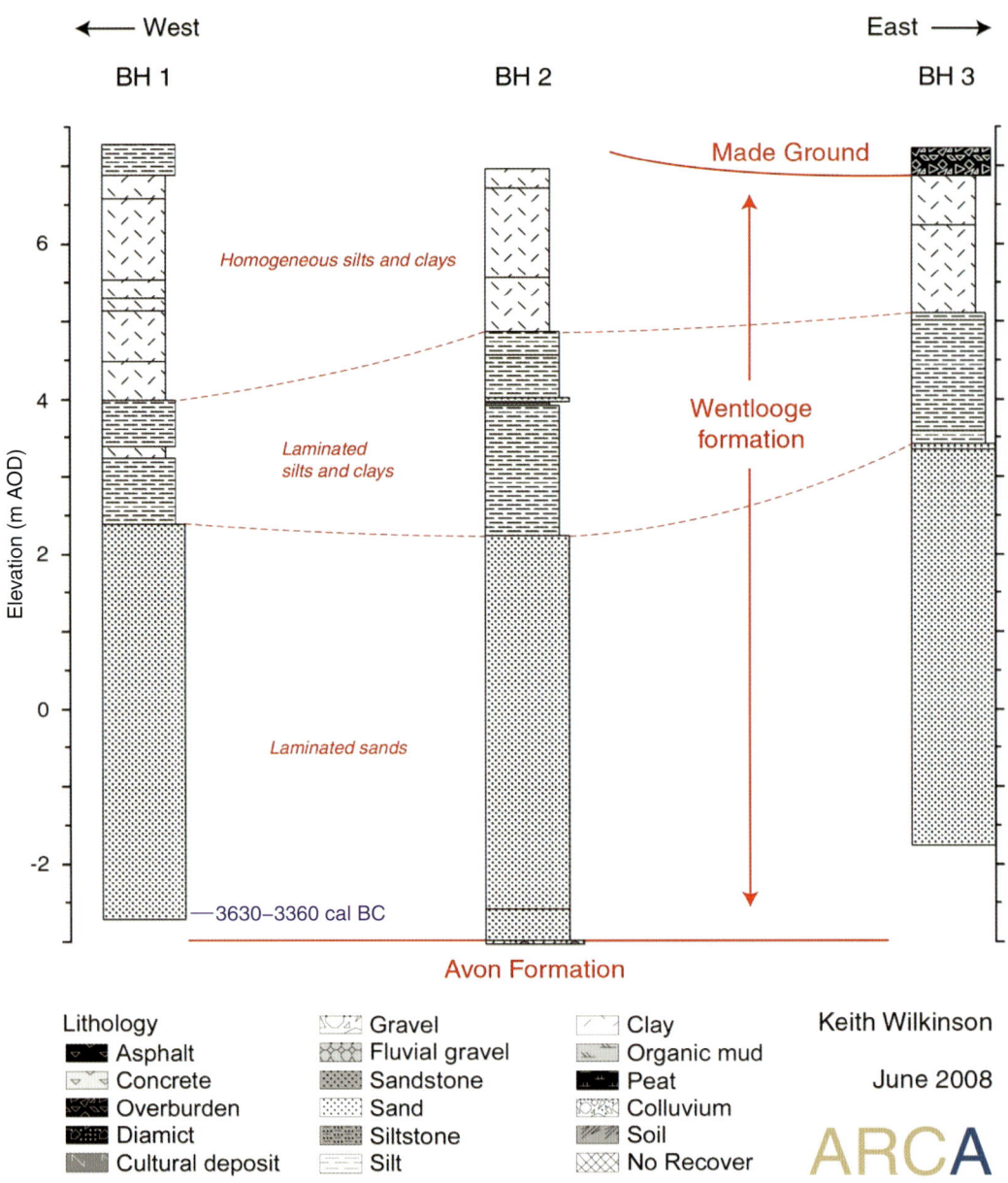

Fig. 5.4 Cross section through the deposits revealed in the geoarchaeological boreholes

Gravel strata with a similar stratigraphic position, elevation and morphological properties to those at the present site have been found in a number of geoarchaeological borehole studies in central Bristol in the last decade. Avon Formation gravels have been found outcropping at Harbourside (Wilkinson 2011a; Wilkinson and Tinsley 2005); Redcliff Backs (Wilkinson 2004); Welshback (Wilkinson 2007b); Broad Quay (Wilkinson 2007c); 55–60 St Thomas Street (Wilkinson 2011b) and Cabot Circus (Wilkinson 2013). It is also probable that deposits of the Avon Formation have been removed from many areas of central Bristol by channel scouring processes in the Holocene.

Wentlooge formation
Silts, clays and fine sands of the informally defined Wentlooge formation (*sensu* Allen and Rae 1987) form the bulk of the sediment succession at Redcliff Street, as they do at most other sites in central Bristol. At the present site the Wentlooge formation can be divided into three lithofacies: laminated silts and sands; laminated silts and clays, and homogeneous, iron-stained silts and clays. Deposits encountered in the cores below +2.5m (BH 3) to +3m AOD (BH 1 and BH 2) almost entirely consist of the first lithofacies. These sediments comprise 200mm-thick sets of laminated reddish brown fine silts/clay and fine sands, with occasional thin beds of fine sand. Within each of the beds, wavy and straight (occasionally

angled), parallel, continuous laminae of alternating silt/clay and fine sand are clustered in 20–50mm thick bundles. The sedimentary characteristics of the laminated sediments suggest that they formed in a deep water channel environment. However, whether deposition was in a predominantly tidal or fluvial system cannot be stated with any certainty on the basis of the descriptive data collected here. It is notable that stratigraphy with almost identical properties to those described above, have been found in borehole cores in several other sites in the Redcliffe area, e.g. 32–36 Victoria Street (Wilkinson 2008a), 55–61 Victoria Street (Wilkinson 2007a) and 55–60 St Thomas Street (Wilkinson 2011b). Not only is the stratigraphy the same at these other Redcliffe sites, but the elevation at which the laminated sands outcrop is comparable. It is thus highly likely that the laminated beds at all these sites formed in the same channel feature, while it is possible that they may correlate with channel gravels noted in cores at Redcliff Backs (Wilkinson 2004).

Overlying the laminated silt and sand sediments at the base of the Wentlooge formation at this site are a series of 400–600mm-thick beds comprised predominantly of laminated silts and clays. These extend from +2.5m to +5.1m AOD. The silt/clay laminae are predominately straight (although wavy laminae were noted in BH 3) and occur in regular-sized bundles. Coarse sand and granular-size charcoal pieces were noted as rare inclusions in the laminated silt/clay layers, perhaps indicating human activity within the wider catchment, while fragmented mollusc shell (unidentifiable) was also present. These structural and morphological properties suggest regular and pulsed deposition, but in this case the most likely depositional environment is on mud flats or on channel margins.

The very top of the Wentlooge formation (i.e. above +5.1m AOD) comprises homogeneous reddish grey to greyish brown silt/clays. Morphological properties are otherwise similar to those described for the underlying laminated silt/clays. It is highly likely that laminae were once present in the homogeneous unit, but that bioturbation and other diagenetic processes have led to their disappearance. If this is the case, it is likely that the homogeneous silt/clays also formed in a mud flat or floodplain environment.

There are several possible scenarios to explain the stratigraphic data:
1. The channel in which the laminated silts and sands were deposited migrated away from the site leading to deposition of laminated silts and clays in a location that was now marginal to the channel. Bioturbation then caused the loss of the lamina structure in the upper 1.8–2.8m of stratigraphy.
2. Sedimentation within the original channel led over time to a shallower, lower energy channel in which silts and clays were deposited.
3. Relative sea level rise caused an evolution from fluvial (laminated silts and sands) to intertidal (homogeneous silts and clays) sedimentation.

It is not possible to determine which of these explanations is correct based on data from the present site, but an examination of the bedding properties and elevation of Wentlooge formation strata from all of the sites that have been geoarchaeologically investigated in Redcliffe may provide an answer.

Made ground

Deposits relating to human activity conformably overlie homogenous silt/clays of the Wentlooge formation at around +6.9m AOD. These were not sampled in ARCA's borehole cores (except in the top of BH 3), but were rather encountered in the gouge auger heads used to start the drilling operations. Nevertheless anthropogenic material was comparatively rare even in these samples as the archaeological excavation had almost completely removed the archaeological strata prior to the borehole survey commencing.

Borehole chronology

In order to provide an absolute chronology for the Holocene part of the sequence and to enable comparison with other sites from Bristol and the surrounding region, AMS radiocarbon dating samples were taken from suitable strata. Unfortunately a single organic lamina from the base of BH 1 proved to be the only possible location for sampling (Table 5.11).

The results demonstrate that organic sedimentation at the margins of the river channel took place in the Early-Middle Neolithic (3630–3360 cal BC). Consequently sand accretion in the channel must have been initiated shortly before this date given that the AMS radiocarbon dated-organic laminae was found just above the unconformable contact with the gravels of the Avon Formation. This chronology suggests that fluvial sands were accreting in the Redcliffe area at the same time as peats were forming in the Cabot Circus, Deanery Road and Harbourside areas (Wilkinson 2013; Wilkinson 2011c; Wilkinson 2011a).

Archaeological significance

While Bates (2003) has demonstrated that Palaeolithic artefacts occur in the Avon Formation, few have been found from the lowest lying terrace. Furthermore those Palaeolithic artefacts that have been found have always been found in a reworked situation and in low densities. The Avon Formation gravels were in any case only found at the very base of BH 2 and are therefore poorly represented in the borehole cores. The deposits of the Wentlooge formation below +3m AOD accumulated in a channel environment in which people are unlikely to have been active. The stratigraphically later silts and clays probably accumulated in a channel marginal location, but there are limited indicators (such as charcoal and other cultural debris) suggesting human activity. Indeed such findings are rare in central Bristol where anthropogenic material is commonly found in the uppermost part of the Wentlooge formation. The charcoal fragments that were noted in the borehole cores between +2.5m and +5.1m AOD are associated with the laminated silts and clays. There are no parts of the stratigraphy with particularly high concentrations, while it appears that the charcoal that was found was washed in from the wider catchment.

The archaeological significance of the 'made ground'/uppermost part of the Wentlooge formation has been proven by the archaeological excavation. On the basis of the borehole evidence, human impact on alluvial/intertidal sedimentation is restricted to stratigraphy overlying +6.80m AOD (Fig. 5.4) and it would therefore appear that in this part of central Bristol, medieval and post-medieval deposits outcrop above this elevation.

Palaeoenvironmental significance

Organic remains were not noted in the Avon Formation strata, while the braided bedform in which such gravels commonly accrete rarely contain beds suitable for palaeoenvironmental study. The Wentlooge formation sediments formed in relatively deep water at the base of a channel and contain no visible organic material. Any microbiological remains present within these channel sediments are likely to have been reworked a number of times while their point of origin is unknown.

Both the laminated and the homogeneous silts and clays at the top of the Wentlooge formation formed in a relatively gentle depositional environment. However, there are no visible organic inclusions while the presence of iron and manganese oxide precipitates suggest that redox processes have impacted on the whole stratigraphy. Such processes will have led to the decay of microbiological remains.

Chapter 6
Thematic Discussion

The excavations covered the sites of ten properties identified on historic mapping, many of which can be traced to the earliest period of occupation in the early 12th century. However, not all these tenement plots were clearly identifiable at the beginning of the archaeological sequence, and evidence for physical boundaries was rare. The earliest evidence suggests that some of the plots were of double width or under single ownership. The boundaries become more visible in the archaeological record in the late 13th to mid 14th century when stone walls were erected. Common themes in activity across the plots suggest that ownership of multiple or adjacent plots may have continued into the later medieval period, and is certainly evident from the post-medieval documents and plans, although the physical plot divisions were largely maintained.

A considerable degree of modern truncation had affected many areas of the site, but where the impact of modern development was less, a well-stratified sequence of activity was present, accompanied by a rich assemblage of pottery and other artefacts. In the deeper parts of the site, and in particular the fills of pits and drains, ground conditions were favourable for the preservation of organic material, including leather, plant remains and insects. Interpretation of the stratigraphic sequence in conjunction with the analysis of the finds assemblages revealed a sequence of almost continuous development from the early 12th century onwards.

Particular focus is given in this chapter to the development of the site through the medieval and early post-medieval periods (Periods 1, 2 and 3), and how this contributes to our wider understanding of the development of Redcliff Street and its relationship to the riverside. It also focuses on analysis of the buildings and changes in construction technique and usage throughout the medieval period. The evidence for the crafts, industry and economy of the tenants is examined with reference to archaeological and historical sources.

6.1 Early Development of the Redcliffe Suburb

The earliest building evidence at Nos 16/17 suggests that construction took place on the east side of Redcliff Street either at the same time as, or shortly after, the development of the wharves on the west side of the street in the early 12th century. In this respect the excavated evidence supports the general impression from previous archaeological investigations in the Redcliffe area that the development of the former marsh coincides with, but does not precede, the establishment of the Temple and Redcliff Fees in the first half of the 12th century. In this context the construction of a Law Ditch to the rear of the plots provided the necessary drainage, and also a back boundary to the plots (which was later followed by the north–south section of Little Thomas Lane). The term 'Law Ditch' is applied to a network of drainage ditches across the Redcliff and Temple suburbs, and it is possible that a dual role as a drainage facility and as a boundary dividing land into suitably-sized pieces for development was envisaged from the outset of the suburb. Some lengths of the Law Ditch also demarcated the parish boundary between the Redcliffe and Temple Fees (Fig. 2.1). The excavation results suggest that this area was amongst the first to be utilised, with the east side of the street probably developed concurrently with the riverside. Leech (2009) has discussed the presence of an earlier development around the bridgehead, possibly with pre-Conquest origins, and has argued that a Law Ditch traced in excavations at the former Courage Brewery/Finzel's Reach site (Fig. 2.1, no. 1) (Kate Brady pers. comm.) followed the circuit of an earlier defensive ditch enclosing the bridgehead (see also Leech 2014, 14–20). The course of this Law Ditch, identified from rentals (Bickley 1900, 7–10), encompassed the first 12 tenements on the eastern side of Redcliff Street. This ditch is postulated to have run across the north side of the development area, but was not identified in the excavations. Amongst the 12th-century pottery in the trampled marsh surface revealed in the excavation was a small assemblage of pottery which was possibly manufactured as early as the later 11th century. Along with a small quantity of animal bone, this material might conceivably have derived from disposal of waste into the marsh directly adjacent to the early bridgehead development.

6.2 Development of the Plots

Period 1 (early 12th to mid 13th centuries)

The earliest physical evidence for the plot boundaries is most clearly seen in the drain 1773 and post alignment between Nos 16 and 17, although the early construction of Building 1A at the street end of the plot across this boundary line implies a single owner from the beginning and throughout Period 1. The plot division between Nos 18 and 18a is demarcated by the post line south of Building 1B. No other boundary construction is in evidence in this period apart from the line of small stakes dividing No. 19 from No. 20 towards the rear of these plots. The plot division between Nos 17 and 18 is suggested by the gap between Buildings 1A and 1B. Further indications of plot divisions are suggested by the alignments of the industrial pits, most obviously in the linear arrangement of pits at Nos 17 and 18, but more hazily implied in the arrangement of some pits to the rear of Nos 12 to 15. The pit lines in Nos 17 and 18 are very closely spaced and overlap the later boundary division, and it is unlikely that any fence or barrier existed at this time. The general impression is that property boundaries were fluid and the industrial pits and dyeing waste found across the whole excavated area may suggest a common endeavour in the backplots that was facilitated by a lack of substantial boundary divisions.

The earliest building work on site was broadly contemporary with the first stone wharfs at the riverside, as recorded at Bristol Bridge (Williams 1982) (Fig. 2.1, no. 2), Dundas Wharf (Good 1991) (Fig. 2.1, no. 3), Buchanan's Wharf (Burchill et al. 1987) (Fig. 2.1, no. 4) and Canynges House at 95–97 Redcliff Street (Jones 1986) (Fig. 2.1, no. 6). At Dundas Wharf timber postholes of the earliest phase of development were replaced by stone buildings and tenement boundaries. At the former Courage Brewery site 12th-century stone buildings precede the first evidence for a quay wall, although earlier wharves or a quay wall cannot be discounted (Jackson 2006b, 55).

The main period of activity at the present site associated with industrial pits and occupation centred on the second half of the 12th and the early 13th centuries, with pottery evidence supported by dendrochronology from timbers within pits and structures. This was broadly contemporary with a second phase of development of the wharves at the riverside. The earliest 12th-century waterfront wall and jetties at Bristol Bridge became choked with silt and as a consequence they were extended in the 13th century (Williams 1982); a similar picture occurred at Dundas Wharf (Good 1991, 37) and Canynges House (Jones 1986). The redeveloped 13th-century wharves were generally more sophisticated than their 12th-century predecessors, involving major investment in stone walls and extensive reclamation to surmount the problems of an extreme tidal range. Where slipways and jetties were built, as at Canynges House, the wharves could have also been in use as ferry terminals (ibid.). At Dundas Wharf the 'Common Slip', a narrow cobbled lane facilitating the transport of material (and possibly passengers), issued out onto Redcliff Street between Nos 128 and 129, directly opposite the present site. These developments at the wharfside were accompanied by the burgeoning of industry connected to the cloth trade, not only at the present site but throughout the Redcliffe suburb, as for instance at Canynges House (ibid.), 82–90 Redcliff Street (Williams and Cox 2001) and Finzel's Reach (Kate Brady pers. comm.). Egan (1991) has suggested in London that dyers may have financed land reclamation in the textile-finishing areas of the waterfront in the 12th and 13th centuries, and this may also have been the case in Bristol. The areas of Temple and Redcliffe further from the riverfront were slower to develop; at Nos 26–28 St Thomas Street (Watts 2011a) (Fig. 2.1, no. 7) and 55–60 St Thomas Street (Davenport et al. 2011) (Fig. 2.1, no. 8), occupation began no earlier than the 13th century (the tenement plots were laid out at this time at the latter site). At the corner of Portwall Lane and St Thomas Street there was no evidence to suggest activity before the 14th century (Good 1989, 22) (Fig. 2.1, no. 10).

At the close of Period 1 in the late 13th century the scale and intensity of industry on site appears to have reduced. Pottery and other artefacts, including the shoes represented in the cobbling waste, support a mid 13th-century date for the backfill of many of the pits. It would appear that only a few pits were still open when the major rebuilding of the late 13th to early 14th century took place.

Period 2 (late 13th to early 15th centuries)

Changes in plot organisation in the late 13th century are manifested by the construction in stone of boundary walls and house footings, anchoring the property boundaries into locations that were thereafter preserved by later developments. At Nos 18, 18a, 19 and 20 the preparation for the new building campaign was accompanied by systematic backfilling and levelling of earlier pits. A pair of well-built double town houses (Buildings 2A and 2B) at Nos 18 and 18a was a joint venture, and the building at No. 19 was constructed on an equally solid scale (survival in No. 20 was less complete). Little was done to alter these buildings for the next two centuries, and common ownership of all three properties is a possibility. The extension of substantial structures into the rear part of the plots implies pressure on available space at the street frontage, as well as increasing prosperity. Whilst the buildings at Nos 18–19 represented stability (the walls at Nos 18 and 18a lasted until the 18th century), the use of space at Nos 16 and 17 appears to be in flux throughout Period 2. The nature of the building in the plots to the north of No. 17 is unclear, but the establishment of Little Thomas Lane suggests that Nos 16 and 17 were no longer jointly occupied. Despite their separation the properties were often utilised for the same activities, and this continued into later periods (where evidence survived), although the changes in each plot occurred at slightly different times.

Little Thomas Lane was a substantial thoroughfare. Investment in the construction of this lane and its solid paving was undertaken at the expense of space in the adjoining plots, and emphasises that a considerable degree of importance was attached to access to the rear of the plots. The impetus for this can only be guessed at, but may stem from the development of the back ends of properties, both on Redcliff Street and St Thomas Street to the west as pressure on space intensified. These changes heralded new entrepreneurial ventures to which the hearths at the west end of the site belonged. At the west end of No. 17 activity relating to the dyeing process was intense in Periods 2a and 2b, with a series of circular hearths built and replaced over a period of 50 years or more. Given the lack of structural evidence, this activity may have taken place within an open yard. In the mid 14th century substantial constructions revised the use of the back plot, and ushered in new activities, of which the copper-working furnace was the most notable feature. These changes were contemporary with the substantial walls enclosing the area at the west end of No. 16, although the area continued to be the location of a hearth. The access provided from Little Thomas Lane to the back plots at Nos 16 and 17 implies that the street frontage was now fully developed.

The new phase of construction that heralded the beginning of Period 2 dates to the mid 13th to early 14th centuries. The late 13th or early 14th-century date obtained by dendrochronology of a timber found in the back-filled pit sealed beneath Building 2A gives the buildings at Nos 18 and 18a an even more precise date range. These developments were no doubt intimately connected with contemporary developments on the west side of Redcliff Street. There is much evidence that the 13th-century reclamation of the waterfront was followed by the construction of buildings with stone foundations over the former river walls, and these extended into the newly claimed land. This was most clearly seen at Bristol Bridge (Williams 1982), Dundas Wharf (Good 1991) and Canynges House, where 14th-century advancement of the river frontage was accompanied by extending the buildings back from the street frontage, replacing possible yards and outbuildings (Jones 1986). This rapid and intensive development of reclaimed land indicates that available land was in short supply. There is abundant evidence for dyeing at these sites, and must reflect the profitability of this trade. In many cases circular hearths, which could have been used to support dye vats, date to this period, as at Bristol Bridge (Williams 1982), Dundas Wharf (Good 1991), and at the former Courage Brewery site (Jackson 2006b). At Dundas Wharf (Good 1991), 90–91 Redcliff Street (Youngs *et al.* 1985), and possibly Canynges House (Jones 1986) this superseded earlier evidence for tanning. At 82–90 Redcliff Street an industrial building (building B4i) with evidence for a loom was built on the Redcliff Street frontage in the late 14th century (Williams and Cox 2001, 20) Two circular hearths probably used for dyeing located behind the street frontage at No. 3 Redcliff also date to this period and were part of a major phase of stone-built construction (see the accompanying report).

This evidence for enterprise and construction is not so evident further from the river where excavations at sites such as 30–38 St Thomas Street (Jackson 2004, 60), 55–60 St Thomas Street (Davenport *et al.* 2011) and Portwall Lane (Good 1989, 23) indicate that the early to mid 14th century heralded a period in which earlier activity ceased, or contracted toward the street frontages, whilst back plots were open spaces used for horticulture or gardens.

Period 3 (early 15th to late 17th centuries)

Nos 16 and 17 Redcliff Street continued in industrial use, with metal casting continuing at No. 17 and now adopted at No 16. The demolition of Building 2E at the west end of this property suggests the new enterprise required a deliberate reorganisation of space possibly at the expense of other uses such as accommodation or storage (unless the structure was ruinous by this time). Little Thomas Lane was maintained, with replacements to the southern wall, although the encroachment of furnace 1530 would have impeded access for wide vehicles to the rear of the properties. The constructions at Nos 16 and 17 were entirely without domestic features; if the small extension at the rear of Building 2F was a staircase, its demolition in this period implies some manner of internal reorganisation. Building 2A survived in its original plan without sign of alteration, but at No. 18a a new structure (Building 3A) was built. At No. 19 the area previously occupied by the western rooms of Building 2C housed a mortar mixing pit and a well, features more consistent with an open yard than a roofed building, although the new south wall was rendered.

Periods 4 and 5 (late 17th to late 20th centuries)

The late 17th century saw changes across the whole of

the excavated area, although plot boundaries were still maintained. At Nos 16 and 17 Redcliff Street metal casting ceased, and although the documentary record for the period between the late 17th and the 19th century lists a series of tenants at No. 16, there is little evidence that the trades practised by the occupants (victualler and cordwainer) prompted any alterations to the back of the plot, which was furnished with a soakaway and a new boundary wall constructed in the 19th century. Elsewhere construction and new enterprise took place. The cellars built at No. 17 were contiguous and represent an extension to the rear of buildings on the street frontage. The mid 19th-century deed plan for this property (Fig. 2.5) shows the ground floor plan where a shop at the street front is backed by a parlour, with a series of warehouses and stores behind. At the back end of the property a yard, stable and tenement are located where the well and soakaway were identified in excavation. The network of drains feeding into Little Thomas Lane from the western cellars may relate to domestic sanitation. The construction of a sugar house in the late 17th century brought Nos 18, 18a and 19 into a common purpose for which redevelopment of all three plots was required. However, extant plans of the period show that the plot divisions were generally maintained, and this is confirmed by the excavated evidence. The excavation also revealed the drains, wells and soakaways required to supply and drain water in the sugar-refining process. When the sugar refinery ceased to operate in the early 19th century, the deeds to the properties show that the three plots became separate tenements, although by 1887 they were again jointly occupied by John Thomas and Sons Ltd (Fig. 2.4).

Widening of the Redcliff Street frontage in 1878 caused the rebuilding of the front end of the properties. Where evidence survived at Nos 16 and 18 cellars extended beneath the buildings. Little Thomas Lane also continued to be maintained.

6.3 The Medieval Buildings

Period 1 (early 12th to mid 13th centuries)

The small corpus of surviving timbers from this period display woodworking belonging to the Saxon and Norman 'treewrighting' tradition (Chapter 4.12), a date supported by the mid to late 12th-century tree-ring dates obtained from some structural timbers (Chapter 4.13). Construction techniques relating to this tradition feature earth-fast posts, with a variety of wall constructions. The earliest building evidence was found towards the west, or street side, of the excavated area. Bearing in mind that the westward limit of excavation lies some 9m from the street frontage as depicted on early 19th-century maps, these remains are assumed to represent the back ends of the buildings. The length of 8.5m for the back wall of Building 1A, and 5–6m for Building 1B compares with domestic buildings from Coppergate, York (Hall 1984, 46) and London (Horsman et al. 1988) where ranges of 4–5m by 8–10m are considered to be average building dimensions. The length to which these buildings extended to the west cannot be estimated, but if both extended to the line of the street preserved in the earliest scaled maps, Building 1A would have a length of almost 12m, a larger building than most, but consistent with the larger average dimensions of buildings recorded at the Guildhall, London (Bowsher et al. 2007, 308).

Buildings 1A and 1B at Nos 16/17 and 18 Redcliff Street employed a variety of building techniques. The most clearly defined corner at the north end of Building 1A comprised a right-angled slot, for which no equivalent construction at the south end of the building could be found. Given the early 12th-century date, this slot is unlikely to represent a timber frame, so the slot may be a post-in-trench construction, or even the robbing of a line of posts. The small dimensions of the original posts of both buildings suggest comparatively insubstantial walls. The spacing of the postholes in Building 1A could denote the bulwark technique of boarding set on edge slotted into grooved posts, but the original back wall of Building 1B was more likely to have been built of wattle and daub secured by small posts and stakes. The later phase of Building 1B suggested a much more robust construction using large posts, more widely spaced, to support the raised sill beams and stave-built walls associated with middling to high-status buildings of the period (Chapter 4.12). Other postholes associated with these buildings are open to interpretation. A series of postholes approximately 1m to the east of the slot, and posts at the rear of Building 1A, could have been a line of external buttress posts which braced the roof, although this function could have equally been served by the some of the internal posts, including 3021 which appears to have been supported on a postpad. Both internal and external roof-supporting posts have parallels elsewhere, including contemporary buildings at the Guildhall site, London (Bowsher et al. 2007), where postpads were a common feature of internal roof-supports. As noted in that report (ibid., 308), it was not uncommon in this period for a variety of constructional techniques to be employed simultaneously in a building, allowing a more flexible approach to the practical considerations of available space, and to the use and adaptation of the buildings. In the later medieval period the introduction of timber framing imposed more regularity in building plans (Chapter 4.12).

Evidence for doorways, or other internal features, in these early buildings is a matter of speculation. The surviving timbers in posthole 2070 of Building 1B have been interpreted as a door jamb and support, but the posthole was curiously positioned to serve as a doorway to the exterior, as it was apparently well within the building's interior (unless it belonged to a re-siting of the outer wall). Additional postholes forming two parallel lines at the rear of Building 1A may denote an extension, although the 5m gap between these posts and the rear posts of Building 1A argue more for a separate outhouse that post-dated the construction of a wattle-lined drain. This may have been a purpose-built, and possibly open-sided, building associated with dyeing or other industrial activity at the rear of the main building. The use of different wood species (maple, oak and beech) and the reuse of an oak timber in the postholes suggest *ad hoc* construction. Wood fragments reused within the drain cast light on aspects of the buildings from which they derived, and included weather boarding and a possible window post. One of a line of three posts cut into the backfill of pits at No. 17 displayed a slot consistent with the upright of a boarded or wattle wall, although it may have been reused. It is unlikely that the buildings were roofed in tile given the almost complete absence of tile fragments from this period. Instead roof coverings may have been of thatch, stone or shingles, occasionally capped with ceramic ridge tiles.

Interpretation of the buildings of Period 1 is further complicated by the longevity of the period over which they were erected, repaired and replaced. The large number of buildings recorded at London Guildhall allowed an average lifespan of 20–40 years to be estimated for those with earth-fast timbers (Bowsher *et al.* 2007, 317). At the present site the small corpus of surviving timbers testifies to the recycling of good wood as buildings were replaced and repaired. The frequency of postpads and other post supports may also be an indicator of the instability of ageing structures, and the propensity of earth-fast timbers to rot from the ground up. No evidence for buildings survived within the plots to the north of No. 16, or to the south of No. 18, although pit 3735 at the west end of the excavated area at No. 19 may indicate that any building here did not extend as far back from the street frontage as those further to the north.

Period 2 (late 13th to early 15th centuries)

The buildings erected in Period 2 were a radical departure from those of the preceding period. At Nos 18 and 18a the stone footings of Buildings 2A and 2B survived above ground. These may have been dwarf walls supporting a timber frame; certainly timber was employed in their construction, as the post sockets in the party wall indicate. Building 2A was partitioned at the west end but internal arrangements did not survive at the rear of the building, which may not have been subdivided. Schofield and Vince (1994, 72–4, based on Pantin 1962–3) identified a type of medieval town house in which the street end was given over wholly to trade, with a two-storey hall at the back. Alternatively all living space may have been on the first floor, including the hall. The footings were clearly robust enough to take a second storey, possibly accessed by stairs in the extensions at the back end of Buildings 2A and 2B. Access to the back of the plot was via the passageway to the north of Building 2A, which was possibly overshot at first storey height. There is no evidence for external doorways into the back rooms of Buildings 2A, and 2B; restricted access would have afforded the security to store valuable goods, if that were their purpose. The circular hearth-base in the west room in Building 2A could have had an industrial use. To the south the arched foundations between Building 2C and the building at No. 20 may have supported a stone wall to full height which was buttressed on its southern side. In Building 2C the western space was also utilised for industrial activity and may have shared the chimney stacks built into the party wall with No. 20. The back end of Building 2C appeared to be subdivided, and the property shared a well with No. 20, accessed via a doorway. It is not clear if the buildings continued to the street, but if so they would have been gable end on, as would buildings at the street frontage at Nos 16 and 17 where the construction of Little Thomas Lane divided the plots and constricted the available widths.

The nature of the buildings at Nos 16 and 17 was not clear. Building 2D at No. 17 appeared to be free-standing, as did Building 2F which replaced it. This construction was robust, representing a square room at the west side, and a much smaller square room to the east separated by a narrow corridor. The small anteroom had particularly solid foundations and may represent a strong-room or the base of a staircase to an upper floor. Building 2E at No. 16 was not built until the end of this period, replacing some more ephemeral evidence for structures, but activity remained industrial rather than domestic in flavour. Roof tiles from this period suggest that some buildings supported a ridge of tiles at their apex, but were roofed in other materials. The mid 13th century saw the replacement of 12th-century timber buildings by ones with stone foundations at some other sites along Redcliff Street. For instance the stone walls at Buchanan's Wharf (Fig. 2.1, no. 4) were also thought to have supported timber-framed walls (Youngs *et al.* 1987, 116).

6.4 Industry, Economy and Trade

Period 1 (early 12th to mid 13th centuries)

The most notable feature of the activity at the rear of the plots revealed in the excavation is the numerous sub-rectangular pits and the associated evidence from waterlogged plant remains for plants associated with the dyeing industry. Over 30 sub-rectangular pits were spread across the excavated area, the densest concentration surviving at Nos 17 and 18 where intercutting shows that dyeing took place over a considerable period of time, probably from the early 12th century to the mid 13th century (the slightly later date for some artefacts relates to the backfill and disuse of the pits). The waterlogged plant remains from within the backfill of these features and from other pits, drain fills and occupation layers are rich in dye plants. There is a general spread of all the dyestuffs represented, although higher concentrations of dyer's greenweed, madder, weld and woad in some features might suggest more frequent use of specific colours. The type of hearths normally associated with medieval dyeing (and which are evident in Period 2) are absent in Period 1. The pits may have been cold vats used for preparatory soaking, for fixing dyes or rinsing. The wattle linings and dividers no doubt relate to the details of these processes. Early illustration of the dyeing processes, for instance the 14th-century 'Holkham Picture Bible' (British Library Add. Ms. 47682), depict cold vats as casks or tubs sitting on the ground, rather than sunk, although Evans (Evans and Tomlinson 1992, 284) suggests that this would aid cooling, and was used in other early chemical processes (Taylor and Singer 1956). The deposits from the wharfsides at Dundas Wharf, Bristol Bridge and Canynges House (Jones and Watson 1987) demonstrate that these dyestuffs were imported, probably ready prepared, although the presence of bran in samples at the present site suggests some preparation of woad may have taken place here. Flax seeds were used in dye production, and are represented in the samples, particularly those from pit 3229 at No. 18, where processing of the seed appears to have taken place (Chapter 5.3). The wattle-lined drain running between Nos 16 and 17 may have served to take waste water to the drainage ditch at the back of the plots, but a similar wattle-lined drain excavated at 33–35 Eastgate, Beverley, was considered to have been used for retting flax, with temporary sluices represented by stakes (Evans and Tomlinson 1992). The wattle lining was replaced after silting up, as was also the case here. A flax retting interpretation is therefore worthy of consideration for the Redcliff Street drain. The dyeing process would have required fresh water but no obvious source was identified in this period, although there may be an earlier phase to the well at the rear of No. 17 which was not excavated to its full depth. There is little direct evidence for cloth processing from the insect remains, whose habitats largely reflect the domestic sphere (such as straw, hay, stored dry goods and woodworm) and rotting settlement waste. The high frequency of saline-tolerant species suggests cess is a major component of the waste material in the pits. While waste of all kinds would have been disposed of in pits once they ceased to be used for their primary functions, the salinity of the pit fills may also have been augmented by the use of urine and salt in dyeing processes. The spread of industrial pits and dye remains across the whole excavated area may represent individual enterprises or a single entrepreneurial venture, as it is evident from other sites that cloth dyeing was a widespread industry along the Redcliffe and Temple waterfront, with supplies of raw materials and exports trafficked via the series of wharves along the river frontage.

Although dyeing appears to be the dominant activity on site, other activities are represented. The possibility that tanning was practised using the rectangular pits for soaking hides cannot be entirely discounted, although the faunal remains do not show the bias towards foot bones that characterise animal bone waste from the tanning process. The only notable bias in the faunal assemblage is towards the skull and sawn horncore tips indicative of the first stage of preparing animal horns for the horners' trade (Chapter 5.1). The first stage of horn preparation could be undertaken by butchers or tanners before selling the core with sheaf attached, and it is evident from later medieval sources that it was profitable to sell the rough horns (core and sheaf attached) abroad (MacGregor 1991, 372). Tanners or butchers could have been operating businesses close-by. Evidence for tanning in the second half of the 12th century was found at Dundas Wharf (Good 1991) and at Canynges House (Jones 1986). The removal of the horn tip aided the process of decay, as the horn was subsequently soaked, and then boiled to remove the sheaf. The removal of the sheaf is normally indicated by large quantities of horncore waste (e.g. Clarke and Carter 1977), which were not present at this site. The tips needed no further preparation before use as handles, and could have been collected and sold on separately (MacGregor 1991, 371).

The quantities of worn-out leather shoes, and off-cuts distributed across the site in the backfills of pits are typical of a cobbler's workshop (Chapter 4.11). Waste material from this activity could be substantial: enormous quantities of off-cuts and shoes were found in the infill of the 14th-century slipway at 95–97 Redcliff Street (Jones 1986). Cobbling required the purchase of old shoes for refurbishment, and was a distinct trade in the medieval period, unconnected to tanning or shoemaking. If a cobbler was working at No. 17, the workshop was probably located on the street frontage to take advantage of passing trade. The two fragmentary shears blades found in Period 1 deposits may have been associated with the cloth trade or cobbling activity, or some purely domestic function. Craft and trade activity doubtless took place alongside, and within, domestic premises, with many small subsidiary activities such as weaving and spinning undertaken to supplement the household income.

The 'west country vessels' ('Bath A' type coarseware BPT 46) with a distinctive in-curved form appear in sufficient quantities in the pottery assemblage to represent another craft activity in this period and were found in the greatest concentration in a small number of pits at the west end of No. 17. The function of these vessels is open to debate (Chapter 4.1), and their presence here raises the possibility that they might have been used in the dyeing industry. Of note in this context are the pierced ceramic discs found at Swan Lane, London, which were perhaps used as coarse filters in textile processing (Pritchard 1982).

Period 2 (late 13th to early 15th centuries)

A smaller body of environmental evidence was available for study from Period 2, with far fewer pits and drains available for sampling. Interpretation of the activities taking place relies more heavily on the physical evidence and some artefacts. The most notable features of this period that could be ascribed to economic activity are the circular stone-built hearths present at Nos 17, 18 and 19, towards the west side of the properties. The hearth remains at No. 16 were too fragmentary to interpret, but could have been of the same type. The better preserved examples at No. 17 suggest that these hearths were all approximately 1.8m to 2m in diameter, with a pitched-stone base and a stoking chamber. The hearths in all properties showed signs of replacement, and at No. 17 more than one hearth may have operated at one time. This type is characteristic of the 14th century and appears to have evolved from the earlier 'keyhole' shaped hearths of which good examples are evident from the late 12th/early 13th century at Swan Lane, London, associated with fulling and possibly dyeing (Egan 1991). The Redcliff Street hearths of Period 2 could have supported cauldrons or vats in which the dye bath was prepared. In this process the cloth might be immersed directly in the dye, or the 'liquor' poured into a separate vat to which the cloth was added (Walton 1991, 336). The wells sunk at No. 17 could have supplied the water necessary for these processes, and the substantial square cistern may also have been for water storage. Both suggest a change to the means by which water was obtained from Period 1. The need to store water on the site might have become more pressing as the distance to the river increased through land reclamation at the riverside. Other uses for the circular hearth bases are also possible, including brewing beer, baking bread or boiling food although there is no distinctive evidence for these activities.

Developments at the riverside suggest that dyeing largely replaced the earlier tanning industry. At Dundas Wharf early evidence for tanning was superseded by cloth-dyeing in the second half of the 13th century when a complex of circular hearths was maintained and replaced probably until the 15th century (Good 1991). At the former Courage Brewery site a similar sequence extended from the late 13th to the 14th century, and contemporary dye vat hearths were found at 85–87 Redcliff Street (Williams 1981) (Fig. 2.1, no. 11). At 90–91 Redcliff Street possible tanning vat-bases were replaced by a 14th-century stone arcade (Youngs et al. 1986). At Canynges House three rectangular shallow pits to the rear of a 12th-century building on the street frontage were tentatively interpreted as tanning pits (but could have served a similar purpose to the Period 1 dyeing pits here). In the 13th century a single 'keyhole' oven was excavated. Six 14th-century circular ovens were also found which were not thought to be linked to the dyeing industry. However, large quantities of madder in the infill of the 14th-century dock indicate either the use or import of this dyestuff (Jones 1986). The interpretation of two contemporary hearths at No. 3 Redcliff Street as dye vats is strengthened by comparison with those at 1–2 Redcliff Street, although associated environmental evidence was not available. Title deed leases and other documents of 15th and 16th-century date add to the picture of an area dominated by the cloth trade, and of particular note is the mid 15th-century reference to three generations of dyers occupying No. 127 Redcliff Street, directly opposite the present site (Chapter 2.1).

In the mid 14th or early 15th centuries the evidence for dyeing diminished. Circular hearths continued to be built and replaced at No. 16, but at No. 17 a completely new industry was represented by a large circular furnace at the east end of the plot and associated evidence of mould fragments for the casting of leaded antimony bronze (lead-bronze) cauldrons or posnets. The clay used for the moulds was from the local alluvium and the moulds were either made locally or at the site itself. The metalworking debris also included fragments of crucibles. These were used to melt the same lead-bronze alloy but are considered to be too small to be used in the casting of the body of these vessels (unless several were used for one cast), but may have been employed in the casting of smaller elements such as the handles and feet. The two properties on the east side of Redcliff Street at its northern end which were occupied by 'brasiers' in the mid 15th century could not, unfortunately, be located with any precision (Chapter 2.1). The 1456 reference to a William Tanner as a potter is ambiguous, as this term was also applied to those practising the metal-casting of domestic vessels. It is interesting to note that William had inherited the surname of Tanner as this was another industry which, although apparently not practised on the present site, was widespread in the area.

The metalworking furnace at No. 17 is the first indication on the site of an industry that gains greater importance in the Redcliffe and Temple suburb in the period between the early 15th century and the 17th century (Period 3). Similar moulds in local clay were found at 3 Redcliff Street (see accompanying report), and at 55–60 St Thomas Street in deposits from this period (Davenport et al. 2011, 43–5); evidence for a copper-alloy foundry was found at 68–72 Redcliff Street (Jones 1983). Large quantities of clay mould fragments from copper-alloy casting were recovered from late 14th to early 15th-century deposits at the corner of St Thomas Street and Portwall Lane and were interpreted as possibly from a bell foundry (Good 1989, 26).

However, recent evidence suggests that the production of large domestic vessels would be the staple of any foundry business, with bell-casting a less frequent event (Dungworth and Nicholas 2004, 25). The burgeoning of this industry is intimately linked to the production of silver. As leaded antimony bronze was a by-product of the extraction of silver from copper, the industry relied on supplies of this material. Ores suitable for the extraction of silver were quarried in Germany and Sweden and the 'liquation' process by which the silver was extracted was in use in Europe by at least the 13th century. As the minting of silver coinage and the rise in the manufacture of silver wares rose during this period, so did the availability of leaded antimony bronze. It is not known if silver extraction from ore took place at this time in Britain or abroad (Chapter 4.6), but in either case the furnaces were in an ideal location to receive supplies transported by boat to Bristol. Evidence from the Broadmead suburb attests to copper-alloy working in the mid 12th to late 13th century at St James Priory, but it is not known if it was for the priory's needs or a commercial venture (Ridgeway and Watts 2013).

Period 3 (early 15th to late 17th centuries)

The metal-casting industry at No. 17 expanded and developed in the early 15th century and new furnaces represent two of the earliest examples of reverberatory furnaces found in Britain. This new style of furnace construction dispensed with bellows and increased heat efficiency. It is generally assumed that the metal for cauldrons was melted in simple furnaces rather than crucibles (Blaylock 1996; 2000). The construction of a third furnace at No. 16 suggests the industry was expanding; the slightly different style of construction of this furnace (Chapter 4.6) either indicates a separate venture, or possibly an earlier date for its construction. All three furnaces are on a north–east/south–west alignment, presumably to take advantage of prevailing draughts. From what is known about these furnaces, it is understood that the molten metal flowed by gravity into the mould via a connecting channel. This necessitated digging a pit to hold the moulds for the larger domestic vessels such as posnets and cauldrons (Dungworth and Nicholas 2004, 25). The surviving evidence for features associated with these furnaces at Redcliff Street is not easily interpreted. The pit immediately adjacent to the furnace at No. 16 is rather shallow but may have served as a casting pit. The pits at No. 17 also appear to be associated with the casting process, but lie several metres from the furnaces and may be more closely associated with the adjacent hearths. Although cauldrons or posnets continued to be produced in Period 3, candlesticks and chafing dishes were added to the repertoire of the metal-casting industry. The context for the candlestick mould fragments suggest production at Redcliff Street may be some of the earliest recorded as it pre-dates the small corpus of comparable material, including the late 16th-century activity at Guildhall, London (Chapter 4.5).

Periods 4 and 5 (late 17th to late 20th centuries)

Deeds demonstrate that Nos 18–20 Redcliff Street were the premises of a sugar refinery established in 1695, and which carried on in operation until 1816 (Chapter 2.1). Some features associated with the necessary supplies of water were found in the excavation, but there is little else amongst the structural evidence that can be linked to any part of the sugar-refining process. Although a number of substantial walls survive from the sugar house construction, these are assumed to have been part of the cellar system. Even less structural evidence survived from the excavated sugar house at Cabot Circus (Ridgeway and Watts 2013, 25–6), although it is apparent from both that large premises were required. The basic process of refining the imported raw muscovado sugar required water, a source of heat and large cauldrons. Plans of contemporary sugar refineries, such as Kroger's Sugar House of 1805 at the former Courage Brewery site (Jackson 2006b, 9), suggest that warehouses, mills, a cooperage, stabling, fuel stores and 'sugar bins' or stores would have been present. The plan of a sugar house at Gloucester Square, Southampton includes a cistern, two stoves and three oblong cauldron bases set into walls with ash pits in front (Platt and Coleman-Smith 1975; Hughes 1986, 43–4). Hearth 1101 at No. 18a is the only surviving evidence for a source of heat within the sugar house premises. Although there is no record of sugar refining at No. 17, the paired ash pits and hearths set into the wall and the network of drainage in the room to the west might have been associated with this activity.

The cessation of sugar refining at Nos 18–20 accords with the general decline of this business in the 19th century. In the mid 18th century the sugar trade with the West Indies was worth twice as much as all other overseas trade, and was the mainstay of Bristol's economy. Shipping, provisioning, confectionery and distilling all relied heavily on the sugar industry, and this economic specialisation proved to be dangerous when the sugar trade with the West Indies suffered a series of blows in the early 19th century. Extra dues on ships and foreign goods were introduced to pay for the costly construction of the Floating Harbour at the beginning of the 19th century. New legislation followed which impacted on the sugar trade, in particular the Abolition of Slavery in 1833, and the Sugar Equalisation Act of 1851 which placed cane sugar from the West Indies on an equal footing with European beet. The refineries themselves were slow to modernise and the sugar house at Redcliff Street had closed some years before the innovations introduced by Conrad Finzel at Counterslip revolutionised sugar production (Penny 1997).

Two other industries are represented in the waste

material found in Period 4 deposits. Tobacco pipe wasters and kiln debris from a clay pipe factory used as backfill at No. 17 represent a corpus of material which can be dated to the period 1651 to 1654. The presence of this material at the present site does not necessarily suggest that the factory used by the Hunt family was close-by, as waste from the clay pipe industry was transported by river for use as hardcore in new constructions such as riverside wharves. Glass waste was also transported for use as hardcore and the waste from this industry found in the excavations could have derived from many sources. Glass houses have been found in a number of locations in the Redcliffe suburb (cf. Jackson 2004; Good 1989). The industry thrived in the early to mid 18th century, but experienced a decline in the 1770s linked to loss of trade with North America. Ash from glass production was used in soap production, and the glass waste at the present site may have some connection with the soap manufacturers recorded on both sides of Redcliff Street (Chapter 2.1).

Excavations at 3 Redcliff Street, 2003

by Peter Davenport, Simon Cox and Richard Young

with contributions from J. Athersuch, N.P. Branch, R. Gale, C.P. Green, L. Higbee, R. Leech, E.R. McSloy, G.E. Swindle, S. Warman, A. Vaughan-Williams and A. Vince

Chapter 1
Introduction

In May and July 2003 CA carried out an archaeological excavation at 3 Redcliff Street on behalf of Westmark Developments Limited (See 1–2 Redcliff Street, Fig. 1.1). The No. 3 Redcliff Street site lay on the opposite side of Thomas Lane to the 1–2 Redcliff Street excavations and was bounded by Redcliff Street to the west, Thomas Lane to the north and standing buildings to the south and east. It was centred on NGR: ST 59086 72727. It was approximately 0.1ha in area and had been occupied by 19th-century buildings. Two separate areas were investigated. Area 1 lay on the western part of the site in a gravelled area formerly used for car parking at the corner of Redcliff Street and Thomas Lane; Area 2 was at the eastern end of the site in a space formerly occupied by a modern garage building (Fig. 1.1). The modern ground level lay at approximately 9m AOD, with the car parking area and the floor of the demolished garage building forming level surfaces prior to the excavation work.

1.1 Previous Work

The historical background for Bristol and the Redcliffe suburb, and a summary of previous archaeological work in the vicinity, is contained above in Chapters 1 and 2 of the 1–2 Redcliff Street report. At the 3 Redcliff Street site a preliminary desk-based assessment (MoLAS 1999a; 1999b) was followed by archaeological monitoring of geotechnical test-pits (MoLAS 1999c) which revealed levelling layers, pit fills and occupation horizons typical of the post-medieval period, which overlay medieval deposits sealing alluvium. The monitoring work also indicated that archaeological deposits over large areas of the site had been destroyed by the construction of basements. This was confirmed by an evaluation trench in the western part of the site in October 2002 (CA 2002), although alluvial deposits survived at a height of 6.50m AOD. Archaeological deposits of medieval and later date survived above the alluvium at the northern end of the evaluation trench to 7.8m AOD, representing a surviving sequence up to 1.3m deep. In the light of these results a condition requiring prior archaeological excavation was attached by Bristol City Council to a planning consent for residential and office development.

1.2 Excavation and Post-Excavation Methodology

Two areas were subjected to archaeological excavation: Area 1 covered 118m² and Area 2 169m² (Fig. 1.1). Modern surfaces and overburden were excavated mechanically under archaeological supervision. The site was then hand-cleaned and the archaeological features thus exposed were manually excavated. Archaeological contexts were described using a single-context recording system. The geological and Holocene sequence encountered at 3 Redcliff Street was similar to that described above for 1–2 Redcliff Street.

Most of the archaeological features had been cut into substantial deposits of silty clays and sands, which had

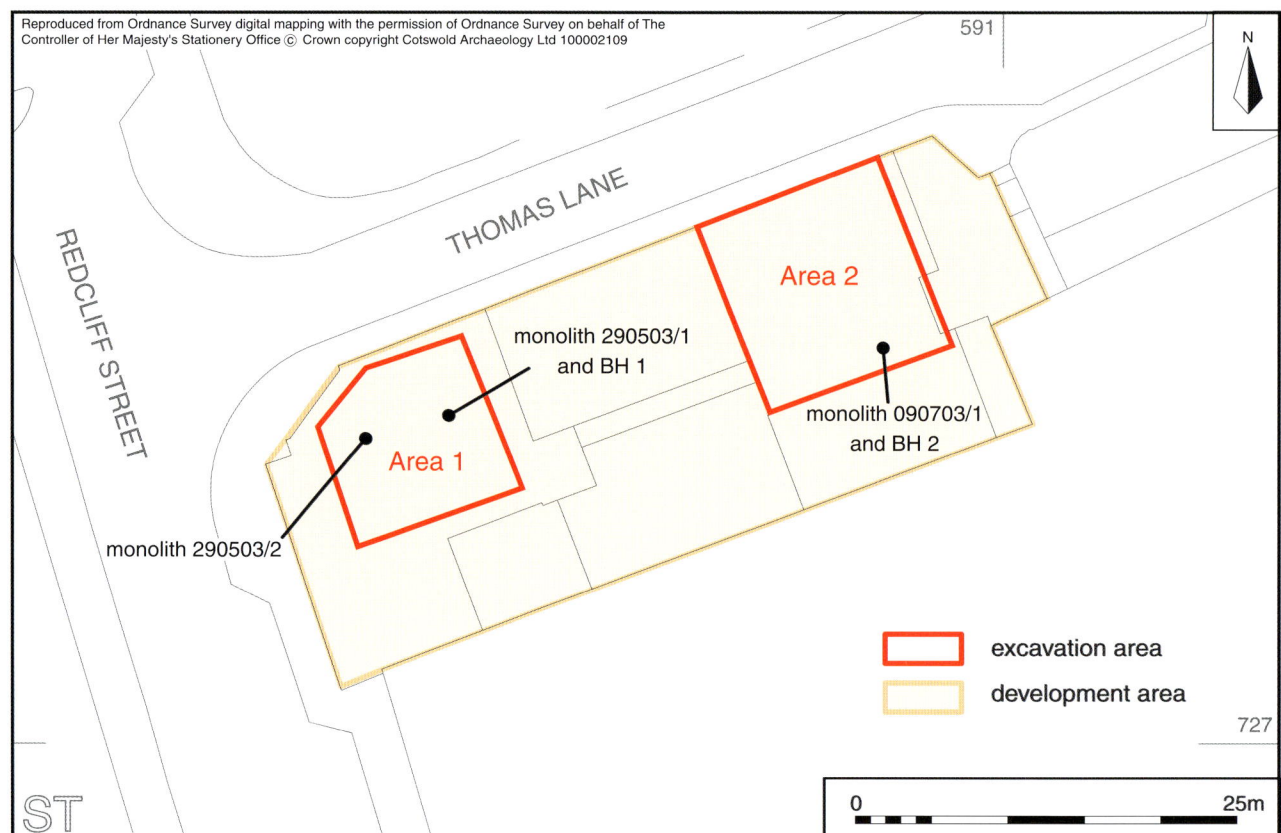

Fig. 1.1   Excavation Areas 1 and 2 showing monolith and borehole (BH) locations. Scale 1:500

been deliberately dumped over the natural alluvium to raise the ground level. These dumps were recorded and removed mechanically, under archaeological supervision, to expose features cutting into earlier dumping and the underlying alluvium. Walls of 19th-century and later date were left *in situ* during this work as their footings continued into the alluvium and there was no advantage to be gained in removing them. Three monolith samples and two borehole samples were also collected in order to examine the form and structure of the pre-medieval sediments (Fig. 1.1; Chapter 5.5). Following the completion of the excavation a watching brief was undertaken during groundworks associated with the redevelopment, but no additional findings were made.

After completion of the fieldwork a post-excavation assessment (CA 2004) was compiled which identified those parts of the archive that were of sufficient significance to warrant analysis and publication. The excavation areas straddled several medieval and early post-medieval tenement plots and documentary sources were consulted to aid interpretation of the site, its boundaries, buildings and other features.

Chapter 2
Documentary Evidence

Roger Leech

2.1 The Redcliff Street Area

Though now referred to as 3 Redcliff Street, the area within which the excavations were situated was, from at least 1775 to the 1880s, numbered as Nos 21–23 Redcliff Street. The site was situated historically entirely within the parish of St Thomas. This locality was first developed as part of the town of Bristol in the 12th century with the establishment of the fees of Temple and Redcliff, the site lying within the Redcliff Fee. The boundary between the two developments was the Law Ditch, which served as a drain and open sewer for the tenements on both sides, in both fees. The tenement plots within which the site was located extended from Redcliff Street on the west to the Law Ditch on the east. The north side of these properties extended along Thomas Lane, for which no street numbers are known for the period before the 1880s.

2.2 Documentary Evidence for the Site

The excavations at 3 Redcliff Street were situated within the plots numbered from 1775 to the 1880s as Nos 21–23 Redcliff Street. These tenements formed part of or abutted a larger block of properties, Nos 21–25, which will be considered here in more detail (see Figs 3.18–3.19 for general orientation). For none of these properties has it been possible to extend the histories of the tenements back beyond the mid 17th century. A discussion of the manuscript and cartographic sources consulted can be found in the References section.

Nos 21 and 22 can be traced back to the 1650s, when they were both possessions of Hugh Smyth of Ashton Court. No. 21 was, in 1656, one of two tenements sold by Hugh Smyth of Long Ashton to Edward Bovey ironmonger, 'with a cellar below, in Redcliff Street and abutting on Saint Thomas Lane, heretofore of William Hawle and then of John Millard'; Millard was still the occupier in 1664 (BRO 05820, abstract; F/Tax/A/1). By 1684 the two tenements had passed to Edward Booth, citizen and clothworker of London, and Elizabeth his wife, daughter and heir of Edward Bovey. From 1685 the two tenements were leased by Booth and his wife to Walter Gunter and others, extending back to a tenement formerly called the Sheremans' Hall. No. 21 adjoined St Thomas Lane, was then of John Griffin, scivier (scribe), and was by him lately new built. By 1696 and in 1699 this was where Elizabeth Griffin widow lived (BRO 05820, abstract). By 1701 it had passed to John Hall, apothecary, and Elizabeth his wife, the sole surviving daughter of Edward and Elizabeth Booth; by 1744, the date of Hall's will, it was of --- Smith widow (BRO 05820, deeds). By 1775 No. 21 was an earthenware shop, occupied by George Plumly. By 1819 it was 'since of Solomon Marwood and now of John Smith earthenware seller' (BRO 05820, deed of 1819 for No. 22 Redcliff Street giving abuttals from No. 22). The property was compulsorily acquired in 1878 for the widening of Redcliff Street (BRO 05839, No. 43 on the plan).

No. 22 was, in 1656, the second of the two tenements sold by Hugh Smyth of Long Ashton to Edward Bovey, ironmonger, 'once of William Blake, since of Samuel Bilfield, and then of Thomas Hucknall haberdasher' (BRO F/Tax/A/1). As above, from 1685 the two tenements were leased by Booth and his wife to Walter Gunter and others. No. 22 adjoined a pavement belonging to a tenement where Walter Gunter then lived, and was then 'of Hannah Hook widow' (BRO 05820, abstract). From 1696 it was leased by Elizabeth Booth to Joshua Cachmay, silkweaver, there in 1699, between 'the tenement where Elizabeth Griffin then lived on the north and a house late of Walter Gunter on the south, extending from the street on the west to a garden late of Walter Gunter on the east'. By 1701 Elizabeth Horneblow now lived in the tenement where Cachmay had lived, this now leased by John Hall, apothecary, and Elizabeth his wife, the sole surviving daughter of Edward and Elizabeth Booth, to John Merrifield, gent. By 1744, the date of Hall's will, it was of --- Milleman, butcher (BRO 05820 deeds). By 1775 it was occupied by John Thatcher, stockingmaker. By 1819 it was the tenement 'formerly of Milleman butcher, since of --- King and now of --- watchmaker, now sold by John Day, descended from John Hall of Dundry, to William Lott'. The property is located from the plan of 1878, for the compulsory acquisition of the property by the Urban Sanitary Authority, for the widening of Redcliff Street (BRO 05820).

No. 21 extended back to the Sheermans' Hall. By 1684 the tenement formerly called 'the Sheermans' Hall', to the east of No. 21 Redcliff Street, was 'now of Walter Gunter ironmonger' (abuttals from No. 21 Redcliff Street). By 1720 it was the 'tenement and garden and an outhouse adjoining, known as the Sheermans' Hall, consisting of an upper room now of --- Tindale writing master, and two cellars under the same, one of John Durban and the other late of Nicholas Tooker grocer and now of John Smith distiller, also a stable at the east end of the garden now of Patience Potter widow, all now owned by Richard Smith mercer, of Haverford West, Pembrokeshire, and Mary his wife, one of the daughters of Walter Gunter ironmonger'. By 1735 the property was used as a writing school, 'of Tobias Newham writing master', part of the bequest made by Mary Smith to the charities of St Mary Redcliffe and St Thomas (BRO 05836). The property fronting Thomas Lane in 1816–17, part of the lands of St Thomas's Church, preserved the footprint of the Sheermans' Hall, and possibly some or all of the fabric (BRO P/StT/Ch/3/31 fol. 20). It was one of the properties in Thomas Lane purchased for the widening of Redcliff Street in 1879 (Nos 45 and 47 on the plan BRO 06494(2) fol. 38; deeds are BRO 05846).

Nos 23–25 Redcliff Street, or a part of these, was by 1685 the tenement where Walter Gunter, ironmonger, lived; by 1699 late of Walter Gunter, and extending also to the east of No. 21 (abuttals from No. 22). By 1720 Nos 23–25 were owned by Richard Smith, mercer, of Haverford West, Pembrokeshire, through his marriage to Mary, one of the daughters of Walter Gunter (BRO 05836). By 1735 Nos 23–25 were the three tenements held by William Smith, distiller, and Henry Gresley, grocer, part of the bequest made by Mary Smith to the charities of St Mary Redcliffe and St Thomas (BRO 05836). The property is shown in detail on a plan of 1816–17. At this stage it appeared to fall into three distinct units. No. 23 was a dwelling house and other buildings connected (by access around the back of No. 22) with the property fronting Thomas Lane, the former Sheermans' Hall and later writing school. No. 23 was, in 1819 and still in 1837, occupied by George Taylor, liquor dealer. No. 24 was probably connected to what may have been industrial buildings, extending back and behind Nos 22 and 23 to the Law Ditch, which ran between the properties fronting Redcliff Street and those fronting St Thomas Street. Close to the Law Ditch was a circular installation, of sufficient prominence to be shown on the plan. In 1831 No. 24 was the house and warehouse occupied by Shute, Edwards and Co., by 1837 of Charles M. Williams. Shute, Edwards and Co. in 1831 was possibly the same company as Edwards and Co., rectifiers (a term for distillers) in Redcliff Street in 1801. The third part was No. 25, a smaller property extending back a much shorter distance. In 1831 and 1837 No. 25 was occupied by Benjamin Bozley. The property is located from the plan of 1878, for the compulsory acquisition of the property by the Urban Sanitary Authority, for the widening of Redcliff Street (BRO 05836).

In the 19th century the landscape of Redcliff Street was much changed by street widening on its eastern side. North of Little Thomas Lane, the east side of Redcliff Street was widened *c.* 1872 as part of the scheme to create Victoria Street. Between Little Thomas Lane and (St) Thomas Lane, the east side of Redcliff Street was widened *c.* 1878. South of Thomas Lane the east side of Redcliff Street was widened *c.* 1880. Most of the purchases of properties to be demolished in advance of widening were made between 1876 and 1879 (BRO 06494(2) fol. 38). No overall plan of this scheme to the south of Little Thomas Lane (Undertaking No. XII) has been traced.

2.3 Conclusions

Over five or more centuries the north end of Redcliff Street was a mix of dwellings and industry. In the later medieval period industry was centred around the production and particularly the finishing of cloth. From the 16th and 17th centuries onwards industrial processes linked to the Atlantic trades predominated, first of soap and then of sugar and its by-products. The excavated sites were most probably closely associated with distilling, maximising the use and potential of the waste from sugar refining for the production of rum.

Chapter 3
Fieldwork Results

3.1 Introduction

Analysis of the site records identified six periods of activity. Features have been assigned to groups within these periods on the basis of the dating evidence (derived from the ceramic assemblage and other dateable artefacts), functional interpretation, and spatial and stratigraphic relationships with other features. The six periods are:

Period 1: geological
Period 2: later 12th to mid 13th centuries
Period 3: mid/late 13th to 15th centuries
Period 4: 15th to 18th centuries
Period 5: late 18th to 19th centuries
Period 6: 19th to 21st centuries

The archaeological sequence presented below is organised by period, with some periods divided into sub-periods of activity (as 'a', 'b' etc.). To aid description and avoid a multiplicity of context numbers, some classes of archaeological feature, such as walls, pits, floors and cellars, have been assigned letters or numbers ('Wall A', 'Cellar 2', for example). Context numbers, when referred to, are shown either as unprefixed numbers or in parentheses.

3.2 Period 1: Geological Strata (not illustrated)

Deposits of naturally accumulated alluvial silts were encountered in both of the excavation areas, including contexts 1144, 1147, 1171 (Fig. 3.2, sections AA and BB), 1045, 1105, 2145 and 2152 (not shown). The upper surface of the silts lay at approximately 6.7m AOD. Molluscan, archaeobotanical and lithostratigraphical analysis of this alluvial material has concluded that it was deposited on the margins of a river channel during intermittent flooding and in a virtually stationary water body, but that the environment was essentially stable (Chapters 5.3–5).

3.3 Period 2: Early Reclamation and Settlement Activity (later 12th to mid 13th centuries)

Period 2a

Substantial evidence for Period 2a was only encountered in Area 1, on the western part of the site, where several features had been constructed upon, or were cut into, the natural alluvium (Fig. 3.1). The surface of the alluvium had been disturbed by human activity and contained charcoal and carbonised seeds (Chapters 5.4 and 5.5).

Period 2a features included an ovoid pit (1177), approximately 1m by 1.5m in plan, whose lower fill of organic silt (1178) had been deliberately capped with a layer of brown clay (1179) (Fig. 3.2, section BB). About 3m to the north-east of this pit, a small circular pit (1049), possibly a posthole, *c.* 0.3m in diameter, had also been cut into the alluvium. There was no clear sign of a post and the profile was bowl-shaped. A beechwood board (1048), with four battens attached, had been placed in a shallow rectangular cut into the alluvium, just to the south of the posthole. This may have been a tread-board or part of a walkway as the battens, although irregularly spaced, were on the upper side (Fig. 3.3). The board, which measured 0.9m by 0.4m and was 0.02m thick, had one chamfered edge and appeared to have been reused. It may originally have formed part of the lining of a pit or well (Chapter 4.9) although equally it could well have been part of a window shutter or similar. Both pits 1049 and 1177 contained pottery of later 12th to mid 13th-century date in their fills. What may have been a gully of this period (1180) ran along the bottom of the baulk (Fig. 3.2, section BB), and only its southern edge was seen. It extended east and west of the excavated area.

To the south of probable gully 1180 was Wall A (Fig. 3.1). This was constructed of rubble, bonded with an orangey-brown mortar and set in a shallow foundation trench 1174, cut into the alluvium (Fig. 3.2, section

Fig. 3.1   Area 1, Period 2a: later 12th to mid 13th centuries. Scale 1:100

AA). The wall was 0.8m wide and aligned roughly at right angles to Redcliff Street. Only a short length of the wall survived, as its east and west ends had been truncated by the modern walls K and N (Fig. 3.20). It was not recorded further to the west, in the small area between Wall N and the robbed foundation trench for Wall D of Period 3b (Fig. 3.6). Its non-existence here suggests that it either ended on the line of Wall N or turned north on the same alignment. The latter interpretation is less likely because it would have had to have been much thinner at this point to have been so completely removed by the modern wall. It was bordered on the south by the deep foundation trench 1129 for Period 6 Wall M, between 3 and 4 Redcliff Street (formerly Nos 22 and 23 Redcliff Street).

The features recorded in Area 1 and the surface of the earlier alluvium in Area 2 were sealed by trampled and mixed alluvium deposits 1119, 1141 and 1170 (Fig. 3.2, section BB), and deposit 2151 (Fig. 3.5, section DD) which contained pottery dated to the later 12th to the 13th century. The pottery recovered from the trampled horizon was essentially the same as that recovered from the underlying features. Sherds from only ten vessels (minimum vessel count) came from this period: Ham Green coarseware and glazed sherds, including a Ham Green A style jug and a Minety type ware tripod pitcher sherd (Chapter 4.1). The earliest pottery found was represented by one sherd of Bristol C ware of 11th to early 12th-century date, but this was found residually in Period 2b.

Period 2b

In Area 1 a small pit 1052 and a posthole 1068 were cut into the Period 2a trampling. Neither feature contained dating evidence (not illustrated). In Area

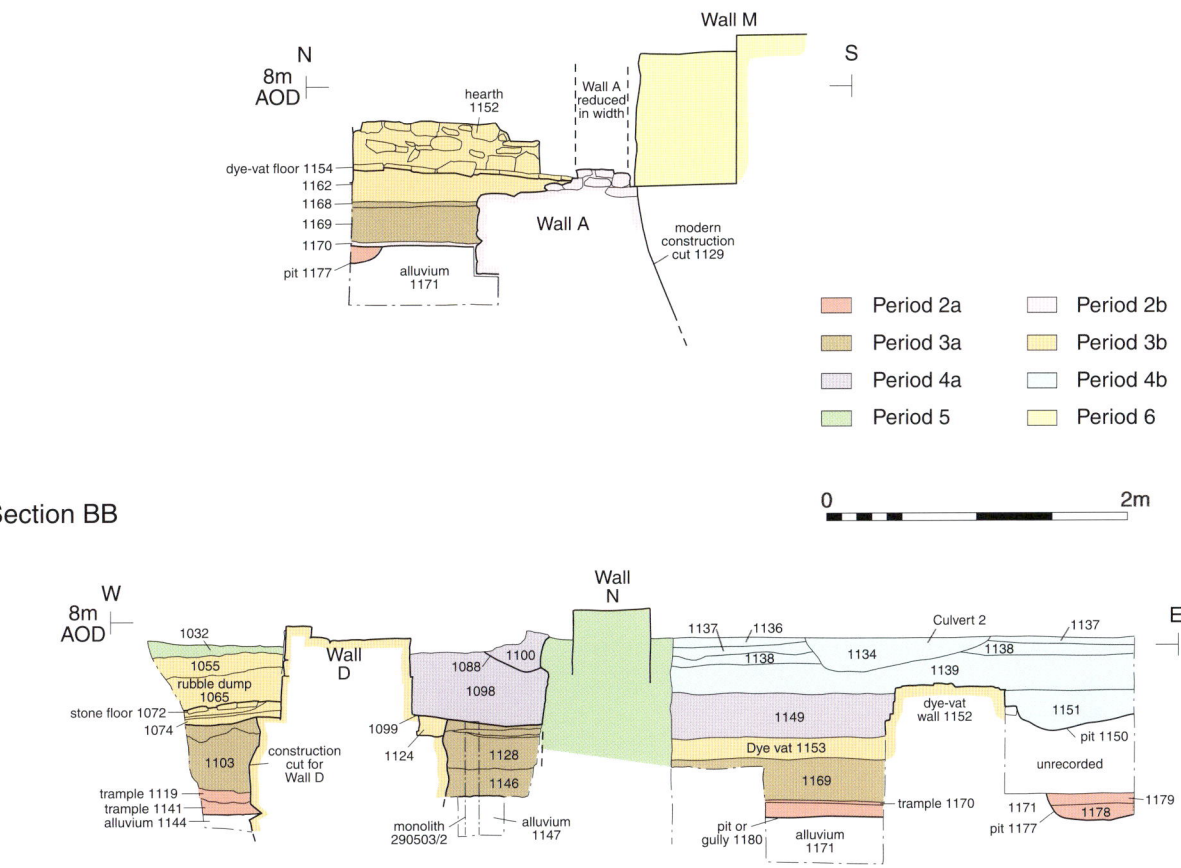

Fig. 3.2   Area 1, Sections AA and BB. Scale 1:50

2 the few features from this period included ditches, a pit and a length of stone wall (Fig. 3.4). In Area 2, all features post-dated the trampled horizon (2151). Pit 2160 was cut into this level (Fig. 3.5, section DD). It had a bowl-shaped profile, was 1.9m in diameter and 0.60m deep. Its basal fills (2162) contained pottery dating to after the mid 13th century, as well as bone and wood, suggesting that the feature was a rubbish pit. It was sealed by deposit 2150, one of the lower levels of the widespread dumping that formed Period 3a. Two linear features were also cut into the alluvium further south. The first was the western terminal of a ditch (2131), only 1.5m of which survived later disturbance. It was filled with a clean clay silt. The second was a ditch (2148), which continued beyond the south and east limits of excavation. A 3.5m-length of the ditch lay within the trench; it was more than 0.7m wide and was 0.20m deep. Its fill was a silty clay. At its western end, ditch 2148 may have turned south, its position against the south baulk precluding certainty on this point. Seeds recovered from the fills of ditch 2148 (2149)

Fig. 3.3   a: Board 1048 and associated pit 1049. b: Board 1048 after lifting. Scales 1m

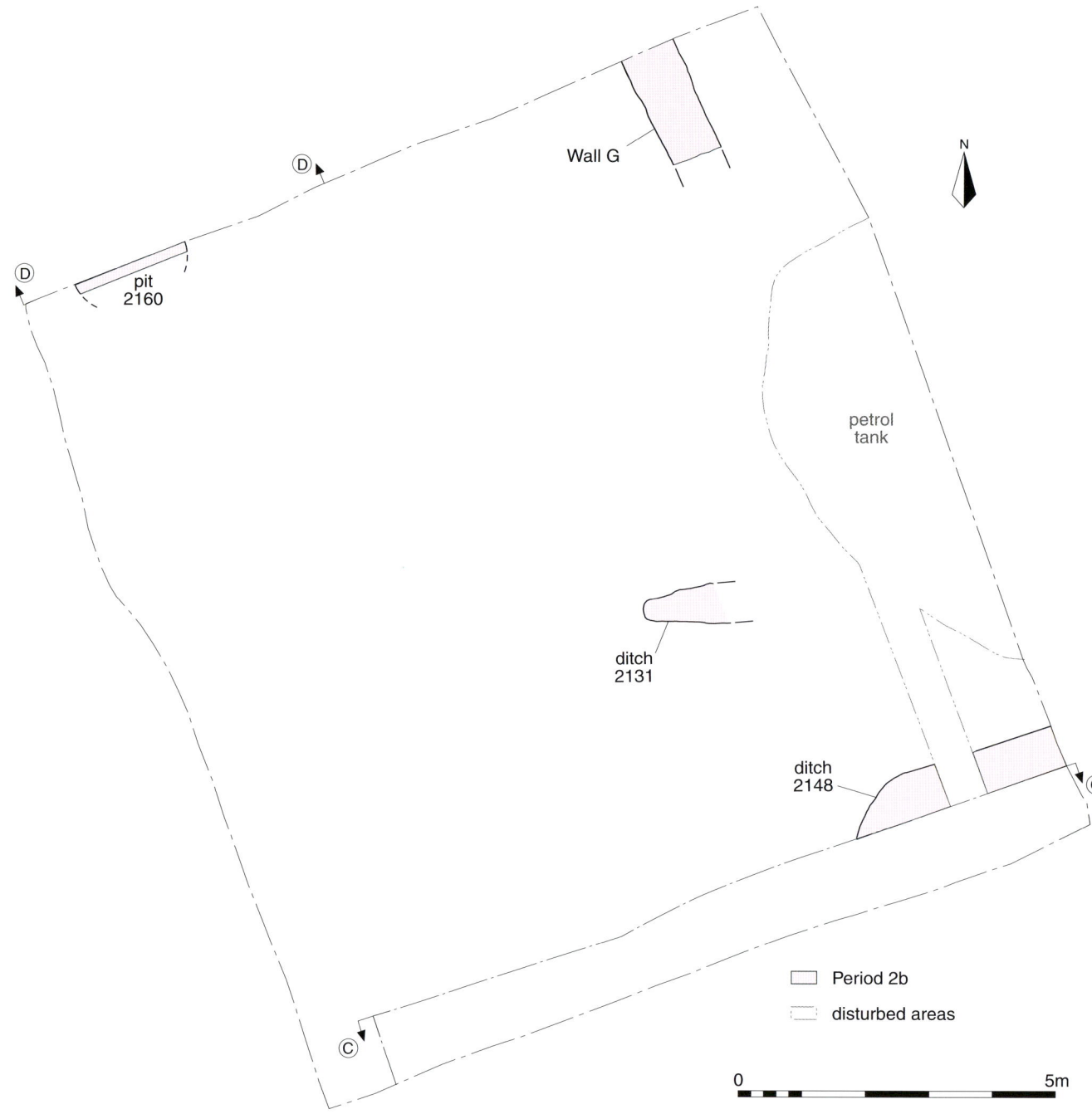

Fig. 3.4 Area 2, Period 2b: later 12th to mid 13th centuries. Scale 1:100

indicate that there had been a damp and waterlogged environment and suggested that it provided drainage (Chapter 5.4). Bristol (Redcliffe) glazed ware recovered from ditch 2131 indicates that it was also filled in after the mid 13th century. Otherwise the pottery was similar to that recovered from Period 2a, although slightly more abundant, at 42 vessels. This suggests a date for the activity of this period of the first half of the 13th century, ending with the infilling of ditches and pit in the second half of that century.

To the north, Wall G was aligned at right angles to Thomas Lane and was truncated at its southern extent. The rough construction of the sandstone blocks suggested only the foundation survived. It was clearly earlier than Wall F of Period 3b, being under layers 2076 and 2123, onto which Walls E and F were built. To which earlier structure it belonged, however, was not clear. No earlier version of Wall F was recorded, for example.

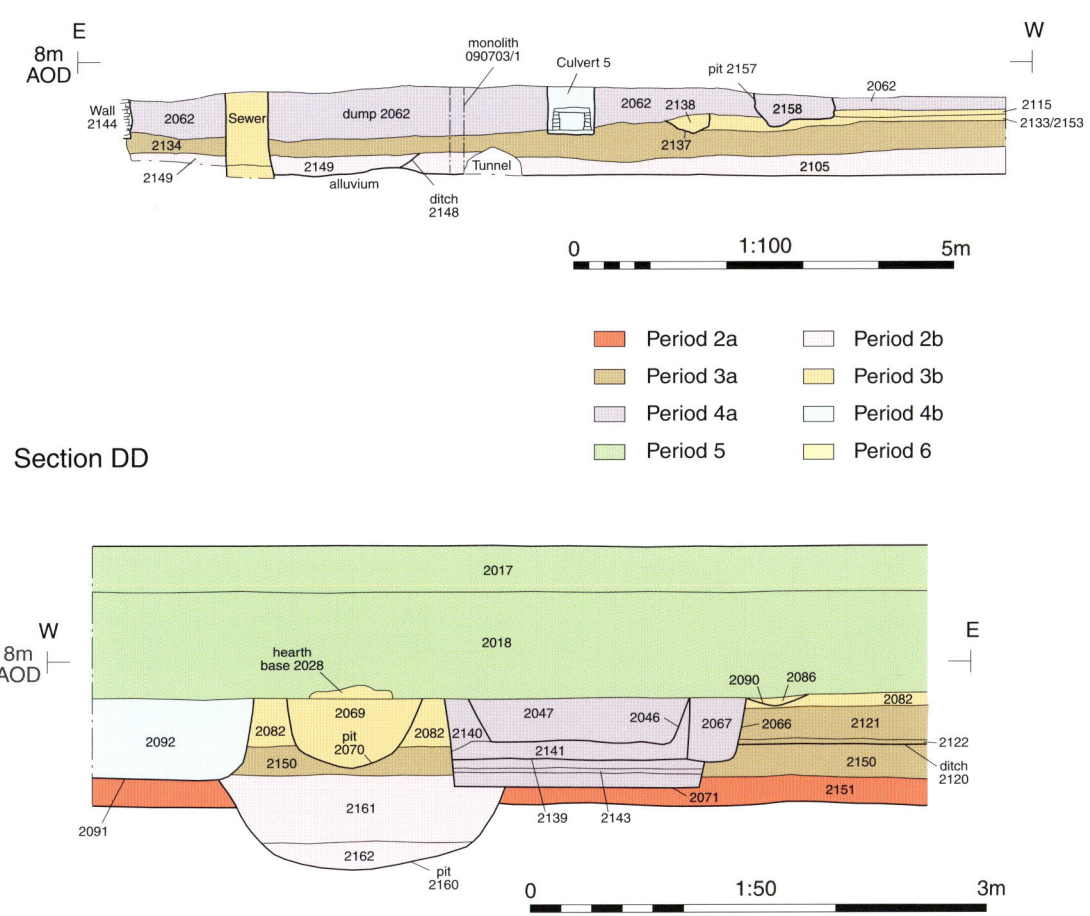

Fig. 3.5 Area 2, Sections CC and DD. Scales 1:100 and 1:50

3.4 Period 3: Medieval Expansion and Industrial Activity (mid/late 13th to 15th centuries)

Period 3a

The Period 2 pits and postholes that cut the dumped levels in Areas 1 and 2 were sealed by an episode of substantial dumping of imported clay, which was recorded right across the site in sections AA, BB, CC and DD (Figs 3.2 and 3.5). The pottery from these deposits is not distinct from that recovered from Period 2b contexts, and the Bristol (Redcliffe) glazed ware indicates a *terminus post quem* no earlier than the second half of the 13th century for their importation. The amount of pottery and the variety of pottery types in the Period 3a assemblage was much greater, with 65 vessels being represented. However, as the material was imported from elsewhere and contained residual material, this dating must be treated with caution. In Area 1, the dumped deposits abutted Wall A of Period 2a, and it seems that the structure it represented remained standing. Lithostratigraphic analysis suggests that some of these deposits (1125, 1126, 1127 and 1128) show evidence of soil formation processes (Chapter 5.5) which might suggest these deposits formed the ground surface for a period of time. Deposit 2134 contained evidence for crop-processing (Chapter 5.4), but was probably derived from off-site activities.

Cut into these make-up deposits in Area 1 were two small rectangular pits 1113 and 1101 (not illustrated). The fills of these features contained large amounts of charcoal, bone and shell, indicating that their final function was as rubbish pits.

In Area 2 the dumped layers were cut by a shallow ditch 2120 (Fig. 3.5, section DD). It lay close to the northern limit of excavation and was 0.65m wide. It oversailed the earlier infilled pit 2160, and from its position, it may have been an early boundary ditch, superseded in Period 3b by Walls E and F. Bristol (Redcliffe) glazed wares recovered from ditch 2120 indicate that it was also filled in after the mid 13th century.

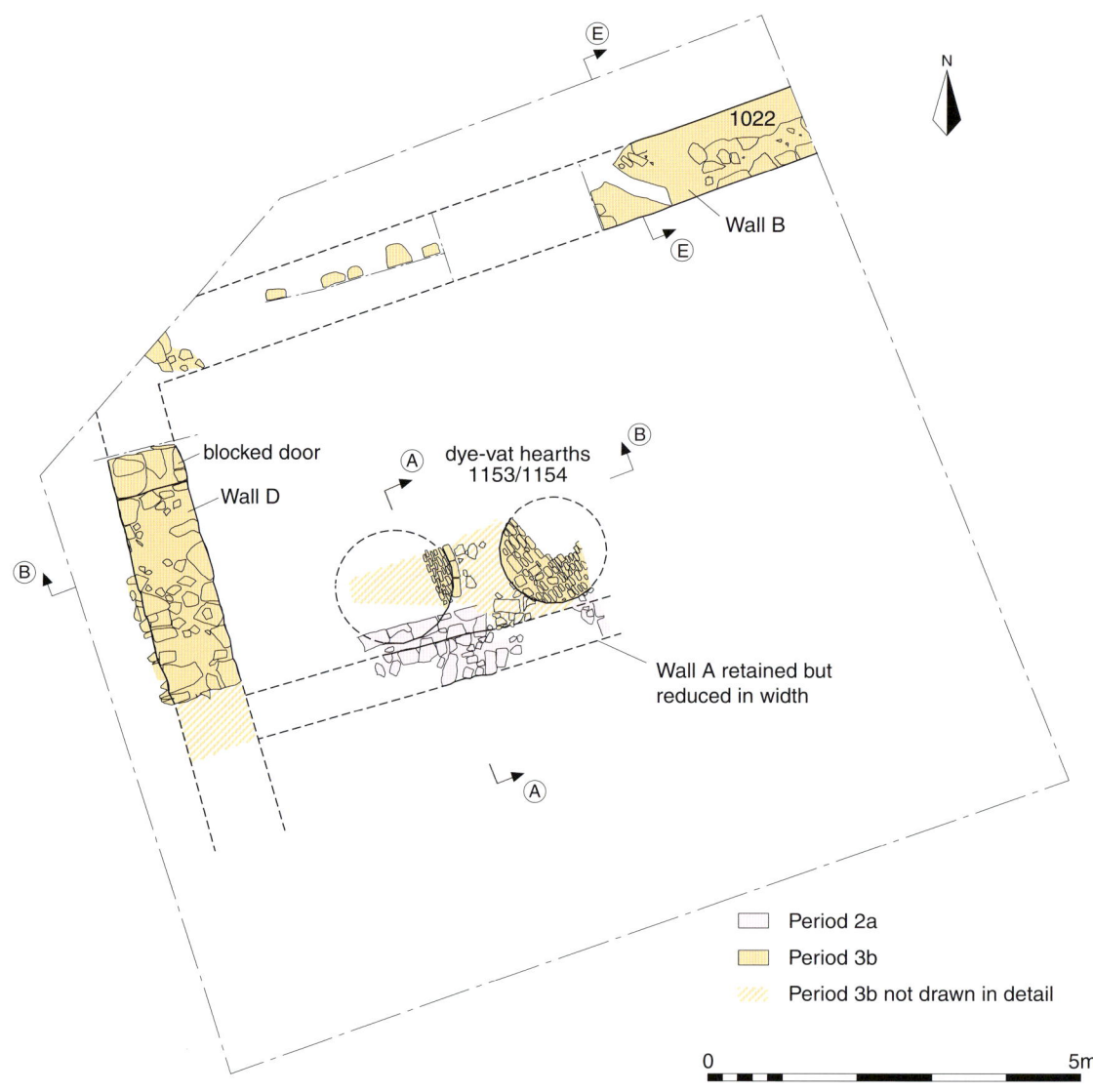

Fig. 3.6 Area 1, Period 3b: mid/late 13th to 15th centuries. Scale 1:100

Period 3b

The ground consolidation represented by the Period 3a make-up deposits was followed by the first clear evidence of extensive development on the site, which consisted of the construction of stone buildings fronting on to Redcliff Street and Thomas Lane, and activity in the rear of the properties including stone-built vat bases.

In Area 1, Wall D was constructed to run north/south, parallel to Redcliff Street, its foundation trench cutting through the dumped layers of Period 3a (Fig. 3.2, section BB). Some deposits containing demolition material were associated with this construction, but their source is unknown. A perforated clay fragment and crucible fragments associated with copper-alloy casting were found in one of these deposits (context 1058; Chapters 4.4 and 4.8). Wall D, which was built of roughly squared sandstone blocks laid in a mortary loam, was 0.9m wide and survived to a length of 3.4m (Figs 3.6 and 3.7). It was removed to the north by pit 1031 of Period 5, and the southern end appeared to have been robbed at some point as its foundation trench 1089 continued a further 0.9m to the south, until cut away by the construction cut for Period 6 Wall M. The fills of the construction cut contained pottery dated to the mid 12th and 13th century but this was probably residual from the imported dumps of Period 3a. A pale pink render on the west face of the wall indicated that this was an internal face. The remnants of a stone slab floor 1072 also survived on the western side of Wall D (Fig. 3.2, section BB). Towards the northern end of the surviving wall, a straight joint separated a short length of wall with redder bonding material, and may represent the south side of a blocked doorway, the north side robbed away with the rest of the wall by Period 5 pit 1031. The overall evidence suggests that Wall D formed

Fig. 3.7   Area 1, Wall D viewed from the south. Scale 1m

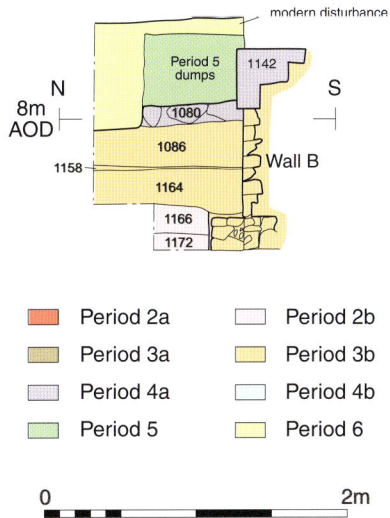

Fig. 3.8   Area 1, Section EE. Scale 1:50

the back wall of a building fronting Redcliff Street to the west. It may be noteworthy that Wall D coincided with a building alignment change plotted on the mid 19th-century mapping of the area (see Fig. 3.18; the wall's position is represented by a kink in the east/west wall between Nos 22, and 23 to the south).

Deposits on the west side of Wall D suggest a sequence spanning several decades. Stone slab floor 1072 was laid in a slight hollow which may have represented the worn-down remains of its beaten-earth predecessor. The pottery from make-up layer 1074 beneath the floors contained Bristol medieval jugs and a possible chafing dish in Bristol (Redcliffe) glazed ware (Fig. 4.1, no. 1) dating to the mid 13th century or later. A layer associated with the beaten earth floor (1090) contained a pair of iron shears of 13th to 14th-century date (Chapter 4.3). The stone floor was sealed by make-up layers that contained a pottery assemblage mainly dated to the late 13th to 14th centuries, but including a Minety type pancheon of late 14th or 15th-century date from rubble dump 1065. Intermittent dumping and a shallow pit 1062 (not illustrated) were part of a sequence associated with alterations to the building that can be dated by pottery to the late 14th to 15th centuries. Wall D seems to have remained in use throughout these alterations and into the post-medieval period, though it is possible that it was rebuilt above its surviving basal level.

An east/west aligned foundation, Wall B, was recorded in the northern part of Area 1 and also cut into the Period 3a dumps. The wall was built from roughly-faced sandstone blocks, survived to a height of c. 1m, and was originally 0.96m in width. Its offset footings, seen on the north side, added another 0.4m to its width on that side. It could be traced (with interruptions due to later disturbances) right across Area 1. Its alignment continued as Wall E/F in Area 2 but there was only 0.48m or so in width. Two mortary, sandy silt layers, 1164 and 1086, separated by a thin mortary layer 1158, were recorded butted up against the north face of Wall B (Fig. 3.8, section EE). These deposits could be make-up layers for a series of surfaces, or even rudimentary surfaces themselves. Altogether these deposits raised the internal floor level to over 0.75m above the offset footings of Wall B, suggesting that they were secondary to the original construction of the wall, although there was no sign of an earlier, lower floor. It is possible that these layers relate to the Period 4a renovations, and if so, the pottery dated to the 14th to 15th centuries recovered from layer 1086 was residual. Based on dating evidence, a 13th to 14th-century date for the construction of Wall B is likely.

Wall B formed the party wall between Nos 21 and 22 Redcliff Street (Fig. 3.18). Most of No. 21 is now under Thomas Lane, lost to widening in the late 19th century.

Deposits contemporary with Wall B to the south had been largely removed by later disturbances, and indeed, the central part of Wall B itself was largely cut away by Cistern D in Period 4. Further to the south, the earlier Period 2a Wall A was retained within structural activity in a possible yard. This was represented by the remains of the bases of two hearths for dye vats, both abutting the north side of Wall A, which was reduced in thickness to accommodate them. The hearths were massively

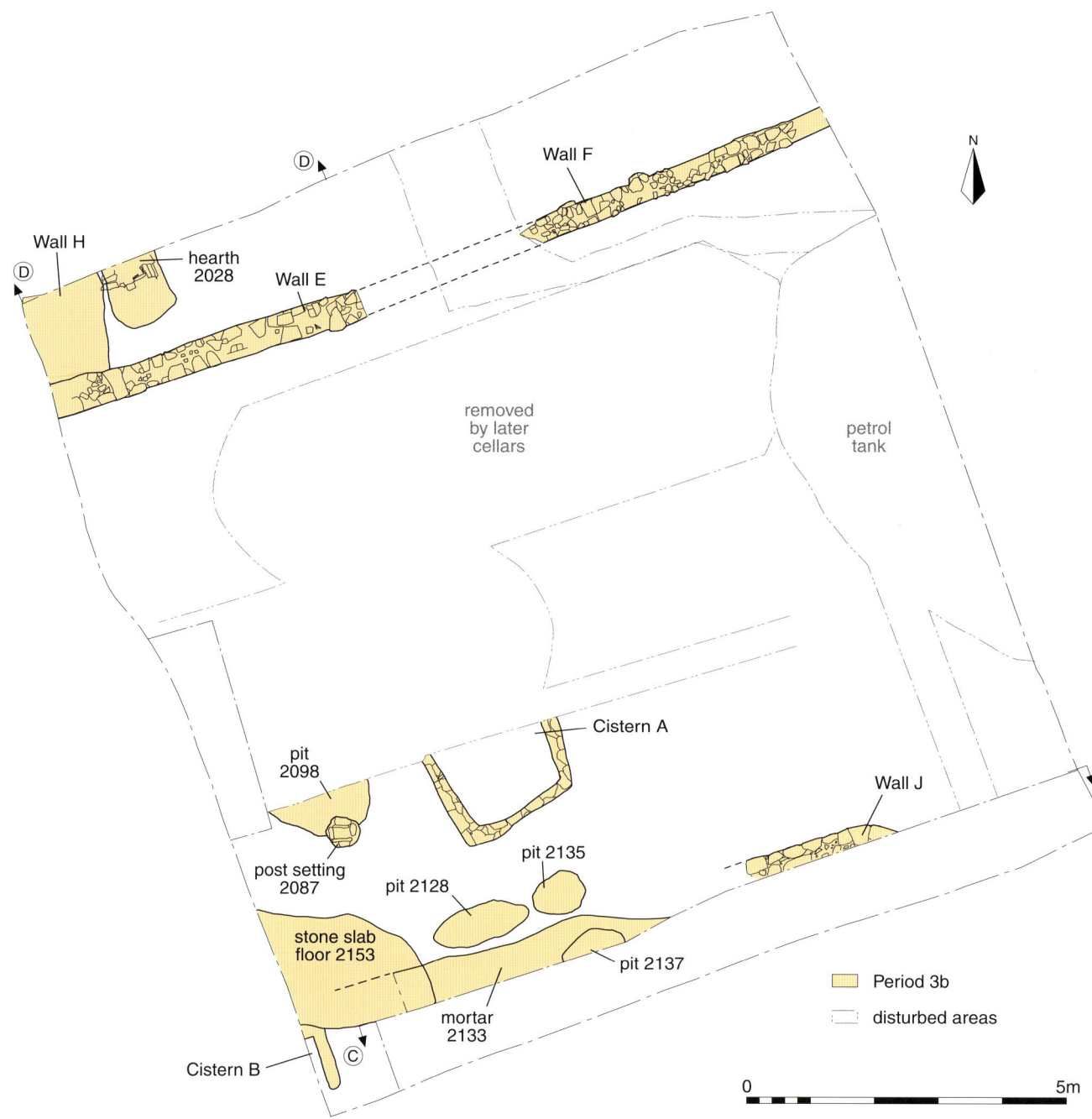

Fig. 3.9 Area 2, Period 3b: mid/late 13th to 15th centuries. Scale 1:100

built of mortared sandstone rubble and the bases were of pitched sandstone, but were poorly preserved, with only part of the curved walls (1152), pitched stone bases (1153 and 1154) and mortar bedding 1162 surviving later disturbance (Fig. 3.2, section BB). The two hearths were part of one integrated structure with an overall width of about 4.5m. The stoke-holes were presumably to the north, in the destroyed sections. The internal diameter of the hearths could be estimated at 1.4m and 1.9m. The pitched stone base 1154 was bedded on mortar that contained pottery from the 13th century.

The construction of the dye vats is consistent with a 14th-century form (Newman 2001, 144) and this would fit the dating evidence for this period (Chapter 4.1). Wall A may have functioned with Wall D to the west and Wall B to the north to form either part of a building or an enclosing wall of a yard. Unfortunately, the physical relationship of Wall A to Wall D was not clear because of later disturbances.

A similar sequence was recorded in Area 2, to the east. In the northern half of Area 2, the line of Wall B in Area 1 was continued by Walls E and F (Fig. 3.9). Both walls

Fig. 3.10 Area 2, Wall E/F viewed from the west. Scale 1m

were of similar construction, rubble in a sandy, orangey-red lime mortar. Both walls were considerably narrower than the walls in Area 1. Wall E, at the western half of the area, was 0.47m wide, while Wall F on the east was only 0.37m wide (Fig. 3.10). Historically, they formed the southern boundary of the Thomas Lane properties (Fig. 3.18; Chapter 2.2).

A length of wall (Wall H) ran northwards from Wall E, in the north-west corner of Area 2. It had been almost completely robbed, however the southern end of the wall against Wall E was still in place. The blocks were laid in a sandy, orange-brown, lime mortar matrix, similar to Wall E. Pottery from the backfill of the robbing trench 2091 dates to the 13th or 14th centuries and while presumably residual, may just hint at a date for the construction of the wall. It was structurally later than Wall E but was probably broadly contemporary with it. A poorly preserved but substantially built, scorched, pitched stone surface, 2028, located to the north of Wall F, is interpreted as the partial remains of another hearth for a dye vat, located within the Thomas Lane properties and set into the corner of Walls E and H. It was set over a deep bowl-shaped construction cut 2070, and it contained pottery of 13th or 14th-century date.

Ditch 2120 was described under Period 3a, but actually cut the same layers as Walls E and F and was sealed by layers that lay against them (2122, 2082). It could therefore have been still open when Walls E and F were built, running alongside them. If so, it was filled in by the time Wall H and hearth 2028 were built over it. Walls E and F in Area 2 could have been contemporary with Wall B, but are not likely to have been the same build on constructional grounds (they are much narrower). Wall E/F formed the southern boundary of the second tenement along Thomas Lane, later known as Sheremans' (Sheermans' or Shearmans') Hall and its neighbour to the east.

Evidence for the superstructure of the buildings associated with the Period 3b walls in Areas 1 and 2 was sparse. All the walls were sufficiently large to have carried a masonry superstructure and timber roof. Roof tiles of Pennant sandstone were recovered from Period 3–5 contexts in Area 2; these were probably used with the glazed ridge tiles found, mostly in later contexts (Chapter 4.2). These latter, with a date range of the 13th to 15th centuries, seem to confirm the broad dating for Period 3.

Against the southern limit of excavation of Area 2, Wall J, aligned east/west, was built of roughly shaped limestone blocks bonded with loam. The wall was over 0.6m wide and only two courses survived. The wall curved slightly to the south at its eastern end and extended beyond the southern limit of excavation, whilst its western extent was uncertain. The function of Wall J is unknown, though the curved northern side might suggest an oven in an outbuilding.

Several irregularly shaped pits lay to the west of Wall J including 2128, 2135, 2137 and 2125 (the latter not shown on Fig. 3.9). The lower fills of these pits contained bone, shell and burnt material, suggesting that they were rubbish pits. Pottery from the pits indicates a 14th to 15th-century date. Pit 2098 contained mortar lenses indicating the disposal of construction or demolition debris. A substantial, stone post setting 2087 cut this pit on its southern edge, suggesting that timber structures were present to the rear of the stone buildings, and this also contained mid 14th to 15th-century pottery.

Two stone-built cisterns A and B were located in the south-western quadrant of Area 2. Both cisterns survived to over one metre in depth. The walls were quite thin and Cistern A was of dry-stone construction (Fig. 3.11). Organic, silty fills within the cisterns suggested that they were cess pits, however, the plastering of the internal faces of Cistern B was unusual, suggesting that it was used for water storage, perhaps related to dye working. The dry-stone construction of Cistern A precluded its use for water storage. A shallow, rectangular-section stone drain ran into its south-west corner, but this was not traced any distance beyond the edge of the cistern.

Fig. 3.11 Cistern A viewed from the north with incoming drain visible top right. Scale 1m

This, and the permeable walls, suggest that it was intended as a soakaway. Cistern A contained 13th to 14th-century pottery and Cistern B contained 14th to 15th-century pottery. A sandstone slab surface, 2153, abutted the northern side of Cistern B. This surface was sealed by a gravel path, 2133, and a mortar surface, 2115 (not illustrated). The mortar surface to the north of Cistern B appeared to post-date the nearby pits 2128 and 2135 and these surfaces are likely to post-date all of the pits in this group. Another set of shallow pits and scoops, 2113 (not shown) and 2137, were cut into these surfaces. They were filled with rubble and may have been repairs of pot-holes.

3.5 Period 4: Early Post-Medieval Industrial Activity (15th to 18th centuries)

Period 4a

In the 16th and 17th centuries the Period 3 buildings represented by Walls B and D in Area 1 either continued in use, or the lower parts of their walls were reused as footings (Fig. 3.12). There was evidence for short lengths of inserted repair work in Wall B (1142) and for the insertion of a new floor at a higher level associated with this repair (1080) (Fig. 3.8, section EE). Material was dumped to raise the level in Area 1. Associated pottery dates to the early 16th century, and the absence of Malvern Chase pink fabric vessels, post-dating 1530, suggests a construction period close to this date.

On the north side of Wall B, a semi-circular pit (1084) was filled with a loose, stony deposit 1085 that may have been associated with the robbing of its lining, dated by associated pottery to the late 17th century, so the pit must have been created sometime before then. On the south side, near the centre of the excavated area, the remains of a mortared rubble raft 1149 (in cut 1148), ran east/west and clearly post-dated the Period 3b dye vats, cutting away their northern side. The raft was constructed from massive sandstone blocks in an orange, sandy lime mortar and extended westwards as raft 1098, where it butted Wall D. The original extent of this rubble raft is unknown due to later truncation, but it covered an area measuring at least 3m north/south and 4m east/west, and probably extended from Wall A to Wall B and some distance eastwards. The upper surface of 1149 was at the same level as the stone dye-vat wall stub (1152–54) of Period 3b, but this was because both had been truncated by later drains; the surviving upper level of raft 1098 shows it was at least 0.4m higher than the hearth bases. The rubble may have been part of a massively-built floor or base for installations that replaced the earlier dye vats in a yard area whose edges continued to be defined by the earlier wall lines to the west, north and south.

Period 4a was represented in Area 2 by several stony, sandy-silt layers (for instance dump 2062, Fig. 3.5, section CC), that represented further measures to raise the ground level and contained late 16th to early 17th-century pottery, suggesting that the dumping in Area 2 was somewhat later than that in Area 1.

To the north of Wall E/F, these layers were cut into by an apparently rectangular pit 2071 (its northern side running beyond the edge of the excavation; Fig. 3.13). It was nearly vertically sided, 1.6m wide at the base and a minimum 1.7m north/south, and was lined with Pennant sandstone slabs set in a hard pink mortar. It appeared to have been built up against the face of Wall E. Its fill was cut by pit 2066 (Fig. 3.5, section DD) which contained a small brick box structure, 2142, which partly sat on the paving. The box was 0.3m square with bricks 8⅔″ by 4⅓″ by 2¾″. Silty fill 2067 had built up around it. Both were truncated by the recutting of a flat-bottomed, vertical-sided pit (2139) not as deep as the paving but removing the top of box 2142 and respecting its western side. The pit was smaller than the earlier ones at 1.5m by a minimum of 1.6m. This had no structure in it, but was filled with very sooty silts and sandstone blocks (2141). An upper fill, 2140, had no soot in it. These fills were again recut by a flat-bottomed, less deep, but not quite so vertical-sided pit, 2046. This was filled with a sandy light brownish/grey lime mortar, 2047. Strictly these structures could have been Period 4b as they were unsealed.

Period 4b

Period 4b included the construction of drainage systems in Areas 1 and 2, further dumping of soil to make up the ground level, and the construction of cellars and other features to the rear of properties in and around Area 2. The rubble raft 1149 of Period 4a was cut by pit 1150 and subsequently buried by the dumping of this period.

There were at least two episodes of drain construction in Area 1, beginning with a linear stone culvert which sloped slightly downwards from south-west to north-

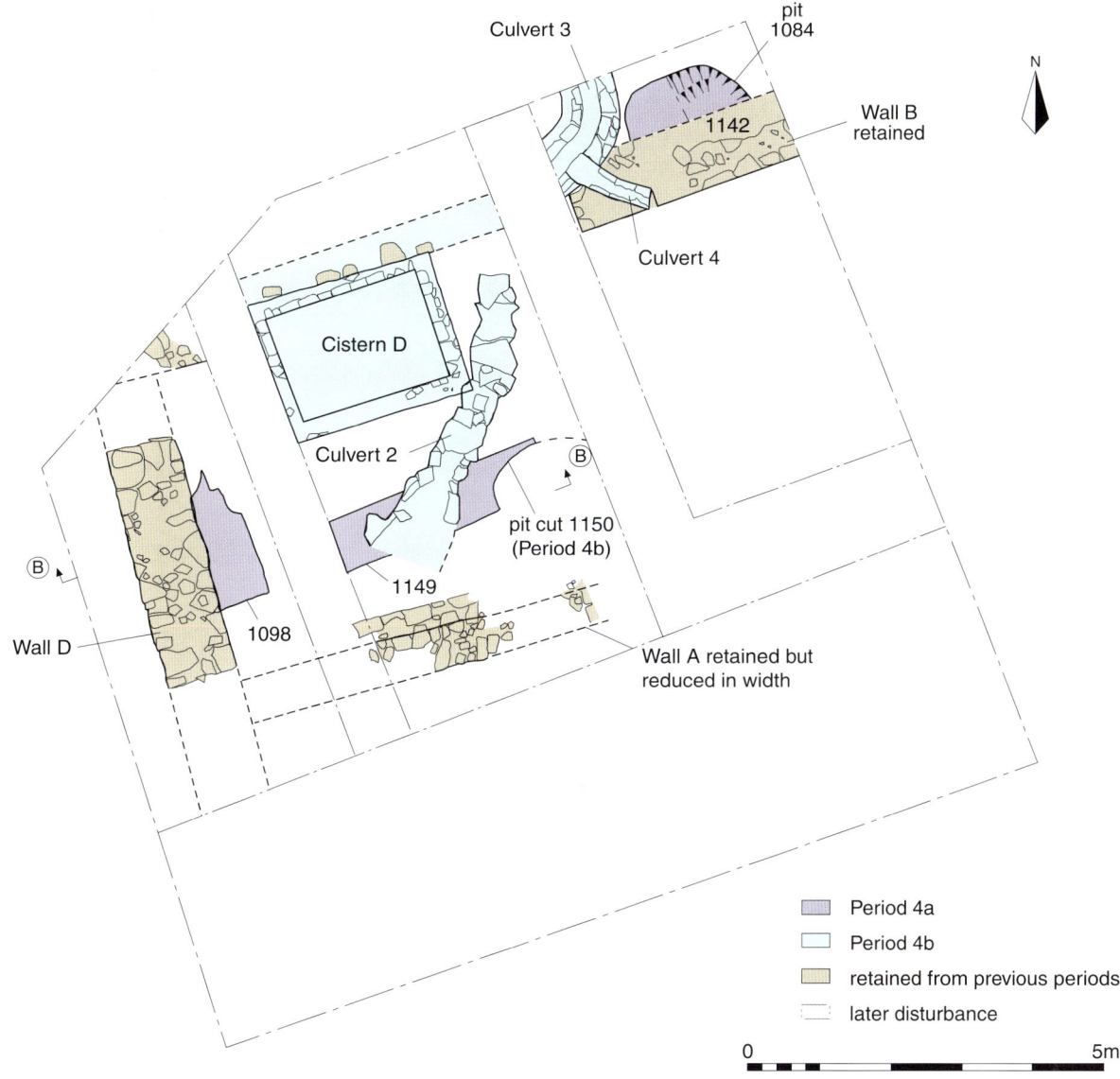

Fig. 3.12 Area 1, Periods 4a and 4b: 15th to 18th centuries. Scale 1:100

east (Culvert 1, not illustrated: little survived the later replacement). It cut through a 0.34m-thick grey-brown mortar layer and sandy make-up deposit, 1138 and 1139, which sealed the underlying Period 4a rubble horizon and contained 18th and 19th-century pottery, though the latter is probably intrusive (Fig. 3.2, section BB). These layers may represent ground preparation for 18th-century rebuilding. The recovery of most of the late medieval roof tiles from this period suggests demolition of the older structures at this time.

The initial drain layout (Culvert 1) was replaced by Culvert 2, cut through a thin layer of mortar and sandy make-up (1136 and 1137) only 0.10m thick, that sealed layer 1138 (Fig. 3.12 and 3.2, section BB). This culvert was built in rubble stone and brick with a stone slab capping and base. A square hole in a capstone towards the middle of the drain indicated where a smaller drain had entered vertically. Culvert 2 originated in the south-west, as had Culvert 1, but curved around Cistern D to a gap in Wall B which seemed to have been specifically made for it.

Cistern D seems to have been inserted in a yard or garden at the back of No. 22 Redcliff Street and was probably used as a cess pit. It cut away the south face of Wall B and much of Culvert 1. It was associated with a mortar floor (1132) which was overlain by a cobbled surface and bedding layers (1115 with 1117 and 1118) (not illustrated). The cobbled surface overlay the capping of Culvert 2. Pottery from layer 1118 was of 18th-century date while the final fill of the cistern contained 17th and 18th-century pottery.

Two similar drains lay to the north-east and cut through Wall B (Culverts 3 and 4). It was clear that the wall remained in use and the culverts were inserted

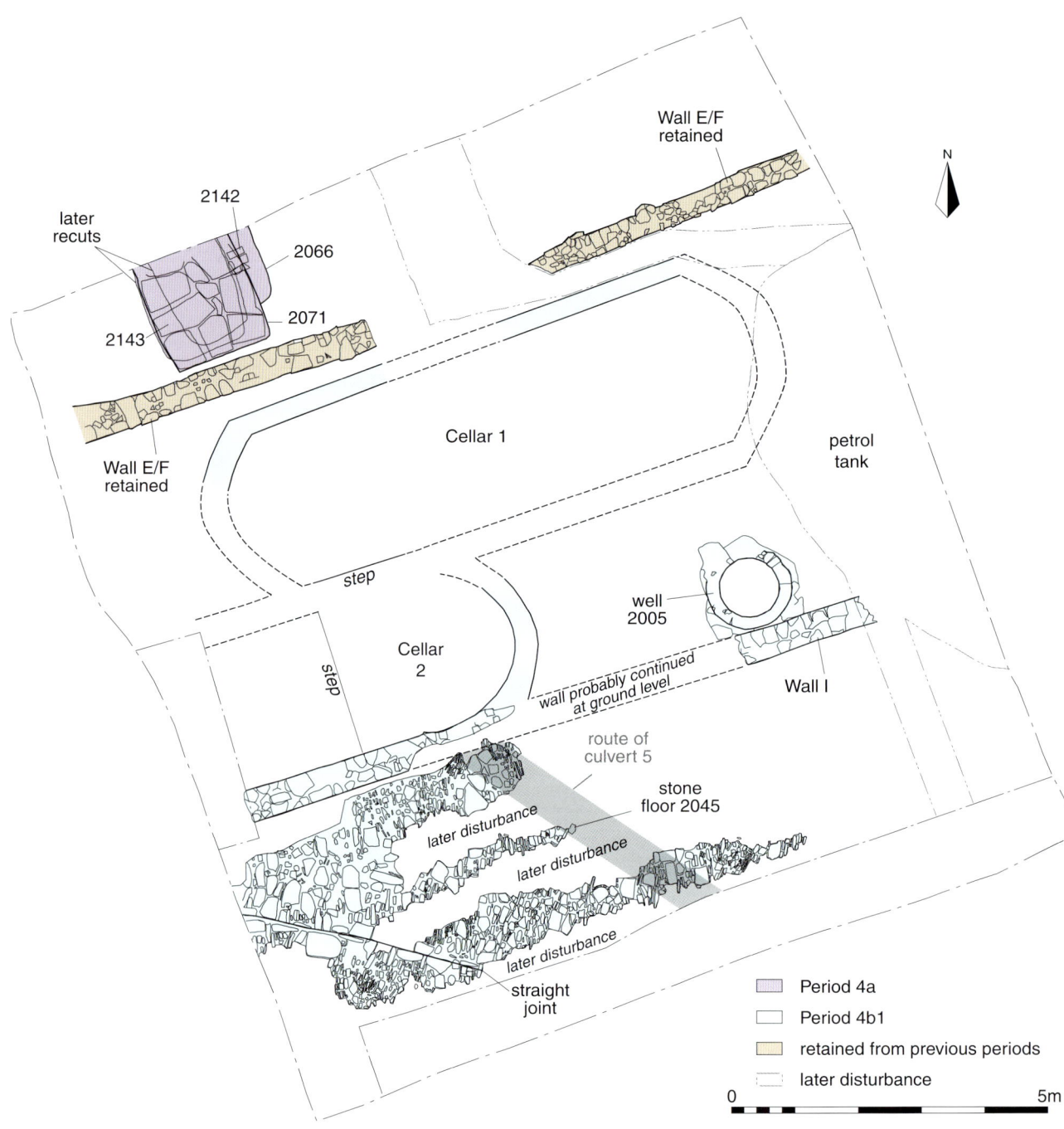

Fig. 3.13 Area 2, Periods 4a and 4b1: 15th to 18th centuries. Scale 1:100

through the standing structure. The culverts were built in rubble stone and brick with a stone slab capping and base, and their contents indicated that their last use was as foul drains. Culvert 4 fed into Culvert 3 and it seems likely that Culvert 2 did as well, although the junction was removed by later disturbance.

To the east, in Area 2, Period 4a features were buried under layers of soil and rubble 2022, 2031, 2104 and new structures were built. These included two small pits 2102 and 2155 (not illustrated) and a sandstone block and slab drain (Culvert 5; Fig. 3.13). Pottery recovered indicates that this activity occurred during or after the middle of the 17th century.

The main features from Area 2 from this period were two abutting stone-built cellars with apsidal ends constructed immediately to the south of Wall E/F. The northern cellar has been labelled Cellar 1 and the southern Cellar 2. These structures were contemporary with those described above and therefore were probably also constructed in the mid 17th century. The cellars

Fig. 3.14 Area 2 cellars, general view from the east

were heavily modified twice, and these modifications are described and illustrated as Periods 4b1 and 4b2 (Figs 3.13 and 3.15). The final changes to the cellars are attributed to Period 5 (see below).

Cellars 1 and 2 were first built of random sandstone rubble in orange lime mortar, with walls surviving to a height of 1.25m above the sandstone slab floor (Period 4b1; Fig. 3.14). The estimated thickness of the Cellar 2 walls was 0.5m (the earth behind Cellar 1 was not excavated). The cellars were constructed through the dump layers of previous periods and rested on the alluvium. Cellar 2 cut away parts of both Cistern A and Culvert 5. A residual late medieval horseshoe was found in the make-up deposits for the construction of the cellars (Chapter 4.3).

Cellar 1 had apsidal ends to the east and west. Cellar 2 had an apse at the east end, and may have matched Cellar 1 in plan, but its western end was beyond the limit of the excavation area. The southern wall of Cellar 2 had a slight spur beyond the line of its eastern apse suggesting that it continued towards the east, where its alignment was continued by Wall I and formed the tenement wall between the two properties. This part of the structure was at ground level, or at least at a higher level, there being no sunken room beyond the apse. Wall I was similar to the walls of Cellars 1 and 2 and was clearly related, although separated from Cellar 2 by a modern intrusion. Later alterations meant that there was no direct relationship between these early cellars, although it seems certain that they were of one build.

An extensive area of stone pitched surfacing (2045) lay to the south of the cellars. It overlay the now-redundant Culvert 5. The floor had a 'straight joint' marked by larger, straight-sided stones, running at an angle across the otherwise irregular slabs and pitched blocks, which seems to be a deliberate change of camber to facilitate better drainage. Three elongated intrusions of unknown date had removed large areas of the surface.

Only the north wall and part of the western apse of the northern cellar survived later changes, whilst the southern cellar retained only its south wall and eastern apse from the Period 4b1 construction. Cellars 1 and 2 were substantially altered in brick in Period 4b2 (Fig. 3.15). The western apse of Cellar 1 was mostly rebuilt in red brick and its northern wall raised in height in the same material (Fig. 3.16). In the centre of the cellar's north wall a very shallow recess was built in similar brick. Judging by the distorted shape of the recess, the brick pier in the centre of this feature may have been built to support it after it started to fail. The eastern apse of Cellar 1 was recognised but could not be excavated for full recording, though it appeared to be built mostly

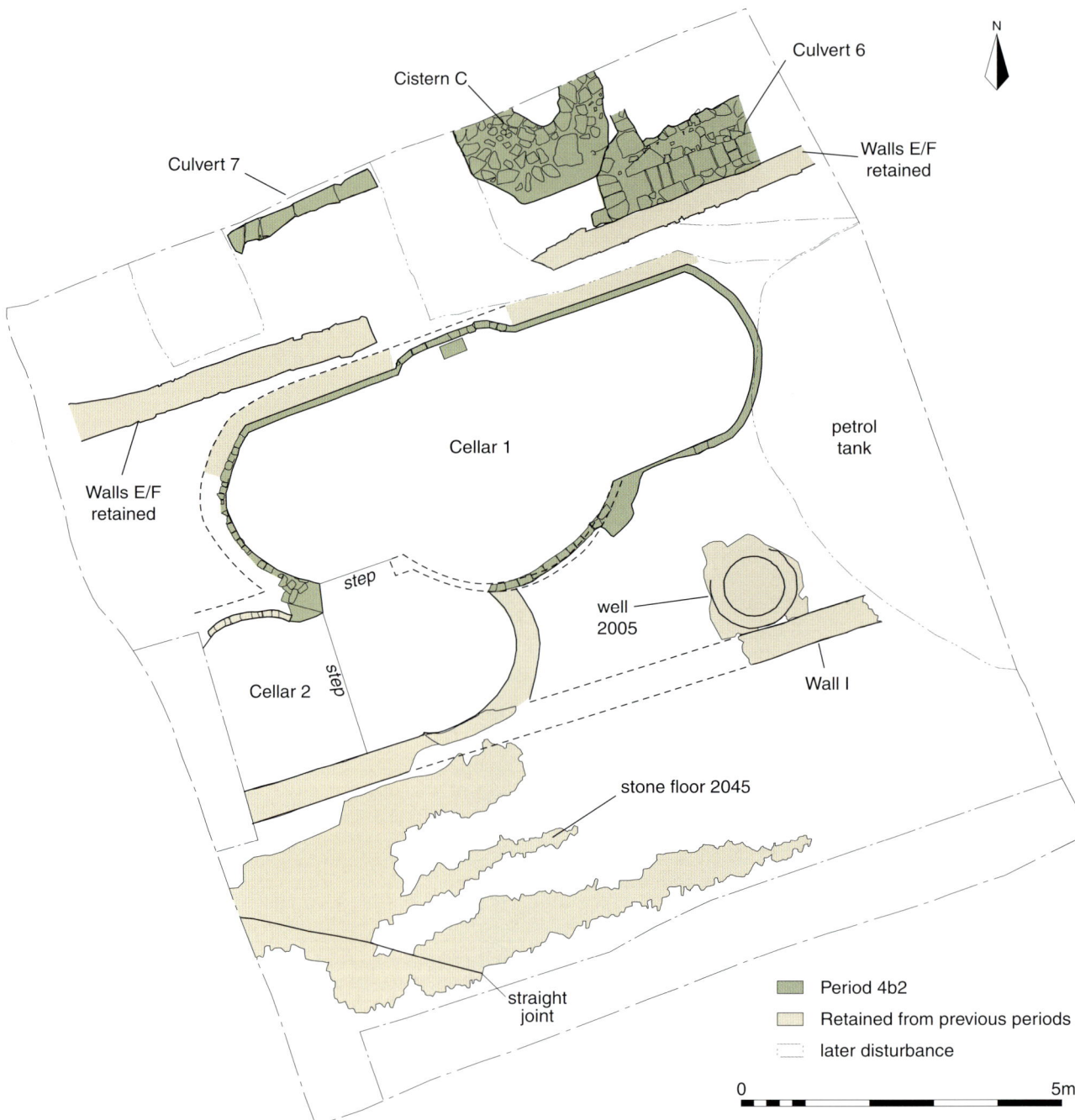

Fig. 3.15 Area 2, Period 4b2: 15th to 18th centuries. Scale 1:100

in yellow brick, the same as the south wall. The south wall contained an integral, larger recess, also located centrally, opposite the smaller, northern recess. In the southern recess was a well-laid Pennant stone tile floor which was only seen in a limited area but probably extended across the whole cellar. The central section of the apse, merely a single brick thick (unlike the rest of the rebuild which was at least 0.25m thick), had slumped forward a few centimetres under pressure of the retained ground behind it. Both of these new walls,

despite their apparent structural inadequacy, were neatly and carefully constructed, although the brick bond itself was irregular with headers and stretchers in no clear pattern. The western end of the southern central apse impinged on the northern end of the eastern apse of Cellar 2 and only one apse could have been complete. It is clear that the northern end of the Cellar 2 apse was removed and was partly rebuilt in brick.

The north wall of Cellar 2 also contained a shallow brick recess. It was built of yellow brick and was integral

Fig. 3.16 Area 2, west end of Cellar 1. Period 4b2 alterations (in brick) to stonework of Period 4b1

with a jamb in the same brick which was created at the south end of the western apse of Cellar 1. This implied an inserted or rebuilt opening between the two cellars, but the other jamb was itself replaced by a later rebuilding in Period 5. Cellar 2 was set at a slightly higher level than the northern one, but there was no threshold stone or other evidence of a step between the two, simply an abrupt change in levels, suggesting that a step may have been robbed out. Cellar 2 was itself at two levels, with a step up just west of the doorway into Cellar 1 (Fig. 3.15).

An uncellared area to the south of Cellar 1 contained a well, adjacent to Wall I (Fig. 3.13). The well (2005) was only partly excavated and its upper backfills contained much 19th and 20th-century material. It was 0.97m in diameter and brick-lined. The lined shaft was set into a mass of mortared rubble butted up against Wall I and occupying much of the space between it and the rebuilt south wall of Cellar 1. The use of brick may mean that it was inserted at the time of the other brick-built alterations in this period.

Structural alterations were also evident in the extreme northern part of Area 2 (Fig. 3.15). Culvert 6, with rubble limestone walls and a slab base, was laid along the north side of Wall E/F. The drain ran from the east side of a substantial, semi-circular, mortared sandstone foundation, falling to the east. The foundation was interpreted as the base for a cylindrical cistern, Cistern C. Its overall shape and extent was not established as it extended beyond the northern limit of excavation. The cistern was at least 0.85m deep and was not bottomed. Culvert 6 probably functioned as a drain for that structure. Another drain of similar design formed from sandstone slabs, Culvert 7, was laid parallel to but further north and to the west of the cistern. Only the basal slabs remained. These had a minimal fall to the east but were to all intents level. Given the minimal survival, they could have been the remains of a slab floor instead.

3.6 Period 5: Later Post-Medieval Activity (late 18th to 19th centuries)

The archaeological findings for Period 5 are supported by extensive historical and documentary evidence, including detailed property plans from the early to mid 19th century (Figs 3.18 and 3.19). The features in Area 1 were retained and there is little evidence of substantial redevelopment in either excavation area until the late 19th century, when those parts of No. 21 Redcliff Street were amalgamated with No. 22 and all the properties that impinged on the excavation area were rebuilt on a different plan. Before this work took place, however, Cellars 1 and 2 in Area 2 were once again modified, probably in the late 18th century (Fig. 3.17).

Modifications consisted of the blocking up of the cellars' side apses (though possibly not all at the same time, as the materials used differed). The northern apse of Cellar 1 had already been given a central pier and the two openings left were filled in with machine-made red bricks laid in an irregular English Garden wall bond in grey cement mortar. The large central southern apse was closed off with a thick sandstone rubble wall. This may have been the earliest change, given the material and the use of a soft lime mortar. Butted up to this was the red brick repair of the eastern apse of the southern Cellar 2 (walls 2008 and 2081), set in grey cement mortar. This replaced the western end of the southern apse of Cellar 1 and must also have replaced the original eastern jamb of the opening between the two cellars. A new Pennant stone slab floor (2010) was laid at a higher level and, when the side apses were all filled in, a brick vault was added to the cellar. The springing for this was clear over the apse blocking, and such a vault could not have been supported until the apses were filled in. The other alterations in Cellar 2 were similar: the northern apse was bricked in and a brick vault was built. A large portion of this still remained when first uncovered.

3.7 Period 6: Modern Development (19th to 21st centuries)

Immediately after the 1878–80 road widening, all the properties south of Thomas Lane were rebuilt. No. 21 Redcliff Street was almost completely lost to road widening, the remaining southern strip of this property being incorporated into No. 22, which was completely rebuilt and became No. 3 in the renumbering that followed. Nos 23 and 24 Redcliff Street were also amalgamated and rebuilt; the rear part of the property was amalgamated with the remains of the Thomas Lane plot.

In Area 1 the Period 4b drains were sealed by layers of rubble (1023). These make-up layers were cut by robbing and ground preparations for new building. A robber cut 1034 associated with the construction Wall N was backfilled with material containing evidence of

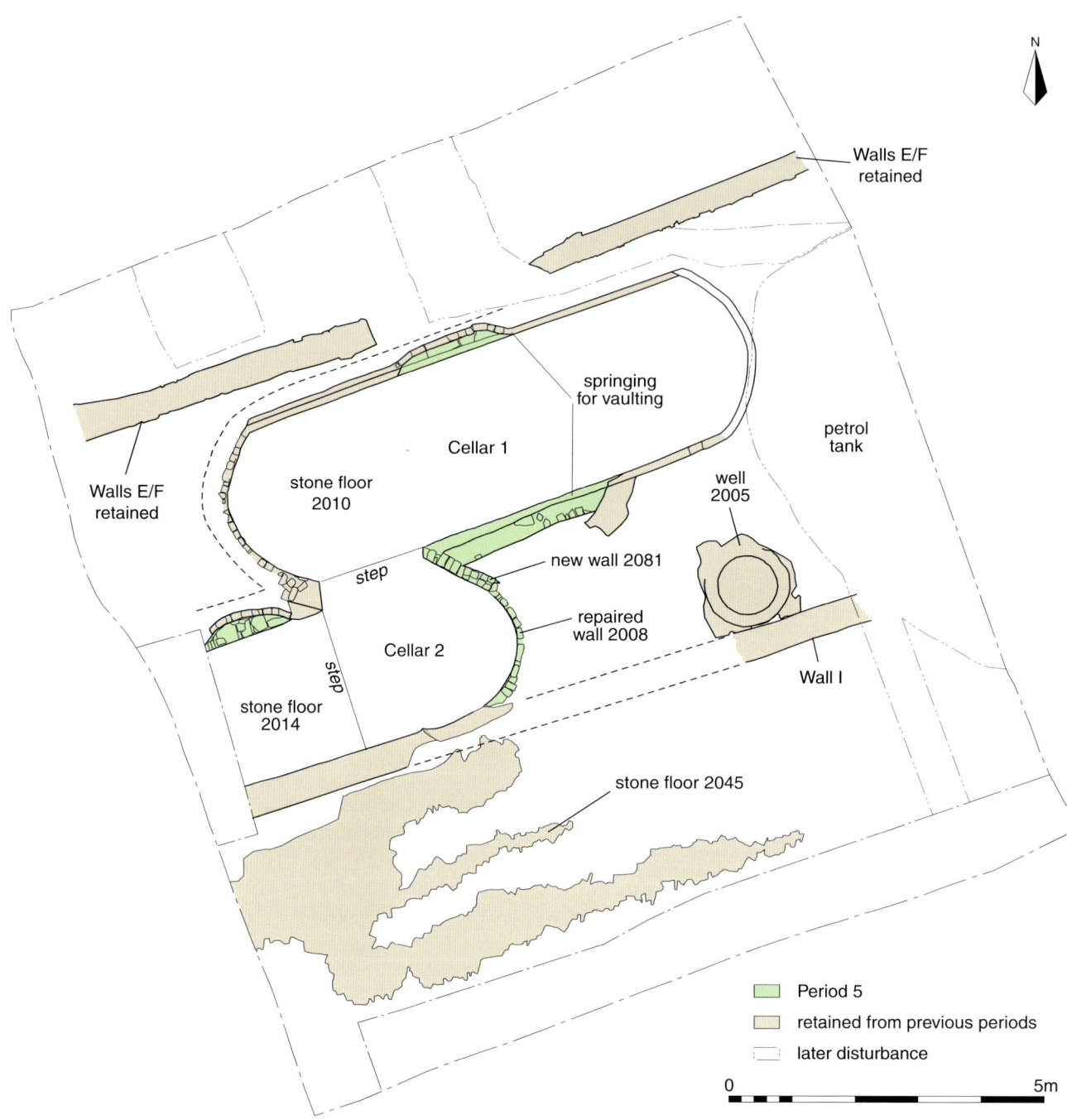

Fig. 3.17 Area 2, Period 5 modification of Period 4 cellars: 15th to 18th centuries. Scale 1:100

copper-alloy working in the form of fired-clay mould fragments and a large quantity of scrap and misshapen lumps probably representing spills or other waste (Chapter 4.4). Four new sandstone foundations topped by brick Walls K, L, M and N represent a complete rebuild of Nos 21 and 22 Redcliff Street, forming a new corner property on the widened Thomas Lane and Redcliff Street (Fig. 3.20). The glazed and unglazed red earthenwares of late 18th-century or later type from Wall N construction deposit 1010 were clearly residual.

Buildings in Area 2 were also rebuilt, with a completely new wall line forming the realigned Thomas Lane frontage (Wall P), and the southern boundary of No. 23 Redcliff Street also rebuilt (Wall Q). Extensive layers of demolition rubble were recorded across the site containing much residual pottery including early to mid 18th-century slipwares and tin-glazed wares, late 18th-

Fig. 3.18 Areas 1 and 2, Period 5: late 18th to 19th centuries, plotted against early 19th-century ground plans (based on BRO P/StT/Chl/3/31, fol. 20). Scale 1:250

168   *Excavations at 3 Redcliff Street, 2003*

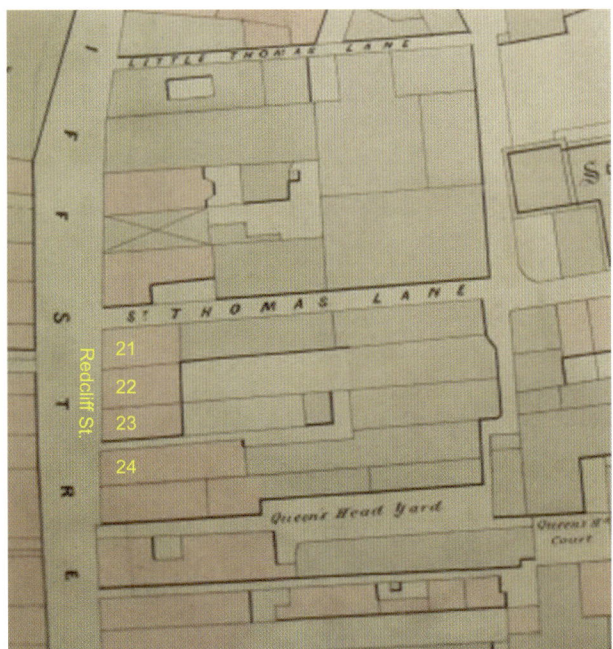

Fig. 3.19 Ashmead's map of 1855

century transfer-printed wares, and sherds of unglazed flowerpots of early modern type. The Area 2 cellars were infilled with rubble, although at least part of the brick vault remained in place over Cellar 2. The east end of the site was excavated for petrol storage tanks, removing all archaeological layers.

Fig. 3.20 Areas 1 and 2, Period 6: 19th to 21st centuries, plotted against the 1884 Ordnance Survey boundaries. Scale 1:400

Chapter 4
Finds

4.1 Medieval and Later Pottery
Alan Vince

The excavations produced a moderate-sized collection of pottery, comprising 611 sherds weighing a total of 11.146kg. The pottery was recorded in an Access database and the wares present were coded according to the system used at the Museum of London and correlated against the Bristol Pottery Type series (Table 4.1). Forms were classified using the Medieval Pottery Research Group dictionary of pottery forms (MPRG 1998).

Analysis of the stratigraphic sequence suggests that a large proportion of the pottery was 'recycled' before final deposition, leading to the presence of mostly small sherds with few being from the same vessels. There are, however, some groups which provide fixed points in the site sequence which can be assigned a date range for the period of deposition.

Assemblage composition

Early 11th to mid 12th centuries
A single probable jar sherd from a distinctive fabric with carboniferous limestone inclusions (Vince 1984, Bristol C; BRISC; BPT 2, 10, 194, 309) was recovered. The end date for the use of this ware in Bristol is considered to be c. 1120, based on its occurrence at Bristol Castle.

Later 12th to mid 13th centuries
Material of later 12th to mid 13th-century date is present as sherds of Ham Green redware, produced in the region of Pill, Bristol (Vince 1984; HGR; BPT 32). All represented sherds come from jars with everted rims, globular bodies and sagging bases. Some of the rim sherds have thumbed decoration. Combed horizontal and wavy lines are commonly found on the vessel shoulders.

Ham Green glazed jug fabrics (HG) include type A (BPT 26) and type B (BPT 27), distinguishable largely on the basis of form. Thirteen sherds of Ham Green A probably dating to the 12th century were present: one collar rim; three roller-stamped bodysherds (one on a corrugated neck), five combed body sherds and the remainder plain sagging bases. Twenty-eight sherds with diagnostic Ham Green B features, including sherds with thumbed bases and bridge-spouts, were present. Of note is a bridge-spout type jug with anthropomorphic decoration (Fig. 4.1, no. 5). Thirty-two sherds were plain bodysherds which could not be reliably assigned to either group.

'Bath A' coarseware (Vince 1984; BATHA; BPT 46, 73), current in Bristol from the 11th century through to the early 14th century, is reasonably abundant. Forms are largely confined to plain jar body sherds but include one jar rim with a T-section more similar to those found in eastern Wiltshire (Newbury B ware). Also of note is one handmade jug sherd with vertical combed lines and a U-sectioned strap handle decorated with knife slashes (Fig. 4.1, no. 2). This handle form suggests a 13th-century date in the West Country.

Examples of Minety type ware (Vince 1984; MINETY; BPT 18, 84), produced between the early 12th to the late 15th or early 16th centuries, largely consist of earlier (12th to mid 13th-century) handmade products. Included are large globular tripod pitchers and globular jars with everted rims. A single residual sherd from the Period 3a imported dumps of material, a tripod pitcher handle formed from two rods of clay with a third strip of clay wrapped around them, is a 12th-century form. No other chronologically diagnostic sherds were present although it is likely that several sherds found in later 13th-century or later contexts derive from wheel-thrown jugs.

The only other wares of this date consist of a sherd of a handmade, unglazed jar containing rounded siltstone fragments (EMEDX) from Period 3a context 1103, part of the imported dumps of material (Fig. 3.2, section BB) and a sherd from an unglazed handmade jar with horizontal wavy combed decoration (found in a residual Period 4a context) which is also possibly from south-

Table 4.1: Basic pottery quantification with concordance with Bristol Pottery Type series (BPT)

Code	BPT	Description	Count	Min. no. vessels	Weight (g)
Medieval					
BRISC	309	Bristol C coarseware	1	1	8
HGR	32	Ham Green redware	100	97	1097
HG	26/27	Ham Green glazed ware (A and B)	106	101	1687
BATHA	46	'Bath A' type coarseware	29	27	402
BR	118	Bristol (Redcliffe) glazed wares	112	98	1067
EMEDX	-	?East Wiltshire sandy coarseware	3	2	12
GLAM	-	Glamorgan glazed ware	7	1	131
MINETY	18/84	Minety type ware	33	25	673
NH	368	Lacock, Nash Hill glazed	2	2	19
SEW	-	South-east Wiltshire sandy coarseware	1	1	8
SAIM	156/157	South-west French Saintonge mottled glaze	5	5	18
SAIP	39/232	South-west French Saintonge polychrome	2	2	16
SAIU	160	South-west French Saintonge unglazed	4	3	107
NFRE	-	?North French micaceous	1	1	6
Sub-total			406	366	5251
Post-medieval and modern					
BORD	-	Coarse Border ware	2	1	29
TUDG	182	'Tudor Green'	3	2	5
CSTN	93/266/275	Cistercian type wares	5	5	30
HERB4	197	Malvern Chase redware	22	22	373
HERB5	-	Malvern Chase 'pink' fabric	47	40	1235
BPT265	265	Local sandy earthenware	4	4	96
AK?	-	Ashton Keynes type ware	1	1	4
NDFW	108	North Devon gravel-free	4	4	91
NDGT	112	North Devon gravel-tempered	53	5	1578
NIMS	82	North Italian marbled slipware	1	1	4
RAER	287	Raeren stoneware	3	2	134
LVAL?	83	Late Valencian lustreware	1	1	65
SNTG	344	South Netherlands tin-glazed	1	1	12
OLIV	81	Seville olive jars	1	1	12
SPAM	282	Algarve micaceous/Merida type ware	3	3	38
SSOM	268	South Somerset glazed earthenware	4	2	24
STCO	100	Yellow slipwares	3	3	26
STMO	211	Mottled brown-glazed earthenware	1	1	7
LONS	-	London stoneware	2	2	254
TGW	99	London/Brislington tin-glazed	5	5	58
PMX	-	Tin-glazed albarello	1	1	2
BRS	277	Bristol stoneware	12	6	1013
TPW	278	Transfer-printed refined whiteware	5	5	18
LPMLOC	201	Local earthenware (flowerpot)	14	10	593
WSM	-	Weston-super-Mare coarseware	6	6	193
MISC	-	Miscellaneous	1	1	1
Sub-total			205	135	5895
Total			**611**	**501**	**11146**

east Wiltshire, although the more common form of decoration on these vessels is scratch marking.

Later 13th to 15th centuries

A total of 112 sherds of Bristol (Redcliffe) glazed wares (BR; BPT 118) were present, representing no more than 98 vessels. The majority come from jugs (97 sherds), with a range of other vessel forms represented by a handful of sherds each. These sherds could come from vessels produced at any point in the later medieval period. Eleven sherds derive from jugs dateable to the 13th to early 14th centuries and similar in form to Ham Green types. A single vessel of this type with an applied, thumbed frill at the base and a number of sherds with applied decoration, of either self-coloured or an iron-rich clay, were identified. Three sherds derive from forms typical of a later (14th-century) period of production, characterised by plainer, more standardised jug forms. A further two sherds from internally-glazed jugs may be representative of the latest, possibly 15th-century period of production. The small number of sherds from non-jug forms includes small condiment dishes; jars; small drinking jugs (perhaps copying Rhenish stonewares); a chafing dish (Fig. 4.1, no. 1) and a dripping dish.

The majority of Bristol sherds were undecorated, decorated with bands of wheel-applied combing, wavy combing or horizontal grooves, and have external copper-mottled glaze. Table 4.2 shows the distribution by period of these various groups and shows that the Period 3b Bristol (Redcliffe) glazed wares have the highest proportion of highly-decorated sherds and that sherds of types dateable to the 14th century only occur residually in Period 4a and later deposits, which also have a high proportion of undiagnostic sherds.

Later medieval regional imports include jug fabrics from Glamorgan (GLAM; Vince 1984; Period 4a, mixed rubble make-up deposit 2062) and Nash Hill, Lacock (NH; BPT 368 McCarthy 1974; Vince 1984; from a clay dump and 2127, fill of pit 2125, both Period 3b). Additionally, one Minety type ware vessel (MINETY; BPT 84), a pancheon comparable to examples from the production site (Musty 1973, 83–4; fig. 1, no. 1) is of certain late medieval date.

Continental material of later medieval date includes south-west French Saintonge mottled glazed jugs (SAIM; BPT 156); Saintonge polychrome jugs (SAIP; BPT 39); Algarve micaceous/Merida type micaceous ware costrels (SPAM; BPT 282; Hurst 1977) and a sherd from a flanged bowl in a highly micaceous fabric, possibly of Breton origin (NFRE; Period 4b, make-up deposit 2022).

Early 16th to early 17th centuries

In the late 15th or early 16th century, the Bristol medieval pottery industry fell into decline and the city was supplied with most of its pottery from the industry based at Hanley Castle, on the west bank of the River Severn between Upton on Severn and Worcester (Vince 1977). The site produced 22 sherds of Malvern Chase redware (HERB4; BPT 197), occurring in a wide range of forms (Table 4.1). Whilst some of these might be of later medieval date, the majority are likely to date to the first third of the 16th century and can be paralleled elsewhere (e.g. Acton Court; Vince and England 2004). The majority of sherds from the Malvern Chase industry are of the characteristically later, lighter, pink-coloured, earthenware fabric with a red slip and a plain lead glaze (HERB5), which is typical of the period c. 1530–1630. Jars are the main form found, followed by pipkins, pancheons and cisterns. A jar-like vessel with complex rim and applied lugs is illustrated (Fig. 4.1, no. 4).

Examples of three other West Country earthenwares were present: South (and East) Somerset ware (SSOM, BPT 96, 220, 268, 274 and 334); Ashton Keynes ware (AK) and a possible local Bristol product (BPT 265), distinguished by a red sandy fabric containing moderate rounded calcareous inclusions.

Black-glazed Cistercian type ware cups (CSTN; BPT 93, 266, 275) were present, possibly originating north of Bristol, at Falfield. The form of some of the vessels suggests influence from mid 16th-century Rhenish stoneware forms and it is likely that this ware is mainly of early to mid 16th-century date.

Non-local British wares were present in the form of 'Tudor Green' ware (TUDG; BPT 182) and Coarse Border ware (BORD), both from the Surrey/Hampshire border (Pearce 1992). Sherds of tin-glazed ware may be of local Brislington or London origin (TGW; BPT 99) and a tin-glazed albarello or jar (PMX; Period 4b, make-up deposit 2022) is of an unidentified fabric.

Imported wares occur as sherds of Raeren stoneware (RAER; BPT 287); South Netherlands tin-glazed ware (SNTG; BPT 344); Late Valencian lustreware (LVAL: BPT 83: Fig. 4.1, no. 3); Seville olive jars (OLIV; BPT 81) and North Italian marbled slipware, probably from Pisa (NIMS; BPT 82).

Later 17th to mid 18th centuries

A total of 63 sherds of later 17th to mid 18th-century wares were present at Redcliff Street, but these represent no more than 15 vessels, since 53 sherds come from five North Devon gravel-tempered vessels (NDGT; BPT 112). These include the complete profile of a pipkin (Period 4b or later, fill 2156 of pit 2155). North Devon gravel-free ware (NDFW; BPT 108) is also present and includes a single sgraffito dish sherd. The North Devon wares, produced at Bideford and Barnstaple from the late 16th century onwards, are uncommon in Bristol until the later 17th century.

Other pottery of this date consists of Staffordshire or Bristol slipwares: a press-moulded combed slip plate (STCO; BPT 100) and a mottled glazed vessel (STMO; BPT 211). Sherds of London stoneware (LONS) probably pre-date the inception of the local Bristol stoneware industry and are therefore likely to be

Table 4.2: Pottery quantification by period (ves. = minimum no of vessels; wt. = weight in grams)

Period	1a		2a		2b		3a		3b		4a		4b		5a	
Fabric	ves.	wt.	ves.	wt.	ves.	wt.	ves.	wt.	ves.	wt.	ves.	wt.	ves.	wt.	ves.	wt.
BRISC					1	8										
HGR	2	18	5	26	24	314	38	488	23	191	1	7	3	50	1	3
HG	1	9	3	30	12	312	18	319	38	559	12	176	14	251	3	31
BATHA			1	6	1	3	3	39	21	341			1	13		
BR					3	35	4	40	26	351	28	319	31	270	4	46
EMEDX					1	10	1	2								
GLAM											1	131				
MINETY			1	15			1	55	12	315	1	3	10	285		
NH									2	19						
SEW													1	8		
SAIM									1	2			4	16		
SAIP													2	16		
SAIU									2	72	1	35				
NFRE													1	6		
BORD															1	29
TUDG													2	5		
CSTN											3	19	2	11		
HERB4									2	16	15	190	4	29		
HERB5													36	952	3	268
BPT265	1	5											2	90		
AK?													1	4		
NDFW									1	4	2	42	1	45		
NDGT											1	1397	3	174	1	7
NIMS													1	4		
RAER													2	134		
LVAL?													1	65		
SNTG													1	12		
OLIV																
SPAM									1	17					1	15
SSOM											1	23	1	1		
STCO													1	8	1	7
STMO													1	7		
LONS															2	254
TGW													5	58		
PMX													1	2		
BRS									1	4			3	146	2	863
MISC									1	1						
TPW									1	1			1	2	3	15
LPMLOC													3	65	7	528
WSM													4	138	2	55

of this date, although London stoneware was produced throughout the 19th century.

Late 18th century and later
Thirty-seven sherds of later 18th and 19th-century date were present. The majority are from unglazed flower-pots (LPMLOC; BPT 201) followed by Bristol stoneware (BRS; BPT 277) and Weston-super-Mare-type coarse-ware (WSM). A stone-ware stamped flagon marked '[TA]YLOR/ [REDCLIFF]E STREET/ [BRIST]OL', almost certainly refers to Wine and Spirit Merchants George and R.C. Taylor, operating in Redcliff Street (Chapter 2.2). Five sherds of transfer-printed refined whiteware were also present (TPW; BPT 278).

Discussion of the pottery assemblage
Pottery from Period 2 indicates that the first activity on site relates to the later 12th to mid 13th century. Assemblages which pre-date the 13th-century are absent, however there is a handful of pottery of this date in later deposits. This might have been disturbed from early deposits on the site or perhaps it was imported to the site with make-up and building materials. Period 3a can be dated to the mid/late 13th century whilst Period 3b is a long-lived period of activity, extending from the later 13th to 14th century into the late medieval period.

Area 2 produced evidence for 16th and early 17th-century activity that was absent from Area 1. This includes a group of early 16th-century date from Period 4a deposits to the rear of buildings fronting onto Thomas Lane; a group of early 17th-century date is from Period 4b horizons associated with the construction of cellars. None of the assemblages are particularly large but in each case they are perhaps unlikely to have been redeposited and therefore provide a fixed point in the stratigraphic sequence.

There is abundant evidence of residuality throughout the stratigraphic sequence and therefore it is difficult to reconstruct complete contemporary assemblages even where the date of deposition can be determined. Additionally there is a small proportion of pottery throughout the sequence which is clearly intrusive.

The character of the pottery is typical of medieval and post-medieval sequences in Bristol and apart from rare non-local English imports the range of sources which supplied the site with the majority of its pottery is similar to that found throughout the city. Despite being located in a suburb of the city noted for its pottery industry, there is no evidence for pottery waste or even seconds in the collection. The composition of pottery groups from Periods 2 and 3 ostensibly shows little variation (Table 4.2). Imported and non-local pottery is absent from the earliest mid 13th-century deposits (one might have expected to find Rouen ware jugs and jars, Normandy gritty ware and the earliest types of south-west French Saintonge ware, all of which are absent). Most abundant throughout are Ham Green and Bath A type wares, the production for each of which did not extend beyond *c*. 1300. Bristol (Redcliffe) glazed wares, which are no earlier than the mid 13th century occur in small quantities in Period 2, only becoming significant in Period 3b. The Period 3b assemblage is modestly diverse compared with the earlier groups, including pottery from north Wiltshire (Minety, Nash Hill) and Malvern Chase and continental imports in the form of unglazed Saintonge vessels and Iberian micaceous ware.

The Period 4 assemblages include Rhenish stonewares; South Netherlands tin-glazed maiolica, North Italian marbled slipware and a probable piece of late Valencian lustreware. As a proportion of the total size of the assemblages (residual and contemporary), there appear to be more imports of 16th/17th-century date than of later medieval date. By comparison with contemporary sites in the surrounding countryside, the site contains a high proportion of imported pottery (although it cannot compare with the frequencies found at Acton Court) but in comparison to other assemblages from medieval ports in the south and west of England (e.g. Southampton), the quantities are modest.

The pottery was mainly used for the standard range of domestic activities: food preparation and cooking; serving at table; the drinking of alcoholic beverages, and by the 16th/17th centuries, display.

Catalogue of illustrated sherds (Fig. 4.1)
1. Chafing dish sherd. Fabric BR. Area 1, Period 3b layer 1074.
2. Jug with U-shaped and knife-slashed handle. Fabric BATHA. Area 2, Period 3b make-up deposit 2082.
3. Dish. Fabric LVAL? Area 2, Period 4b make-up layer 2038.
4. Jar-like vessel with complex rim and lug. Fabric HERB5. Area 2, Period 4b make-up deposit 2022.
5. Jug with anthropomorphic applied decoration. Fabric HG. Area 2, Period 2b 'dirty alluvium' 2105 (Fig. 3.5, section CC).

4.2 Ceramic Building Material
Alan Vince

Late 13th to 15th centuries
Forty-six fragments of ceramic building material of later 13th to 15th-century date were recovered from the site. Forty-one of these fragments are of Bristol medieval ware ridge tiles with applied knife-cut crests, copper-mottled glaze and applied diagonal clay strips. A single fragment of this type was recovered from a Period 3a deposit and six were found in Period 3b deposits. The remaining 33 fragments were found in 16th and early 17th-century deposits of Period 4a and 4b. These may be residual, or it may be that they were still in use on the ridges of the Redcliff Street buildings at this date.

Four fragments of Malvern Chase ridge tile, of the sandy, medieval fabric, were found in Period 4b and 5 deposits. These may indicate a reroofing or rebuilding

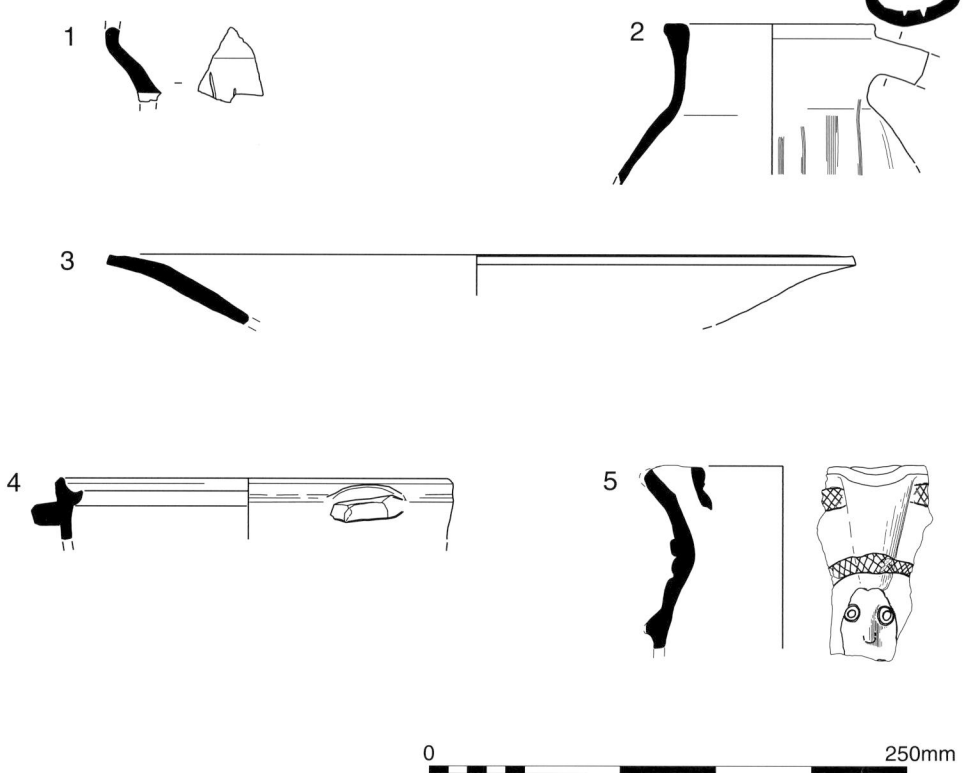

Fig. 4.1   Medieval pottery. Scale 1:4

in the early 16th century. A single fragment of unglazed hearth tile, also of sandy, medieval Malvern Chase fabric, was recovered from a Period 3b deposit. Such tiles were used as an alternative to pitched tile or roof slate to form the base for open hearths.

16th to early 17th centuries

Two fragments of floor tile can be dated to this period. The first is a Canynges-type tile, produced perhaps in the Worcester area in the early decades of the 16th century (Vince 1984). The tile has an overall white slip and is worn. It was recovered from a Period 5 deposit. The second is in BPT 265 fabric and has a burnt surface (perhaps therefore having been used as a fire surround). It was recovered from a Period 6 deposit but the similarity in fabric suggests that it has a similar date to the pottery vessels, i.e. 16th to early 17th century.

Late 18th century and later

Four fragments of pantile and two fragments of brick were recovered from Period 4b, 5 and 6 deposits. The pantiles include examples made from calcareous estuarine mud (similar to the Weston-super-Mare-type ware, WSM, and finer textured than the 19th-century Bridgwater products) and both the brick fragments were also made from fine-textured calcareous clays. In both cases it is likely that the material was brought to Bristol up the Avon.

4.3 Metalwork
E.R. McSloy

A total of 38 objects of metalwork and worked bone are listed fully in the site archive. The majority of recovered items were fragmentary and of uncertain function. Selected items of individual interest or which are dateable by form are described below. None of the finds described have been illustrated.

Copper alloy

Joining fragments from rectangular sheet. X-ray image shows five uneven hexagonal sheet-metal rivets. Almost certainly a patch-repair for a metal vessel. Similar patches with folded rivets are known from London from medieval contexts as early as the mid 12th century (Egan 1998, 176–7). Length: 51mm; width: 43mm (approx.). Period 2b, 'dirty alluvium' layer 2105 (Fig. 3.5, section CC).

Wire dress pin. The X-ray indicates the head is formed from a coil of wire, shaped to globular form (Crummy's Type 2). Wire pins, used for fastening clothing or for haberdashery, are used from the medieval period onwards, with later, post-medieval, examples generally shorter (Crummy 1988, 7). The form and length of this example are consistent with a medieval date. Length: 33mm. Period 3a, layer 1103 (Fig. 3.2, section BB).

Complete thimble from thin, machine-stamped sheet metal. Dutch type II (dateable c. 1650–1730) or the outwardly identical English type dateable *c.* 1690–1730 (Holmes 1999, 4). Height: 21.5mm; diameter at base: 15mm; weight: 4g. Period 5, layer 1063.

Possible needle, with spatulate head. There is no 'eye', suggesting breakage beyond this point or that the object is unfinished. Compares in form to needles from Exeter from medieval and 15th to 16th-century contexts (Allan 1984, 345). Length: 40mm. Residual in Period 6, context 1035 of robber cut 1034 (not shown).

Iron

Joining fragments, comprising the looped bow and portions of the blades of a pair of shears. The blades are narrow, straight backed, characteristics of Goodall's Type 3b/c, however the blade tips are absent, preventing full classification (Goodall 1980, 96–7). Type 3 shears were most common in the 13th and 14th centuries (ibid., 97). Surviving length: 127mm. Period 3b, layer 1090.

Fragment (the larger part of one arm is missing) of horseshoe. The surviving arm exhibits three rectangular and tapering nail holes. The inner profile is of the pointed arch type which can be characteristic of some Type 4 shoes as defined by Clark (1995, 88–91). Type 4 shoes are common from the late medieval period, between the late 13th and 15th centuries. Length: 119mm. Period 4b, residual in preparatory layers for Cellars 1 and 2.

4.4 Crucibles and Copper-Alloy Casting Waste
E.R. McSloy

Crucible sherds were recovered from three contexts: Period 2a mixed alluvial deposit 1119; Period 3a deposit 1128 (part of the dumps of imported clay) and Period 3b deposit 1058, providing evidence for casting of metals. All sherds are of a similar pale grey fabric with surfaces part-vitrified from use. The sherd from layer 1119 is identified by Alan Vince as from a Tertiary kaolinitic clay possibly deriving from southeast Wiltshire (Vince 1984). Only the sherd from layer 1058 exhibits (greenish) metal residues, indicating the use of copper alloys.

Period 6 fill 1035 of robber cut 1034 produced later evidence for copper-alloy working in the form of fired-clay mould fragments and a large quantity of scrap and misshapen lumps probably representing spills or other waste. Further copper-alloy casting waste in the form of solidified runs or spills was recovered as unstratified material. The scrap from deposit 1035 includes sheet metal off-cuts, vessel fragments and the probable needle described above. The mould fragments are of 'piece mould' type, comprising separate halves permitting reuse. A quantity of organic-tempered clay cladding, required to join the mould during casting, was also recovered.

4.5 Clay Tobacco Pipes
E.R. McSloy

A total of 30 fragments of clay pipe was recovered, including seven complete or partially complete bowls. Of the bowls, two examples are marked with the pipe maker's initials. All clay pipe fragments derive from contexts dating to Period 4 (21 fragments) and Period 5 (9 fragments).

Clay pipe bowl forms were compared to Oswald's simplified typology (Oswald 1975, 37–43). There is a single example of Oswald's type 4 form, dateable to the early to middle 17th century (Period 4a, from deposits dumped to raise the level in Area 1). The remainder comprise larger bowled forms (Oswald's types 11 and 12) dateable to after *c.* 1660. Two bowls (Period 4b fill 1109 of Culvert 2; Period 4b, layer 2031, part of the make-up deposits for Cellars 1 and 2 in Area 2, not shown) are stamped with the initials 'RT' to the heel, one of which also has a three-line mark 'R/TIPP/ET'. Both pipes are attributable to Robert Tippet, almost certainly the second of three pipe makers bearing this name, active in Bristol between 1678 and 1722 (Jackson and Price 1974, 73–4).

4.6 Stone Roof Tile
E.R. McSloy

A total of 25 fragments of stone roofing and other building material was recovered. Most fragments are of local Pennant sandstone. Three fragments retain circular peg holes, indicating the means of securing. The use of Pennant stone throughout the medieval period is widely recorded in Bristol (Price and Ponsford 1998, 24). The bulk of fragments in this instance derive from Period 3 (7 fragments) and Period 4 (11 fragments), with only one fragment from Period 2.

Fragments of roofing slate were recovered from Period 3 (1 fragment) and Period 4 (3 fragments). The slate probably derives from the Delabole quarries on the north Cornish coast (Reid *et al.* 1910). Use of slate from this area is recorded in Bristol from contexts as early as the 12th century (Good 1991, 35).

4.7 Glass
E.R. McSloy

Vessel glass amounting to 21 fragments was recovered from Period 4 and 5 contexts. The majority of fragments are dark green 'high lime, low alkali' (HLLA) glass typically used for wine or spirits bottles in the late 17th and 18th centuries. The remainder consists of cobalt ('Bristol') blue, natural blue-green or clear bottle or vessel glass which is almost certainly of 19th or 20th-century manufacture.

4.8 Perforated Fired-Clay Fragment
E.R. McSloy

A flat fragment of fired clay with three perforations, 20mm in diameter, was recovered from demolition deposit 1058 (Period 3b). The function of this item is unclear, however it may have served as the floor of an oven or similar structure.

4.9 Wooden Artefact
E.R. McSloy

A wooden artefact from Period 2a layer 1048, which comprised a board braced by a series of four squared lengths to the underside, was recovered (Fig. 3.3). The wood has been identified as beech (*Fagus sylvatica*) by R. Gale. This item appears to have functioned as a 'tread board', providing access over locally wet or marshy ground. Aspects of the structure's construction, particularly the chamfering of the longer edges of the upper board, indicate that it had been reused, possibly from a wood-lined pit or well.

Chapter 5
Environmental Evidence

5.1 Overview
Sylvia Warman

The earliest evidence for the character of the environment at 3 Redcliff Street comes from the borehole and monolith samples. The Period 1 mollusca comprise a mixture of aquatic and terrestrial taxa, providing a picture of intermittent flood events from a broad, slow flowing, probably base-rich river adjacent to open dry grassland and/or a floodplain. The lithostratigraphic assessment identified three main types of deposit: natural clean alluvium, bioturbated natural alluvium, and dumped deposits. Similar deposits have been identified from other sites in this part of Bristol. The plant remains from the Period 2 assemblage include aquatic and marshland plants, but also charcoal and charred seeds indicating anthropogenic activity. Evidence for cereal cultivation was limited, charred seeds were present but no chaff. Animal bones, although present in all periods, are most numerous in Periods 3 and 4. A range of species are present: dog, horse, cattle sheep/goat, pig, fallow deer, rabbit, wild boar, both domestic and wild birds, and fish. Much of the animal bone is likely to represent food waste, cattle and sheep/goat being important in the diet and pig less so. Evidence for bone/horn working is present in Period 3 but limited to two specimens.

5.2 Animal Bone
Lorrain Higbee

A small assemblage of animal bone was recovered from the site during the normal course of hand excavation and in addition a small number of fragments were retrieved from sample residues, with 264 fragments recovered in total. The entire assemblage was rapidly assessed. Methods used follow Davis (1992) and further details are available in the archive.

Results

The material from all periods is well-preserved, showing very little weathering. Gnaw marks were noted on *c.* 11% of all bones, mostly caused by dogs, but also with occasional rodent gnaw marks seen in Periods 3b and 4b.

Period 1
Animal bone was recovered from a single deposit and is likely to have been intrusive.

Period 2
Animal bone was recovered from 14 separate contexts, mostly from the fills of cut features and a small number of layers. The majority of the animal bone was hand collected but a small quantity was recovered from environmental bulk samples. Sheep/goat bones are relatively common and major meat-bearing bones are more frequent than waste elements. Many distal epiphyses are unfused suggesting the presence of juvenile individuals of less than 13–16 months. Cattle bones are fairly common and major meat-bearing bones are common especially those from the hind limb. Pig is represented by a single radius from an immature animal and two fragments of ulnae. An articulated hind limb from an adult horse was recovered from fill 2132 of ditch 2131, and an atlas vertebra from a small dog was identified from alluvial deposit 2151. Bones from domestic bird species (chicken, goose and duck) and a small number of fish bones were also recovered.

Period 3
Thirty-eight separate contexts, mostly layers and dump deposits, produced diagnostic animal bone. Sheep/goat bones are relatively common; major meat-bearing bones are more frequent than other elements. Three metapodials were differentiated from the general sheep/goat category and all belong to sheep. One of these bones, a metatarsal from dump deposit 2150, has a circular perforation through the proximal surface but no other signs of working. Cattle bones are represented by a wide range of skeletal elements. One cattle horncore from make-up deposit 2082 had been sawn through at

the base to detach it from the skull. Some cattle and sheep vertebrae had been chopped dorso-ventrally, a professional butchery practice that requires the animal to be hung from its hind limbs whilst the main trunk of the carcass is split into left and right sides. A small number of pig bones were identified and the majority are from the hind limb. Horse, dog, rabbit and fallow deer were also identified. Of the two bird species identified, chicken bones are more common than goose bones. Fish bones were present but not identified to species.

Period 4

Animal bone was recovered from ten separate contexts, mostly rubble dumps and a small number of cut features. Cattle bones are more common than the other livestock species and limb bones of high meat value are more common than other body parts. Two sheep/goat ankle bones were positively identified. Four pig bones were identified, all are from immature individuals, including one very large metatarsal which could be from a wild boar or very large domestic male. Chicken, duck, wood pigeon, and fish bones were also identified.

Period 5

Five separate contexts associated with the alterations in Area 2 produced animal bone. The only bones identified were sheep/goat limb bones.

Period 6

Context 2037 associated with the 20th-century garage produced sheep/goat limb and foot bones.

Conclusions

A relatively wide range of taxa have been identified from the assemblage, although in common with most animal bone assemblages of this date domestic livestock species predominate. Cattle and sheep/goat are clearly important in the diet and to a lesser degree pig. With a small assemblage little can be said about any chronological changes in the frequency of these three species. Other mammalian species include horse, dog, fallow deer (*Dama dama*) and rabbit. The bird species are mostly domesticates: chicken, goose and duck. A small quantity of fish bone was also recovered but has not been further identified. Similar small assemblages of animal bone have been recovered from a number of sites in the Redcliffe area of the city over the past few years (Insole 2001; Higbee 2004). The smaller assemblages from the area should be considered alongside the considerably larger assemblage reported above from 1–2 Redcliff Street to give a fuller understanding of animal husbandry, provisioning, dietary preferences and craft activities within this part of the city during the medieval and post-medieval periods.

5.3 Mollusca
N.P. Branch, C.P. Green, G.E. Swindle, A. Vaughan-Williams and J. Athersuch

A research aim of the project was to establish whether any sediment successions might provide potential for improving our understanding of changes in the local depositional environment during Periods 1 and 2 at the site. It was hoped that mollusca would inform upon water flow velocity, depth and temperature, as well as changes in the local vegetation cover (Ložek 1986).

Methodology

Sixteen sub-samples were taken from monolith sample 290503/1 and borehole 1 core sample (see Fig. 1.1 for location). Details of the methods used are available in the archive. The residues were examined under a low-power zoom stereo microscope. For each taxa an estimation was made of relative abundance and preservation.

Results

Mollusca were recovered from only five samples, between 6.08m and 6.59m AOD (Period 1); the overall concentration was low and preservation was 'moderate'. The taxa present include *Pupilla muscorum, Helicella itala, Vallonia costata, Clausilla bidentata* and *Trichia hispida*. These are all terrestrial mollusca, with the majority of these species being typical of open country. *Clausilla bidentata* is classified as shade loving and is common in a wide range of habitats, sheltered places, hedges, among rocks and on walls. *Valvata picinalis, Bithinia* spp and *Gyraulus albus* are all truly aquatic, and are common and widely distributed taxa. *Valvata picinalis* in particular is typical of large bodies of slow moving water (but not ponds or lakes) often with muddy or silty substrates.

Discussion

The assemblage indicates a mixture of aquatic and terrestrial taxa. The former were probably deposited during intermittent flood events (overbank channel deposits) from a broad, slow flowing, probably base-rich river. The terrestrial taxa indicate open (treeless) dry grassland and/or floodplain undoubtedly located in close proximity to the river. This interpretation is entirely consistent with the results of the geoarchaeological assessment (Chapter 5.5), and suggests a relatively stable floodplain surface during Period 1 with a well-developed soil profile and grassland (meadow and/or pasture). It is entirely likely, based upon the results of the geoarchaeological assessment, that similar conditions were present at 3 Redcliff Street during Period 2 (although no mollusca were recovered). These results provide a useful contribution to the growing archive of environmental archaeological information for the Bristol area.

5.4 Archaeobotanical Remains
N.P. Branch, C.P. Green, G.E. Swindle, A. Vaughan-Williams and J. Athersuch

The aim of analysing archaeobotanical samples was to establish whether any deposits could provide potential for improving our understanding of the former local environment, diet and economy. Contexts were selected for analysis based on visual inspection on site.

Methodology

The samples were processed by flotation using 1mm and 300μm mesh sizes. The residues were sorted 'by eye'. The flots were scanned using a low-power zoom stereo microscope. The analysis involved identification of the main taxa present in the samples, and an evaluation of their relative abundance and preservation.

Results

Period 2

Sample 11 from deposit 2105, a layer of bioturbated alluvium, contained moderate quantities of small charcoal (unidentifiable) and three wheat grains (*Triticum* sp.). Sample 13 from ditch 2148, fill 2149 provided abundant waterlogged seeds (main taxa: *Carex* sp., *Eleocharis palustris* and *Stellaria* sp.). These were well preserved, and accompanied by frequent waterlogged wood (*Quercus* sp., oak) and occasional charcoal fragments (*Quercus* sp., oak). The presence of charcoal and charred seeds marks the onset of 'intensive' anthropogenic activities on what has been interpreted as a relatively stable land surface (Chapter 5.5; Branch *et al.* 2004a; 2004b). Unfortunately, the poor preservation and low concentration of charcoal and charred seeds of wheat provides very little information on the local economy and diet, and there is no evidence to suggest that wheat was being grown locally.

Sample 13 was recovered from fill 2149 of ditch 2148, and provided abundant waterlogged seeds. The plant taxa represented by the seeds indicate a mainly damp or waterlogged environment e.g. sedges (*Carex* sp.), common spike rush (*Eleocharis palustris*) and stitchwort (*Stellaria* sp.). These plant taxa probably indicate conditions within the ditch, and are not necessarily representative of the surrounding vegetation cover.

Period 3

Sample 8 from 2112, a fill of Cistern B, provided only a single unidentifiable, poorly preserved charred grain. It also provided frequent charcoal (unidentifiable). Sample 7 from pit 2128 fill 2129 provided only occasional (<10) poorly preserved unidentifiable charred grain. Charcoal was also abundant (*Quercus* sp., oak). These remains may indicate discarded waste materials from a hearth, but unfortunately provide very little information on local economy and diet. Sample 10 from 2134, a dumped layer, contained moderate quantities of charcoal (unidentifiable), and charred seeds of wheat (*Triticum* sp.), wild grasses (Poaceae sp.) and plantain (*Plantago* sp.). These remains may be by-products of cereal crop processing which were burnt and then discarded. This interpretation must be viewed with caution, however, due to the absence of other diagnostic indicators of cereal processing, such as chaff, glumes and spikelet forks.

Period 5

Sample 6 from 2095, a fill of Cistern A, provided only occasional (<10) poorly preserved charred seeds of wheat (*Triticum* sp.) and wild grasses (Poaceae sp.). Sample 6 also provided abundant charcoal (*Quercus* sp., oak). This sample provides some evidence for the utilisation of wheat. The presence of wild grass seeds may simply represent their accidental inclusion within the cereal crop during harvesting. Together with the charcoal (oak), these remains probably represent domestic waste that was discarded into the cess pit.

Summary

Preservation was by charring in all but one sample, which provided abundant and well-preserved waterlogged seeds, frequent waterlogged wood and occasional charcoal fragments. The waterlogged seeds suggest a mainly damp or wetland environment. Samples taken from alluvium horizons contain moderate quantities of charred wood and seeds/grains. Preservation was average to good; however, there was some contamination by modern seeds, in samples 10 and 11. Other samples provided frequent or abundant charcoal but only occasional, poorly preserved seeds.

5.5 Lithostratigraphy
N.P. Branch, C.P. Green, G.E. Swindle, A. Vaughan-Williams and J. Athersuch

The aim of the lithostratigraphic analysis was to establish whether the excavations revealed any sediment successions that provide potential for improving our understanding of changes in the local depositional environment. Samples were obtained from two monolith samples (290503/1 and 290503/2) and a borehole core sample (BH 1) in Area 1; and one monolith sample (090703/1) and a borehole core sample (BH 2) in Area 2 (Fig. 1.1).

Methodology

Sub-samples were extracted from the monolith and borehole samples to determine the organic matter content following standard procedures (Bengtsson and Enell 1986); further details can be found in the archive. Particle size analysis was carried out on monolith sample 290503/1 and borehole 1 core sample, and monolith sample 290503/2.

Results

The base of the recorded sequence in borehole 1 and monolith sample 290503/1 (contexts 1105 and 1045; Period 1) is composed of slightly sandy clayey silt (silt: 85.83 to 82.36%) with a low organic matter content (<5.6%), and is interpreted as natural 'clean' alluvium. It is characterised by an absence of anthropogenic material, the presence of well-developed root channel networks and evidence for clay translocation typical of pedogenic processes within a soil profile. These contexts are overlain (gradual or 'diffuse' transition) by a compacted clayey silt (silt: 82.99%) with a higher organic matter content (7.5%), and 'contaminated' throughout by anthropogenic material (context 1051, Period 2b: a trampled deposit associated with the construction of Wall A). This deposit is interpreted as natural alluvium which has been bioturbated by human activities. The two upper contexts in monolith sample 290503/1 (1044 and 1043) are Period 3b deposits associated with the construction of Cellars in Area 2, and will not be discussed in detail.

The base of the sequence in monolith sample 290503/2 (context 1147; Period 1; Fig. 3.2, section BB) is composed of slightly sandy clayey silt (silt: 80.27%) with a low organic matter content (6%), and is interpreted as natural 'clean' alluvium. It is characterised by an absence of anthropogenic material, the presence of well-developed root channel networks and evidence for clay translocation typical of pedogenic processes within a soil profile. This layer is overlain (very gradual or 'diffuse' transition) by a clayey silt (silt: c. 83%) with a slightly higher organic matter content (7.2%), but which cannot be differentiated from the layer below on the basis of colour. It is 'contaminated' by anthropogenic material and is interpreted as natural alluvium which has been bioturbated by human activities (e.g. presence of charcoal particles) and weak pedogenic processes (e.g. presence of root channels). This context is overlain by clayey silt with low organic matter content (silt: c. 70–83%; organic matter: <6.7%) and composed of anthropogenic materials (e.g. mortar; context 1146; Period 3a). This deposit undoubtedly indicates introduced or redistributed material associated with ground preparation (dumping associated with human activities). This interpretation is confirmed by the sharp transition from layer 1147 to deposit 1146. Overlying deposit 1146, there is evidence for soil-forming processes in contexts comprising fine sand and clayey silt with very low organic matter content (deposits 1128, 1127 and 1126; Period 3a). Although anthropogenic material is lacking in these contexts they seem likely to be artificially redistributed sediment (dump/make-up) as they overlie, with a sharp contact, layer 1146. Deposit 1125 (Period 3a) rests upon this layer and is composed of a thin layer of clayey silt in which there are weakly developed indications of soil-forming processes. The uppermost context in monolith sample 290503/2 (deposit 1098, Fig. 3.2, section BB; Period 4a) is bright red clayey sand and is probably further dumped material/make-up.

The base of the recorded sequence in borehole 2 and monolith sample 090703/1 (context 2145; Period 1) is composed of clayey silt with a low organic matter content (<6.2%), and is interpreted as natural 'clean' alluvium. It is characterised by an absence of anthropogenic material, the presence of well-developed root channel networks and evidence for clay translocation typical of pedogenic processes within a soil profile. Above this (context 2105; Period 2b; Fig. 3.5, section CC) and undifferentiated by colour, the alluvium is 'contaminated' by anthropogenic material and is interpreted as natural alluvium which has been bioturbated by human activities and weak pedogenic processes. The upper part of monolith sample 090703/1, is a mixture of building debris and clayey silt (context 2134 Period 3a and context 2062 Period 4a).

Discussion

Three main types of deposit have been recorded and can be summarised, from the base upwards, as: (1) natural 'clean' alluvium; (2) bioturbated natural alluvium; and (3) dumped deposits. The natural alluvium was undoubtedly deposited on the margins of a river channel during intermittent flood events, with the fine-grained sediments deposited in a virtually stationary ('low-energy') water body. The mineral deposits have occasional fragments of organic detritus, which may represent either long-distance transportation of organic matter or *in situ* deposition of detritus from plants growing on the floodplain surface. The presence of well-developed root channel networks, evidence for clay translocation typical of pedogenic processes within a soil profile and earthworm activity indicates that the floodplain surface was relatively stable (e.g. an alluvial flood meadow/pasture). Similar deposits have been recorded in geoarchaeological investigations at 26–28 St Thomas Street (Branch *et al.* 2004c), indicating that the height of the upper surface of the natural alluvium is between 6.5–7.1m AOD in this part of Bristol. Further discussion is provided in Chapter 5.5 of the 1–2 Redcliff Street report).

The heavily bioturbated upper surface of the natural alluvium marks the onset of intensive anthropogenic activity. The presence of root channel networks and evidence for clay translocation suggests that pedological processes, similar to those described above, were clearly active prior to human disturbance. However, compaction, partial obliteration of the root channel network and the introduction of anthropogenic materials to the surface layer are all typical of natural ground surfaces affected by human occupation.

Chapter 6
Discussion

6.1 Early Landscape Reclamation and Settlement

The evidence from the site suggests that occupation in the second quarter of the 12th century (Period 2) followed on very closely from the legal establishment of the suburb (for discussion of the early establishment of the Redcliffe suburb see Chapter 1.2 of the 1–2 Redcliff Street report). This period is one of preparation of the muddy alluvial banks of the Avon, the digging of pits and gullies, the latter possibly marking new plot boundaries or for drainage, and the construction of at least two substantial masonry structures (represented by Walls A and G). Period 2a features provide an overall date of the later 12th century for this activity. Period 2b pottery was similar except for a small number of sherds which date after the mid 13th century, suggesting that Period 2, despite the lack of evidence for intensive activity, lasted for about a century. It may be that initial activity was concentrated on the western side of the street, by the foreshore. Scarcity of pottery supply might be indicated in this early period as riveted pot-repair plates were found in Period 2b, but the limited area investigated in Period 2 deposits and the correspondingly small pottery assemblage prevent meaningful comparison with the later periods.

A detailed picture of activity at the site in this period is lost to us, but the fills of the pits and ditches suggest domestic occupation. The short lengths of gully on, or near, later tenement boundaries strongly suggest that the tenement boundaries laid out at this early date were those that endured until the late 19th century, a conservatism also seen on other sites in Redcliffe, including 1–2 Redcliff Street. Only very limited exploration of the lowest levels was possible, but these are clearly of high potential, with waterlogged conditions and good survival of organic material.

6.2 Expansion of the Medieval City and the Early Industrialisation of the Redcliffe Suburb

Period 3 marks the onset of a recognisable organised pattern of occupation at the site. Associated pottery dating includes Ham Green ware sherds thought to be later 12th century in date, but these are associated with 13th-century types from Wiltshire. The earlier pottery in Period 3a is residual and is most likely to have been brought to the site with the material that was dumped to raise the general ground surface. The most acceptable date for this dumping is therefore the later 13th century. This activity is followed by the laying out of masonry buildings whose property boundaries are those identified in historical records. The eastern end of Wall B formed part of the south wall of the Sheermans' Hall plot, and Wall E/F performed the same function for the Thomas Lane property to its east. Excavation work in Area 1 encountered the rear of properties at Nos 21 and 22 Redcliff Street. Area 2 included a small part of the Thomas Lane property but fell mostly in the rear of what was probably originally Nos 22 and 23 Redcliff Street, but had become part of No. 24 by the later 17th century.

The recognisable medieval activity in Period 3b seems to be dated somewhere within the 14th to 15th centuries. The earlier part of the period is the most likely for expansion, as the general optimism and dynamism of the time was indicated by the investment in the mid 13th century in rerouting the Frome, building the Port Wall and providing new quay facilities at Broad Quay. The later 14th and 15th centuries by contrast were a period of economic decline, reversed by aggressive exploitation of Atlantic possibilities in the 16th century.

The pottery supply is similar to that seen elsewhere in Bristol, being predominantly local and regional wares with rare imports, mostly indicative of Bristol's trading contacts in Wales and the South West; the more exotic Saintonge and Spanish wares reflect the wine trade and were not uncommon in important English ports. Not only did pottery become more common in Period 3b, it came in more varied forms, suggesting increasing sophistication and wealth. This probably coincides with the peak of the cloth trade in the Redcliffe suburb.

The two dye-vat bases in Area 1 show that groups of these dyeing vats were built in the rear of the tenements, to the east of Wall D. The external face of a loam-bedded wall normally needs to be rendered if it is not mortar-pointed, but the east face of Wall D had neither, suggesting an enclosed, rather than an open yard. Although there is only a small amount of evidence for roofing materials, it should be noted that, even if the ovens were in an open yard, the surrounding walls were also the external walls of the neighbouring buildings and the scarcity of tiles may simply show that other materials such as thatch or shingles were in use, both here and in the neighbouring buildings at this period. Another possibility, inferred from the presence of medieval tiles in post-medieval deposits, is that the roofs were removed at a much later date, presumably when the houses were demolished. The glazed ridge tiles found, mostly in later contexts, some with cut coxcomb finishing, provided high quality and relatively expensive roof finishes (Chapter 4.2).

Almost complete examples of identical hearth bases were found at the 1–2 Redcliff Street site, where environmental material includes plant remains associated with a number of dyestuffs. A similar but even more fragmentary hearth floor was also thought to be a dye-vat base in the property on Thomas Lane, to the east of Sheermans' Hall.

As early as the 13th century, guild regulation was causing the loss of cloth workers to the (unregulated) hinterland (Bettey 1986, 63, 115). No recognisable structures or finds relating to cloth manufacture were found on site certainly later than the 14th century. Nevertheless, the cloth *trade*, finishing and exporting the product of the surrounding areas, along with the importation of wine, appears to have filled the gap in Bristol (ibid., 142) and dyers in particular congregated in Redcliffe, possibly processing cloth passing through the town. Bristol did considerably better than Southampton for example, in dealing with changes in trade and manufacturing patterns in the late Middle Ages (Carus-Wilson and Coleman 1963).

The dyeing of cloth is well attested archaeologically and historically in Redcliffe and it is no surprise that the remains of dye-vat bases should have been uncovered on site. It would be usual in the medieval and post-medieval period for this industrial activity to have taken place in a workshop that was also part of a residential and domestic setting. The quality of the building construction, the rubbish pits and stone-built cess pits are indicative of a reasonable to good standard of living for the occupants. The lack of high-status goods, however, may show the middling level of the occupation itself, but is as likely to reflect the relatively few rubbish pits or other repositories for rubbish within the excavated area. Redcliff Street was a centre of the cloth trade in general and was occupied by affluent cloth merchants as well as cloth workers from at least the 15th century and well into the 17th (see Chapter 1.2 of the 1–2 Redcliff Street report). The tenement called (by 1685) Sheermans' Hall and the finding of a medieval example of a pair of shears in a layer from Period 3b in Area 1, typically used to trim the nap on worsted cloths, shows that that skill had a long history on the site (Chapter 4.3). However, the occupations attested are those of cloth finishing, and trading, not manufacture.

There was some evidence of other medieval crafts from the excavations at 3 Redcliff Street. Casting in copper alloy is attested by crucible sherds, mould fragments and small quantities of solidified spills and runnels of the metal. The copper-alloy casting furnaces at 1–2 Redcliff Street provide a possible source for the material recovered from Periods 3 and 5, although the crucible fragment from Period 2a pre-dates the earliest furnace there, which was established in the mid 14th to early 15th century. Metalworking was a widespread occupation in the Redcliffe suburb between the early 15th and 17th centuries (1–2 Redcliff Street report Chapter 6), and the material is not necessarily all derived from one location. A needle from a Period 5 context, unfinished but of medieval type, might suggest specialised production for the cloth trade, but is hardly evidence of specialisation by itself.

Animal bone was recovered from many medieval contexts and was predominantly meat-bearing bone from domestic animals, elements from domestic fowl tending to confirm the picture of consumption debris that might be expected in an affluent urban site. An articulated horse leg and a sawn-through horncore hint at processing activities although evidence for this was not abundant. The practice of dorso-ventral section butchery in some bones from the late medieval contexts suggest the early adoption of this practice.

6.3 Industrial Activity in the Post-Medieval Period

The pattern of development in the post-medieval period is mixed (Period 4). The frontages were increasingly residential but occupied by tradespeople or their widows. Whether this increase in small tradespeople, such as ironmongers, silk weavers, mercers or writing masters, is genuine or a result of better documentation is unknown, but there were clearly changes in the larger-scale trades practised in the area. The cloth trade seemed to die out and the new industries of sugar refining and distilling take over. Soap manufacture, dependent on imported whale oil, is also a significant industry in Redcliffe (1–2 Redcliff Street report, Chapter 2.1). Apparent rebuilding of the properties in the excavated area may reflect these changes.

The local medieval Bristol pottery industry declined and, by the 16th century, pottery came predominantly from Malvern Chase, transported down the Severn. Although the quantities of pottery are small from this period, the trend of more complex forms and variety continued, although none of the pottery indicated high-status living (Chapter 4.1). Later in the century and into the earlier 17th century, pottery came from further afield in the south of England and from the Continent. As supply centres rose and fell, so did the supply to Bristol in this period. The presence of North Devon ware reflected coastal trade, and pottery from the proto-industrial centres in Staffordshire and London makes its appearance. In the later 18th century and after, the pottery is mostly flowerpots and varieties of stoneware, and transfer-printed whiteware, reflecting the increased industrialisation of supply.

Modifications, including new yard surfaces and alterations to the party wall of Nos 21/22 Redcliff Street (Wall B) were carried out in the yard area in the 16th to 18th centuries (Periods 4a and 4b). The first phase provided little evidence of actual building, and Period 4a may have been one of little activity. The alterations to Wall B strongly suggest that the buildings were eventually rebuilt on the old footings. No. 21 Redcliff Street was 'new-built' in 1685 and these alterations could well be reflecting that. Culverts and cess pits (Area 1, Culvert 2 and Cistern D, in the rear of No. 22) probably indicate drainage and sewerage works of the 18th century.

The yard at the rear seems to have continued in existence, as it was still mapped as a yard or garden on the Ashmead map of 1855 (Fig. 3.19), a conclusion supported by the cobbled surfaces in this area. On the other hand, the lease plan of c. 1818 (BRO P/StT/Ch/3/31 fol. 20; Fig. 3.18), while it does not show Nos 21 and 22 in detail, suggests that the 1855 map was simplified to the point of distortion, although the differences may be partly explained by demolitions or other alterations between c. 1818 and 1855. What is clear from the cartographic research and property documentation, is that Area 2 was part of No. 24 Redcliff Street property from at least the mid 17th century and not of No. 22. This property angled around the east of Nos 22 to 23 Redcliff Street, abutting the south side of the narrow Thomas Lane plots. No. 22 was further separated from the rear of No. 24 by the similar angling around of No. 23 Redcliff Street to include the plot immediately east of No. 21 on Thomas Lane, which by the 17th century was called Sheermans' Hall (Chapter 2.2). However, the alignment of substantial internal masonry walls on the c. 1818 plan, some also found during excavation, strongly suggests that this arrangement was a modification of an original layout of narrow, parallel tenement plots running back from Redcliff Street to the Law Ditch. The first three plots south of Thomas Lane were approximately 18′ 4″ (5.58m) wide and the next two, 24′ (7.32m). It is not known how much earlier than the mid 17th century the plots were reallocated, but the different stratigraphic histories in Period 4 suggest that it may have occurred by the early 16th century. It seems probable, although it cannot be proved, that the Thomas Lane plots were at some date formed out of a long tenement that originally stretched back alongside Thomas Lane but fronted onto Redcliff Street.

Sheermans' Hall had, by this stage, two separately-let cellars, stables, a garden and an outhouse, all of which, apart from the cellars, are identifiable on the c. 1818 lease plan. Little was recognisable in the excavations apart from the south wall, represented by the eastern end of Period 3b/4 Wall B in Area 1.

Nos 23 to 25 were held by a grocer and a distiller in 1735. It seems likely that No. 23 would have been the one occupied by the grocer as by the time of the 1818 survey it was clearly fitted with a shop front. No direct evidence of sugar refining and distilling was found at the site, but No. 24 Redcliff Street, being the larger of the two properties, was the more suitable premises for distilling. It is certainly at around this time that the cellars in Area 2 were given their curvilinear recesses and good quality Pennant sandstone floors, and these cellars could have accommodated some part of the fermentation or distilling process. There was a great deal of space available at the rear of No. 24 for manufacturing and storage. In the early 19th century it seems that the premises were still in the hands of distillers, and No. 23 was occupied from at least 1819 to 1837 by George Taylor, Liquor Dealer (Chapter 2.2). A complete stoneware bottle stamped 'H Taylor 23 Redcliff St Bristol' found in the Broadmead excavations refers to Henry in residence at No. 23 in 1850 (Jarrett 2013, 180). A sherd from the present site was stamped with the name 'Taylor' and 'Redcliff Street', and Vince had noted a sales ledger showing that Taylor had moved from here by 1867 (Vince, pers. comm.).

The small amount of animal bone from this period indicated that beef consumption was increasing at the expense of sheep and goat, and again meat-bearing bones indicate consumption rather than processing. This presumably shows that the tenements were just as much residential as the bases for industrial and commercial operations.

6.4 Late Post-Medieval and Modern Redevelopment

By the early 19th century much of Redcliff Street had been rebuilt and most buildings were probably of 17th and 18th-century date, though significant and important late medieval buildings clearly still survived (Period 5). The distillers and sugar refiners were still the dominant industries in the area. In the later 19th century the narrow streets were a hindrance to traffic struggling to reach Bristol Bridge and the quays, and schemes were designed to widen many of the streets in Redcliffe. In 1878 and 1880 properties on the east side of Redcliff Street and the south side of Thomas Lane were bought up by the Corporation for this purpose. The buildings on the site of Nos 21–25 Redcliff Street and Thomas Lane were clear-felled and the replacement structures were built on completely new footprints unrelated to the older tenement boundaries. South of the excavation area, the historic plots were replaced by large warehouses and workshop buildings amalgamating several older tenements, a process that took place throughout the 20th century, but predominantly before the Second World War (Period 6). The recent redevelopment replaced the late 19th-century buildings but largely on the plots established by their construction.

References

Abbreviations

BRO Bristol Record Office
BRSMG Bristol City Museum and Art Gallery
TNA The National Archives

Printed Maps

Millerd 1673
John Rocque 1742
Ashmead and Plumley 1828 (extract reproduced as Fig. 2.3)
Ashmead 1855 (extract reproduced as Fig. 3.19)
Ordnance Survey 1884, 1:500, and later Ordnance Survey maps
Goad Insurance Map 12, January 1887 and later revisions (extract reproduced as Fig. 2.4)
Hoefnagle map 1581 (extract reproduced as Fig. 2.2)

Manuscript Sources

Within the Bristol Record Office the topographical card index provided references for plans and deeds immediately to the north and south of the site. The property on the north side of Thomas Lane, No. 20 Redcliff Street, was identified (BRO 00508(8)g) as forming part of the lands of Lord Lisle acquired by the Corporation in 1544, before that part of the Cheddar family lands. To the south of the site No. 28 Redcliff Street is documented from 1672 onwards (BRO 5918(4)).

Within the Bristol Record Office the various antiquarian collections of deeds were searched, but contained few records for the site. The custumals, enrolled deeds, plan books, leases, rentals, surveys and other records relating to the landholdings of the City Corporation contained records relating to the lands of Lord Lisle at No. 20.

The records of all the church, charitable and institutional property owners listed by Manchee (1831) were searched. Folio 20 of the St Thomas Plan Book (BRO P/StT/Ch/3/31) is of the site, of Nos 23–25 Redcliff Street, extending back behind Nos 21–22 to Thomas Lane. This property came to the two parishes through the will of Mary Smith, 12th March 1735. Records relating to the site were not otherwise identified either in the parish records of St Mary Redcliffe or St Thomas.

The collections of deeds acquired by the City as the result of various highway improvement schemes provided several references to the deeds for properties within the site (all within the BRO).

Searching the 'Planning Deeds' for properties acquired in the post-War clearance of heavily bomb-damaged areas provided no references to the site or its immediate environs.

The Hearth Tax contained within F/Tax/A/1 (the Chimney Book) provided the first house by house listing of inhabitants, and hearths, for 1662, 1664, 1668 and 1672. The entries for the parish of St Thomas were used with limited success to identify the properties Nos 11–20 Redcliff Street, and those in Thomas Lane. The survey of 1837 was especially useful for confirming the occupation of Nos 23–25 Redcliff Street, as noted by Manchee in 1831.

Works cited in the text

Ainsworth, A. and Redvers-Higgins, N. (eds) 2005 *Main Scheme and Quakers Friars: Broadmead Expansion, Bristol* Unpublished Oxford Archaeology report

Albarella, U. 2003 'Tawyers, tanners, horn trade and the mystery of the missing goat', in Murphy and Wiltshire (eds) 2003, 71–86

Albarella, U. 2005 'Alternate fortunes? The role of domestic ducks and geese from Roman to medieval times in Britain', in Grupe and Peters (eds) 2005, 249–58

Alcock, N.W., Warwick University, Howard, R.E., Laxton, R.R., Litton, C.D., Nottingham University Tree-ring Dating Laboratory and Miles, D.H. 1991a *Leverhulme Cruck Project* Unpublished site chronology COSBSQ05 for Coates' Barn, Cosby, Leics

Alcock, N.W., Warwick University, Howard, R.E., Laxton, R.R., Litton, C.D., Nottingham University Tree-ring Dating Laboratory and Miles, D.H. 1991b 'List 41 no 1 –Leverhulme Cruck Project Results: 1990', *Vernacular Architect.* **22**, 45–7

Allan, J.P. 1983 'The importation of pottery to southern England, *c.* 1200–1500', in Davey and Hodges (eds) 1983, 193–207

Allan, J.P. 1984 *Medieval and Post-Medieval Finds from Exeter 1971–1980* Exeter Archaeological Report **3**. Exeter, Exeter City Council/University of Exeter

Allen, J.R.L. and Rae, J.E. 1987 'Late Flandrian shoreline oscillations in the Severn Estuary: A geomorphological and stratigraphical reconnaissance', *Philosophical Transactions of the Royal Society of London* **B315**, 185–230

Anderberg, A-L. 1994 *Atlas of Seeds: Part 4* Uddevalla, Swedish Museum of Natural History

ARCA 2007 *1–2 Redcliff Street, Bristol: Borehole Survey. Assessment Report* ARCA typescript report **070816**

Armitage, P. 2013 'Fish bone', in Ridgeway and Watts (eds) 2013, 283–8

Arnold, A.J. and Howard, R.E. 2007 *St John's Hospital and Chantry, Cirencester, Gloucestershire: Tree-ring Analysis of Timbers* Engl. Heritage Res. Dep. Report **14/2007**

Arnold, A.J., Howard, R.E., Laxton, R.R. and Litton, C.D. 2003 *Tree-ring analysis of timbers from Exeter Cathedral, Exeter, Devon: Part 3 (western roof, bays 1–4)* Engl. Heritage Centre for Archaeol. Rep. **49/2003**

Arnold, A.J., Howard, R.E. and Litton, C.D. 2005 *Tree-ring analysis of timbers from 7–9 Stourport Road, Bewdley, Worcs* Engl. Heritage Centre for Archaeol. Rep. **45/2005**

Atkinson, E. and Atkinson, M.D. 2002 '*Sambucus nigra* L.', *J. Ecol.* **90(5)**, 895–923

Baas, P., Gasson, P.E. and Wheeler, E.A. 1989 'IAWA list of microscopic features for hardwood identification', *International Association of Wood Anatomists Bulletin* **10**, 219–332

Baillie, M.G.L. and Pilcher, J.R. 1982 *A master tree-ring chronology for England* Unpublished computer file MGB-EOI, Belfast, Queens University

Balaam, N., Levitan, B. and Straker, V. 1987 *Studies in palaeoeconomy and environment in south-west England* Brit. Archaeol. Rep. Brit. Ser. **187**. Oxford

BaRAS (Bristol and Region Archaeological Service) 2002a *Archaeological Evaluation at 25 Redcliff Street/14 St Thomas Street, Redcliffe, Bristol* BaRAS typescript report **081/2002**

BaRAS (Bristol and Region Archaeological Service) 2000b *Archaeological Evaluation at Timber Yard to rear of No. 18 St Thomas Street, Bristol* BaRAS typescript report **1064/2002**

Barber, B. and Thomas, C. (eds) 2002 *The London Charterhouse* Museum of London Archaeology Service Monograph **10**. London, Museum of London Archaeology Service

Barnwell, P.S. and Airs, M. (eds) 2006 *Houses and the Hearth Tax: The later Stuart house and society* Counc. Brit. Archaeol. Res. Rep. **150**. York, Council for British Archaeology

Barton, K.J. 1963 'The medieval pottery Kiln at Ham Green, Bristol', *Trans. Bristol Gloucestershire Archaeol. Soc.* **82**, 95–126

Bates, M.R. 2003 *A brief review of deposits containing Palaeolithic artefacts in the Shirehampton area of Bristol and their regional context* Unpublished report for Terra Nova, Brecon

Bayley, J. 1989 *Preliminary Analysis of Copper Alloy Waste from the Deansway Project, Worcester* Anc. Mon. Lab. Rep. **32/1989**. London, English Heritage

Bayley, J. 1992 'Metalworking ceramics', *Medieval Ceram.* **16**, 3–10

Bayley, J. 1996 'Innovations in later medieval urban metalworking', *Hist. Metall.* **30**, 67–71

Bayley, J. and Rehren, T. 2007 'Towards a functional and typological classification of crucibles', in La Niece *et al.* (eds) 2007, 46–55

Bayley, J., Dungworth, D. and Paynter, S. 2001 *Archaeometallurgy Guidelines* Swindon, English Heritage

Bayley, J., Crossley, D. and Ponting, M. (eds) 2008 *Metals and Metalworking. A research framework for archaeometallurgy* London, Historical Metallurgy Society

Behre, K-E. 2008 'Collected seeds and fruits from herbs as prehistoric food', *Vegetation History and Archaeobotany* **17**, 65–73

Behrensmeyer, A.K. 1978 'Taphonomic and ecologic information from bone weathering', *Paleobiology* **4(2)**, 150–62

Bekker, R.M., Cappers, R.T.J. and Gronigen, J.E.A. 2006 *Digital seed atlas of the Netherlands* Archaeological Studies **4**. Eelde, Barkhuis Publishing

Belshaw, R. 1989 'A note on the recovery of *Thoracochaeta zosterae* (Haliday) (Diptera: Sphaeroceridae) from archaeological deposits', *Circaea* **6**, 39–41

Bengtsson, L. and Enell, M. 1986 'Chemical analysis', in Berglund (ed.) 1986, 423–54

Berggren, G. 1981 *Atlas of Seeds: Part 3* Arlöv, Swedish Museum of Natural HistoryBerglund, B.E. (ed.) 1986 *Handbook of Holocene Palaeoecology and Palaeohydrology* Sussex, Wiley

Bernick, C. (ed.) 1998 *Hidden Dimensions* University of British Columbia Press, 130–8

Bettey, J.H. 1986 *Wessex from AD 1000* London, Longman

Bettey, J. (ed.) 2001 *Historic Churches and Church Life in Bristol: Essays in Memory of Elizabeth Ralph, 1911–2000* Bristol, Bristol and Gloucestershire Archaeological Society

Bickley, F.B. 1899 *A Calendar of Deeds (chiefly relating to Bristol), collected by George Weare Braikenridge, F.S.A.* Edinburgh, Constable

Bickley, F.B. (ed.) 1900 *The Little Red Book of Bristol, volumes 1 and 2* Bristol and London, Hemmons and Sotheran and Co.

Blades, N. 2004 'Chemical analysis of the copper alloys', in Dalwood and Edwards 2004, 378–81

Blair, J. and Ramsay, N. (eds) 1991 *English Medieval Industries* London, Hambledon

Blaylock, S.R. 1996 'Bell and cauldron founding in Exeter', *Hist. Metall.* **30**, 72–82

Blaylock, S.R. 2000 'Excavation of an early post-medieval bronze foundry at Cowick Street, Exeter, 1999–2000', *Proc. Devon Archaeol. Soc.* **58**, 1–92

Boessneck, J. 1969 'Osteological differences between sheep (Ovis aries Linné) and Goat (Capra hircus Linné)', in Brothwell and Higgs (eds) 1969, 331–58

Bowen, D.Q. (ed.) 1999 *A revised correlation of Quaternary deposits in the British Isles* Geological Society Special Report **23**

Bowsher, D., Dyson, T., Holder, N. and Howell, I. 2007 *The London Guildhall: An archaeological history of a neighbourhood from early medieval to modern times* Museum of London Archaeology Service Monograph **36**

Branch, N.P., Green, C.P., Swindle, G.E., Vaughan-Williams, A. and Athersuch, J. 2004a 'Appendix 9: Geoarchaeology' in CA 2004, 47–52

Branch, N. P., Green, C. P., Swindle, G. E., Vaughan-Williams, A. and Athersuch, J. 2004b 'Appendix 10: Archaeobotany' in CA 2004, 53–5

Branch, N.P., Canti, M.G., Green, C.P., Kemp, R.A., Swindle, G.E., Vaughan-Williams, A. and Warman, S. 2004c *26–28 St Thomas Street, Bristol: Environmental Archaeological Investigations* Unpublished report, ArchaeoScape

Bridge, M. 1988 'The dendrochronological dating of buildings in Southern England', *Medieval Archaeol.* **32**, 166–74

Bridge, M.C. 1999 *Tree-ring analysis of timbers from the Isaac Lord Complex, Ipswich, Suffolk* Anc. Mon. Lab. Rep. **49/1999**

Bridge, M.C. 2000 *Tree-ring analysis of timbers from St Andrew's Church, Ford, West Sussex* Anc. Mon. Lab. Rep. **27/2000**

Bronk Ramsey, C. 2008 *OxCal 4* https://c14.arch.ox.ac.uk/oxcal.html (accessed 24 July 2008)

Brothwell, D.R. and Higgs E.S. (eds) 1969 *Science in Archaeology* London, Thames and Hudson

Brothwell, D.R., Dobney, K. and Ervynck, A. 1996 'On the causes of perforations in archaeological domestic cattle skulls', *Int. J. Osteoarchaeology* **6**, 471–87

Brown, D.H. 2002 *Pottery in Medieval Southampton c. 1066–1510* York, Counc. Brit. Archaeol. Res. Rep. **133**; Southampton Archaeology Monograph **8**

Brownsword, R. 1985 *English Latten Domestic Candlesticks 1400–1700* Finds Research Group Datasheet **1**

Brunning, R. 1996 *Waterlogged Wood Guidelines* London, English Heritage

Bryant, V. 2004 'Medieval and early post-medieval pottery', in Dalwood and Edwards 2004, 281–339

Buckland, P.C. and Perry, D.W. 1989 'Ectoparasites of sheep from Storaborg, Iceland and their interpretation: piss, parasites and people, a palaeoecological perspective', *Hikuin* **15**, 37–46

Burchill, R. 2006 'The ceramic roof tiles', in Jackson 2006a, 132–3

Burchill, R., Coxah, M., Nicholson, A. and Ponsford, M. 1987 'Excavations at Bristol 1985–6', *Bristol and Avon Archaeol.* **6**, 11–30

Butler, R. and Green, C. 2003 *English Bronze Cooking Vessels and their Founders 1350–1830* Honiton, Roderick and Valentine Butler

CA (Cotswold Archaeology) 2002 *3 Redcliff Street, Bristol: Archaeological evaluation* Unpublished CA Report **02112**

CA (Cotswold Archaeology) 2004 *3 Redcliff Street, Bristol: Post-excavation assessment and updated project design* Unpublished CA Report **04106**

CA (Cotswold Archaeology) 2010 *1–2 Redcliff Street, Redcliffe, Bristol: post-excavation assessment and updated project design* Unpublished CA report **09013**

Campbell, S., Hunt, C.O., Scourse, J.D., Keen, D.H. and Croot, D.G. 1999 'Southwest England', in Bowen (ed.) 1999, 66–78

Carrott, J. and Kenward, H.K. 2001 'Species associations amongst insect remains from urban archaeological deposits and their significance in reconstructing the past human environment', *J. Archaeol. Science* **28**, 887–905

Carus-Wilson, E.M. 1937 *The Overseas Trade of Bristol in the Later Middle Ages* Bristol Record Soc **7**

Carus-Wilson, E. M. and Coleman O. 1963 *England's Export Trade 1275–1547* Oxford, Clarendon Press

C.J. Associates 2007 *Site investigation No. T1024. Factual report, 2 Redcliff Street, Bristol* Unpublished document, C.J. Associates Geotechnical Ltd, Bristol

Clark, J. 1995 *The Medieval Horse and its Equipment c. 1150–1450* Medieval Finds from Excavations in London **5**. London, Her Majesty's Stationery Office

Clarke, H. and Carter, A. 1977 *Excavations in Kings Lynn 1963–1970* Society for Medieval Archaeology Monograph **7**

Clason, C.A. (ed.) 1975 *Archaeozoological Studies* Amsterdam, North-Holland Publishing Company

Connor, A. and Buckley, R. 1999 *Roman and Medieval Occupation in Causeway Lane, Leicester* Leicester Archaeological Monographs **5**. Leicester, Leicester University Press

Courtney, P. 2004 'Small finds', in Rodwell and Bell 2004, 365–97

Cox, S. 1998 'Excavations on the medieval waterfront at Bridge Parade, Bristol, 1999', *Bristol and Avon Archaeol.* **15**, 1–26

Crackles, F.E. 1986 'Medieval gardens in Hull: Archaeological evidence', *Garden History* **14(1)**, 1–5

Crawford, A. 2014 'Pottery', in Hardy and Dungworth 2014, 127–9

Crellin, J.K., Philpott, A.L. and Bass, T. 1997 *Herbal Medicine Past and Present: A Reference Guide to Medicinal Plants* Durham, US, Duke University Press

Cronne, H.A. (ed.) 1946 *Bristol Charters 1378–1499* Bristol Record Society **11**

Crummy, N. 1998 *The Post-Roman Small Finds from Excavations in Colchester 1971–85* Colchester Archaeological Report **5**. Colchester, Colchester Archaeological Trust

Cutler, D.F. and Gale, R. 2000 *Plants in Archaeology: Identification Manual of Artefacts of Plant Origin from Europe and the Mediterranean* Kew Westbury Scientific Publishing

Dalwood, H. and Edwards, R. 2004 *Excavations at Deansway, Worcester, 1988–89: Romano-British Small Town to Late Medieval City* London, Counc. Brit. Archaeol. Res. Rep. **139**

Davenport, P., Leech, R. and Rowe, M. 2011 '55–60 St Thomas Street, Redcliffe, Bristol: Excavations in 2006', in Watts (ed.) 2011b, 1–72

Davey, P. and Hodges, R. (eds) 1983 *Ceramics and Trade: The production and distribution of later medieval pottery in north-west Europe* University of Sheffield

Davis, S.J.M. 1992 *A rapid method for recording information about mammal bones from archaeological sites* Anc. Mon. Lab. Rep. **19/92**

Day, J. 1991 'Copper, zinc and brass production', in Day and Tylecote (eds) 1991, 144

Day, J. and Tylecote, R.F. (eds) 1991 *Metals in the Industrial Revolution* London, Institute of Metals

de Boe, G. and Verhaeghe, F. (eds) 1997 *Urbanism in Medieval Europe. Papers of the 'Medieval Europe Brugge 1997' Conference* **1**, Zellik

Defelice, M.S. 2004 'Common Chickweed, Stellaria media (L.) Vill.: "Mere Chicken Feed"', *Weed Technology* **18(1)**, 193–200

Dickson, C. 1996 'Food, medicinal and other plants from the 15th century drains of Paisley Abbey, Scotland', *Vegetation History and Archaeobotany* **5**, 25–31

Dobney, K. and Rielly, K. 1988 'A method for recording archaeological animal bones: the use of diagnostic zones', *Circaea* **5(2)**, 79–96

Duke, J.A. 1973 'Utilization of Papaver', *Economic Botany* **27(4)**, 390–400

Dungworth, D. 2000 'A note on the analysis of crucibles and moulds', *Hist. Metall.* **34**, 83–6

Dungworth, D. 2005 *Assessing Evidence for Post-Medieval Glassworking* Unpublished course notes

Dungworth, D. and Nicholas, M. 2004 'Caldarium? An antimony bronze used for medieval and post-medieval cast domestic vessels', *Hist. Metall.* **38**, 24–34

Dungworth, D. and White H. 2007 'Scientific examination of zinc-distillation remains from Warmley, Bristol', *Hist. Metall.* **41**, 77–83

Dunning, G.C. 1974 'Other finials, water pipe and louver', in McCarthy 1974, 128–31

Dyer, C. 2000 *Everyday Life in Medieval England* London, Hambledon

Edmonds, J. 2003 *Medieval Textile Dyeing* Historical Dyes Series **3**. Buckinghamshire, J. Edmonds

Edmonds, J. 2006 *The History of Woad and the Medieval Woad Vat* Historical Dye Series **1**. Buckinghamshire, J. Edmonds

Egan, G. 1991 'Industry and economics on the medieval and later London waterfront', in Good *et al.* (eds) 1991, 9–18

Egan, G. 1998 *The Medieval Household, Daily Living c. 1150–c. 1450* Medieval Finds from Excavations in London **6**. London, Her Majesty's Stationery Office

Egan, G. 2007 'Late 16th-century candleholder manufacture', in Bowsher *et al.* 2007, 351–2

Egan, G. and Pritchard, F. 1991 *Dress Accessories c. 1150–c. 1450* Medieval Finds from Excavations in London **3**. London, Her Majesty's Stationery Office

EH (English Heritage) 1991 *Management of Archaeological Projects II*

Ellis, B.M.A. 1995 'Spurs and Spur Fittings', in Clark 1995, 124–50

Ellis, P. (ed.) 2000 *Ludgershall Castle: Excavations by Peter Addyman 1964–1972* Wiltshire Archaeol. Natur. Hist. Soc. Monograph Series **2**. Devizes, Wiltshire Archaeol. Natur. Hist. Soc.

Ervynck, A., van Neer W., Hüster-Plogman, H. and Schibler J. 2003 'Beyond affluence: the zoo-archaeology of luxury', *World Archaeology* **34(3)**, 428–41

Esling, J., Howard, R.E., Laxton, R.R., Litton, C.D. and Simpson, W.G. 1990 '*List 33 no 8a/b - Nottingham University Tree-ring Dating Laboratory Results: general list*', Vernacular Architect. **21**, 37–40

Evans, D.H. and Tomlinson, D.G. 1992 *Excavations at 33–35 Eastgate, Beverley, 1983–1986* Sheffield Excavations Reports **3**. Dorchester, The Dorset Press

Evison, V.I.H.H. and Hurst, J.G. (eds) 1974 *Medieval Pottery from Excavations: Studies presented to Gerald Clough Dunning, with a bibliography of his works* London, John Baker

Fabiš, M. and Thomas, R. 2009 'Not just cattle: Cranial perforations revisited', *Int. J. Osteoarchaeol.* 21 (2011), 347–50. Published online (2009): Doi: 10.1002/oa.1133

Fock, J. 1966 *Metrische Untersuchungen an Metapodien einiger Europäischer Rinderrassen* Unpublished dissertation, University of Munich

Freestone, I.C. and Tite, M.S. 1986 'Refractories in the Ancient and Preindustrial world', in Kingery (ed.) 1986, 35–63

Giorgi, G. 2013 'Plant macro remains', in Ridgeway and Watts (eds) 2013, 288–301

Good, G.L. 1987 'The excavation of two docks at Narrow Quay, Bristol, 1978–9', *Post-Medieval Archaeol.* **21**, 25–126

Good, G.L. 1989 'An excavation at the corner of St Thomas Street and Portwall Lane', *Bristol and Avon Archaeol.* **8**, 20–9

Good, G.L. 1991 'Some aspects of the development of the Redcliffe waterfront in the light of excavations at Dundas Wharf', *Bristol and Avon Archaeol.* **9**, 29–42

Good, L. 1998 'Worked bone' in Price with Ponsford 1998, 172–3

Good, G., Jones, R. and Ponsford, M. (eds) 1991 *Waterfront Archaeology: Proceedings of the third international conference, Bristol 1988* Counc. Brit. Archaeol. Res. Rep. **74**

Goodall, I.H. 1980 *Ironwork in Medieval Britain: An Archaeological Study* Unpublished PhD thesis, University College, Cardiff

Goodburn, D. 1991 'New light on early ship and boat building in the London area', in Good *et al*. (eds) 1991, 105–11

Goodburn, D. 1992 'Woods and woodland: Carpenters and carpentry', in Milne 1992, 106–31

Goodburn, D. 1997 'London's early medieval timber buildings. Little known traditions of construction', in de Boe and Verhaeghe (eds) 1997a, 249–57

Goodburn, D. 1998a 'The death of the wildwood and birth of woodmanship in south east England', in Bernick (ed.) 1998, 130–8

Goodburn, D. 1998b *Woodwork analysis report for Regis House, Excavations, City of London* Unpublished report

Goodburn, D. 1999 'A summary of the early-medieval woodworking', in Hill and Woodger 1999, 47–51

Goodburn, D. 2007 'Treewrighting and woodland management in the 11th and 12th Centuries', in Bowsher *et al*. 2007, 303–18

Goodburn, D. 2008 *Initial notes and observations supplied for the site archive following site visits to Oxford Archaeology excavations at Counterslip, Bristol, 2008* Unpublished report

Goodburn, D. 2013 'Historic woodwork', in Ridgeway and Watts (eds) 2013, 247–57

Goubitz, O., van Driel-Murray, C. and Groenman-van Waatering, W. 2001 *Stepping through Time* Zwolle, Stichting Promotie Archeologie

Grant, A. 1982 'The use of tooth wear as a guide to the age of domestic ungulates', in Wilson *et al*. 1982, 91–108

Grew, F. and de Neergaard, M. 1988 *Shoes and Pattens Medieval Finds from Excavations in London* **2**. London, Her Majesty's Stationery Office

Grinsell, L.V. 1986 *The History and Coinage of the Bristol Mint* Bristol City Museum and Art Gallery

Grupe, G. and J. Peters (eds) 2005 'Feathers, Grit and Symbolism: Birds and Humans in the Ancient Old and New Worlds', *Documenta Archaeobiologiae* **3**

Hall, A.R. 1996 'A survey of palaeobotanical evidence for dyeing and mordanting from British archaeological excavations', *Quaternary Science Reviews* **15**, 635–40

Hall, A. and Kenward, H. 2003 'Can we identify biological indicator groups for craft, industry and other activities?', in Murphy and Wiltshire (eds) 2003, 114–30

Hall, R.A. 1984 *The Viking Dig: The Excavations at York* London, Bodley Head

Halstead, D.G.H. 1963 *Histeroidea* Handbooks for the Identification of British Insects **5(10)**. London, Royal Entomological Society of London

Hansen, M. 1986 'The Hydrophilidae (Coleoptera) of Fennoscandia and Denmark Fauna', *Fauna Entomologyca Scandinavica* **18**

Harde, K.W. 1984 *A Field Guide in Colour to Beetles* London, Octopus

Hardy, A. and Dungworth, D. 2014 'A medieval iron production site in Little Snarlton Farm, East Melksham, Wiltshire: Excavations in 2010', *Wilts Archaeol. Natur. Hist. Mag.* **107**, 118–45

Harvey, J.H. 1984 'Vegetables in the Middle Ages', *Garden History* **12(2)**, 89–99

Haslam, J. (ed.) 1984 *Anglo-Saxon towns in Southern England* Chichester, Phillimore

Heller, I., Kienast, F., Schoch, W. and Schweingruber, F.H. 2004 *Wood Anatomy of Central European Species* Online version http://www.woodanatomy.ch (accessed 30 September 2015)

Herrnbrodt, A. 1958 *Der Husterknupp: Eine Niederrheinische Burganlage des Frühen Mittelalters* Köln, Böhlau

Higbee, L. 2004 'The faunal remains', in Jackson 2004, 45–7

Hill, J. and Woodger, A. 1999 'Excavations at 72–75 Cheapside/83–93 Queen Street City of London', *MoLAS Archaeological Studies* **2**

Hillam, J. 1984 'Bristol Bridge dendrochronology: analysis of the reused boat timbers', *Anc. Mon. Lab. Rep.* **4168**

Hillson, S. 1986 *Teeth* Cambridge, Cambridge University Press

Hinton, D.A. 1984 'The towns of Hampshire', in Haslam (ed.) 1984, 149–65

Holbrook, N. and Jurica, J. (eds) 2006 *Twenty-five Years of Archaeology in Gloucestershire: A Review of New Discoveries and New Thinking in Gloucestershire, South Gloucestershire and Bristol, 1979–2004* Bristol Gloucestershire Archaeol. Rep. **3**. Cirencester, Cotswold Archaeology

Holmes, E.F. 1999 'Datasheet 9: Sewing Thimbles' in MacGregor (ed.) 1999, 1–4

Horsman, V., Milne, C. and Milne, G. 1988 *Aspects of Saxo-Norman London 1: Building and Street Development near Billingsgate and Cheapside* London Middlesex Archaeol. Soc. Spec. Pap. **11**

Howard, R.E. 1995 *Site chronology for the Barbican and Gatehouse, Warwick Castle* Unpublished computer file WRKCSQ01, Nottingham University Tree-Ring Dating Laboratory

Howard, R.E., Laxton, R.R., Litton, C.D. and Simpson, W.G. 1986 *Site chronology for Sandwell Priory, West Midlands* Unpublished computer file SANPSQ0/2/3/4, Nottingham University Tree-Ring Dating Laboratory

Howard, R.E., Laxton, R.R., Litton, C.D. and Simpson, W.G. 1991 'List 39 no 8 - Nottingham University Tree-Ring Dating Laboratory: results', *Vernacular Architect.* **22**, 40–3

Howard, R.E., Laxton, R.R., Litton, C.D. and Simpson, W.G. 1992 'List 44 no 12 - Nottingham University Tree-Ring Dating Laboratory: results', *Vernacular Architect.* **23**, 51–6

Howard, R.E., Laxton, R.R., Litton, C.D. and Simpson, W.G. 1994 'List 57 no 13 - Nottingham University Tree-Ring Dating Laboratory: results', *Vernacular Architect.* **25**, 36–40

Howard, R.E., Laxton, R.R., Litton, C.D. and Simpson, W.G. 1995 'List 60 no 14 - Nottingham University Tree-Ring Dating Laboratory: general list', *Vernacular Architect.* **26**, 47–53

Howard, R.E., Laxton, R.R., Litton, C.D. and Simpson, W.G. 1996a 'List 65 no 12 - Nottingham University Tree-Ring Dating Laboratory: results', *Vernacular Architect.* **27**, 78–81

Howard, R.E., Laxton, R.R., Litton, C.D., Morrison, A., Sewell, J. and Hook, R. 1996b 'List 66 no 6b - Nottingham University Tree-Ring Dating Laboratory: Derbyshire, Peak Park and RCHME Dendrochronological Survey 1995–96', *Vernacular Architect.* **27**, 81–4

Howard, R.E. Laxton, R.R. and Litton, C.D. 1998 *Tree-ring analysis of timbers from Naas House, Lydney, Gloucestershire* Anc. Mon. Lab. Rep. **36/1998**

Howard, R.E., Laxton, R.R. and Litton, C.D. 1999 *Tree-ring analysis of timbers from The Manor House, Medbourne, Leicestershire* Anc. Mon. Lab. Rep. **63/1999**

Howard, R.E., Laxton, R.R. and Litton, C.D. 2002 *Tree-ring analysis of timbers from Blackfriars Priory, Ladybellegate Street, Gloucester* Centre for Archaeology Report **43/2002**

Hughes, M. (ed.) 1986 *Archaeology in Hampshire Annual Report for 1984/5* Hampshire County Council

Hurst, J.G. 1974 'Sixteenth- and seventeenth-century imported pottery from the Saintonge', in Evison and Hurst (eds) 1974, 221–56

Hurst, J.G. 1977 'Spanish pottery imported into medieval Britain', *Medieval Archaeol.* **21**, 68–105

Insole, P. 2001 *Archaeological excavation of land at 98–103 Redcliff Street, Bristol, 2000* BaRAS Report **731/2001**

Jackson, R. 2004 'Archaeological excavations at Nos 30–38 St Thomas Street and No. 60 Redcliff Street, Bristol, 2000', *Bristol and Avon Archaeol.* **19**, 1–64

Jackson, R. 2006a *Excavations at St James's Priory, Bristol* Oxford, Oxbow Books

Jackson, R. 2006b 'Archaeological excavations at the former Courage Brewery, Bath Street, Bristol, 2000–2001', *Bristol and Avon Archaeol.* **21**, 1–58

Jackson, R.G. and Price, R.H. 1974 *Bristol Clay Pipes: A Study of Makers and their Marks* City Bristol Mus. Art Gall. Res. Monogr. **1**. Bristol

Jarrett, C. 2013 'Post-medieval pottery', in Ridgeway and Watts (eds) 2013, 176–97

Jenkins, R. 1934 'The reverberatory furnace with coal fuel', *Trans. Newcomen Soc.* **34**, 67–81

Jones, A.P., Tucker, M.E. and Hart, J.K. 1999a 'Guidelines and recommendations', in Jones *et al.* (eds) 1999b, 27–76

Jones, A.P., Tucker, M.E. and Hart, J.K. (eds) 1999b *The Description and Analysis of Quaternary Stratigraphic Field Sections* Quaternary Research Association technical guide **7**

Jones, J. 2010 'Appendix 18: The plant macrofossils', in CA 2010, 130–57

Jones, J. 2011 'Charred and waterlogged plant remains', in Davenport *et al.* 2011, 48–9

Jones, J. and Watson, N. 1987 'The early medieval waterfront at Redcliffe, Bristol: A study of environment and economy', in Balaam *et al.* 1987, 135–62

Jones, R.H. 1983 'Excavations at 68–72 Redcliff Street, 1982 Bristol', *Bristol and Avon Archaeol.* **2**, 37–9

Jones, R.H. 1986 *Excavations in Redcliffe 1983–5: Survey and Excavation at 95–97 Redcliff Street, Bristol: An Interim Report* City of Bristol Museum and Art Gallery

Jones, R.H. 1991 'Industry and environment in medieval Bristol', in Good *et al.* (eds) 1991, 19–26

Jones, R.H. 2006 'Bristol', in Holbrook and Jurica (eds) 2006, 189–209

Jorgensen, G. 1986 *The Archaeology of Svendborg, Denmark* **4** Odense University Press

Kenward, H.K. 1978 *The Analysis of Archaeological Insect Assemblages: A New Approach* The Archaeology of York, Principles and Methods **19/1**. London, Council for British Archaeology for York Archaeological Trust

Kenward, H.K. 1997 'Synanthropic insects and the size, remoteness and longevity of archaeological occupation sites: applying concepts from biogeography to past "islands" of human occupation', *Quaternary Proceedings* **5**, 135–52

Kenward, H.K. and Hall, A.R. 1995 *Biological Evidence from Anglo-Scandinavian Deposits at 16–22 Coppergate* The Archaeology of York **14/7**. York, Council for British Archaeology for York Archaeological Trust

Kenward, H.K. and Hall, A.R. 1997 'Enhancing bioarchaeological interpretation using Indicator groups: stable manure as a paradigm', *J. Archaeol. Sci.* **24**, 663–73

Kenward, H.K., Hall, A.R. and Jones, A.K.G. 1980 'A tested set of techniques for the extraction of plant and animal macrofossils from waterlogged archaeological deposits', *Science and Archaeology* **22**, 3–15

Kenward, H.K., Hall, A.R. and McComish, J.M. 2004 'Archaeological implications of plant and invertebrate remains from fills of a massive post-medieval cut at Low Fishergate, Doncaster, UK', *Environmental Archaeology* **9**, 61–74

Kingery, W.D. (ed.) 1986 *High-Technology Ceramics: Past, Present and Future: The nature of innovation and change in ceramic technology* Westerville, The American Ceramic Society

Koch, K. 1992 *Die Kafer Mitteleuropas (Ökologie Band 3)* Krefeld, Goecke and Evers

Kowaleski, M. 2000 'Fishing and fisheries in the Middle Ages. The Western Fishery', in Starkey *et al.* (eds) 2000, 23–8

La Niece, S., Hook, D. and Craddock, P. (eds) 2007 *Metals and Mines: Studies in Archaeometallurgy* London, Archetype

Latimer, J. 1903 'The Maire of Bristowe is Kalendar: its list of civic officers collated with contemporary legal MSS', *Trans. Bristol Gloucestershire Archaeol. Soc.* **26**, 108–37

Laxton, R.R. and Litton, C.D. 1988 *An East Midlands Master Tree-ring Chronology and its use for Dating Vernacular Buildings* University of Nottingham Dept of Classical and Archaeol. Studies Monograph Series **3**

Laxton, R.R., Litton, C.D., and Simpson, W.G. 1984 'List 12 no 13 - Nottingham University Tree-Ring Dating Laboratory: tree-ring dates for buildings in Eastern and Midland England', *Vernacular Architect.* **15**, 65–8

Leech, R. 2004 'Tenement Histories' in Jackson 2004, 57–9

Leech, R. 2006 'Bristol: the Hearth Tax as a decodeable street directory', in Barnwell and Airs (eds) 2006, 83–94

Leech, R. 2009 'Arthur's Acre: A Saxon bridgehead at Bristol', *Trans. Bristol Gloucestershire Archaeol. Soc.* **127**, 11–20

Leech, R. 2014 *The Town House in Medieval and Early Modern Bristol* Swindon, English Heritage

Leech, R. forthcoming *The topography of medieval and early modern Bristol. Part 3: Property holdings in the walled town and suburbs south of the Avon* Bristol Record Society

Lewis, E. (ed.) 1991 *Custom and Ceramics: Essays presented to Kenneth Barton* Bristol, Wickham

Lewis, J.M. 1973 'Some types of metal chafing-dish', *Antiq. J.* **53**, 59–70

Libois, R.M., Hallet-Libois, C. and Rosoux, R. 1987 Éléments *pour l'identification des restes crâniens des poissons dulçaquicoles de Belgiquie et du Nord de la France 1* Fiches d'Ostéologie Animale pour l'Archéologie **3**. Juan-les-Pins, Centre de Recherches Archéologiques

Lobel, M.D. and Carus-Wilson, E.M. 1975 'Bristol', in *The Atlas of Historic Towns* **2** London, Scolar Press

Locker, A. 2008 *The fish bones from excavations at 55–61 Victoria Street, Bristol* Unpublished report, BRSMG (Bristol City Museum and Art Gallery)

Lowe, B.J. 1987 'Keynsham Abbey: Excavations 1961–1985', *Proc. Somerset Archaeol. Natur. Hist. Soc.* **131**, 81–156

Ložek, V. 1986 'Quaternary malacology and fauna genesis in Central Europe', *Proc. of the 8th Internat. Malacological Congress Budapest 1983*, 143–5

Lucht, W.H. 1987 *Die Käfer Mitteleuropas (Katalog)* Krefeld, Goecke and Evers

McCarthy, M.R. 1974 'The medieval kilns on Nash Hill, Lacock, Wiltshire', *Wiltshire Archaeol. Natur. Hist. Soc.* **69**, 97–160

McCutcheon, C. 2006 *Medieval Pottery from Wood Quay, Dublin: The 1974–6 Waterfront Excavations* Dublin, National Museum of Ireland/Royal Irish Academy

McDonnell, J.G. and Dungworth, D. 2006 'Metalworking evidence', in Saunders 2006, 417–19

McGrail, S. 1993 *Medieval boat and ship timbers from Dublin* Dublin, National Museum of Ireland

MacGregor, A. 1985 *Bone, Antler, Ivory and Horn: The technology of skeletal materials since the Roman period* London, Croom Helm

MacGregor, A. 1991 'Antler, Bone and Horn', in Blair and Ramsay (eds) 1991, 355–78

MacGregor, A. (ed.) 1999 *Datasheets 1–24: A consolidated reprint of Datasheets issued by the Finds Research Group between 1985 and 1998* Oxford, Finds Research Group 700–1700

McSloy, E. 2013 'Metal and other small finds', in Ridgeway and Watts (eds) 2013, 237–43

Manchee, T.J. 1831 *The Bristol Charities, Volumes 1 and 2* Bristol, T.J. Manchee

Margeson, S. 1993 *Norwich Households: The Medieval and Post-Medieval Finds from Norwich Survey Excavations 1971–1978* E. Anglian Archaeol. Rep. **58**

Marsden, P. 1996 *Ships of the Twelfth to Seventeenth Centuries AD* London, English Heritage

Martinón-Torres, M. and Rehren, T. 2009 'Post-medieval crucible production and distribution: a study of materials and materialities', *Archaeometry* **51**, 49–74

Meirion-Jones, G.I., Pilcher, J.R., Guibal, F., Heward, J. and Taylor, R. 1987 'The Dating by Dendrochronology of three Northamptonshire Halls', *Vernacular Architect.* **18**, 34–40

Miles, A.E.W. and Grigson, C. 1990 (eds) *Colyer's Variations and Diseases of the Teeth of Animals* Cambridge, Cambridge University Press

Miles, D.H. and Worthington, M.J. 1997 'Tree-ring dates', *Vernacular Architect.* **28**, 159–81

Milne, G. 1992 *Timber Building Techniques in London c. 900–1400* London Middlesex Archaeol. Soc. Spec. Pap. **15**

Milne, G. and Hobley, B. (eds) 1981 *Waterfront Archaeology in Britain and Northern Europe* Counc. Brit. Archaeol. Res. Rep. **41**

Mitich, L.W. 1997 'Intriguing world of weeds: Fumitory (*Fumaria officinalis* L.)', *Weed Technology* **11**, 843–5

MoLAS (Museum of London Archaeology Service) 1999a *One Redcliff Street, Bristol, BS1: An archaeological assessment*

MoLAS (Museum of London Archaeology Service) 1999b *2 and 3 Redcliff Street, Bristol, BS1: An archaeological assessment and supplementary report to inform a design for geotechnical test pits*

MoLAS (Museum of London Archaeology Service) 1999c *2 and 3 Redcliff Street, Bristol, BS1: An archaeological assessment and report of the observation of geotechnical test pits*

Moore, J.S. 1982 'The medieval forest of Kingswood', *Avon Past* **7**, 6–16

Morris, E.L. 2011 'Clay mould fabric', in Davenport *et al*. 2011, 45

Mould, Q. 2001 *The Leather from 3–5 Welsh Back, Bristol (BUAD 3581)* Unpublished typescript report for Avon Archaeological Unit

Mould, Q. 2008a *Assessment of the leather from Broad Quay, Bristol (BQB06)* Unpublished typescript report for Cotswold Archaeology

Mould, Q. 2008b *Assessment of the leather from 32–36 Victoria Street, Bristol (BRSMG 2007/18)* Unpublished typescript report for Bristol and Region Archaeological Services

Mould, Q. 2010a *The leather from Finzel's Reach, Bristol (BRSMG2007/28)* Unpublished typescript report for Oxford Archaeology

Mould, Q. 2010b *The leather from Oxford Castle and Paradise Street* Unpublished typescript report for Oxford Archaeology

Mould, Q. 2013 'Leather', in Ridgeway and Watts (eds) 2013, 260–3MPRG (Medieval Pottery Research Group) 1998 'A Guide to the Classification of Medieval Ceramic Forms', *Medieval Pottery Research Group Occasional Paper* **1**

Mulkeen, S. and O'Connor, T.P. 1997 'Raptors in Towns: Towards an Ecological Model', *Int. J. Osteoarchaeology* **7**, 440–9

Munsell Color 2000 *Munsell Soil Color Charts* New Windsor, Munsell Color

Murphy, P. and Wiltshire E.J. (eds) 2003 *The Environmental Archaeology of Industry* Symposia of the Association for Environmental Archaeology **20**. Oxford, Oxbow Books

Musty, J. 1973 'A preliminary account of a medieval pottery industry at Minety, North Wiltshire', *Wiltshire Archaeol. Natur. Hist. Mag.* **68**, 79–88

Newman, P.B. 2001 *Daily Life in the Middle Ages* Jefferson, McFarland

Nicholson, R. 2004 'The fish remains', in Jackson 2004, 47–50

Nicholson, R.A. and Hillam, J. 1987 'A dendrochronological analysis of oak timbers from the early medieval site at Dundas Wharf, Bristol', *Trans. Bristol Gloucestershire Archaeol. Soc.* **105**, 133–45

Noël Hume, I. 1969 *A Guide to Artifacts of Colonial America* Philadelphia University of Pennsylvania Press

Osborne, P.J. 1983 'An insect fauna from a modern cesspit and its comparison with probable cesspit assemblages from archaeological sites', *J. Archaeol. Sci.* **10**, 453–63

Oswald, A. 1975 *Clay Pipes for the Archaeologist* Brit. Archaeol. Rep. Brit. Ser. **14**. Oxford

Ottaway, P. and Rogers, N. 2002 *Craft, Industry and Everyday Life: Finds from Medieval York* The Archaeology of York: The Small Finds **17/15**. York, York Archaeological Trust and the Council for British Archaeology

Pantin, W.A. 1962–3 'Medieval English Town-House Plans', *Medieval Arch*aeol. **6–7**, 202–39

Patrick, C. and Ratkai, S. 2009 *The Ring Uncovered: Excavations at Edgbaston Street, Moor Street, Park Street and the Row, Birmingham 1997–2001* Oxford, Oxbow Books

Patterson, R.B. 1973 *Earldom of Gloucester Charters: The Charters and Scribes of the Earls and Countesses of Gloucester to A.D. 1217* Oxford, Clarendon Press

Peacey, A. 1996 *The Development of the Clay Tobacco Pipe Kiln in the British Isles* Brit. Archaeol. Rep. Brit. Ser. **246**. Oxford

Peacock, D.P.S. (ed.) 1977 *Pottery and Early Commerce: Characterisation and Trade in Roman and Later Ceramics* London, Academia Press

Pearce, J. 1992 *Border Wares*, Post-Medieval Pottery in London, 1500–1700 **1**. London, Her Majesty's Stationery Office for Museum of London

Pearce, J. and Vince, A. 1988 *A Dated Type-Series of London Medieval Pottery. Part 4: Surrey Whitewares* London, London and Middlesex Archaeological Society

Pearson, K.L. 1997 Nutrition and the early-medieval diet', *Speculum* **72(1)**, 1–32

Penny, J. 1997 *Is the Economic History of Bristol Region between 1780 and 1850 a Story of Relative Decline?* Bath Spa University http://fishponds.org.uk/brisecon.html (accessed 5 February 2015)

Peterken, G. 1996 *Natural Woodland* Cambridge, Cambridge University Press

Platt, C. and Coleman-Smith, R. 1975 *Excavations in Medieval Southampton 1953–1969, Vol 1: The Excavation Reports* Leicester, Leicester University Press

Ponsford, M. 1981 'Bristol', in Milne and Hobley (eds) 1981, 103–04

Ponsford, M. 1983 'North European pottery imported into Bristol', in Davey and Hodges (eds) 1983, 219–24

Ponsford, M.W. 1988 'Pottery', in Williams 1988, 124–45

Ponsford, M.W. 1991 'Dendrochronological dates from Dundas Wharf, Bristol and the dating of Ham Green and other medieval pottery', in Lewis (ed.) 1991, 81–103

Ponsford, M.W. 1998 'Pottery', in Price with Ponsford 1998, 136–56

Press, B. 2002 *Herbs of Britain and Ireland* London, New Holland Publishers

Price, R. with Ponsford M.W. 1998 *St Bartholomew's Hospital, Bristol: The Excavation of a Medieval Hospital 1976–8* Counc. Brit. Archaeol. Res. Rep. **110**. York, Council for British Archaeology

Price, R. and Jackson, R. and P. 1979 *Bristol Clay Pipe Makers: A Revised and Enlarged Edition* Privately published by the authors

Pritchard, F. 1982 *Building material: Swan Lane car park, Upper Thames Street* Unpublished MoLAS report

Pritchard, F.A. 1991 'Small finds', in Vince (ed.) 1991b, 120–278

Rackham, O. 1976 *Trees and Woodland in the British Landscape* London, Dent

Rackham, O. 1986 *The History of the Countryside* London, Phoenix Press

Reid, C., Barrow, G. and Dewey, F.I. 1910 *Geology of the Country around Padstow and Camelford* Memoir of the Geological Survey of Great Britain. London, Her Majesty's Stationery Office

Reimer, P.J., Baillie, M.G.L., Bard, E., Bayliss, A., Beck, J.W., Bertrand, C., Blackwell, P.G., Buck, C.E., Burr, G., Cutler, K.B.P., Damon, E., Edwards, R.L., Fairbanks, R.G., Friedrich, M., Guilderson, T.P., Hughen, K.A., Kromer, B., McCormac, F.G., Manning, S., Bronk Ramsey, C., Reimer, R.W., Remmele, S., Southon, J.R., Stuiver, M., Talamo, S., Taylor, F.W., van der Plicht, J. and Weyhenmeyer, C.E. 2004 'IntCal04 terrestrial radiocarbon age calibration, 0–26 cal. kyr. BP', *Radiocarbon* **46**, 1029–58

Riddler, I. 1998 'Bone styli', in Egan 1998, 270–4

Ridgeway, V. and Watts, M. (eds) 2013 *Friars, Quakers, Industry and Urbanisation: The Archaeology of the Broadmead Expansion Project, Cabot Circus, Bristol 2005–2008* Cirencester and London, Cotswold Archaeology and Pre-Construct Archaeology

Robinson, P. and Griffiths, N. 2000 'The copper alloy objects', in Ellis (ed.) 2000, 124–37

Rockware 2008 *RockWorks v2006* https://www.rockware.com (accessed 20 May 2008)

Saunders, A. 2006 *Excavations at Launceston Castle, Cornwall* London, Society for Medieval Archaeology

Scofield, J. and Vince, A.G. 1994 *Medieval Towns: The Archaeology of British Towns in Their European Setting* Leicester, Leicester University Press

Seeley, D., Phillpotts, C. and Samuel, M. (eds) 2006 *Winchester Palace: Excavations at the Southwark Residence of the Bishops of Winchester* Museum of London Archaeology Service Monograph **31**. London, Museum of London Archaeology Service

Serjeantson, D. 1989 'Animal remains and the tanning trade', in Serjeantson and Waldron (eds) 1989, 129–45

Serjeantson, D. and Waldron, T. (eds) 1989 *Diet and Crafts in Towns: The evidence of animal remains from the Roman to the post-medieval periods* Brit. Archaeol. Rep. Brit. Ser. **199**. Oxford

Serjeantson, D. and Woolgar, C.M. 2006 'Fish consumption in medieval England', in Woolgar *et al.* (eds) 2006, 102–30

Shoesmith, R. 1991 *Excavations in Chepstow 1973–1974* Cambrian Archaeol. Monogr. **4**. Bangor, Cambrian Archaeological Association

Silver, I.A. 1969 'The ageing of domestic animals', in Brothwell and Higgs (eds) 1969, 283–302

Singer, C., Holmyard, E.J., Hall, A.R. and Williams, T.I. 1956 *A History of Technology Vol 2* Oxford, Clarendon Press

Sketchley, J. 1775 *Sketchley's Bristol Directory* Bristol, James Sketchley

Skidmore, P. 1999 'The Diptera', in Connor and Buckley 1999, 341–3

Smith, D. 1997 'The insect fauna', in Thomas *et al.* (eds) 1997, 245–7

Smith, D.N. 2001 *The Insect Remains from 5–7 Welsh Back, Bristol* Unpublished report for Avon Archaeology Unit

Smith, D.N. 2002a 'Insect remains', in Barber and Thomas (eds) 2002, 113–15

Smith, D.N. 2002b *The insects from Cathedral School/ College Square Bristol* Unpublished report for Avon Archaeology Unit

Smith, D.N. 2006 'The insect remains', in Seeley *et al.* (eds), 142–4

Smith, D. 2009 'Chapter 14: The Insect Remains from Edgbaston and Park Street', in Patrick and Ratkai 2009, 269–75

Smith, D. 2010 *The Insect Remains from Finzel's Reach, Bristol* Unpublished report for Oxford Archaeology

Smith, D.N. and Morris M. 2007 'Insects', in Bowsher *et al.* 2007, 480–2

Smith, K.G.V. 1973 *Insects and Other Arthropods of Medical Importance* London, British Museum

Smith, K.G.V. 1989 *An introduction to the Immature Stages of British Flies* Handbooks for the Identification of British Insects **10(14)**. London, Royal Entomological Society of London

Soderberg, J.A. 2003 *Feeding Community: Urbanization, Religion, and Zooarchaeology at Clonmacnoise, an early Medieval Irish Monastery* Unpublished PhD thesis, Minneapolis, University of Minnesota.

Spink 2009 *Coins of England and the United Kingdom* London, Spink

Spry, N. 2003 'Eighteenth century slag construction blocks in Gloucestershire – a survey', *Gloucestershire Society for Industrial Archaeology Annual Journal* 2003, 36–58

Stace, C. 1997 *A New British Flora* Cambridge, Cambridge University Press

Stace, C. 2010 *New Flora of the British Isles* (3rd edition) Cambridge, Cambridge University Press

Starkey, D.J., Reid, C. and Ashcroft, N. (eds) 2000 *England's Sea Fisheries: The Commercial Sea Fisheries of England and Wales since 1300* London, Chatham Publishing

Stoddard, S. 2001 *Bristol before the Camera: The City in 1820–30* Bristol, Redcliffe Press

Stone, D.J. 2006 'The consumption of field crops in late medieval England', in Woolgar *et al.* (eds) 2006, 11–26

Taylor, F.S. and Singer C. 1956 'Pre-scientific industrial chemistry', in Singer *et al.* 1956, 364–9

Taylor, G. 1996 'Medieval bronzefounding at Deansway', *Hist. Metall.* **30**, 111–15

Taylor, G. 2004 'Bronzeworking crucibles', in Dalwood and Edwards 2004, 384–6

Taylor, J. 1875 'The Church of Holy Cross, Temple, Bristol', *J. Brit. Archaeol. Soc.* **31**, 275–82

Teichert, M. 1975 'Osteometrische Untersuchungen zur Berechnung der Widerristhöhe bei Schafen', in Clason (ed.) 1975, 51–69

Thomas, C., Sloane, B. and Philpotts, C. (eds) 1997 *Excavations at the Priory and Hospital of St. Mary Spital, London*, Museum of London Archaeology Service Monograph **1**. London, Museum of London Archaeology Service

Timson, J. 1966 '*Polygonum hydropiper* L.', *J. Ecol.* **54(3)**, 815–21

Tottenham, C.E. 1954 *Coleoptera. Staphylinidae, Section (a) Piestinae to Euaesthetinae* Handbooks for the Identification of British Insects **4(8a)**. London, Royal Entomological Society of London

Tucker, M.E. 1982 *Sedimentary Rocks in the Field* Chichester, Wiley

Tyers, I. and Groves C. 1999 *England, London* Unpublished computer file LON1175, Sheffield University

Ure, A. 1844 *A Dictionary of Arts, Manufactures, and Mines* New York, Appleton

Vander Voort, G.F. 1999 *Metallography: Principles and Practice* Materials Park, ASM International

Van Walt, V. 2005 *Window sampling* http://www.vanwalt.co.uk/motorised_window.htm_(accessed 24 August 2006)

Veale E.W.W. (ed.) 1950 *The Great Red Book of Bristol, Text Part 3* Bristol, Bristol Record Society **16**

Veale E.W.W. (ed.) 1953 *The Great Red Book of Bristol, Text Part 4* Bristol, Bristol Record Society **18**

Vince, A.G. 1977 'The medieval and post-medieval ceramic industry of the Malvern region: the study of a ware and its distribution', in Peacock (ed.) 1977, 257–305

Vince, A.G. 1984 *The Medieval Ceramic Industry of the Severn Valley* Unpublished PhD thesis, University of Southampton

Vince, A.G. 1991a 'The medieval pottery', in Shoesmith 1991, 93–139

Vince, A.G. (ed.) 1991b *Aspects of Saxo-Norman London: 2 Finds and Environmental evidence* London Middlesex Archaeol. Soc. Spec. Pap. **12**

Vince, A. and England, S. 2004 'Medieval and later pottery', in Rodwell and Bell 2004, 294–348

von den Driesch, A. 1976 *A guide to the measurement of animal bones from archaeological sites* Peabody Museum of Archaeology and Ethnology Bulletin **1**, Cambridge, Harvard University

Wadley, Rev. T.P. 1886 *Notes or abstracts of the wills contained in the Great Orphan Book of Wills* Bristol, C.T. Jefferies and Sons

Walton, P. 1991 'Textiles', in Blair and Ramsay (eds) 1991, 319–54

Warman, S. 2010 'Appendix 8: The animal bone', in CA 2010, 79–81

Warman, S. 2013 'The Animal Bone', in Ridgeway and Watts (eds) 2013, 268–83

Watts, M. 2011a '26–28 St Thomas Street, Redcliffe, Bristol: Excavations in 2002' in Watts (ed.) 2011b, 73–8

Watts, M. (ed.) 2011b *Medieval and Post-Medieval Development within Bristol's Inner Suburbs* Bristol Gloucestershire Archaeol. Rep. **7**. Cirencester, Cotswold Archaeology

Watts, L. and Rahtz, P. 1985 *Mary-le-Port Bristol: Excavations 1962/3* City of Bristol Museum and Art Gallery Monograph **7**. Bristol, City of Bristol Museum and Art Gallery

Webb, S.C., Hedges, R.E.M. and Robinson, M. 1989 'The Seaweed Fly *Thoracochaeta zosterae* (Hal.) (Diptera: Sphaerocidae) in Inland Archaeological Contexts: $\delta 13C$ and $\delta 15N$ Solves the Puzzle', *J. Archaeol. Science* **25**, 1253–7

White, H. and Kearns, T. 2010 *Legge's Mounts, Tower of London, London. Scientific examination of the crucibles* Res. Dep. Rep. **76/2010**. Portsmouth, English Heritage

Whitehead, R. 1996 *Buckles, 1250–1800* Chelmsford, Greenlight Publishing

Williams, B. 1981 *Excavations at the medieval suburb of Redcliffe, Bristol, 1980* Bristol, City of Bristol Museum and Art Gallery

Williams, B. 1982 'Excavations at Bristol Bridge, 1981', *Bristol Avon Archaeol.* **1**, 12–15

Williams, B. 1988 'The excavation of medieval and post-medieval tenements at 94–102 Temple Street, Bristol, 1975', *Trans. Bristol Gloucestershire Archaeol. Soc.* **106**, 107–68

Williams, B. (ed.) 1992 'Archaeology in Bristol 1990–92', *Bristol Avon Archaeol.* **10**, 53–6

Wiliams, B. and Cox, S., 2001 *Excavations at Redcliff Street, Bristol 1980 and 1999* Unpublished BaRAS report **456/2001**

Williams, B. and Ponsford, M. 1988 'Clay roof tiles', in Williams 1988, 145–9

Williams, E.E. 1950 *The Chantries of William Canynges in St Mary Redcliffe Bristol* Bristol, William Georges Sons Ltd

Williams, J.T. 1963 '*Chenopodium album* L.', *J. Ecol.* **51(3)**, 711–25

Wilkinson, K.N. 2004 *Huller House, Bristol: An assessment of stratigraphy revealed in bore holes and evaluation trenches* Unpublished report, University College Winchester

Wilkinson, K.N. 2007a *55–61 Victoria Street, Bristol: Borehole survey. Assessment Report* Unpublished ARCA Report **0607-7**, University of Winchester

Wilkinson, K.N. 2007b *O and M Sheds, Welshback, Bristol: Borehole survey. Assessment Report* Unpublished ARCA report **0708-5**, University of Winchester

Wilkinson, K.N. 2007c *7–11 Broad Quay, Bristol: A geoarchaeological assessment of borehole stratigraphy* Unpublished ARCA report **0708-8**, University of Winchester

Wilkinson, K.N. 2008a *32–36 Victoria Street, Bristol: Borehole survey and monolith sampling. Assessment report* Unpublished ARCA report **0809-1**, University of Winchester

Wilkinson, K.N. 2008b *Mitchell Lane, Bristol: Borehole survey. Assessment report* Unpublished ARCA report **0708-15**, University of Winchester

Wilkinson, K.N. 2011a 'Geoarchaeological sequence', in Alexander, M. and Harward, C. 2011 'Harbourside, Bristol: Investigations from 2003–2008', in Watts (ed.) 2011b, 82–3

Wilkinson, K.N. 2011b 'Borehole stratigraphy', in Davenport, P., Leech, R. and Rowe, M. 2011 '55–60 St Thomas Street, Redcliffe, Bristol: Excavations in 2006', in Watts (ed.) 2011b, 51–4

Wilkinson, K.N. 2011c 'Period 1: pre-18th century development (pre- *c*. 1770)', in Holt, R. and Leech, R. 2011 'Cabot House, Deanery Road, Bristol: Investigations in 2008', in Watts (ed.) 2011b, 125–6

Wilkinson, K.N. 2013 'Geological Background', in Ridgeway and Watts (eds) 2013, 3–4

Wilkinson, K.N. and Tinsley, H. 2005 *Harbourside Development Area, Bristol: The geoarchaeology of borehole stratigraphy* Unpublished ARCA report **05/06 1**, University of Winchester

Wilson, B. Grigson, C. and Payne, S. 1982 *Ageing and Sexing Animal Bones from Archaeological Sites* Brit. Archaeol. Rep. Brit. Ser. **109**. Oxford

Woolgar, C.M. 2000 '"Take this penance now, and afterwards the fare will improve": Seafood and late medieval diet', in Starkey *et al.* (eds) 2000, 36–44

Woolgar, C.M., Serjeantson, D. and Waldron, T. (eds) 2006 *Food in Medieval: England Diet and Nutrition* Oxford, Oxford University Press

Wright, E.P. 1891 *The Ocean World: Being A Description of the Seas and Some of its Inhabitants* London, Cassell Petter and Galpin. Revised from the French work of Louis Figuier published in 1889

Youngs, S.M., Clark, J. and Barry, T. 1985 'Medieval Britain and Ireland in 1984', *Medieval Arch*aeol. **29**, 158–230

Youngs, S.M., Clark, J. and Barry, T. 1986 'Medieval Britain and Ireland in 1985', *Medieval Arch*aeol. **30**, 114–98

Youngs, S.M., Clark, J. and Barry, T. 1987 'Medieval Britain and Ireland in 1986', *Medieval Arch*aeol. **31**, 110–91

Index

Page numbers in roman refer to text and tables; page numbers in *italics* refer to illustrations.
Property numbers, eg No.16, refer to Redcliff Street (in the main excavated site, Nos 1-2 Redcliff Street).
The entry for No.3 Redcliff Street includes all the excavated periods on that particular site.

animal bone 96-101, 142, 177-8, 182, 183
   cat 97
   cattle 16, 96, 97, 98, 99-100, 101, 177-8, 183
   deer 100, 101
   dog 97, 98, 99, 177, 178
   fallow deer 96, 97, 98, 177, 178
   hare 101
   horse 96, 97, 98, 99, 100, 177, 178, 182
   pigs 16, 96, 97-8, 99, 100-1, 177, 178
   rabbit 96, 97, 98, 99, 100, 101, 177, 178
   rat 96, 97, 99, 100
   sheep/goat (ovicaprids) 16, 96, 97, 98, 99, 100, 101, 177, 178, 183
   wild boar 177, 178
   see also bird bone; fish bone; No.3 Redcliff Street; *and* Redcliff Street property numbers
antler tine 58, *58*
architectural stone 76-8
Arthur's Fee 6
Ashmead map (1828) *9*, 10, 14, 22
Ashmead map (1855) *168*, 183
Avon Formation 1, 3

bead, glass 76
bee 'skep' bases 19, 52
Benson, Richard, soapmaker 8
Bilfield, Samuel 149
bird bone 96, 97, 98, 100, 101, 177, 178, 182
black dye production 118, 120
Blake, William 149
boat planking, reused 17, 84, 87
bone and horn working 97, 99, 100, 101, 142, 177; *see also* hornering
bone (worked) 54-60, *57*, 99
   pointed implement (textiles) 57-8, *58*
Booth, Edward and Elizabeth 149
Bovey, Edward 149
Bozley, Benjamin 150
bran 105, 115, 116, 117-18, 120, 142
brasiers *7*, 9, 63, 143
brick 174
Bridges, George, distiller 9, 10

Bright, Henry 10
Bristol Bridge 3, 6, *7*, 12, 13, 138, 139, 142, 184
Bristol Castle 3
Bristol Distilling Company 8, 9
Brook, Thomas 10
Buchanan's Wharf *7*, 12, 138, 141
buckles
   copper-alloy 29, 55, *57*
   lead alloy 55-6, *57*
Building 1A *see under* Nos 16/17, Period 1
Building 1B *see under* No.18, Period 1
Building 2A *see under* No.18, Period 2a
Building 2B *see under* No.18a, Period 2a
Building 2C *see under* No.19, Period 2a
Building 2D *see under* No.17, Period 2b
Building 2E *see under* No.16, Period 2c
Building 2F *see under* No.17, Period 2c
buildings, medieval 140-1
burh and defences 3
Burton, Thomas 9
Bushe, John 9

Cabot Circus 3, 144
Cachmay, Joshua, silkweaver 149, 150
candlesticks, metal (moulds for) 29, 55, *56*, 60, 61, 62, 63, 64, *64*, 71, 72, 144
Canynges House, 95-97 Redcliff Street *7*, 12, 13, 138, 139, 142, 143
carpentry 84-6, 89
Carter, Edward 10
casting pits/water stores 29, 144
Catcott, Hannah 10
cauldron handles 62, 143
cauldrons/posnets, metal (moulds for) 28, 29, 61-2, 63, *63*, *64*, 66, 67, 71, 143, 144
Cave, Thomas, wine merchant 9, 10
ceramic building materials 173, 174; *see also* brick; floor tiles; hearth tile; roof tiles
chafing dishes, metal (moulds for) 29, 31, 55, 60, 62, 63, 61, *63*, 144
   drop handle mould 31, 55, *56*, 62, 63, *63*
chape, copper-alloy 55, *57*

197

charcoal 117, 119, 121
cheese making (dishes) 19, 52
church architectural fragments 76-9
cistern (1604) see No.17, Period 2b
clay mould fragments (for copper-alloy working) 13, 28, 29, 60-4, 65, 66, *66*, 68-70, 72, 143, 144, 166, 175, 182
   clay pattern 62
   fabric 60
   handle mould fragments 61, 62
   marks 62-3, *63*, *64*
   tenons/mortices 62, *64*
   see also candlesticks; cauldrons/posnets; chafing dishes; sprues and sprue cups
clay tobacco pipes 32, 34, 51, 73-5, *75*, 175; see also pipe kiln waste
cloth trade and cloth finishing 6-7, 12, 118, 138, 142, 143, 150, 182; see also dyeing industry; shears
clothworkers 149-50
cobbler's workshop (No.17, Period 1) 78-9, 142
cobbling and waste 16, 19, 78, 79, 138; see also leather
coins 34
   Cnut 3
   James I farthing 32
   Short Cross penny 24, 48, 54
   Victorian 36
   see also jetton
comb, ivory *57*, 60
container, wooden 19, 89, *90*
Cook, Temperance 10
Copnor, John, baker 10
copper-alloy objects 54-5, 174-5, 181, 182
copper-alloy working debris (casting and waste) 13, 65-72, 166, 175, 182
   spills (metal waste) 67, 72, 166, 175
   see also clay mould fragments; crucibles; reverberatory furnaces; slag
Courage Brewery site *7*, 12, 13, 137, 138, 139, 143, 144
Croft, John 9, 10
crucibles 29, 65, *66*, 67-70, *67*, 71, 72, 143, 156, 175, 176, 182

Day, John 150
deed plan, 19th century 12, *12*, 140
dendrochronology (tree-ring analysis) 6, 12, 18, 19, 20, 24, 26, 29, 46, 52, 84, 86, 87, 89, 90, 92-5, 138, 140
distilling and distillers 8-9, 13, 150, 182, 183
Droys, John 10, 12
Dundas Wharf 6, *7*, 8, 12, 13, 52, 138, 139, 142, 143
Durban, John 150
dye residues (red and blue) 115, 116, 118
dye vats: No.3, hearths/bases 13, 139, 143, 157-8, *159*, *160*, 182; see also No.19, Period 2a, hearths
dyeing industry and dye working 13, 16, 46, 99, 117-18, 120, 131, 138, 141-2, 159, 182
dyeing plants (weld, dyer's greenweed, madder, woad) 16, 19, 105, 116, 117-18, 120, 141, 142, 182; see also madder; woad
dyers 7, 138, 139, 143

Edwards and Co., rectifiers 150
egg shell 105, 115, 117
Elsworthy, Bridget 10
Elyot, John, brasier 9

Elyot, Thomas, brasier 7, 63
Elyott, Nicholas 7

Fear and Burgum 8
fees, of Temple and Redcliff 3, 6, 14, 137, 149
Finzel, Conrad 144
Finzel's Reach *7*, 13, 137, 138
fired clay, perforated 176
fish bone 24, 101-4, 177, 178
FitzHamon, Robert 3
Fitzharding, Robert 6
flax 19, 105, 116, 117, 118, 119, 142; see also linseed oil production
flax retting 142
floor tiles 13, 174
footwear see leather
Frome river 3
fuel 29, 72, 119-20
furnaces see No.16 (1426), Period 3; No.17 (1845), Period 2c; No.17 (1530, 1535), Period 3
furniture or machinery fragment, with red pigment 29, 90
Fysshe, Thomas 9

geoarchaeology (boreholes) 14, 132-6
glass
   bead 76
   pharmaceutical phial 34, 76
   vessel 32, 76, 175
   window 34, 76
glass houses 145
glass waste and crucible fragments 76, 145
Glover, Joseph 9, 10
Goad Insurance map (1887) 8, 10, *11*, 12, 14, 36
Godwin, Richard 10
Gresley, Henry, grocer 150
Griffin, John, scivier, and Elizabeth 149
Gunter, Walter 149, 150
Guylham, William 7

Hall, John, apothecary, and Elizabeth 149, 150
Hampton, John 9
handle fragment, bone 56-7, *57*
handle or staff, yew 89
Haubury, Capel 9, 10
Hawle, William 149
hearth tile 174
herbs and herbalism 118, 119
Hoefnagle's map (1581) *8*
Holbyn, Thomas, baker 10
Holocene 1, 3
hone, stone 73
Hone, William, weaver 9
Hook, Hannah 149
Horneblow, Elizabeth 150
hornering 13, 14, 16, 20, 98-9, 100, 101, 142
horse harness ring 55, *56*
horseshoes 163, 175
Hucknall, Thomas, haberdasher 149
Hunt family, pipemakers 145
Hunt, Flower, pipemaker 74, 75, *75*
Hunt, John I 74, 75, *75*
Hyle, Nicholas 9

industry, economy and trade 141-5, 150, 182-3
inlays, goose bone 20, 100
insect remains 121-31
iron objects 54, 55, 175, 182
iron slag 65
ironworking 13
ivory *see* comb

J. and G. Thomas 10
jetton, French 28, 29, 54
jetton mould, stone 19, 73, *73*
John Thomas and Sons Ltd 10, *11*, 140
Jones, Charles, soapmaker 8
Jones, Daniel, elder and younger 10
Jones, Humphrey 7

Keene, Allis and Thomas, sugar refiners 10
Keene, Thomas, sugar baker 10
knife handle, bone 24
knife/shears blade 55, *56*

Law Ditch 6, 17, 137, 149, 150, 183
lead/lead alloy objects 54, 55-6
leather
    footwear, scraps and cobbling waste 14, 16, 19, 78-84, *82, 83*, 84, 142
    straps 80, *82*, 84
Lewis, Joseph, soapmaker 8
lime (production) 13, 32, 34
linseed oil production 19, 118, 120; *see also* flax
lithostratigraphy 155, 177, 179-80
Little Thomas Lane 6, 9, 10, 17, 20, 32, 34, 36, 48, 137, 140, 150
    Period 2: *21*, 22, *22*, 28, 29, 139, 141
Lott, William 150
Ludlow, William 9

madder 19, 22, 26, 105, 116, 117, 118, 120, 142, 143
marsh 137-8
Marwood, Solomon 149
Merrifield, John 150
metalworking 12, 13, 63; *see also* clay mould fragments; copper-alloy working debris; slag
Millard, Daniel 10
Millard, Edward 9
Millard, John 149
Milleman, --, butcher 150
Mills, William, baker 9
molluscs 105, 115, 116, 178
mortar-mixing pits (lime) 32, 34, 139
moss 115
moulds *see* clay mould fragments

nails 54
Naish, William, cooper 9
Need, Bridget 10
needle, copper-alloy 175, 182
Newe, Alexander, Edmund and Richard, dyers 7
Newham, Tobias, writing master 150
Newport, John 10
Newport, Robert 3, 12

Olyver, Thomas, baker 7
oyster 19, 105, 115

Page, John 10
panel fragment, waste *57*, 58-9
Parkhous, Thomas 9
patch-repair plates, copper alloy, for pottery 174, 181
Period 1: 14-20, *15*, 138, 140-3
    animal bone 14, 16, 96-9, 100-1, 142
    cobbling 16, 19, 78, 138
    dendrochronology (tree-ring analysis) 18, 19, 20, 46, 52, 87, 89, 138, 140
    dyeing industry 16, 46, 118, 120, 138, 141-2
    dyeing plants 16, 19, 118, 141, 142
    finds 19, 54-5, 56-7, *56, 57*, 76, 142
    hornering 14, 16, 98-9, 101, 142
    insect remains 121-31, 142
    iron slag 65
    leather (footwear and scraps) 14, 16, 19, 78-84, 142
    pits, linings and wattlework 14, *15*, 16-20, *16*, 86-9, 91, 141-2
    plant remains 16, 19, 105-116, 118, 119, 120, 141, 142
    pottery 14, 17, 20, 37, 38-40, 41, 43, 44, 45-6, *47*, 48, *49*, 52, 53, 138
    roof tiles 54
    and see No.12; Nos 12-15; Nos 13-15; No.16; Nos 16/17; No.17; No.18; No.18a; No.19
Period 2a-c
    animal bone 20, 96, 99-101
    clay mould fragments 23, 28, 60, 61, 65, 143
    coins and jetton 24, 28, 29, 48, 54
    crucibles 65, 143
    dendrochronology 20, 22, 24, 26, 48, 89, 139
    dyeing 20, 118, 120, 139, 143
    finds 20, 24, 28, 55, 57-8, *57, 58*, 59-60, 73, 76, 100
    fish bone 24, 102, 103, 104
    hornering 20, 100, 101
    insect remains 121, 122-9, 131
    leather 22, 48, 78, 79, 80
    madder 22, 118
    plant remains 20, 26, 111-20
    pottery 20, 22, 24, 26, 28-9, 37, 38-40, 43, 44, 45, 48, *49*, 50, *51*, 52, 53
    roof tiles 54, 141
Period 2a: 20-4, 138-9, 141, 143-4, *and see* No.15; No.16; No.17; No.18; No.18a; No.19; No.20
Period 2b *see* No.17
Period 2c: 26-9, 65, *and see* No.16; No.17; No.20
Period 3: 29-32, 139
    animal bone 96, 100
    clay mould fragments 29, 32, 55, 60, 61, 62, 63-4, *63, 64*, 65, 66, 67-70
        candlestick (in No.16) 29, 55, *56*, 62, 64, *64*, 144
        cauldron/vessel, failed casting waste (No.17) 29, 67
        cauldrons/posnets (Nos 16 and 17) 29, 63, *63*, *64*, 66, 144
        chafing dishes (in No.17) 29, 31, 55, 63, 144
        drop handle (chafing dish) 31, 55, *56*, 62, 63, *63*
        marks 62, 63, *63, 64*
        sprue cup (cover) 62, 67, 72
    clay tobacco pipes 32, 34, 51, 73-5, *75*
    coin 32

Period 3 (cont.):
   crucibles 29, 65, 66, *66*, 67-70, *67*, 143
   dendrochronology 29, 31, 32, 90
   dyeing 118
   finds 29, 55, *57*, 73, 90
   fish bone 102, 103, 104
   glass 32, 76
   hearth deposits (3523) 51
   leather 80
   metalworking 29, 65, 120, 139, 144
   pipe kiln waste 31, 73, 74
   plant remains 111-15, 117, 118, 119, 120
   pottery 29, 31, 32, 37, 38-40, 44, 45, 50-2, *51*, 53
   roof tiles 54
   slag 29, 67, 69, 70
   window glass 76
   and see No.16; No.17; No.18a; No.19; No.20
Period 4: 32-4, 139-40, 144-5, 150
   animal bone 96, 100
   architectural stone reused 34, 76-8
   clay mould fragments 61
   coin 34
   copper-alloy working debris 65
   finds 55, *57*, *59*, 60, 73
   fish bone 102, 103, 104
   glass pharmaceutical phial 34, 76
   pipe kiln waste 31, 32, 34, 74-5, *75*, 145
   pottery 34, 45, *51*, 52, 53
   roof tiles 54
   window glass 34, 76
   and see No.16; No.17; Nos 18-19; No.20
Period 5 (19th-20th centuries) 34-6, 139-40, 144-5
   buckle, lead-alloy
   clay pattern 62
   coin, Victorian 36
   finds 55-6, *57*, 73, *73*
   pottery 36, 52
   roof tiles 54
   slag 65
   Nos 11-15, oil store 36
   No.16, buildings 36, 140
   No.17, drains 36
   No.18, cellars 36, 140
   No.20, cellars 36
pinner's bone *59*, 60
pins
   copper-alloy 28, 55
   dress 174
pipe kiln waste 31, 32, 34, 73, 74-5, *75*, 145
plant remains and charcoal 104-21; *and see under Redcliff Street property numbers*
Plumly, George 149
Poole, Nicholas 10
Portwall 3, 181
Portwall Lane *7*, 13, 138, 139, 143
Potter, Patience 150
pottery
   copper-alloy patch-repair plates 174, 181
   medieval 137-8
     'Bath A' glazed (BPT 134) 26, 39, 41, 44, 48, *49*
     'Bath A' type coarseware (BPT 46) 20, 39, 41, 42, 46, 48, *49*, 50, 52, 53
     'Bath A' type coarseware (BPT 46) 169, 170, 172, 173, *174*
     Bristol C coarsewares (BPT 309) 20, 37, 39, 46, *47*, 52, 152, 169, 170, 172
     Bristol (Redcliffe) glazed wares (BPT 85, 118, 118L, 120, 123, 126, 127, 128) 26, 28, 39, 40, 41, 43-4, 48, 50, *51*, 52, 53, 154, 155, 157, 170, 171, 172, 173, *174*
     East Wiltshire Sandy coarseware (EMEDX) 169, 170, 171, 172
     French jug fabric (BPT 192) 39, 41, 43, *47*, 48, 50, *51*, 52
     Glamorgan (GLAM) 170, 171, 172
     Ham Green A and B glazed ware (BPT 26 and 27) 20, 24, 39, 41, 42, 46, *47*, 48, *49*, 50, *51*, 53, 152, 169, 170, 172, 173, *174*
     Ham Green redware (BPT 32) 20, 39, 41, 42, 46, 48, *49*, 50, 53, 169, 170, 172
     Ham Green redware (large jars) (BPT 305) 39, 42, 50, *51*
     incurved dishes/'west country vessels' (BPT 46) (for cheese making/bee hives/dyeing) 19, 52, 142-3
     Lacock, Nash Hill glazed ware (BPT 368) 39, 41, 44, 48, *49*, 50, 53, 170, 171, 172, 173
     Minety type ware (BPT 18) 39, 41, 42-3, 48, 50, *51*, 52, 152, 157, 169, 170, 171, 172, 173
     Minety type ware (wheelthrown) (BPT 84) 26, 39, 41, 44, 48, 50, *51*, 52, 53, 170
     miscellaneous north French jugs (BPT 366) 39, 41, 43, 46, *49*, 50, *51*, 52
     miscellaneous unidentified medieval wares (BPT 252d/e) 39, 41, 43
     'motte ditch' type coarseware type (BPT 6) 20, 37, 39, 41, 46, *47*
     Normandy green glazed (BPT 239) 39, 41, 43, *47*, 48, 52
     ?North French micaceous/Breton (NFRE) 170, 171, 172
     Paffrath 'blaugrau' type (no BPT) 39, 41, 43, *47*, 48, 52
     Pill/'Proto-Ham Green' coarseware (BPT 114) 20, 39, 41, 42, 46, 48, *49*, 50
     South-east Wiltshire sandy coarseware (SEW) 170, 172
     South-east Wiltshire tripod pitchers (BPT 18c) 39, 41, 42, *47*, 48
     South-west French Saintonge polychrome (SAIP) (BPT 39/232) 170, 171, 172
     South-west French wares/Saintonge (SAIM/ SAIU) (BPT 156/157/160) 28, 39, 44, 48, 50, *51*, 52, 53, 170, 171, 172, 181
     Thornbury type glazed ware (BPT 121) 39, 44, 48, 50, 53
     'Tudor Green' (BPT 182) 28, 32, 40, 45, 50, 51-2, *51*, 53, 170, 171, 172
     unsourced Saxo-Norman coarseware 1 (BPT 252a) 37, 39, 46, *47*, 52
     unsourced Saxo-Norman coarseware 2 (BPT 252b) 37, 39, 48
     unsourced Saxo-Norman 3 (BPT 252c) 42
     Worcester type glazed ware (BPT 168) 39, 41, 44, 48, *49*, 53
   post-medieval to modern
     Algarve micaceous/Merida type ware (BPT 282) 40, 45, 53, 170, 171, 172, 173, 181

pottery (cont.)
  post-medieval to modern (cont.)
    Ashton Keynes ware (AK) 170, 171, 172
    Bristol (BPT 265) 171
    Bristol stoneware (BPT 277) 170, 172, 173
    Cistercian type wares (BPT 93/266/275) 32, 40, 45, 51, 53, 170, 171, 172
    Coarse Border ware (BORD) 170, 171, 172
    English tin-glazed earthenware (BPT 99) 45
    figurine jug 44, *51*, *52*
    flowerpots (BPT 201) 168, 170, 172, 173
    Frechen stoneware (BPT 286) 40, 45
    Late Valencian lustreware (BPT 83) 170, 171, 172, 173, *174*
    local sandy earthenware (BPT 265) 170, 172
    London/Brislington tin-glazed (BPT 99) 170, 171, 172
    London stoneware (LONS) 170, 171, 172, 183
    Malvern Chase 'pink' fabric (HERB5) 160, 170, 171, 172, *174*
    Malvern Chase redwares (HERB4) (BPT 197) 28, 32, 40, 44-5, 50, 51, 53, 170, 171, 172, 173, 183
    miscellaneous (MISC) 170, 172
    Nether Stowey (West Somerset) glazed earthenwares (BPT 280) 40, 45, 51, 53
    North Devon gravel-free (BPT 108) 40, 51, 170, 171, 172, 183
    North Devon gravel-tempered (BPT 112) 40, 51, 170, 171, 172, 183
    North Italian marbled slipware (BPT 82) 170, 171, 172, 173
    Raeren stoneware (BPT 287) 32, 40, 45, 51, 53, 170, 171, 172
    red earthenwares 166
    slipwares 166
    South Netherlands tin-glazed (BPT 344) 170, 171, 172, 173
    South Somerset glazed earthenware (BPT 268) 40, 170, 171, 172
    Spanish (Seville) amphorae and olive jars (OLIV) (BPT 81) 40, 45, 170, 171, 172
    Staffordshire (or Bristol) mottled brown-glazed earthenwares (BPT 211) 45, 170, 171, 172, 183
    Staffordshire (or Bristol) yellow slipwares (BPT 100) 45, 170, 171, 172
    tin-glazed wares 166, 170, 171, 172
    transfer-printed wares (BPT 278) 168, 170, 172, 173, 183
    Wanstrow (East Somerset) glazed earthenwares (BPT 96) 40, 45, 51, 52, 53
    Western-super-Mare coarseware (WSM) 170, 172, 173
pottery supply 52-3, 181-2, 183
Puxton, Thomas 10

radiocarbon dating 132
reclamation of land 139, 143, 181
Redcliff fee 3, 6, 14, 137, 149

Redcliff Street
  documentary background 6-12
  widening 9, 10, 12, 34, 36, 149, 150, 165, 184
Nos 1-2 Redcliff Street (see after 7 Redcliffe Street)

No.3 Redcliff Street *7*, 13, 147-84, *148*
  animal bone 177-8, 182, 183
  ceramic building material 173-4, 182
  clay tobacco pipes 175
  copper-alloy, casting waste 174-5, 182
  crucibles 156, 175, 182
  documentary evidence 149-50
  dye-vat bases (hearths) 13, 139, 143, 157-8, 159, 160, 182
  finds 174-6, 182
  geological and Holocene 147
  hearths 143
  industrial activity 182-3
  iron objects 175, 182
  lithostratigraphy 155, 177, 179-80
  metalwork 174-5, 182
  mollusca 177, 178
  mould fragments 143, 182
  perforated fired clay 176
  plant remains 177, 179
  as plot Nos 21-23: 149
  pottery, medieval and later 169-73
  stone roof tile and slate 175
  vessel glass 175
No.3 Redcliff Street fieldwork (Areas 1 and 2, monolith and boreholes) 13, 151-68
  Period 1
    animal bone 177
    geological strata 151
    mollusca 177, 178
  Period 2a-b reclamation and settlement 151-4, 157, 181
    animal bone 177
    crucible 175, 182
    patch-repair, copper alloy 174, 181
    plant remains 153-4, 177
    pottery 151, 152, 153, 154, 173, *174*, 181
    stone roof tile 175
    'tread board' 151, *153*, 176
  Period 3a-b 155-60, 181-2
    animal bone 177-8
    bone/horn working 177, 182
    ceramic building material 173, 174
    cisterns (dye-working) 159-60
    crop-processing 155
    crucibles 175, 176
    dress pin 174
    fired-clay, perforated 156, 176
    hearths for dye vats 157-8, 159, 160, 182
    pottery 155, 156, 157, 158, 159, 160, 169, 171, 173, *174*, 181-2
    shears blades 157, 175, 182
    stone roof tile and slate 175, 182
  Period 4 industrial activity 160-5, 182-3
    animal bone 178, 183
    brick box structure 160
    cellars 160, 162-5, *163*
    cistern 157, 161, 165, 183
    drains/culverts 160-2, 165, 183
    horseshoes 163, 175
    pottery 160, 161, 162, 171, 173, *174*, 183
    roof tiles 161, 173, 174
    stone roof tile and slate 175
    vessel glass 175

202 Index

No.3 Redcliff Street fieldwork (cont.)
  Period 5 post-medieval 165, 183-4
    animal bone 178
    cellars 165
    clay tobacco pipes 175
    thimble 174-5
    tiles 173, 174
    vessel glass 175
  Period 6 (modern) 165-8, 184
    animal bone 178
    clay mould fragments 166, 175
    copper-alloy working 166, 175
    floor tile 174
    needle 175, 182
    pottery 166, 168
    tiles 174
5 Redcliff Street 8
7 Redcliff Street 6

Nos 1-2 Redcliff Street *(formerly Nos 11-20)* 6, 13, 181, 182
11 Redcliff Street 9-10, 14
11-15 Redcliff Street, Period 5, oil store 36
11-20 Redcliff Street 6, 9, *9*, 14
No.12 Redcliff Street 9-10
  Period 1, plant remains 105, 106-10
No.12-15 Redcliff Street
  leather 79, 80, *82*, *83*, 84
  Period 1
    dyeing plants 118
    leather and cobbling 16
    pits 16, 88
    weather board reused 16
Nos 13-15 Redcliff Street
  Period 1
    insect remains 121, 122, 129-31
    plant remains 105, 106-10, 118, 119
13 Redcliff Street 10
14 Redcliff Street 10
No.15 Redcliff Street 10
  Period 2a, pits and surfaces 20
No.16 Redcliff Street 9, 10
  Period 1: 16, 141
    animal bone 98
    yew handle or staff 89
  Period 2a 20, 22, 139, 141
    hearths 20, 139, 143
    wells 20
  Period 2c
    bone stylus/parchment pricker 28, 59-60
    Building 2E 26, *27*, 28, 139, 141
    hearths 26, 28
    industrial waste 26
  Period 3: 29, 139
    buckle, copper-alloy 29, 55, *57*
    casting pit/water for cooling (1436) 29, 144
    charcoal 29, 117, 119
    clay mould fragments 29, 60, 61, 62, 63-4, *64*, 144
    crucible 29
    drain 29
    furnace (1426), for melting copper alloy 29, *31*, 32, 52, 60, 61, 62, 71-2, 117, 119, 139, 144
    furniture/machinery with red pigment 29, 90
    plant remains 117
  Period 4: 32, 34, 140
  Period 5, buildings 36, 140
Nos 16/17 Redcliff Street
  Period 1: 17-19, 86, 137
    animal bone 98
    Building 1A and features at rear 14, *15*, 17-19, 86, 138, 140-1
    dendrochronology 18
    dyeing or industrial building 141
    pits *16*, 17-19
    pottery 17
No.17 Redcliff Street 10, 12, *12*
  Period 1: 18, 19
    animal bone 96, 98
    bone, worked 99
    ceramic dishes, incurved (BPT 46), for dyeing? 19, 52, 142-3
    cobbler's workshop 78-9, 142
    fish bone 102-3, 104
    insect remains 122-9, 130
    jetton mould, stone 19, 73, *73*
    leather and cobbling waste 19, 78, 79, 82-3, 84, 142
    plant remains 105, 106-10, 119
    plots 138
    shears blade 19, 55, *56*, 142
    well 142
    woad 118
    wooden container 19, 89, *90*
    worked wood and wattlework 86-9
  Period 2, plant remains 116-17, 118
  Period 2a 22
    dendrochronology 22
    drain (1911) 22, 48
    fish bone 103
    hearths 22, 139, 143
    leather (shoes) 22, 48, 78, 79, 80
    madder 22, 118
    plots 139, 141
    pottery 22, 48
    wells (1822, 1914) 22, 24, 29, 48, 143
    worked timber 89, *90*
  Period 2b 24-6
    Building 2D 24, *25*, 141
    cistern (1604) 24, *25*, 26, *26*, 28, 76, 89, 103, 116, 121, 122, 131, 143
    fish bone 24, 102, 103
    glass bead 76
    hearths 24, 26, *26*, 103, 116, 139
    insect remains 121, 122-9, 131
    leather 78, 80
    madder 26
    metalworking 65
    plant remains 26, 116
    plots 139
    pottery 26, 38-40, 44, 50, 52, 53
    roof tiles 54, 141
    tenon (carpentry) 26, 89
    wood and organic 26
  Period 2c
    animal bone 100

No.17 Redcliff Street Period 2c (cont.)
  Building 2F *27*, 28, 29, 139, 141
  clay mould fragments 28, 60, 61, 65, 143
  crucibles 143
  fish bone 102, 103
  furnace (1845), copper-alloy working 26, 28, *28*, 29, 50, 60, 61, 71, 100, 116, 117, 139, 143
  jetton, French 28, 29, 54
  lead weights 28, 55
  pins 28
  pottery 28-9
  water butt (barrel) *26*, 28, 116, 117, 119
  Period 3
    casting pit/water store (1340) 29
    clay mould fragments 29, 55, 60, 61, 62, 63-4, *64*, 144
    clay tobacco pipes 32, 34, 51, 73-5, *75*
    coin 32
    copper slag 29, 31
    dendrochronology 29, 90
    drain 29
    fish bone 103
    furnaces (1530, 1535) 29, *30*, 31, *31*, 32, 34, 44, 51-2, *51*, 60, 61, 62, 71-2, 90, 117, 139, 144
    glass 32
    hearths 29
    pipe kiln waste 31, 73, 74
    plant remains 117
    pottery 29, 31, 32, 44, 51-2, *51*
    vessel/cauldron, failed casting? 29, 67
    weather board, plank 29, 31, 90
  Period 4
    architectural stone reused 34, 76-8
    cellars 34, 140
    clay tobacco pipes 34
    coin 34
    hearths 34, 144
    metal pot 34
    mortar-mixing pit (lime) 34
    pin 55
    pipe kiln waste 31, 32, 34, 74-5, *75*, 145
    pottery 34
    well 34, 36, 140
  Period 5, drains 36
Nos 17-20 Redcliff Street 10
No.18 Redcliff Street 10, 12, *12*
  leather 80, 83, 84
  Period 1: 14, 16, 18, 19, 20, 86, 141-2
    animal bone 98
    Building 1B *15*, 19, 138, 140-1
    coopered vessel 19, 89
    dyeing plants 19, 118, 142
    fish bone 102, 103
    flax 19, 142
    hearth, stone 19
    insect remains 122-9, 130-1
    oyster shell 19
    pits 19, 142
    plant remains 105, 118
    plots 138
    worked wood 87-8, 89
  Period 2a 22-3, 138-9
    Building 2A 20, *21*, 22, *23*, 29, 138, 139, 141
    clay mould fragment 23
    dendrochronology 48, 139
    hearth (1201) 23, 143
    well 23
  Period 5, cellars 36, 140
No.18a Redcliff Street
  leather 80
  Period 1: 14, 19-20, 138
    worked wood 19-20, 87-8, 89
  Period 2a, Building 2B 20, *21*, 23, *23*, 29, 31, 138-9, 141
  Period 3: 29, 31, 139
    Building 3A 19, *30*, 31, 52, 90, 139
    dendrochronology 31, 32, 90
    hearth 31
Nos 18-19 Redcliff Street 10, 12, *12*, 140
  Period 4: 34, 140
    hearth *33*, 34, 144
    sugar house (refinery) 3, 8, 10, 12, 32, 34, 140, 144
    sugar warehouse 34
    well 34
No.19 Redcliff Street
  Period 1: 14, 20, 138
    hearths 20
    insect remains 122-9, 131
    pits 20, 141
    plant remains 116, 118
  Period 2, plant remains 117
  Period 2a 23-4, 138-9
    animal bone 99
    buckle 24
    Building 2C *21*, 23-4, *23*, 139, 141
    charcoal 119
    drain 24
    fish bone 102, 103
    hearths, for dye vats (3597, 3651) 23, 24, 48, 99, 102, 103, 117, 119, 139, (3534) 143
    plant remains 117
    well (3550) 23, 24, 32, 141
  Period 3: 29, 31-2, 139
    fish bone 103
    hearths (3480) 32
    lime 32
    pottery 32
    well (mortar mixing pit) 32, 139
    wooden structure? 32
No.20 Redcliff Street 9, 10, 12
  Period 2a 24, 138-9, 141
    drains 24
    pottery 24, 48
    Short Cross penny 24, 48, 54
  Period 2c 26, 28
    drains and surfaces 28, 32
  Period 3, hearth (3503) and pits 32
  Period 4, and pottery 34
  Period 5, cellars 36
21 Redcliff Street
  documentary evidence 7, 12, 149, 150, 183, 184
  fieldwork 157, 165, 166, 181, 183
22 Redcliff Street 149-50, 157, 165, 166, 181, 183, 184
  Cistern D 161
23 Redcliff Street 149, 150, 165, 166, 181, 183, 184
24 Redcliff Street 149, 150, 165, 181, 183, 184

Index

25 Redcliff Street 149, 150, 183, 184
26 Redcliff Street 6
28 Redcliff Street 8
68-72 Redcliff Street, foundry *7*, 13, 143
82-90 Redcliff Street 138, 139
85-87 Redcliff Street 143
90-91 Redcliff Street 139, 143
95-97 Redcliff Street *see* Canynges House
98-103 Redcliff Street *7*
127 Redcliff Street, dyers 143
128 and 129 Redcliff Street 8, 138
130 Redcliff Street 8
134 Redcliff Street 9
138 Redcliff Street 8
reverberatory furnaces 71-2, 144, *and see* No.16, Period 3, furnace (1426); No.17, Period 3, furnaces (1530, 1535)
Rich, Henry, soapmaker 8
Rigbye, James 10
Rigge, Joseph 10
Robert Earl of Gloucester 3, 6
Rogers, Robert, soapmaker 10
roof shingle 18, 141
roof tile, stone 182
roof tiles (ceramic) 53-4, 141, 159, 161, 173-4, 182
    Bristol medieval ware ridge tiles 173
    glazed ridge tiles 53, 182
    louvre 54
    Malvern Chase fabric 53, 54, 173-4
    miscellaneous (BRF 14) 53, 54
    pantiles, post-medieval 53, 54, 174
    ridge tiles and crests 53, 141, 159
    roof furniture (finials) 54
roofing slate 175

St Thomas's Church 13, 34, 76, 150
St Thomas Street 6, 150
14 St Thomas Street *7*, 13
18 St Thomas Street *7*, 13
26-28 St Thomas Street *7*, 13, 138, 180
30-38 St Thomas Street *7*, 13, 139
55-60 St Thomas Street *7*, 13, 132, 138, 139, 143
shears blades 19, 55, *56*, 142, 157, 175, 182
Sheerman's (Shereman's) Hall 7, 149, 150, 159, 181, 182, 183
shoes *see* leather
Shute, Edwards and Co. 150
silver extraction 71, 144
slag 29, 31, 65, 66-7, *67*, 69, 70, 72
Smith, John, distiller 150
Smith, John, earthenware seller 149
Smith, Mary 150
Smith, Richard, mercer 150
Smith, William, distiller 150
Smyth, Hugh 149
soap trade and soapmakers 7, 8, 10, 12, 145, 150, 182
spindlewhorls 20, 73, *73*
sprues and sprue cups 62, 67, *67*, 72
stone, architectural 76-8
straps, leather 80, *82*, 84
stylus/parchment pricker, bone 28, 59-60
suburbs 3, 6, 137-8, 181
sugar house *see* Nos 18-19, Period 4
sugar trade and refining 8, 10, 12, 34, 150, 182, 183

Tadleton, Thomas, latimer 9
Taillour, Thomas 9
Tamworthe, William 10
Tanner, William, brasier and potter 63, 143
tanning 13, 97, 131, 142, 143
Taylor, George, liquor dealer 150, 183
Taylor, Henry 183
Temple Fee 3, 6, 137, 149
Thatcher, John, stockingmaker 150
thimbles 55, 174-5
Thomas Lane (St) 149, 150, 157, 159, 165, 166, 181, 182, 183, 184
45 and 47 Thomas Lane 150
Thomas, Richard, victualler 10
tiles *see* floor tiles; hearth tile; roof tiles
timber hauling 88, *89*, 91
Tindale, --, writing master 150
Tippet, Robert, pipemaker 175
Tipton, Cole and Feddens 10
Tooker, Nicholas, grocer 150
topography and geology 1-3
'tread board' 151, *153*, 176
treewrighting 84-6, 91, 140
12 and 13 Tucker Street 6
Tyte, George, grocer 10

Uphyll, John 10
urine 16, 117, 142

vessel, coopered 19, 89
Victoria Street 3, 9, 150
Vyell, Thomas 9

Warminstre, William 10
Warton, Michael 10
water butt *see* No.17 Redcliff Street, Period 2c
waterfront and wharves 12-13, 138, 142, 145
Watson, George 9, 10
weights, lead 28, 55
Wentlooge Formation 1, 14, 134-5, 136
Whitchurch, James 9, 10
Williams, Charles M. 150
Willis, Thomas 10
Willoughby, John 8
window glass 34, 76
window post 141
wine trade 181, 182
wire dress pin, copper-alloy 174
woad 105, 117, 118, 120, 142
wood (worked), reused 84-92
    boat planking reused 17, 84, 87
    building posts 17, 18, 84, 91, 141
    roof shingle reused 18, 141
    small woodwork fragments 90-1
    wattlework 84, 85, 86, 88-9, 91, 141, 142
    weather boarding reused 16, 29, 31, 84, 88, 90, 141
    window post 141
    see also dendrochronology (tree-ring analysis)
woodland management and wildwood 88, 91-2, *92*
Woodson, Richard 10
wool preparation waste (insects) 129, 130, 131